500153

STUDENT STUDY GUIDE

Forrest Shull and Roseanne Tesoriero
Revised by Maria Augusta Vieira Nelson for Third Edition
Revised by Eduardo Barrenechea for Fourth Edition

SOFTWARE ENGINEERING

THEORY AND PRACTICE

FOURTH EDITION

Shari Lawrence Pfleeger
Joanne M. Atlee

Prentice Hall

Upper Saddle River   Boston   Columbus   San Francisco   New York
Indianapolis   London   Toronto   Sydney   Singapore   Tokyo   Montreal
Dubai   Madrid   Hong Kong   Mexico City   Munich   Paris   Amsterdam   Cape Town

Vice President and Editorial Director, ECS: Marcia J. Horton
Executive Editor: Tracy Dunkelberger
Assistant Editor: Melinda Haggerty
Director of Team-Based Project Management: Vince O'Brien
Senior Managing Editor: Scott Disanno
Production Liaison: Jane Bonnell
Senior Operations Specialist: Alan Fischer
Operations Specialist: Lisa McDowell
Marketing Manager: Erin Davis
Marketing Assistant: Mack Patterson
Art Director: Kenny Beck
Art Editor: Greg Dulles
Media Editor: Daniel Sandin
Media Project Manager: Danielle Leone

Prentice Hall
is an imprint of

PEARSON

www.pearsonhighered.com

10 9 8 7 6 5 4 3 2 1

ISBN-13: 978-0-13-815166-9
ISBN-10: 0-13-815166-0

Table of Contents

Course Summary

This course is organized so as to, first, provide a general introduction to software development and identify the important phases of any software project. Then, each of the phases is examined in detail, in order to give the reader a picture of the current state of our understanding of software development.

Chapter 1 provides a general introduction to the field in order to give some sense of the magnitude and importance of software in today's world, the kinds of problems that make software development difficult, and an outline of how software development is undertaken. Chapter 2 provides more detail on the idea of a "software process"--that is, on the various stages software goes through, from the planning stages to its delivery to the customer and beyond. Different models of the process are introduced, and the types of project features for which each is most appropriate are discussed.

Chapters 3 through 10 follow, in order, the major phases in the life of a software system. Chapter 3 deals with the planning stages: how resources and cost are estimated, how risks are identified and planned, and how schedules are created. Chapter 4 details how the problem to be solved by the system (not the system itself) is defined. This chapter concentrates on the methods that are necessary to fully capture the customer's requirements for the system, and how to specify them in a way that will be useful for future needs. Once the problem is sufficiently well understood, the system that solves it can be designed. Chapter 5 discusses the design of the software, introducing broad architectural styles that may be useful for different types of systems as well as more specific design characteristics. This chapter sketches the roles of the people involved in producing the design, as well as measures that can be used to assess a design's quality. Chapter 6 explores an important design paradigm, object-orientation, in more detail and shows how the design notation captures useful information about several aspects of the problem and the resulting system. Chapter 7 discusses the general principles by which a system design is turned into working code. Chapters 8 and 9 discuss testing, an important activity for ensuring the quality of the code, in some detail. An overview of different types of testing, as well as testing tools and methods, are presented. Finally, Chapter 10 describes different types of training and documentation and what should happen when the system is delivered to the customer.

For many systems the responsibility of the developers does not stop at delivery. Chapter 11 discusses system maintenance--that is, the part of the life cycle that comes after delivery. The nature of the problems that may arise with the system in this phase, as well as techniques and tools for performing maintenance, are presented. Special emphasis is placed on what can be done during system development to minimize the effort required during maintenance.

Having presented a wide array of tools and techniques that can be used during the software process, the course next presents some guidelines for how an effective set of tools can be selected. Key to this idea of process improvement is the concept of empirically evaluating the different tools available. Chapter 12 presents the basic concepts behind empirical evaluation, including the different types of empirical studies. More specific guidelines are presented for evaluations of products, processes, and resources. Chapter 13 further illustrates this discussion by presenting specific process improvement examples in each of these categories. Chapter 14 examines what progress has been made in better understanding software development and the consequences of development decisions, and presents the efforts in the professionalization of software engineering.

Course Learning Objectives

This course should help you understand:
- What is encompassed by the field of study within computer science known as "software engineering." Your understanding of this field should include its past contributions, a sense of what is understood today about software development, and an overview of important and promising areas of future research.
- What it means to be a software engineer:
  - What kinds of activities are necessary for the production of a software system;
  - What the relationship with the customer should be like, and when to involve the customer in the software development process to ensure that the system meets his or her needs;
  - What the relationship with other members of the development team should be like, in order to achieve the complex, collaborative tasks that are necessary for developing large systems.
- What it means to be a software engineering researcher:
  - What kind of working relationship is needed with practitioners;
  - What types of research problems are of interest to researchers, and stand to give practical benefit to practitioners;
  - A general idea of how software engineering research is done.
- What is meant by a "software life cycle":
  - What the important phases of software development are, and why each is necessary;
  - What types of intermediate products are produced in each phase;
  - How the phases relate to each other and to the finished product;
  - What type of activities a software engineer must complete in each phase.
- Particular techniques and tools that have been applied to software development, and the circumstances under which they may be more or less appropriate.
- How software projects are planned and managed:
  - What types of resources are involved in software development projects;
  - How risks are identified and assessed;
  - How predictions and assessments are made.
- How software process improvement can be achieved. You should also have an understanding of the role of empirical studies in process improvement, including the general types of empirical studies and the kinds of answers each is able to give to software problems.

Chapter 1: Why Software Engineering?

Learning objectives:
After studying this chapter, you should be able to:
- Define what is meant by software engineering and describe the differences between computer science and software engineering.
- Understand the track record of software engineering.
- Identify the characteristics of "good software."
- Define what is meant by a systems approach to building software and understand why a systems approach is important.
- Describe how software engineering has changed since the 1970s.

Summary:
This chapter addresses the track record of software engineering, motivating the reader and highlighting key issues that are examined in later chapters. In particular, the chapter uses Wasserman's key factors to help define software engineering. The chapter also describes the differences between computer science and software engineering and explains some of the major types of problems that can be encountered. The chapter explores the need to take a systems approach to building software. The main emphasis of this chapter is to lay the groundwork for the rest of the book.

Software engineers use their knowledge of computers and computing to help solve problems. For problem solving, software engineering makes use of *analysis* and *synthesis*. Software engineers begin investigating a problem by analyzing it, breaking it into pieces that are easier to deal with and understand. Once a problem is analyzed, a solution is synthesized based on the analysis of the pieces. To help solve problems, software engineers employ a variety of methods, tools, procedures and paradigms.

To understand where software engineering fits in, it is helpful to consider the field of chemistry and its use to solve problems. A chemist investigates various aspects of chemicals while a chemical engineer applies the chemists' results to a variety of problems. In a similar manner, computer scientists provide the theories and results that are used by software engineers to solve problems.

The development of software involves requirements analysis, design, implementation, testing, configuration management, quality assurance and more. Software engineers must select a development process that is appropriate for the team size, risk level and application domain. Tools that are well-integrated and support the type of communication the project demands must be selected. Measurements and supporting tools should be used to supply as much visibility and understanding as possible.

Software engineering has had both positive and negative results in the past. Existing software has enabled us to perform tasks more quickly and effectively than ever before. In addition, software has enabled us to do things never done before. However, software is not without its problems. Often software systems function, but not exactly as expected. In some cases, when a system fails, it is a minor annoyance. In other cases, system failures can be life threatening. This has led software engineers to find methods to assure that their products are of acceptable quality and utility. Quality must be viewed from several different perspectives. Software engineers must understand that technical quality and business quality may be very different.

Exercises:

1. What is software engineering and how does it fit into computer science?
2. What is the difference between technical and business quality? Explain why each is important.
3. Give two or three examples of failures you have encountered while using software. Describe how these failures affected the quality of the software product.
4. Examine failures that have occurred in software that you have written. Identify and list the faults and errors that caused each failure.
5. Look through several issues of software magazines (*IEEE Computer* and *IEEE Software* are good choices) from the 1970s, 1980s as well as recent issues. Compare the types of problems and solutions described in the older issues with those described in the more recent issues.

Answer Guidelines:

1. To answer this question, you may find it useful to re-read Section 1.1. Software engineering is the study or practice of using computers and computing technology to solve real-world problems. Computer scientists study the structure, interactions and theory of computers and their functions. Software engineering is a part of computer science in that software engineers use the results of studies to build tools and techniques to meet the needs of customers.

2. Technical quality emphasizes the technical performance of a software product. Often, it is measured by the number of faults, failures and timing problems. Business quality focuses on the value of the software product for the business. It is measured by return on investment (ROI). ROI may be viewed very differently depending on the organization. In the Brodman and Johnson (1995) study, different views of ROI were found with the U.S. government and U.S. industry. The U.S. government views ROI in terms of dollars saved while U.S. industry views ROI in terms of effort savings.

   Both technical and business qualities are important. A software product may have technical quality in that it performs the way it is intended or specified to perform. But, if the software system is not used for business functions, the system is not providing value to the business. In this case, the system would have technical quality, but not business quality. Similarly, a software product can provide functionality that is vital to the business, yet the technical quality may be poor. Ideally, a software product should have both technical and business quality.

   You may find it useful to re-read Section 1.3.

3. Answers to this question will vary depending upon your experiences. In your answer, you should include the following:

   - A description of the failure. Explain how the system performed in a way that was different from its required behavior.
   - A list of quality characteristics that have been violated by the failure.

   You may find it useful to use McCall's quality model (from Figure 1.5 of the textbook) as a checklist. That is, use the items listed in the model to ask questions about the failures you describe. For example, was the failure that you experienced related to correctness? Were the results incomplete or inconsistent? Did the failure affect the system's usability? These are a sample of the questions that you may want to consider.

4. Answers will be specific to the types of failures that you identify. The purpose of this exercise is to make the distinction between errors, faults and failures clear. Review the definitions for errors, faults and failures. These definitions can be found in Sidebar 1.1 of the textbook.

5. Answers to this question will vary depending upon which articles are involved. To answer this question, you may want to use the seven key factors that have altered software engineering (from Wasserman (1996) and presented in Section 1.8 of the textbook) to make your comparison among articles from the past and recent articles. In your comparison, cite specific examples of how the problems and solutions have changed.

Chapter 2: Modeling the Process and Life Cycle

Learning Objectives:
After studying this chapter, you should be able to:
- Define what is meant by the term "process" and how it applies to software development.
- Describe the activities, resources and products involved in the software development process.
- Describe several different models of the software development process and understand their drawbacks and when they are applicable.
- Describe the characteristics of several different tools and techniques for process modeling.

Summary:
This chapter presents an overview of different types of process and life-cycle models. It also describes several modeling techniques and tools. The chapter examines a variety of software development process models to demonstrate how organizing process activities can make development more effective.

A process is a series of steps involving activities, constraints and resources that produce an intended output of some kind. A process usually involves a set of tools and techniques. Processes are important because they impose consistency and structure on a set of activities. The process structure guides actions by allowing software engineers to examine, understand, control, and improve the activities that comprise the software process. In software development, it is important to follow a software development process in order to understand, control and improve what happens as software products are built for customers.

Each stage of software development is itself a process (or a collection of processes) that can be described by a set of activities. A process can be described in a variety of ways, using text, pictures or a combination. In the software engineering literature, descriptions of process models are prescriptions (or the way software development should progress) or descriptions (the way software development is done in actuality). In theory, the two should be the same, but in practice, they are not. Building a process model and discussing its subprocesses helps the team to understand the gap between the two.

Every software development process model includes system requirements as input and a delivered product as output. Some of the more common models include the waterfall model, the V model, the spiral model and various prototyping models. The waterfall model was one of the first models to be proposed. The waterfall model presents a very high-level view of what goes on during development and suggests the sequence of events a developer should expect to encounter. The V model is a variation of the waterfall model that demonstrates how testing activities are related to analysis and design. The spiral model combines development activities with risk management. No matter what process model is used, many activities are common to all.

In opposition to the rigor introduced by software processes, developers in the late nineties proposed several processes that focused on flexibility and adaptability instead of planning and predictability. The main goal in these "agile methods" is to produce executable software as quickly as possible, with a high level of customer participation, and then improve the software through many iterations. Examples of agile methods are Extreme programming, Crystal, Scrum, and Adaptive Software Development.

There are many choices for modeling tools and techniques. There are two major categories of model types: static and dynamic. A static model depicts the process, showing that the inputs are transformed to outputs. A dynamic model can enact the process, so that the user can see how intermediate and final products are transformed over time. The Lai notation is an example of a static modeling notation. The systems dynamics approach has also been applied to dynamically model software development processes.

Exercises:
1. Describe the process you use to get to ready for class or work in the morning. Draw a diagram to capture the process.
2. Describe three software development life-cycle models. For each, name the main activities performed, and the inputs and outputs of each activity. For each give an example of the kind of software development project where the life-cycle model would be well-suited, and an example of where the life-cycle model would be inappropriate; explain why.
3. What are the similarities between the life cycles of systems developed following the spiral model and systems developed using extreme programming? What are the major differences?
4. What is the difference between static and dynamic modeling? Explain how each type of modeling is useful.
5. Use the five desirable properties of process modeling tools and techniques identified by Curtis, Kellner and Over(1992) and presented in Section 2.4 of the textbook to evaluate one process modeling tool or technique. You may use an example from the book and/or consult outside sources.
6. Explain the difference between prescriptive and descriptive process models. What is the purpose for each? When is it appropriate to use each?

Answer Guidelines:
1. When answering this question, consider the definition of a process. Your answer should include the following:
   - the activities involved
   - the steps required to complete the tasks
   - the inputs and outputs to each activity
   - the constraints involved

   You may find it useful to re-read Section 2.1.

2. Answers to this question will vary depending upon the life-cycle models chosen. Section 2.2 describes several life-cycle process models. Your answer should include the activities, the inputs and the outputs involved with each process model. In addition, you should provide examples and reasons why a particular process model would be appropriate as well as situations where a process model would be inappropriate. For example, if a development project is highly risky (development team is inexperienced with the domain, time pressures exist) a spiral life-cycle model would be appropriate because development activities are combined with risk management to minimize and control risk. However, if the development project is low risk, a spiral model may not be the best choice.

3. Both are iterative, going through the same phases several times during development. Both require prioritizing the requirements and revising the priorities at each iteration. Both concentrate on building an artifact at each iteration. However, in the spiral model this is a prototype, and in extreme programming this should be an executable program that has functionality that is useful to the client. The iterations in the spiral model are for planning and for gradually increasing the level of

understanding about the system; the model does not consider changing requirements explicitly. On the other hand, the iterations in extreme programming are for building incremental releases of a working system, and the planning that happens in each iteration deals mainly with changing requirements.

4. A static process model describes the elements of a process. It depicts where the inputs are transformed to outputs. A dynamic process model enacts the process and allows the user to view how the products are transformed over time. A static model is useful to identify the elements of the process. A dynamic model may be useful to simulate how changes to the process affect the outputs of the process over time.

   For more details on static and dynamic process models, re-read Section 2.3.

5. Your answer to this question will depend upon which process modeling technique or tool is chosen. Your answer should address the five desirable properties of process modeling tools and techniques outlined in Section 2.4. Does the tool or technique you are evaluating possess the desirable characteristic? Which features of the tool or technique satisfy the desirable property? Are there areas where the tool or technique lacks support for a desirable property?

6. Descriptive models attempt to describe what is actually happening in the process. Prescriptive process models attempt to describe what should be happening with the process. For more details on prescriptive and descriptive process models, you may find it helpful to re-read Section 2.2. In your answer to this question, use the reasons for modeling a process (in Section 2.2) to describe how and when prescriptive and descriptive models are useful. Can you think of cases where a prescriptive process model may be inappropriate? How does a descriptive model help in building a prescriptive model?

Chapter 3: Planning and Managing the Project

Learning Objectives:
After studying this chapter, you should be able to:
- Understand how to track project progress.
- Identify different communication styles of personnel and how these styles affect team organization.
- Apply several effort and schedule estimation models.
- Identify risks and understand what is meant by risk management.
- Describe how process models and project management fit together.

Summary:
This chapter looks at project planning and scheduling by examining the activities necessary to plan and manage a software development project. It introduces some of the key concepts in project management, including project planning, cost and schedule estimation, risk management, and team organization. The chapter introduces notations that support project management activities. It also presents several examples of estimation models used to estimate cost and size.

The software development cycle includes many steps, some of which are repeated until the system is complete and the customers and users are satisfied. However, before committing funds for a software development or maintenance project, a customer usually wants an estimate of how much the project will cost and how long the project will take.

A project schedule describes the software development cycle for a particular project by enumerating the phases or stages of a project and breaking each into discrete tasks or activities to be done. The schedule is a time-line that shows when activities will begin and end, and when the related development products will be ready.

A systems approach of analyzing and synthesizing can be used to determine a project schedule. In the analysis of a project, a clear distinction between milestones and activities must be made. An activity is a part of the project that takes place over a period of time, whereas a milestone is the completion of an activity--a particular point in time. An analytical breakdown of the project into phases, steps and activities gives software engineers and the customers an idea of what is involved in building and maintaining a system. The analytical breakdown of the project is sometimes referred to as the work breakdown structure. From the work breakdown structure, an activity graph depicting the dependencies can be drawn. To make the activity graph more useful, the estimated time to complete each activity can be added to the graph. Then, the critical path method (CPM) can be used to determine the minimum amount of time it will take to complete the project, given the estimates of each activity's duration. In addition, the CPM reveals those activities that are most critical to completing the project on time. There are many tools available to support the tracking of a project's progress.

The number of people that will be working on the project, the tasks they will perform, and the abilities and experience they must have to do their jobs effectively are all factors that are used to determine a project schedule and estimate the associated effort and costs. As the number of people on a project increases, the number of possible lines of communication grows quickly. Breakdowns in communication can affect a project's progress. The degree of communication and the work styles of project team members should be considered when deciding on the organizational structure of the team. There are several choices for team structure, from a hierarchical chief programmer team to a loose, egoless approach. Each has its benefits, and the appropriateness of each depends to some degree on the uncertainty and size of the project.

One of the crucial aspects of project planning and management is understanding how much the project is likely to cost. Cost estimation should be done early and often, including input from team members about progress in specifying, designing, coding and testing the system. To address the need for producing accurate estimates, software engineers have developed techniques for capturing the relationships among effort and staff characteristics, project requirements, and other factors that can affect the time effort and cost of developing a software system. Many effort-estimation methods rely on expert judgment, estimates based on a manager's experience with similar projects. Algorithmic methods are based on data from past projects. With algorithmic methods, models that express the relationship between effort and the factors that influence it are generated. The models are usually described using equations, where effort is the dependent variable, and several factors (such as size, experience, and application type) are the independent variables. Most of these models acknowledge that project size is the most influential factor. Machine learning methods are another alternative to expert judgment and algorithmic methods.

Project managers take steps to ensure that their projects are done on time and within effort and cost constraints. Managers must also determine whether any unwelcome events may occur during development or maintenance, and make plans to avoid these events or, if they are inevitable, minimize their negative consequences. A risk is an unwanted event that has negative consequences. Project managers engage in risk management to understand and control risks in a project. As with cost estimation, the project team can work to anticipate and reduce risk from the project's beginning. Redundant functionality, team reviews, and other techniques can help the team catch errors early, before they become embedded in the code as faults waiting to cause failures. Cost estimation and risk management can work hand in hand; as cost estimates raise concerns about finishing on time and within budget, risk management techniques can be used to mitigate or even eliminate risks.

Exercises:
1. Describe the process of getting a degree (bachelor's, master's or PhD) as a work breakdown structure. Draw an activity graph for the process. What is the critical path?
2. Describe the organizational structure for your work environment. Classify the working styles of several of your co-workers. What are the advantages to this structure? Do you see any problems with the current structure?
3. Discuss two techniques for making a prediction for effort. In particular, explain where during the development process the prediction is made, and when (if at all) the prediction is repeated.
4. Any prediction generates an estimate, E, that can be compared eventually to an actual value, A. Name two values that can be calculated from E and A to help determine the accuracy of the estimating process. Define the two values and discuss how the values for each are used to tell us that a prediction is acceptable.
5. Describe two different size measures and the advantages and disadvantages of using each.

Answer Guidelines:

1. The answer to this question will depend on the degree chosen and the process involved. Your work breakdown structure should include phases, steps, activities and milestones. You must also consider constraints such as time limits and prerequisites. For example, to get a PhD, you may have to complete coursework, pass comprehensive exams, pass a preliminary exam, and defend your dissertation. There may be constraints, such as a two-year time limit to complete all coursework or all comprehensive exams must be successfully completed before a preliminary exam can occur.

   For more details on work breakdown structures, activity graphs and critical paths, re-read Section 3.1.

2. Your answer will depend on your work environment. Use the descriptions of organizational structures to characterize your work environment. In Section 3.2, chief programmer teams are described. Section 3.6 describes several management structures such as matrix organizations and integrated product development teams. When evaluating the structure, you should consider whether the environment is highly or loosely structured. You should consider the number of potential lines of communication.

   When describing the working styles of your co-workers, keep in mind the styles described in the chapter: rational introverts, rational extroverts, intuitive introverts, and intuitive extroverts. Consider how these working styles affect communication in your work environment.

3. The chapter covers several different techniques for predicting effort. Algorithmic models and machine-learning models are presented in Section 3.3. Project planning is covered in Section 3.8.

4. Two measures of an estimate's accuracy are the mean magnitude of relative error (MMRE) and the percent of projects with estimate values within x percent of the actual value (PRED). The MMRE is the average of $|E-A|/A$ for each project. The PRED(x) is n/N where n is the number of projects with $|E-A|/A < x$ and N is the total number of projects. When the MMRE < 0.25, the technique is considered fairly good. Some researchers would like the MMRE to be less than 10%. For the PRED, a PRED(0.25) > 0.75 is considered good. The PRED(0.25) criterion means that 75% of the project estimates were within 25% of the actual values.

5. When estimating effort, it is often necessary to estimate size. Examples of size measures include lines of code, function points and object points. Object points can be calculated early in the process, but object points are a coarse measurement. Lines of code are not available early in the process, but are relatively easy to calculate. Function points can be calculated earlier than lines of code and provide a richer system description than object points.

Review Exam 1

1. If a system is being developed where the customers are not sure of what they want, the requirements are often poorly defined. Which of the following would be an appropriate process model for this type of development?
   a. prototyping
   b. waterfall
   c. V model
   d. spiral

2. The project team developing a new system is experienced in the domain. Although the new project is fairly large, it is not expected to vary much from applications that have been developed by this team in the past. Which process model would be appropriate for this type of development?
   a. prototyping
   b. waterfall
   c. V model
   d. spiral

3. Which of the following are potential barriers to the consumer of a reusable component?
   a. It is unclear where the responsibility for component failures lies.
   b. Sometimes, it takes more time to find a reuseable component than it would to build it.
   c. It can be costly to understand the intended behavior of a reuseable component.
   d. a and b only
   e. b and c only
   f. a and c only
   g. a, b and c

Suppose a library system is being developed. The system has three major subsystems: one that handles the check-out/check-in transactions; one that handles inventories; and one that handles reports. During the development of the system, several problems occur. Identify the problems as errors, faults or failures.

4. In the code for calculating late fees, the *fine_total* variable is not initialized.
5. While a librarian is attempting to add a new book title to the inventory, the system shuts down.
6. The requirements writer is unaware that a library card is not necessary for the check-in transaction.
7. In the requirements document, a late fee is specified as $0.25 per day with a maximum of $15. The code for calculating the late fee does not check for the maximum fee.
8. Every evening at 11 pm, the library system is supposed to perform a backup of the daily transactions. The backup for Tuesday night did not occur.

9. Paul, a manager of the development team, decides to use a COTS product
    developed by Reports 2 U, a third-party vendor, as part of the inventory
    subsystem. Which of the following are valid concerns?
    a. The COTS product may no longer be supported by the vendor at some
       later date.
    b. In order for the COTS product to work with the new system, a
       modification or enhancement to the COTS product may be needed. The
       vendor may be unwilling to make the change.
    c. The COTS product may not function as specified.
    d. a and b only
    e. b and c only
    f. a and c only
    g. a, b, and c

Jenna, a project manager, has developed a new technique for estimating
project size. She has been using the new technique on several projects. Her
estimates and the actual values for project size are shown below. The
criteria for a good estimating technique are: 75% of the estimates should be
within 25% of the actual; and the mean magnitude of the relative estimate
errors should be less than 25%. Use the table of project size estimates and
the criteria given to answer the questions about Jenna's estimating
technique.

Project	Estimate	Actual
A	8060	8000
B	9000	10000
C	7000	7200
D	15000	13000
E	10000	9600

10. Given the table of estimates and actuals, what is the MMRE? Round to the
    nearest 1/100.
    a. 0.01
    b. 0.05
    c. 0.06
    d. 0.07
    e. 0.10

11. What is the PRED(.25)?
    a. 0.05
    b. 0.25
    c. 0.33
    d. 0.75
    e. 1.00

12. Based on the criteria for a good estimation technique and the estimate
    data gathered so far, is the new technique a good one? (Yes/No)

Suppose Madeline, Andrew and Jason are three managers asked to estimate
effort required to build a 50,000 lines of code project. Each manager uses a
different estimating technique.

13. Madeline uses the basic, Walston/Felix model. What will her estimate (in person-months) be? Round to the closest month.
    a. 185 person-months
    b. 572 person-months
    c. 620 person-months
    d. 79634 person-months
    e. 99134 person-months

14. Andrew uses the Bailey and Basili basic model. What will his estimate (in person-months) be? Round to the closest month.
    a. 65 person-months
    b. 74 person-months
    c. 1189 person-months
    d. 1246 person-months
    e. 206129 person-months

15. Jason uses expert judgment to arrive at a 400 person-month estimate for the project. Using the estimates of Madeline, Andrew and Jason, what is the Delphi estimate for this project? Round to the closest month.
    a. 220 person-months
    b. 400 person-months
    c. 720 person-months
    d. 755 person-months
    e. 101888 person-months

16. If Madeline's estimate is used and there are 12 team members working on the project, how many months will the project take? Assume all team members can work concurrently. Round to the closest month.
    a. 15
    b. 48
    c. 52
    d. 6636
    e. 8261

17. Answer TRUE or FALSE:
    a. A development project is just beginning. An initial prototype of the user interface has been completed. It would be appropriate to use the COCOMO 2.0 stage 1 at this point in the development.
    b. A design has been chosen and development has begun. Detailed information about the design is known. The COCOMO 2.0 stage 2 model would be appropriate at this point in the development.

18. System A has 4 screens and 3 reports. Of the 4 screens, 3 are medium and 1 is difficult. Of the reports, 2 are medium and 1 is difficult. System B also has 4 screens and 3 reports. For system B, 2 screens are medium and 2 are difficult. The 3 reports for system B are medium difficulty. Which system has more new object points (COCOMO 2.0, stage 1 model)?
    a. System A
    b. System B
    c. System A and B have the same number of new object points.
    d. It is impossible to determine from the information given.

Consider the following descriptions of different employees' work styles.

19. Kristie seeks out evidence to support her decisions. She is currently considering rearranging the office space to make the working environment more comfortable for the members of her team. While carefully considering

the objective aspects of the change are important to her, she is also concerned about the opinions of the people who work for her. The members of Kristie's team consider her to be a good listener and often consult her when they have problems. Kristie's work style is:
    a. rational extrovert
    b. rational introvert
    c. intuitive extrovert
    d. intuitive introvert

20. Shane is an efficient leader. He knows what he wants and relies on his own experiences and logic to make decisions. He does not feel the need for extensive information before making a decision. He is capable of making fast decisions. Shane's work style would be described best as:
    a. rational extrovert
    b. rational introvert
    c. intuitive extrovert
    d. intuitive introvert

21. Jessica is a developer who enjoys trying new technology. She often finds inventive ways of incorporating new tools and techniques into the development process. After trying a new design tool, she immediately forms a positive opinion of the tool and attempts to get others to use the tool. Jessica's work style could best be described as:
    a. rational extrovert
    b. rational introvert
    c. intuitive extrovert
    d. intuitive introvert

22. Matthew is considering a new process for code reviews. He carefully seeks and reviews evidence to determine the potential benefits. He prides himself on being accurate and thorough. Matthew rarely looks to others for opinions. He would rather rely on information that can be objectively observed. Matthew's work style can be described as:
    a. rational extrovert
    b. rational introvert
    c. intuitive extrovert
    d. intuitive introvert

Activity graphs are used to depict the dependencies among the activities and milestones of a project. The nodes of the graph represent the milestones of the project. The edges linking the nodes represent the activities. The numbers adjacent to the edges represent the number of days required for the activity. For example, in the activity graph below, it will take 6 days to complete the activity starting at milestone A and ending in milestone C. Use this activity graph to answer the following questions:

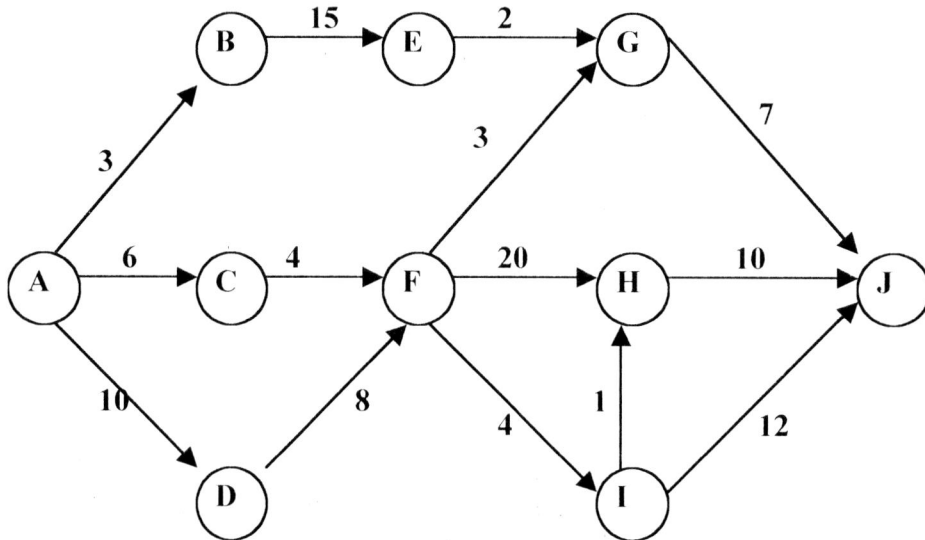

23. Which of the following is a critical path from milestone A to milestone J?
    a. ACFHJ
    b. ACFIHJ
    c. ABEGHJ
    d. ADFHJ

24. What is the slack time for the activity starting at milestone C?
    a. 7
    b. 8
    c. 15
    d. 20

25. What is the length of the critical path identified in question 23?
    a. 32
    b. 40
    c. 48
    d. 55

26. What is the latest start time for the activity starting at milestone E?
    a. 10
    b. 18
    c. 25
    d. 40

14

27. What is the earliest start time for the activities starting at milestone F?
    a. 11
    b. 19
    c. 33
    d. 37

28. Which milestones are precursors to H?
    a. A
    b. B
    c. C
    d. A and B
    e. A and C
    f. All of the above

29. If there are seven team members assigned to a project team, how many potential lines of communication are there?
    a. 6
    b. 7
    c. 21
    d. 49

Determine whether or not each of the following statements is describing a risk. Answer TRUE if the statement describes a risk, FALSE otherwise.

30. To catch defects early, requirements inspections have been incorporated into the process.

31. The customers are not clear about what they want. The requirements may be volatile.

32. The delivery of a subsystem being developed by another group may be delayed and cause the whole project schedule to slip.

33. The project team is inexperienced. A requirement may be misunderstood and designed incorrectly.

34. The development team is using a CASE tool for the first time on the design.

35. To aid the customer in identifying requirements, several prototypes are planned.

Review Exam 1 Answers

1. a, prototyping [Section 2.2]

2. b, waterfall [Section 2.2]

3. g; [Section 1.8]

4. fault [Sidebar 1.1]

5. failure [Sidebar 1.1]

6. error [Sidebar 1.1]

7. fault [Sidebar 1.1]

8. failure [Sidebar 1.1]

9. g; (COTS concerns)

10. d; MMRE = ((60/8000) + (1000/10000) + (200/7200) + (2000/13000) + (400/9600)) / 5 = 0.07 [Section 3.3]

11. e; All estimates are within 25% of actual values. [Section 3.3]

12. Yes; using criteria MMRE < 0.25 and PRED(0.25) > 0.75. [Section 3.3]

13. a; 185 person-months (Walston/Felix) [Section 3.3]

14. b; 74 person-months (Bailey/Basili basic model) [Section 3.3]

15. a; 220 person-months is the average of the three estimates [Section 3.3]

16. a; 15 months (duration on Madeline's estimate) [Section 3.3]

17. COCOMO [Section 3.3]
    a. TRUE
    b. FALSE, stage 3 would be more appropriate than stage 2 because detailed information about the design is known.

18. a; difficulty of reports is weighted more heavily than difficulty of screens in the COCOMO 2.0 model. [Section 3.3]

19. d; intuitive introvert [Section 3.2]

20. a; rational extrovert [Section 3.2]

21. c; intuitive extrovert [Section 3.2]

22. b; rational introvert [Section 3.2]

The following table can be used to answer questions 23 to 28:

Activity	Earliest Start Time	Latest Start Time	Slack
A	1	1	0
B	4	25	21
C	7	15	8
D	11	11	0
E	19	40	21
F	19	19	0
G	22	42	0
H	39	39	0
I	23	37	14
J(finish)	48	48	0

An activity label in the table should be read, "the activity beginning at milestone <label>." For example, the activity beginning at milestone B has an earliest start time of 4.

23. d; ADFHJ is the critical path [Section 3.1]

24. b; 8 is the slack time for the activity starting at milestone C. [Section 3.1]

25. c; 48 is the length of the critical path. [Section 3.1]

26. d; latest start time for the activity starting at milestone E is 40. [Section 3.1]

27. b; earliest start time for the activity starting at F is 19 [Section 3.1]

28. e; B is not a precursor to H [Section 3.1]

29. c; $(n(n-1))/2 = (7(6))/2 = 21$ lines of communication [Section 3.2]

30. FALSE; This is a risk control. [Section 3.4]

31. TRUE; Requirements volatility is a risk. [Section 3.4]

32. TRUE; Late delivery is a risk. [Section 3.4]

33. TRUE; Team inexperience is a risk. [Section 3.4]

34. TRUE; First use of a new technology is a risk.

35. FALSE; Prototyping is a risk control. [Section 3.4]

Chapter 4: Capturing the Requirements

Learning Objectives:
After studying this chapter, you should be able to:
- Explain why it is necessary to elicit requirements from software customers, and the role of requirements in the software life cycle.
- Describe the types of requirements that should be included in a requirements document.
- Appreciate the importance of the context in which a proposed system is expected to operate, and how that context affects the system's requirements.
- Explain how to express acceptance criteria to test whether the requirements are met.
- Use modeling notations to capture requirements, and understand the types of situations in which each notation may be appropriate.
- Describe which techniques can be employed to perform requirements validation and verification.
- Evaluate requirements with respect to general characteristics of well-documented requirements.
- Explain how to document requirements as defined by the customer and how to document requirements for use by the design and test teams.

Summary:
This chapter focuses on capturing system requirements, an important component of any model of the software development process. It is important to remember that the purpose of requirements is to specify the problem that the system is intended to solve, leaving the details of the solution to the system designers. Formulating a useful set of requirements will require working closely with all stakeholders. They are the clients (who pay for the software to be developed), the customers (who buy the software), the users (who will use the system), the domain experts (who are familiar with the problem that the software must automate), the software designers (who will design the software based on the requirements specification), the testers (who will write test plans to evaluate whether the implementation meets the requirements), and the documentation writers (who will write user's manuals from the specifications). To elicit requirements is to collect all the different views of the stakeholders in a coherent document that expresses what the requirements are. Everyone involved must understand and agree on the requirements.

Any requirements document should include different types of requirements. Functional requirements explain what the system will do. Quality or nonfunctional requirements describe quality attributes that the system must possess, such as safety, reliability, performance, cost, and maintenance. Design constraints restrict the solution dictating some of its design aspects that have already been decided. Process constraints restrict the techniques or resources that can be used to develop the system.

Mistakes made during the requirements process can cause additional--and expensive--problems later in the software life cycle. Thus, requirements must be validated to ensure that they reflect the expectations of customers. The set of requirements should also be validated by checking for completeness, correctness, consistency, realism, and other attributes. Measures reflecting requirements quality are especially important since they may indicate useful activities; e.g., when indicators show that the requirements are not well understood, prototyping of some requirements may be appropriate.

A specification describes what software is needed to fulfill the requirements. The specification must adhere to the requirements as defined by the customers, and we should verify that it does so. While the requirements definition is meant to be read and understood by clients and users, the specification is written for designers and programmers. The requirements focus on the environment where the system will be used, whereas the specification focuses on the interface of the system with its environment.

There are many different types of definition and specification techniques that can be used for capturing requirements. Some are models based on prescriptive notations that allow for expressing the expected behavior of a system (e.g., event traces). Others use a descriptive notation to express properties of a system (e.g., logic). Finally, algebraic specifications describe the interactions between pairs of operations instead of modeling individual operations. We can also think of techniques as being informal (e.g., data-flow diagram) or formal, based on mathematics (e.g., temporal logic). The techniques that are used on a particular software-development project should be chosen carefully, based on a number of factors. For example, the specification techniques differ in terms of their tool support, maturity, understandability, ease of use, and mathematical formality. Projects vary in terms of size and scope. The right technique must be chosen based on the needs of the current project, keeping these factors in mind. In some cases, it may be desirable to use a combination of techniques to specify different aspects of a system.

Because requirements typically contain many disparate elements that are integrated into a comprehensive whole, requirements must be written in a way that allows them to be linked and controlled. For example, a change to one requirement may affect other related requirements, and the techniques and tools must support these changes to ensure that errors are caught as early as possible.

Exercises:
1. Most of a system's requirements specify that the system should do what it is intended to do. Is it also appropriate to specify that the system should *not* do what it is *not* intended to do? If your answer is no, explain why; if your answer is yes, give an example.
2. Describe the different consumers of software requirements (e.g., the different users, or types of users, of a software requirements document). For each consumer, explain how he or she would use the requirements, and how the requirements should be documented to make them useful for his/her needs.
3. Looking at Figure 4.1, explain how requirements validation is related to requirements elicitation. Can the validation be based solely on the specification document?
4. What is the role of a domain expert during requirements elicitation?
5. Comment on the phrase: "Good requirements analysis requires excellent 'people skills' as well as solid technical skills."
6. One source of problems in the requirements phase can be the relationship between system developers and their customers. What are some negative stereotypes customers may hold about developers? What could you, as a developer on a project, do to minimize the impact of those negative stereotypes?
7. Download and read the Robertsons' requirements definition template (from http://www.**systemsguild**.com). Write a short report in which you summarize for a software developer how he or she can use the template to validate requirements. Your report should address practical concerns about how to use the template in the requirements process. For example, you should

address questions such as: At what point in the requirements process can the template be helpful? What activities are necessary in order to use the template for validating requirements? What skills will a developer have to possess in order to apply the template effectively? What types of errors and faults will the template help uncover?

8. What are fit criteria? Give an example of a quality requirement and its fit criteria.

9. Pamela Zave has proposed a classification scheme for organizing the different types of research that go on in the area of software requirements (P. Zave (1997). "Classification of research efforts in requirements engineering." ACM Computing Surveys, 29(4): 315-321). Choose one of the categories she presents and write a brief (one paragraph) description of how research in this area is of use to software developers. Track down one of the papers she cites as an example of research in this category, and summarize the problem it addresses and the results it presents.

10. Bashar Nuseibeh and Steve Easterbrook have presented an overview of the area of requirements engineering (Nuseibeh and Easterbrook (2000) "Requirements Engineering: A Roadmap" In Proceedings of the Conference on The Future of Software Engineering, ACM Press, 35-46, Limerick, 2000). They described the main areas of requirements engineering practice. Which of these areas do you think is the hardest to practice in a software development company? Which of these practices do you think would bring the most benefit to a software development company? Justify your answers presenting your rationale.

Answer Guidelines:

1. Yes. An example of the latter type of requirement is a security requirement. In this case, it is necessary to specify exactly what the system should NOT allow a user or other system to do.

2. Requirements need to be used by
   a. The client, the customer, the domain expert, and the users, whose input is necessary to produce the requirements definition document, which is a record of the requirements expressed in the customer's terms. These people must review the document to validate the requirements, and their software expertise may be limited, so the document should be easy to understand, with a minimum of jargon, to facilitate clear communication with the customers.
   b. The analyst and the specifier, who are responsible for writing the requirements definition document and the requirements specification document, which covers the same problem as the requirements definition document, but from the point of view of the developers. They must verify that the specification fulfills the requirements as defined by the customers.
   c. The designers, who need to construct a design that satisfies the requirements as expressed in the requirements specification document. The requirements will need to be as complete, clear, and correct as possible. Also, they will need to identify all of the constraints on the system, so that the design can correctly incorporate them.
   d. The testers, who need to develop test plans. To support testers, the requirements specification document should be as precise as possible, so that the values that need to be tested and the expected system behavior are well specified.

e. The maintainers, who may not be familiar with the system when starting the maintenance work and who need to understand the underlying requirements of the system, any assumptions made, and any constraints on solutions, so that changes to the design don't accidentally invalidate the requirements. Both types of documents (requirements definitions and specifications) are used by maintainers and should be as complete as possible. Maintainers may also need to update these documents to reflect changes.

f. The documentation writers, who will write the user's manuals based on both requirements documents. The requirements should clearly communicate the features of the system.

3. Requirements validation is the process of checking that the specification matches what the customer expects to see in the final product. It cannot be done by reviewing only the specification document. The requirements specification itself can be internally correct and yet not reflect the customer's needs. That is, we may be developing correct software (i.e., software that is free of bugs) that is not the right software, because it does not meet the customer's demands.

4. The domain expert should provide information about the properties, the facts, and characteristics of the application domain of the customer's problem. He should also be able to demystify any wrong assumptions that non-experts tend to believe. Requirements can be met only if the domain properties are correctly taken into account for the definition of the requirements.

5. Both technical and "people skills" are necessary during requirements elicitation, to ensure the successful acquisition of quality requirements. People skills are necessary because human interaction, communication, conflict resolution, interviewing, and apprenticing with users play an important role in gathering information from the stakeholders. A customer may not volunteer information that he believes is well known to everyone. An analyst with good people skills will show interest in the customer's world and will involve the customer in conversations that will reveal as much information as possible.

6. Use Table 4.1 as a starting point for your answer. For each point listed on the table under the category of "How users see developers," think about whether the prejudice is justified, and, if so, whether it always holds. If not, ask what you could do to change that perception. For example, the first point, "Developers don't understand operational needs," is often true, in that software engineers don't always have extensive training in the customer's application domain or way of doing business. However, a serious effort by the developer to learn about the customer's needs in order to support the customer is not only helpful for reversing negative stereotypes, but is also a prerequisite for building quality software.

7. The template is useful during requirements reviews, but it can also be helpful if given to the writers of requirements as a guide for what information should be included. The categories and items of the template can be used as a checklist for ensuring that all of the appropriate issues have been addressed and the correct information has been included in the requirements document. The reviewer of the requirements will have to have a sufficient understanding of the requirements in order to find the pertinent information for each item of the template. The template

will be most helpful for finding defects of omission, that is, for identifying types of information that should be included in the requirements but were left out.

8. A fit criterion quantifies a requirement. It is a goal that distinguishes between a system that passes a test of, for example, possessing a desired property and a system that does not. A fit criterion defines the threshold that the system must reach in order to be accepted by the customer. It can be applied to functional and to quality requirements.
   Example:
   Description of a usability requirement: The system shall be easy to use, and intuitive.
   Fit criterion: After taking the one-day training course on the system, the users shall be able to use the system to complete each of their tasks within 2 minutes.

9. Answers will vary depending on the category chosen and papers selected.

10. To guide your first answer, think about the limitations that software companies have to deal with. To guide your second answer, think about the benefits of each of the practices presented in the paper.

Chapter 5: Designing the Architecture

Learning Objectives:
After studying this chapter, you should be able to:
- Describe the design process, and the different decompositions and architectural views.
- Describe the different ways we can use an architectural model.
- Describe an overview of important architectural styles and techniques, and the conditions under which different choices may be appropriate.
- Explain the different quality attributes of architectural styles.
- Identify and explain the different types of analysis used when evaluating an architectural design.
- Explain what the software architecture document is and what information it should contain.
- Explain why validating architectural design is necessary, and a general overview of how this task can be accomplished.

Summary:
This chapter focuses on the process by which the requirements specification (the description of what the customers want the system to do) are translated into a design (a description of a system that will satisfy the customers' needs). There are many different ways to design a system, such as basing it on a reference model, cloning, reusing previous designs or adapting generic ones. These generic design solutions, referred to as architectural styles, provide ideas on how to better model the requirements specification. This can be accomplished by finding one or more architectural styles that support the properties and constraints present in the requirements specification. This chapter also provides some commonly used sample architectural styles, such as pipe-and-filter, client-server, peer-to-peer, publish-subscribe, repositories and layering.

If no suitable architectural styles can be found then an innovative design can be created, guided by basic design principles and assisted through different design techniques. Decomposition, one of such techniques, is used to identify the main concerns of the system. There are many different decomposition methods, with one of the most well-known being object-oriented decomposition. Decomposition has the purpose of breaking the system into different components or software units. Each resulting software unit can be further decomposed into even smaller software units. Multiple levels of decomposition can be achieved through this process.

When modeling architectures, it is useful to create different models to represent different aspects or facets of the architecture. These models, referred to as architectural views, relate to properties and constraints in the requirements specification. These views depict the interaction between software units and are dependent on each other--changes in one view may affect other views. Such coupling between views is a desired property, and results in a more coherent design.

Once the design is underway, its attributes can be analyzed and matched against the desired system attributes. Tactics can be applied to ensure that the required quality attributes are supported in the design. Quality attributes include modifiability, performance, security, reliability, robustness, usability and business goals. The overall quality of the design can also be analyzed, providing feedback on how to improve the design according to the requirements specification. Some analyses of design quality are:

- Measuring design quality: use metrics to assess aspects of the design quality
- Safety analysis: fault detection, tolerance and correction
- Security analysis: threats and vulnerability assessment, risk analysis
- Trade-off analysis: experiment with different alternate designs
- Cost-benefit analysis: return on investment between different designs
- Prototyping: clarifies questions about a specific part or aspect of the system

This chapter also emphasizes that design is an activity that involves other developers. Other developers are an implicit factor in the design process, since the choice of design method depends on who will have to read and understand the design. Also, since designs comprise multiple software units, the interrelationships among these software units and data must be well-documented.

The software architecture document is used as an information repository, helping different members of the design team to understand the architectural design of the system and its purpose. Cross-referencing may be necessary to help explain which parts of the design affect what software units and data. The software architecture document can also be used to both validate and verify the architectural design. Validation is used to assert that the architectural design of the system fulfills all of the specified requirements. Validation is performed by the requirements analysts, systems architects and designers. Verification is used to ensure that the design follows good design principles and to detect any inconsistencies or faults in the design with respect to the requirements specification.

Exercises:
1. What does it mean to say that a design review should be "egoless"? Why are egoless reviews necessary? Suggest some steps that may help achieve egoless reviews.
2. Choose a software system that you use and for which there is some feature of the interface that you, as a user, dislike. Briefly describe the software and why you consider this feature of the interface to be a problem. Speculate as to whether the problem could have been avoided during design. If so, what changes to the design process would have been necessary?
3. Read the account by Nancy Leveson and Clark Turner of the Therac-25 accidents (N. Leveson and C. Turner (1993). "An investigation of the Therac-25 accidents." *IEEE Computer*, 26(7) (July): 18-41). Give a brief summary of some of the important lessons that can be learned for design.

Answer Guidelines:
1. "Egoless" reviews occur when criticisms are directed at the design process and the design itself, not at the designers and other participants. Egoless reviews are useful since they remind participants that they are moving toward a common goal and keep them focused on the software under review, rather than encouraging them to make excuses or defend themselves. Egoless reviews enhance communication and allow more time to be spent discussing the software itself. Egoless reviews can be facilitated by any measure that reminds participants that the software and not the individuals are under discussion. Examples include making a statement of the review goal at the beginning of the review, or making sure that comments during the review remain centered on the software.

Egoless reviews are also facilitated by not inviting a representative of management, to make sure that participants do not feel their performance is being judged based on other participants' comments.

2. Answers will vary depending on software system chosen and interface problem discussed. In any case, you should first make sure that the problem you've selected is in fact a problem from the user's point of view (i.e., one that results from a poorly defined interface). For example, suppose you work with a piece of software that, at certain times, will not allow you to interact with the system while some computation is going on. The fact that you have to wait for the computation to complete may not be a user interface problem; the computation may simply require a large amount of time to complete the calculation. However, if the user is not given a chance to cancel the computation after it has started, then a frustrating problem can occur in which a user has decided that it is not necessary to run the computation at this point but has to wait for it to complete anyway. Many such problems can be caught in the design phase if resources are expended on user interface design and review.

3. The Leveson and Turner paper contains many lessons that can be applied to design. You should select some of these lessons, and cite experiences with the Therac-25 that support them. For example, page 503, Sidebar 9.11 contains a list of five basic software engineering principles that were violated in development of the Therac-25. Which of these can be applied to design? What kind of conditions did their absence from the development of the Therac-25 lead to? You should use these principles as a starting point but also identify other lessons. For example, what kind of lessons can be found about reuse? About timing problems?

Chapter 6: Designing the Modules

Learning Objectives:
After studying this chapter, you should be able to:
- Describe design principles.
- Describe object-oriented design heuristics.
- Understand what use cases are, discuss why they can be useful in software development, and use them to describe system functionality.
- Use and understand UML diagrams.
- Explain what design patterns are, and apply them in module-level designs.
- Explain how measurement is useful in object-oriented development, give examples of some object-oriented metrics, and explain the concepts those metrics are capturing.

Summary:
This chapter describes approaches to design and develops the modules of the system by decomposing its architectural design units. While in the architectural design phase we focus on system-level properties of the requirement specification, in the module design phase it is necessary to include detailed design specifications so that the design can be implemented in code. Modules are less generic entities than architectural styles and, as a result, less likely to have pre-built solutions. It is necessary, therefore, to use more creativity and innovation in designing modules. Due to this volatile nature, module design decisions often need to be revised and changed. This process is called refactoring.

When creating the modules, good design properties, referred to as design principles, are used to help decompose the specified system functionality into modules. Design principles can help in achieving desired module characteristics such as low coupling, high cohesion, modularity and generality. A system with such characteristics is easier to understand and, as a result, maintain. The design principles are:
- Modularity
- Interfaces
- Information hiding
- Incremental development
- Abstraction
- Generality

Design methodologies that both encode and encourage the use of design principles were put in place to help developers create quality designs. Object-oriented design is one such methodology, and it contains features that implement and enforce the design principles. It uses the concept of an object to encapsulate data and functionality through attributes and methods. Objects have specific features that differentiate them from other system components, such as runtime identification, composition, and extension through inheritance and polymorphism.

Object-oriented solutions are often described using a notation support known as the Unified Modeling Language (UML). UML provides diagrams that capture information about the system in a series of dynamic and static views. The UML diagrams include activity diagrams, domain models, component diagrams, deployment diagrams, class diagrams, interaction diagrams, sequence diagrams, communication diagrams, activity diagrams, state diagrams and package diagrams.

Despite the lack of pre-built solutions, analogous to architectural styles, there do exist several design conventions that help designers make the most of object-oriented features and to avoid certain object-oriented design pitfalls. Conventions include substitutability, law of Demeter and dependency inversion. Another type of aid is design patterns. A design pattern is a template to solve a design problem, which encapsulates best practices according to the design principles. A design pattern is not a finished solution, but a framework that can be applied to many different situations. Design patterns are usually described through UML and object-oriented design. Some design patterns are: template method, factory method, strategy pattern, decorator pattern, observer pattern, composite pattern, and visitor pattern.

Finally, the measurement of object-oriented design characteristics can help in selecting a design and refining it to achieve desirable features such as low coupling and high cohesion. The measurement of design characteristics can help in understanding, prediction or control of the module. Object-oriented metrics can be classified into size and design metrics, with many metrics defined in each category. Unfortunately there is no single best set of metrics, and developers must consider what is useful and feasible to measure in their context before selecting which to use.

Exercises:
1. The following statements describe modules in a (hypothetical) program. For each, decide whether the module is likely to have a high or low degree of cohesion. If cohesion is low, explain why.
    a. Module "InventorySearchByID" searches the records in inventory to see if any match the specified range of ID numbers. A data structure is returned containing any matching records.
    b. Module "ProcessPurchase" removes the purchased product from inventory, prints a receipt for the customer and updates the log.
    c. Module "FindSet" processes the user's request, determines the set of items from inventory that match the request, and formats the items into a list that can be shown to the customer.
2. In what ways do the object-oriented characteristics of encapsulation and information hiding support reuse? What kind of criteria would you use in deciding whether to reuse a class in a new system?
3. Why is it useful to have separate phases for architectural and module designs?
4. Find a paper or book that deals with design patterns in more detail. Summarize briefly one of the patterns presented. Explain what it is useful for, when it can be used, and its effects on the rest of the program. What are some of the difficulties you might expect to encounter if using design patterns in practice?
5. You are designing a system to help run a bookstore. Revenue for the store comes from two distinct services: customers can purchase books, or bring their books in for rebinding. You are considering making a separate class for each service, both of which would be subclasses of a general "sale item" class. What are the likely benefits of such an approach? Are there any possible arguments against using inheritance in this case? Be sure to specify what factors could influence your decision.
6. Section 6.7 discusses Chidamber and Kemerer's metric of depth of inheritance. Why does it seem likely that a class that is deeper in the hierarchy is harder to understand and maintain than one that is less deep?

Answer Guidelines:

1.

    a. Module "InventorySearchByID" can be expected to have high cohesion; it performs only one type of functionality (a search).

    b. Module "ProcessPurchase" can be expected to have relatively low cohesion, since it involves very different functionalities: printing a receipt for use by the user is logically quite different from updating a data store.

    c. Module "FindSet"can be expected to have relatively low cohesion, since it invokes very different functionalities: parsing input, a search-through data, and output formatting.

2. A good way to answer this question would be to turn it around and begin by thinking of what would make for an ideal reuse situation. Some goals could be: it should be easy for the developer to understand what functionality is available to be reused, related functionalities should be somehow reusable together, it should be easy to understand how to reuse the functionality, and the reusable components should be of high quality. Then, address whether it would be harder or easier to achieve these characteristics in an OO environment, and why.

3. Architectural design gives developers a chance to solidify the broad outlines of the proposed system before having to decide on more specific details of the implementation. Use the beginning of Section 6.6 to understand what decisions are reserved for module design. Then consider what negative outcomes could result if developers began debating these issues earlier. What factors, later in development, could make the answers to these issues more or less relevant? Would it ever be a drawback to come to an early decision on these issues, even if the system could be implemented without changing these decisions in later life-cycle phases?

4. The definition of a design pattern almost always includes context information, a definition of the pattern itself, and tradeoffs associated with its use, so be sure to address each of these points in your summary. Design patterns suffer from some of the same difficulties that are experienced in any reuse situation: it is often hard to recognize situations that could benefit from reuse, and it is difficult to search a repository of components (including patterns) to find the best match to the current situation. As with any other type of reuse, developers may not be sufficiently motivated to overcome these difficulties with design patterns.

5. The likely benefits involve shared functionality, perhaps for pricing and revenue, which could be implemented once in the superclass and shared in each of these two classes. On the other hand, there are enough differences between the two services that it could be argued that joining such dissimilar classes in an inheritance hierarchy would be confusing, since very little functionality could be shared through the superclass. (For example, book sales might involve updating inventory, tracking the space required for sale, and ordering more copies of a book when it is close to being sold out. Bookbinding would not track inventory but would need another set of methods to deal with expected due dates for the service and scheduling the time of a suitable expert at the shop.) Many factors should be taken into account to make the decision, but in this case a particularly important one is the anticipated future needs of the store. If it is possible that the range of sale items might increase in

the future, then it becomes more cost effective to encapsulate the common functionality in a superclass for sharing among the classes that might be added.

6. To answer this question, think about how someone reading an OO program knows where the specific definition of a method is located. If there is no inheritance involved, a method is defined within the class to which it belongs. But if that class is part of an inheritance hierarchy, the method need not be defined in the class. Is there any indication of which parent class contains the definition of a method? Can a method be redefined multiple times within a particular hierarchy? How do those factors contribute to the ease and accuracy with which a method definition can be found?

Review Exam 2[1]

The following questions are in reference to a hypothetical "Gas Station Control System" (or GSCS) that will be used to help manage an American-style gasoline or service station. Our hypothetical gas station basically provides two services:

- There is a small store that carries car parts. Inside the store is at least one cash register, operated by a cashier who is an employee of the gas station.
- There are a number of gas pumps, at which customers can park their cars, interact with the system to pay via credit card, and then pump their own gas. Alternatively, the customer can pay for his or her gas via cash or credit card by going into the store and paying directly to the cashier.

Thus, the GSCS has two main classes of users. The first is the cashier, who uses the GSCS to record purchases of car parts by customers. The GSCS must allow the cashier to enter the type and number of parts purchased, then compute the total purchase price and handle the payment. Customers purchasing gasoline are the second type of user. These customers interface with the system at the gas pump by specifying the amount and type of gas they will buy, paying either at the pump or to the cashier, and then pumping the gas themselves.

The system also has to interact with other automated systems to perform its tasks. For example, in order to accept credit card payments, the GSCS must interface with a system maintained by the credit card company. The credit card system is responsible for checking that the customer's account is in good standing and can accommodate the amount of the purchase, and for debiting the customer's account and eventually reimbursing the gas station. The operation of these external systems is beyond the scope of the GSCS, although the GSCS needs to know how the external systems will communicate the success or failure of their tasks.

The first step that the development team decides to undertake is to create a requirements document.

1. Which of the following statements best describe the benefits that the development team may expect from the requirements process?
   a. The requirements process can help team members understand how the different types of functionality in the system relate to each other.
   b. The requirements process can help the team make programming decisions, such as which is the best algorithm to use for computations, at an early point.
   c. The requirements process can help the team avoid omitting necessary functionality.
   d. a and b
   e. a and c
   f. b and c
   g. a, b, and c

[1] The design diagrams for the GSCS used in this exam are adapted from ones created by Prof. Guilherme Travassos, of the Federal University of Rio de Janeiro, and Jeffrey Carver, of the University of Maryland, College Park. The diagrams are reprinted from *Advances in Computers*, volume 54, Travassos, Shull, and Carver, "Working with UML: A Software Design Process Based on Inspections for the Unified Modeling Language," 2001, by permission of the publisher Academic Press London.

2. Which of the following statements best describe the benefits that the owner of the gas station may expect from the requirements process?
    a. The requirements process can help the gas station owner think more clearly about the set of functionality that should be included in the GSCS.
    b. The requirements process can help the gas station owner and the development team in communicating while discussing the system.
    c. The requirements process gives the owner a guarantee that the final system will behave as he expects it to.
    d. a and b
    e. a and c
    f. b and c
    g. a, b, and c

3. The development team needs to pick a representation for the requirements. Which of the following is a valid choice and rationale?
    a. Data flow diagrams, since major system functionality will involve data interfaces among hardware (e.g., cash register, pumps, credit card readers).
    b. Decision tables, because the system will need to handle many events happening concurrently (e.g., multiple customers at multiple gas pumps).
    c. Z, because it is easily understandable by the gas station owner and will aid communication about the system.
    d. Entity-relationship diagrams, since this will make sure that the system response is specified for every situation.

4. In temporal logic, how do you express the fact that after the customer pays for gas at the cashier, the pump's counters must be reset to zero to serve the next customer?
    a. $\Box(\text{paid\_gas} \Rightarrow \bigcirc(\text{pump\_value} = 0))$
    b. $\Box(\text{pump\_value} = 0 \Rightarrow \bigcirc(\text{paid\_gas}))$
    c. $\Box(\text{paid\_gas} \Rightarrow \Diamond(\text{pump\_value} = 0))$
    d. $\Box(\text{pump\_value} = 0 \Rightarrow \Diamond(\text{paid\_gas}))$

Mark the following TRUE if they belong in the requirements for the GSCS, and FALSE if they do not.

5. How much documentation the development team is required to produce.
6. The level of training that will be necessary for the cashiers to use the system effectively.
7. The constraint that new customers, paying for gasoline, must be able to learn how to use the system from simple directions posted at the gas pumps.
8. The maximum cost of the system.
9. The hardware constraints that are necessary for interfacing with the cash registers and gas pumps.
10. The format of the data received from the cash registers and gas pumps.
11. How maintenance to the system will be performed.

12. Which of the following excerpts could be considered valid requirements?
   a. "Once the payment process is complete, the system should respond in the following way: If the user has paid the cashier directly, or has paid at the pump but does not desire a receipt, then return to the initial state. Otherwise, print a receipt."
   b. "A record should be kept for each cashier. Each record should store the last name, first name, and employee ID number. The records should be maintained in a linked list."
   c. "After the user has selected a payment option, the system should check if the input is valid (i.e., a number between one and three)."
   d. a and b only
   e. a and c only
   f. b and c only
   g. a, b, and c

13. Which of the following are examples of valid nonfunctional requirements?
   a. "The display must update within three seconds after the user has selected a payment option."
   b. "When car parts have been purchased, the count of inventory remaining must be updated. A warning message will be displayed if the count drops below the pre-set limit."
   c. "The user must replace the nozzle when finished pumping gas."
   d. a and b only
   e. a and c only
   f. b and c only
   g. a, b, and c

A requirements review is undertaken to make sure that the requirements adequately describe the system to be built.

In questions 14 through 18, review the given excerpt from the requirements and decide whether it is an adequate requirement or not. If it should be rewritten, mark all the reasons that apply.

14. "After the payment process is complete, the relevant information should be appended to a log file."
   a. This requirement should be rewritten; it is incorrect.
   b. This requirement should be rewritten; it is ambiguous or inconsistent.
   c. This requirement should be rewritten; it is unrealistic.
   d. This requirement should be rewritten; it is unverifiable.
   e. This requirement is fine.

15. "The system should be constructed so that it will be easy to add new functionality in the future."
   a. This requirement should be rewritten; it is incorrect.
   b. This requirement should be rewritten; it is ambiguous or inconsistent.
   c. This requirement should be rewritten; it is unrealistic.
   d. This requirement should be rewritten; it is unverifiable.
   e. This requirement is fine.

16. "The price of a gasoline purchase is computed as the price per gallon for the type of gas purchased, multiplied by the number of gallons purchased (use two decimal points for representing fractions of gallons)."
    a. This requirement should be rewritten; it is incorrect.
    b. This requirement should be rewritten; it is ambiguous or inconsistent.
    c. This requirement should be rewritten; it is unrealistic.
    d. This requirement should be rewritten; it is unverifiable.
    e. This requirement is fine.

17. "The system should be easy for new customers to use."
    a. This requirement should be rewritten; it is incorrect.
    b. This requirement should be rewritten; it is ambiguous or inconsistent.
    c. This requirement should be rewritten; it is unrealistic.
    d. This requirement should be rewritten; it is unverifiable.
    e. This requirement is fine.

18. "The system should be available 24 hours a day, 7 days a week."
    a. This requirement should be rewritten; it is incorrect.
    b. This requirement should be rewritten; it is ambiguous or inconsistent.
    c. This requirement should be rewritten; it is unrealistic.
    d. This requirement should be rewritten; it is unverifiable.
    e. This requirement is fine.

After the requirements review, 23 changes are made and a new version of the requirements is created. This version was reviewed again, and 9 changes were suggested. After these were changed, the latest version was shown to the customer, who recommended 5 more changes.

19. Based on the above measurements, what can we conclude?
    a. The requirements should be reviewed again, since there are still defects being found.
    b. The development team should begin working on the design based on these requirements, since the number of changes is decreasing and the requirements are becoming more stable.
    c. It is impossible to say whether the requirements should be reviewed without knowing the types of changes being made.

The development team decides that the next step is to create an architectural design.

20. The first draft of the design has the following characteristics. Which are NOT appropriate?
    a. It is written in a formal design notation, so that functionality can be specified as precisely as possible.
    b. It makes multiple references to the requirements document, in order to provide the reason for including certain system components.
    c. It uses some of the built-in features of C++, in order to better make the argument for choosing this language for use in the implementation.
    d. a and b
    e. a and c
    f. b and c
    g. a, b, and c

21. The team has not decided on a general approach to creating the design. Which are NOT valid choices and rationales?
    a. Modular decomposition, because the system can be divided into separate types of functionality that are relatively independent (for example, the operation of the cashier versus the operation of the gas pumps).
    b. Outside-in design, because the set of user inputs is fairly well understood.
    c. Object-oriented design, because the emphasis will mainly be on the flow of data through the system (for example, how the central system tracks purchases at each of the individual gas pumps).
    d. a and b
    e. a and c
    f. b and c
    g. a, b, and c

22. The team leader decides that the logical next step is to decide on an architectural style for the system. Which of the following are NOT valid choices and rationales?
    a. Object-oriented, since the problem can be decomposed into several different entities, each responsible for its own data access and manipulation routines.
    b. Pipe and filter, since most of the required functionality involves "piping" data between subsystems in preset ways.
    c. Implicit invocations, since the system is event-driven and depends on the reliability of the subcomponents.
    d. a and b
    e. a and c
    f. b and c
    g. a, b, and c

23. TRUE or FALSE: Having decided on an architecture, the team leader decides that the architecture should be frozen for the life of the project. That is, once code design starts, no changes to the architecture will be permissible so that there will be no inconsistencies. This is a reasonable strategy.

The development team decides to divide the system into three subsystems:
- A gas purchase subsystem that takes care of customer interaction with the gas pumps;
- A cashier subsystem that interacts with the cashier to accept payment for the purchase of car parts and gasoline;
- A tracking subsystem that logs all purchases and tracks the inventory remaining.

Each of these subsystems is expected to be a relatively complicated system in its own right, but this design was chosen to minimize the communication among subsystems. Both the gas purchase and cashier subsystems will communicate with the tracking subsystem, but not with each other.

24. Which of the following best describes the design at this level of abstraction?
    a. High coupling, high cohesion
    b. High coupling, low cohesion
    c. Low coupling, high cohesion
    d. Low coupling, low cohesion

25. TRUE or FALSE: The above combination of coupling and cohesion will make programming and maintenance easier than if the system had been designed otherwise.

26. The team leader realizes that the team does not have much experience building systems able to handle concurrency, as the gas purchase subsystem will have to do. He therefore decides that the best way to proceed will be for the team to develop a basic design for the subsystem that demonstrates that concurrency can be handled, but does not include the full range of customer functionality. The full range of functionality can be added once the team is sure they have achieved an adequate design for handling concurrency. This strategy is an example of:
    a. A prototype design
    b. A throwaway prototype
    c. Fault-tree analysis
    d. Design by contract

27. The gas purchase subsystem needs to be able to handle the situation in which the customer pays by credit card, but the remote system that validates the credit card information is unreachable, perhaps because of a temporary network failure. This situation is an example of:
    a. An exception
    b. A fault
    c. A failure

28. It would be reasonable to design the system so that the first time the situation described in question 27 occurs, the system responds by:
    a. Retrying
    b. Correcting
    c. Reporting
    d. Active fault detection
    e. Passive fault detection

29. After more work has been done on the design, the team leader decides it is time to hold a design review. Who among the following need NOT be invited?
    a. The requirements analysts
    b. The developers
    c. The gas station owner
    d. a and b
    e. a and c
    f. b and c
    g. a, b, and c

30. Which of the following items of information are NOT appropriate for inclusion in the Software Architecture Document?
    a. The maximum cost the gas station owner is willing to pay for the system
    b. The layout of the cashier's screen
    c. The general layout of the network that supports communication within and among subsystems
    d. None of the above (all are appropriate)
    e. a and b
    f. a and c
    g. b and c
    h. a, b, and c

31. Which of the following are valid rationales for creating a module design?
    a. The architectural design will be useful for communicating with the gas station owner but not very useful as a basis for implementing the system.
    b. The module design should contain more information about the gas pumps and their interfaces to the software.
    c. The module design should contain more detail about the likely data structures that will be used.
    d. a and b
    e. a and c
    f. b and c
    g. a, b, and c

32. In the initial design, the gas purchase subsystem is assumed to handle all of the details of the purchase, and need send only a record containing the amount of gas purchased, purchase price, and time of purchase to the tracking subsystem. The relationship between the gas and purchase subsystem and the tracking subsystem is best described as:
    a. Content coupled
    b. Control coupled
    c. Stamp coupled
    d. Logically coupled
    e. Temporally coupled
    f. Functionally cohesive

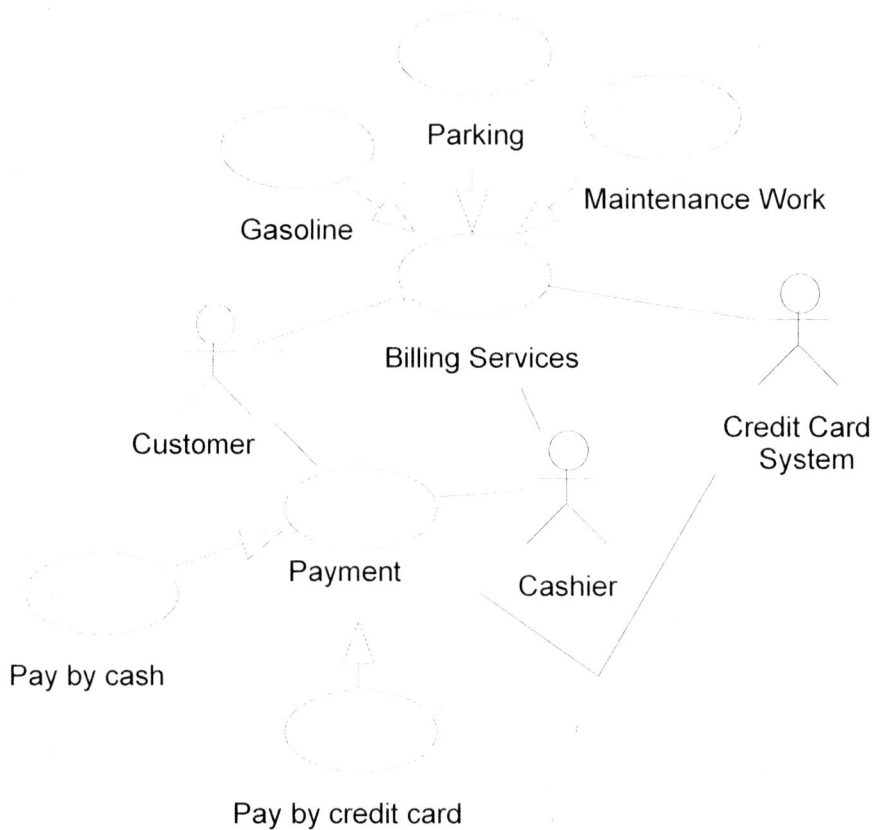

Parking

Maintenance Work

Gasoline

Billing Services

Credit Card System

Customer

Payment

Cashier

Pay by cash

Pay by credit card

The team decides to use an object-oriented methodology to create the design. The figure on the previous page shows the first draft of the use-case diagram for the gas station system. Use it to answer questions 33 and 34.

33. Each of the ovals represents a particular high-level functionality of the system, and
    a. the lines between them represent the order in which they would typically be executed.
    b. a scenario should be constructed for each, to show the details of how the functionality would be supported by the system.
    c. each should have a specified start condition.
    d. a and b only
    e. b and c only
    f. a, b, and c

34. To check for any problems with the use cases, the team should:
    a. Review the customer's description of the "Credit Card System" to see if it can participate in the appropriate way in the functionality described in billing services.
    b. Make sure that the expected start conditions for each use case are well understood.
    c. Combine "Cashier" and "Customer" into a single entity, since they are involved in the same set of use cases.
    d. a and b only
    e. b and c only
    f. a, b, and c

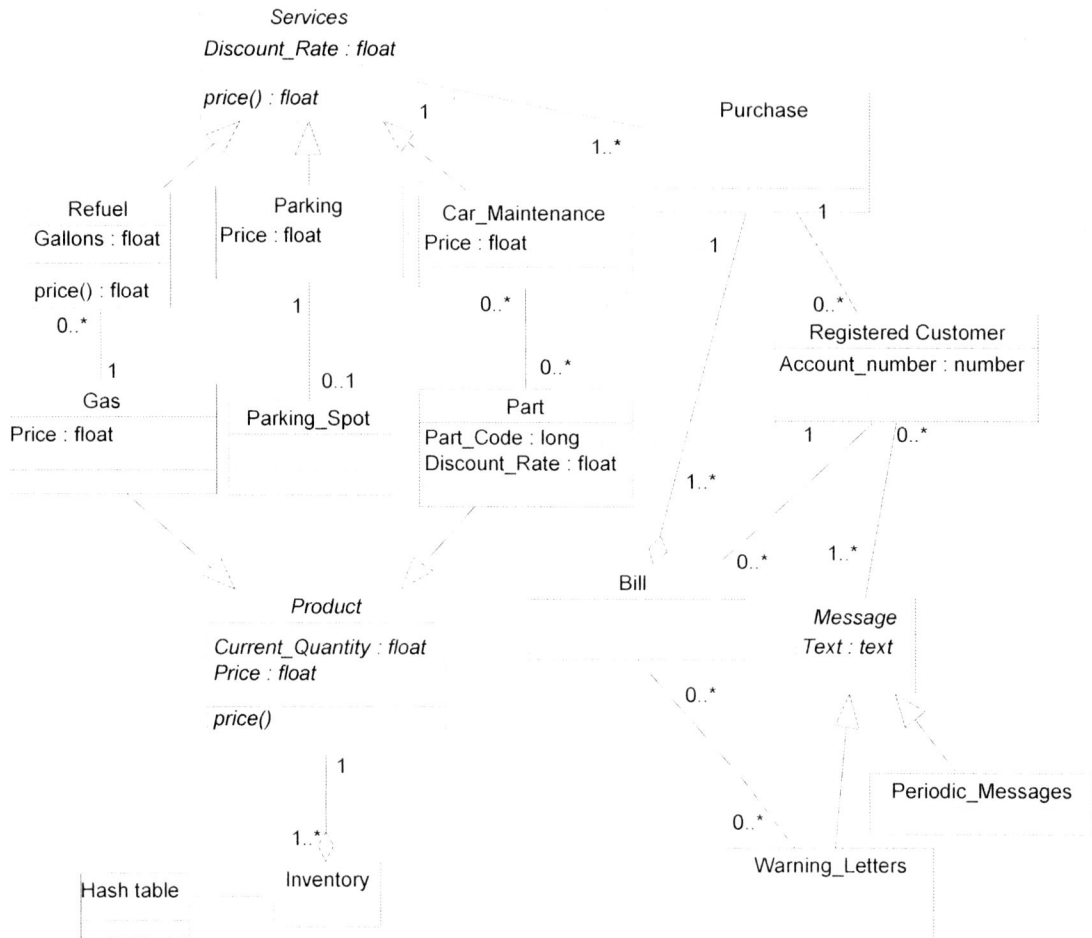

Services
Discount_Rate : float

price() : float

Refuel
Gallons : float

price() : float

Gas
Price : float

Parking
Price : float

Parking_Spot

Car_Maintenance
Price : float

Part
Part_Code : long
Discount_Rate : float

Purchase

Registered Customer
Account_number : number

Bill

Message
Text : text

Product
Current_Quantity : float
Price : float

price()

Periodic_Messages

Warning_Letters

Hash table

Inventory

The figure above shows the first draft of the class diagram for the gas station system. Use it to answer questions 35 through 37.

35. The relationship between classes "Message" and "Registered Customer" is that:
    a. A registered customer can have no associated message.
    b. Multiple messages can be associated with a registered customer.
    c. A message might exist, but be associated with no registered customer.
    d. a and b only
    e. b and c only
    f. a, b, and c

36. Which of the following statements are true about the GSCS, as described in this class diagram?
    a. Any subclass of "Service" must be associated with at least one instance of "Purchase".
    b. A "Bill" refers to exactly one "Registered Customer".
    c. Both "Part" and "Gas" are specializations of "Product".
    d. a and b only
    e. b and c only
    f. a, b, and c

38

37. Once the first draft of the class diagram is completed, the team undertakes an internal review. Which of the following is a valid criticism and rationale?
    a. Classes "Parking" and "Car Maintenance" should be combined into a single class, since they have the same attributes and inherit from the same superclass.
    b. Class "Hash Table" introduces too much detail into the model, since that is an implementation detail that should not be decided in the object-oriented design.
    c. Method "price" does not need to be defined in class "Refuel" since a method with the same name and interface is inherited from superclass "Services".
    d. a and b only
    e. b and c only
    f. a, b, and c

The figure below shows the first draft of a sequence diagram for the gas station system. Use it to answer questions 38 and 39.

38. Which of the following statements are valid interpretations of the sequence diagram?
    a. An object of type "Gas Station" attempted to send an "IsClientRegistered" message to a "Bill" object, but was unsuccessful.
    b. The "update_bill" message is sent only if the information is OK.
    c. An object of type "Bill" is created at the time a "Gas Station" class sends the "update_bill" message.
    d. a and b only
    e. b and c only
    f. a, b, and c

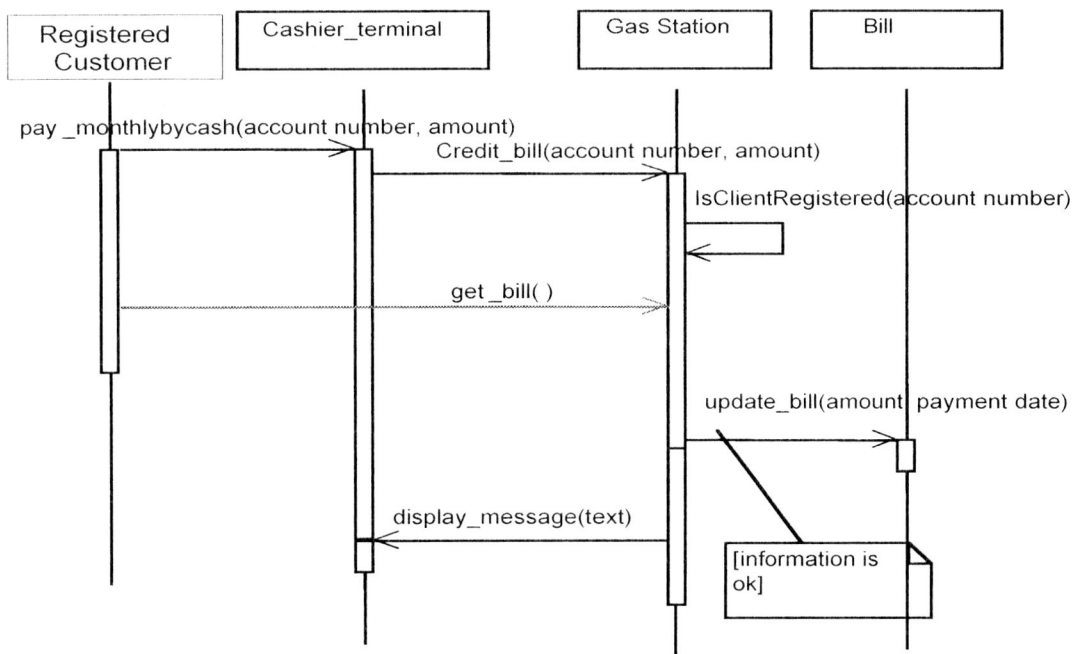

39. TRUE or FALSE: A "Cashier_terminal" object will send a "credit_bill" message only after having received a "pay_monthlybycash" method.

40. Which of the following items of information is NOT appropriate for inclusion in the design?
    a. The maximum amount of time the cashier can be made to wait for a response from the system
    b. How the record of each day's transactions will be archived
    c. What happens if the network connections to any of the gas pumps are severed
    d. None of the above (all are appropriate)
    e. a and b
    f. a and c
    g. b and c
    h. a, b, and c

Based on the design, the gas station owner responds with some critiques of the user interface.

41. The main critique is that it will be hard for the cashiers to learn the system because each screen is laid out differently. For example, on the cashier's initial screen the options are laid out across the bottom. But when the cashier is inputting data about the purchase of car parts, the cashier's options are on the left side of the screen from top to bottom, which is confusing. What the owner is really saying is that the system needs a consistent
    a. Metaphor
    b. Mental model
    c. Navigation rule
    d. Look
    e. Feel

42. TRUE or FALSE: The team lead has monitored several design metrics over the course of the design effort. As the design seems to be nearing completion, he reviews his notes and notices that the metric for "weighted methods per class" for class "Parking" has increased from 6 to 12 at the start of the detailed design phase. The next step should be to split "Parking" into several classes, each with fewer methods.

Review Exam 2 Answers

1. e; Choice b is false. It says that the requirements process can help the team make programming decisions. However, the requirements cover only what functionality is implemented, not how. [Section 4.1]

2. d; The requirements should not be assumed to give any guarantee that the system will behave as expected. We need to verify that the system actually meets the requirements. The requirements process cannot guarantee anything about the system itself. [Section 4.1]

3. a; Decision tables are not well suited to concurrent environments; Z is very formal and does not assist communication with people who are unfamiliar with the notation; ER diagrams do not contain any specific methods for ensuring completeness. [Section 4.5]

4. a; b means that gas will be paid after pump is reset; c means that the pump will be reset at some point after payment but not necessarily in time for the next customer; d means that if the pump is reset, at some point in the future a customer will make a payment. [Section 4.5]

5. TRUE; This is a process constraint type of requirement that refers to the documentation of the system. [Section 4.3]

6. TRUE; This is a quality type of requirement that refers to the human factors or usability of the system. [Section 4.3]

7. TRUE; This is a quality type of requirement that refers to the human factors or usability of the system. [Section 4.3]

8. TRUE; This is a quality type of requirement that refers to the maximum cost of the system. [Section 4.3]

9. TRUE; This is a design constraint type of requirement that refers to the interface with the hardware devices. [Section 4.3]

10. TRUE; This is a functional type of requirement that refers to data formats. [Section 4.3]

11. TRUE; This is a quality type of requirement that refers to the maintenance of the system. [Section 4.3]

12. e; Choice b contains details about how the system should be implemented (i.e., using a linked list), which is outside the scope of the requirements. [Section 4.1]

13. a; Choice b is a functional requirement; Choice c describes something outside the control of the system. [Section 4.1]

14. b and d; The phrase "relevant information" is ambiguous. (How is the developer to know what information is relevant?) This ambiguity also serves to make the requirement unverifiable. [Sections 4.4 and 4.9]

15. d; The phrase "easy to add new functionality" is unverifiable. How is "easy" defined? What types of functionality?[Section 4.3 and Sidebar 4.3]

16. e; The formula described can be verified for correctness, and is not ambiguous. [Sections 4.3 and 4.9]

17. d; The phrase "easy to use" is unverifiable. The requirements should be rewritten using a measurable criterion, e.g., that a new user must have less than a certain number of faults, or that a new user should not take more than a specified amount of time to complete the transaction. [Sections 4.3, 4.4 and 4.9]

18. c; Guaranteeing 100% availability is generally impossible. The requirements should specify concrete measures of reliability, such as the mean time between failures. [Sections 4.3 and 4.9]

19. c; Where possible, requirement measures should be categorized by requirement type, so that it can be understood whether change and uncertainty are product-wide or rest solely with a specific type of requirement. [Section 4.10]

20. e; Architectural design should be written in the customer's language and be independent of the implementation. [Section 5.1]

21. c; Choice c is not valid since object-oriented design is not particularly well-suited to describing data flow (although data-oriented decomposition is). [Section 5.3]
22. g; Pipe and filter is not an appropriate choice because it is not well-suited to interactive applications. Implicit invocation is not a good choice because one of its drawbacks is that there is no assurance that a component will respond to an event. Object-oriented design is not an architectural style. [Section 5.4]
23. FALSE; This process is likely to be iterative. [Section 5.3]
24. c; The components are loosely coupled since they are relatively independent, with some interconnections. The components are cohesive since all of their subcomponents will be directed toward (and presumably essential for) supporting a particular functionality of the GSCS. [Section 5.3]
25. TRUE; Components are easier to understand if they are not intrinsically tied to others (i.e., not tightly coupled). Similarly, cohesive components, with logically related subcomponents, are generally easier to understand than non-cohesive ones. [Sections 5.5 and 5.7]
26. a; Prototypes omit some details of functionality and performance, so that particular system aspects can be focused on. The omitted details are then filled in later (unlike throwaway prototyping, in which the final system is not built directly from the initial prototype). [Section 5.7]
27. a; The situation is not a fault or failure because it does not represent a defect in the GSCS. It is an exception because it does not occur in normal system operation. [Section 5.5]
28. a; Since the network problems may only be temporary, it makes sense to restore the system to its previous state and try contacting the credit card company again, before taking more extreme measures. [Section 5.5]
29. c; The design review allows designers to receive feedback from other designers, analysts, and programmers. The requirements analyst serves as the expert on the customer's needs, and is also able to comment on the technical details of the design. [Section 5.5]
30. a; The design should describe the system in such a way that it can be validated whether the system will meet the requirements of the user. The design should address how users interact with the system (including display-screen formats) and network issues (such as topology). [Section 5.8]
31. g; The module design is better suited to describing issues such as major hardware components and data structures. [Section 6.1]
32. c; Components exhibit stamp coupling when a data structure is used to pass information from one component to another. [Section 6.2]
33. e; No ordering is implied by the use case diagram. [Section 6.4]
34. d; Combining "Cashier" and "Customer" for the reason given in choice c is not valid, since these actors can have unique roles in the scenarios in which they both take part. [Section 6.4]
35. e; The cardinality notation for these two classes indicates that an instance of class "Message" can be associated with 0 or more "Registered Customer" objects, and an instance of class "Registered Customer" can be associated with one or more "Message" objects. [Section 6.4]
36. f; All of the choices are consistent with the class diagram (a subclass inherits its parent's associations). [Section 6.4]
37. b; It is not appropriate to combine "Parking" and "Car Maintenance" because they have different associations with other classes. Method "price" would need to be defined in "Refuel" because it is an abstract class in the superclass "Services." [Section 6.4]

38. b; The message "IsClientRegistered" is NOT an unsuccessful message; it is a message from the "Gas Station" object back to itself. The lifeline of the "Bill" starts at the top of the diagram, so the object exists well before it receives the "update_bill" message. [Section 6.4]

39. TRUE; Sequence diagrams convey chronological information, with methods lower in the diagram occurring after those closer to the top. [Section 6.4]

40. d; The design should describe the system in such a way that it can be validated whether the system will meet the requirements of the user. The design should address how users interact with the system (including performance constraints, and how output are stored) and network issues (including prescriptions for system integrity in the event of a network failure). [Section 6.6]

41. d; The "look" of a system refers to the "characteristics of the system's appearance that convey information to the user." [Section 6.6]

42. FALSE; The fact that the metric has increased is not enough information to justify automatically splitting the class. It should be monitored closely, and compared to other classes in the system and other classes this team may have had experience with in the past. If the value is high relative to other classes, it is a strong indication that the class may be more difficult to implement and may need to be tested more thoroughly than others. [Section 6.7]

Chapter 7: Writing the Programs

Learning Objectives:
After studying this chapter, you should be able to:
- Describe why programming standards and procedures are important for you and for others.
- Define the two types of reuse: producer and consumer.
- Understand the characteristics that influence whether or not a component can be reused.
- Understand how the design is used to frame the code.
- Understand what should be included as part of the internal and external documentation.

Summary:
This chapter addresses issues in implementing the design to produce high-quality code. Standards and procedures are discussed and some simple programming guidelines are suggested. Examples are provided in a variety of languages, including both object-oriented and procedural. The chapter contains discussions on the need for program documentation and an error-handling strategy. This chapter does not teach how to program; rather, it explains some of the software engineering practices that should be kept in mind as code is written.

The task of writing the programs that implement the design can be daunting for several reasons. First, the designers may not have addressed all of the idiosyncrasies of the platform and programming environment; structures and relationships that are easy to describe with charts and tables are not always straightforward to write as code. Second, code must be written in a way that is understandable not only to the author when it is revisited for testing but also to others as the system evolves over time. Third, programmers must take advantage of the characteristics of the design's organization, the data's structure, and the programming language's constructs while still creating code that is easily reusable.

When writing code, the following items should be considered:
- organizational standards and guidelines
- reuse of code from other projects
- writing code to make it reusable on future projects using the low-level design as an initial framework, and moving in several iterations from design to code
- incorporating a system-wide error-handling strategy
- using documentation within programs and in external documents to explain the code's organization, data, control and function, as well as design decisions
- preserving the quality design attributes in the code
- using design aspects to suggest an implementation language

Many corporate or organizational standards and procedures focus on the descriptions accompanying a collection of programs. Program documentation is the set of written descriptions that explain to a reader what the programs do and how they do it. Internal documentation is descriptive material written directly within the code. All other documentation is external documentation. Internal documentation includes summary information to describe its data

44

structures, algorithms and control flow. With external documentation, the summary information is provided from a system rather than component perspective.

Exercises:

1. A *stack* is a data structure used to store elements. A stack is a last-in, first-out data structure. That is, the last element placed on the stack is the first element that can be removed from the stack. Elements can be placed on or removed from the top of the stack only. The allowable operations for a stack are *empty*, *full*, *push*, *pop* and *top*.

    The empty operation returns true if there are no elements in the stack, false otherwise.

    The full operation returns true if the stack is filled to capacity; false otherwise.

    The push operation takes an element as an argument and places the element on top of the stack, if the stack is not full. If the stack is full, the push operation returns an error.

    The pop operation removes an element from the top of the stack, if the stack is not empty. If the stack is empty, the pop operation returns an error; otherwise, the top element is returned.

    The top operation returns the element on the top of the stack without removing the element from the stack, if the stack is not empty. The top operation returns an error if the stack is empty.

    Use an array to implement a stack data structure whose elements are integers. The stack may contain a maximum of 100 elements. Keep in mind the guidelines for programming style that are presented in this chapter.

2. One difficulty with reuse is selecting an appropriate component. Describe a strategy for finding a reusable component. What guidelines or styles would help in the process of selecting a component for reuse?

3. Explain the relationship between the design and implementation. Why is it important to match the implementation to the design? What would you do to keep the two consistent?

4. Consider a case where you have attempted to reuse code written by someone else. What kind of reuse was it? What problems did you encounter? How did you resolve the problems? Are there any guidelines in this chapter that may have helped to eliminate or mitigate the problems you encountered?

5. When writing code, many people are usually involved. Writing code usually requires a great deal of cooperation and coordination. It is important for others to be able to understand what you have written, why you have written it, and how your work fits in with their work. For these reasons, many organizations have coding standards and procedures. Using the guidelines from this chapter, write a set of coding standards for a language of your choice. Explain why you have included the standards you have chosen.

Answer Guidelines:

1. To implement the stack data structure, you should have followed the guidelines presented in the chapter. You should use meaningful variable names, provide good documentation of your code, use efficient algorithms, and maintain good design principles (low coupling and high cohesion).

2. When reusing a component, you may want to examine the documentation, look at the test history, or test the software before you actually commit to using it. It is important to understand whether or not you will have access to the source code, to know who is responsible for changes and to understand the limitations of the reusable component. In Section 7.3, some of the key characteristics you should consider when selecting a reusable component are described. Use this list of characteristics to develop your strategy for selecting a component. How would the strategy be different for white-box versus black-box reuse?

3. The code should implement the design. Design characteristics such as high cohesion, low coupling and well-defined interfaces should be program characteristics as well. It is important that the design and code match for other activities such as maintenance and testing. To maintain traceability, you may want to include design information in the program comments. Configuration management may also help to maintain consistency between the code and design. Section 7.1 describes the relationship between design and implementation.

4. There are many types of problems that may be encountered when you are a consumer of a reusable component. The documentation may be misleading or incorrect. There may be missing functionality that is required by your system. You must determine how to fit a reusable component into the design of the new system. These are only a few of the problems that may occur. Section 7.3 describes characteristics that should be considered when reusing components. Based on the problems that you encountered and the guidelines and programming styles described in this chapter, can you describe ways that the reusable component could have been changed to eliminate or mitigate the problems that you encountered?

5. To write the standards, make the guidelines presented in the chapter operational. For example, to make the guideline of meaningful variable names operational, you might have a standard which requires all variable names to be greater than 5 characters and less than 10 characters. Your reasons for including this standard might be that variable names less than 5 characters are cryptic and anything over 10 characters may be difficult to remember.

Chapter 8: Testing the Programs

Learning Objectives:
After studying this chapter, you should be able to:
- Define different types of faults and how to classify them.
- Define the purpose of testing.
- Describe unit testing and integration testing and understand the differences between them.
- Describe several different testing strategies and understand their differences.
- Describe the purpose of test planning.
- Apply several techniques for determining when to stop testing.

Summary:
This chapter explores several aspects of testing programs. A distinction is made between conventional testing approaches and the cleanroom method. A variety of testing strategies are presented. The chapter also presents definitions and categories of software problems and discusses how orthogonal defect classification can make data collection and analysis more effective. The difference between unit testing and integration testing is explained. The chapter also describes the need for a testing life cycle and describes how automated test tools and techniques can be integrated into it.

Testing is not the first place where fault-finding occurs; requirements and design reviews help to ferret out problems early in development. But testing is focused on finding faults, and there are many ways to make testing efforts more efficient and effective. It is important to understand the difference between a fault (a problem in the requirements, design, code, documentation or test cases) and a failure (a problem in the functioning of the system). Testing looks for faults, sometimes by forcing code to fail and then seeking the root cause. Unit testing is the development activity that exercises each component separately; integration testing puts components together in an organized way to help isolate faults as the combined components are tested together.

Testing is both an individual and a group activity. Once a component is written, it can be inspected by some or all of the development team to look for faults that were not apparent to the person who wrote it. The research literature clearly shows that inspections are very effective at finding faults early in the development process. But it is equally clear that other techniques find faults that inspections often miss. So it is important for team members to work with the team in an egoless way, using the many available methods, to find faults as early as possible during development.

The goal of testing is to find faults, not to prove correctness. Indeed, the absence of faults does not guarantee correctness. There are many manual and automated techniques to help find faults in code, as well as testing tools to show how much has been tested and when to stop testing.

Exercises:
1. Examine faults from code that you have written. For each fault, identify the type of fault (as in Section 8.1, Types of Faults) and classify the fault using a defect classification. Provide the details of the defect classification used. (You may use the IBM defect classification presented in Table 8.1 or the one from HP illustrated in Figure 8.1.) Describe any difficulties encountered in classifying the faults.

2. Based on the faults identified in the previous question, which type of fault occurred most frequently? How might you change your software development approach to eliminate or reduce the occurrence of this type of fault?
3. Describe the differences between unit and integration testing. Give the goals for each type of testing and describe when and how each should occur.
4. Describe the differences between object-oriented and traditional testing.
5. Choose a piece of code and write test cases for the code to satisfy the requirements of statement testing. Write the test cases for all-uses testing. Which testing strategy is stronger? Which strategy requires more test cases?

Answer Guidelines:
1. Chapter 8 describes many different types of faults. The purpose of this exercise is to give you a better understanding of how these descriptions can be used to identify and understand faults in actual code. It will also help you to understand the difficulties in classifying defects. Sometimes it is difficult to classify faults, especially when the defect classification is not orthogonal. The chapter presents two defect classifications. You may use one of these classifications or any other reasonable classification. Be sure your answer clearly describes the defect classification you are using. When answering this question first decide which type of fault you have found. Then, determine if the fault is one of omission or commission. Finally, based on the fault type and your classification of omission or commission, use your defect classification to classify the fault. Did you have difficulties in determining the fault type? Did any of your faults seem to fit in multiple categories?

2. Answers to this question will vary depending on your fault profile. Your fault profile can be used to identify areas of improvement for yourself. Based on your profile, which type of fault had the highest frequency? Would any of the techniques described in this chapter or previous chapters be useful in helping you to reduce the frequency of this type of fault? Which type of fault occurs least frequently? Have you done anything in the past to prevent this type of fault from occurring?

3. The main purpose of unit testing is to make sure that the component is functioning properly. The component is tested in isolation to make sure that the inputs produce the expected outputs. The main purpose of integration testing is to verify that the system components work together as specified by the design. Integration testing occurs after unit testing. Sections 8.3 and 8.4 describe unit and integration testing in greater detail.

4. Section 8.5 addresses the differences between testing object-oriented systems and traditional systems. Most of the techniques used for traditional testing also apply to object-oriented systems. Object-oriented programs have special characteristics that need several additional steps. Some of the characteristics that must be considered with OO programs that may not be included with traditional testing techniques are: missing objects, unnecessary classes, missing or unnecessary associations, or incorrect placement of associations or attributes. Test case adequacy must also be considered more carefully with OO systems. As Perry and Kaiser (1990) found, when a subclass is added or modified, the inherited methods from the ancestor superclasses

must be retested. As noted by Graham (1996a), objects tend to be small and low in complexity. However, the complexity often is pushed to the interfaces among components. This shift of complexity means that unit testing may be easier with OO systems, but integration testing must be more extensive.

5. Section 8.3 describes the different types of test strategies for test thoroughness. Statement testing and all-uses testing are two of the options described. With statement testing, every statement is executed at least once in a test case. With all-uses testing, the test set includes at least one path from every definition to every use that can be reached by the definition. In general, all-uses is stronger and requires more test cases than statement testing.

Chapter 9: Testing the System

Learning Objectives:
After studying this chapter, you should be able to:
- Describe how system testing differs from unit and integration testing.
- Classify tests as function testing, performance testing, acceptance testing or installation testing.
- Understand the purposes and roles of function testing, performance testing, acceptance testing, and installation testing.
- Define software reliability, maintainability and availability.
- Describe different techniques for measuring reliability, maintainability and availability.
- List the different types of test documentation and know what items belong in test documentation.
- Understand the special problems associated with testing safety-critical systems.
- Describe the principles of cleanroom and how it differs from conventional testing.

Summary:
This chapter looks at the system testing process: its purpose, steps, participants, techniques and tools. The chapter describes the principles of system testing, including reuse of test suites and data, and the need for careful configuration management. The concepts introduced include function testing, performance testing, acceptance testing and installation testing. The chapter examines the special needs of testing object-oriented systems. Several test tools are described, and the roles of test team members are discussed. The reader is introduced to software reliability modeling. The issues of reliability, maintainability and availability are discussed. The chapter describes how to use the results of testing to estimate the likely characteristics of the delivered product. Several types of test documentation are described.

Testing the system is very different from unit and integration testing. When unit testing components, the developer has complete control over the testing process. The developer creates the test data, designs the test cases, and runs the tests. When integrating components, the developer sometimes works individually, but often collaborates with a small part of the test or development team. However, when testing a system, the developer works with the entire development team, coordinated and directed by the test team leader.

The objective of unit and integration testing is to ensure that the code implements the design properly. In system testing, however, the objective is to ensure that the system does what the customer wants it to do. Test procedures should be thorough enough to exercise system functions to everyone's satisfaction: the user, customer, and developer.

The steps involved in system testing include function testing, performance testing, acceptance testing, and installation testing. Each step has a different focus. Function testing checks that the integrated system performs its functions as specified in the requirements. Performance testing compares the integrated components with the nonfunctional system requirements. Acceptance testing assures the customers that the system they requested is the system that was built for them. Installation testing allows users to exercise system functions and document additional problems that result in the actual operating environment.

Often, a system is tested in stages or pieces. System testing must also take into account the several different system configurations that are being developed. A system configuration is a collection of system components delivered to a particular customer. During testing, configuration management, the control of system differences to minimize risk and error, is especially important. Configuration management helps to coordinate efforts among the testers and developers.

Techniques such as cleanroom require a great deal of team planning and coordination, in developing the box structures and in designing and running the statistical tests. And the activities involved in acceptance testing require close collaboration with customers and users; as they run tests and find problems, the team must quickly determine the cause so that corrections can allow testing to proceed. Thus, whereas some parts of development are solitary, individual tasks, testing the system is a collaborative, group task.

Exercises:
1. How does system testing differ from unit and integration testing?
2. Explain the purposes and roles of function testing, performance testing, acceptance testing, and installation testing.
3. What is the difference between verification and validation? Which types of testing address verification? Which types of testing address validation?
4. Describe the principles of cleanroom and how it differs from conventional testing.
5. Read the press release and failure report for the Ariane-5 Flight 501. An electronic copy of the failure report is available at http://www.esrin.esa.it/htdocs/tidc/Press/Press96/ariane5rep.html. The joint ESA/CNES press release is available at http://www.esrin.esa.it/htdocs/tidc/Pres/Press96/pres19.html. What kinds of tests might have exposed the problems that caused each of the failures?

Answer Guidelines:
1. The emphasis for unit and integration testing is to make sure the code implements the design properly. With system testing, the focus is shifted to the customer. System testing looks to verify that the system implements the requirements properly.
   For more details on the differences, re-read Section 9.1.

2. The purpose and roles of the different types of testing are presented throughout the chapter. For each type of system testing mentioned, describe the purpose and role. Explain when during the system testing process each type of test should occur. Describe how and why each type of test is performed.

3. A verified system implies that the system operates the way the designers intended it to operate. A validated system implies that the system meets the customers' expectations. The various types of unit and integration tests focus on verification. System testing focuses on validation. Review the descriptions of the types of unit and integration tests and the types of system testing to determine which tests contribute to verification and validation.

   Section 9.1 contains more information on verification and validation.

4. Cleanroom reflects the ideas used in the manufacturing of chips. The goal is to keep faults at a minimum. For software, the goals are to certify software before unit testing and to produce as few faults as possible. With cleanroom, verification replaces unit testing. Cleanroom also makes use of statistical testing.

   Section 9.9 describes the principles and the advantages and drawbacks to the cleanroom process in greater detail. Use this information to compare the cleanroom process against traditional testing.

5. The most obvious failure from the Ariane-5 flight was the explosion of the space rocket itself. The failure report describes additional faults and failures that contributed to the explosion. Use the descriptions of the types of testing in this chapter to determine which tests may have uncovered the faults. Explain how the testing would have uncovered the fault. Be sure to consider whether or not the type of test you describe would have been feasible.

Chapter 10: Delivering the System

Learning Objectives:
After studying this chapter, you should be able to:
- Describe different types of training and training aids.
- Understand the differences between user and operator training.
- Describe special training needs and guidelines for training.
- Describe the types of documentation needed for training.

Summary:
This chapter discusses the need for training and documentation, two issues key to successfully transferring the system from the developer to the user. The chapter presents several examples of training and documentation that could accompany a software system.

Many software engineers assume that system delivery is a formality. However, even with turnkey systems (where the developers hand over the system to the customer and are not responsible for its maintenance), delivery involves more than putting the system in place. It is the time during development when the development team helps users to understand and feel comfortable with the product. If delivery is not successful, users will not use the system properly and may be unhappy with its performance. In either case, users are not as productive or effective as they could be, and the care taken to build a high-quality system will have been wasted.

As the system is designed, aids that help users learn to use the system are planned and developed. Accompanying the system is documentation to which users refer for problem-solving or further information. Training and documentations should be done from two perspectives: the user and the operator. Sometimes, the same person is both user and operator. However, user and operator tasks have very different goals, so the training for each job should emphasize different aspects of the system.

Training can be done in many ways. No matter how training is provided, it must offer information to users and operators at all times, not just when the system is delivered. At some time, if users forget how to access a file or use a new function, training includes methods to find and learn this information. Formal documentation, icons and on-line help, demonstrations and classes, and expert users are examples of training aids that may be provided.

Exercises:
1. Examine the documentation and training resources for a software system of your choice. What resources are available to the users? What resources are available to the operators?
2. What kinds of training aids and resources would be useful for users with little or no computer experience? Give examples of aids or documentation meant for novice users.
3. Suppose a system has functions that are rarely executed by users or operators. What types of resources would be appropriate for these rarely used functions?
4. Often, the training and documentation needs for novice users are very different from the needs of expert users. Give examples of cases where training aids or documentation for one user group are inappropriate for the other.

5. Think about experiences you have had with training and documentation resources. Are there any cases where these aids have interfered with your usage of the software system? If so, how would you change the documentation or training aid?

Answer Guidelines:

1. This exercise is intended to help you to identify the different training and documentation resources available with software systems. Use the descriptions of training and documentation presented in this chapter to help you identify the resources available with the system of your choice. You should be able to distinguish between resources that are meant for users and those resources that are meant for operators.

2. In this exercise, you should focus on the training and documentation aids appropriate for novice users. Throughout the chapter, there are descriptions of various resources. When reviewing these descriptions, think about how each resource described might be useful for an inexperienced user. Try to find examples of support for novice users in software systems that you have used.

3. The knowledge gained in training can be forgotten easily over time if the system functions are not exercised regularly. There are several training options that may be useful in this situation. You should review the different resources described throughout the chapter and comment on the resources that would be useful in this situation. In addition, you may want to include examples from your own experiences.

4. To answer this question, review the training aids and documentation examples presented throughout the chapter. As you review the resources, think of examples that you have experienced in software that you have used. Categorize these examples as resources for novices or resources for expert users.
    Use this information to describe reasons why resources for one group may not be appropriate for the other user group. For example, "wizards" may be useful for novices; however, expert users may find them cumbersome to use. Similarly, documentation meant for expert users may be incomprehensible to novice users.

5. The answers to this question will vary based upon your experiences with training aids and resources. Use the chapter descriptions to help you identify different types of training aids. Have you encountered resources that have hindered you use of a software system? For example, was the user documentation incorrect? Were there aids that were meant for novice users that you were unable to disable? Was information missing from the documentation that made the system impossible to use? Once you have answered these questions, think about things that you would do to eliminate some of the problems that you have encountered.

Review Exam 3

The following questions are in reference to a hypothetical "Gas Station Control System" (or GSCS) that will be used to help manage an American-style gasoline or service station. Our hypothetical gas station basically provides two services:

- There is a small store that carries car parts. Inside the store is at least one cash register, operated by a cashier who is an employee of the gas station.
- There are a number of gas pumps, at which customers can park their cars, interact with the system to pay via credit card, and then pump their own gas. Alternatively, the customer can pay for his or her gas via cash or credit card by going into the store and paying directly to the cashier.

Thus, the GSCS has two main classes of users. The first is the cashier, who uses the GSCS to record purchases of car parts by customers. The GSCS must allow the cashier to enter the type and number of parts purchased, then compute the total purchase price and handle the payment. Customers purchasing gasoline are the second type of user. These customers interface with the system at the gas pump by specifying the amount and type of gas they will buy, paying either at the pump or to the cashier, and then pumping the gas themselves.

The system also has to interact with other automated systems to perform its tasks. For example, in order to accept credit card payments, the GSCS must interface with a system maintained by the credit card company. The credit card system is responsible for checking that the customer's account is in good standing and can accommodate the amount of the purchase, and for debiting the customer's account and eventually reimbursing the gas station. The operation of these external systems is beyond the scope of the GSCS, although the GSCS needs to know how the external systems will communicate the success or failure of their tasks.

The team has finished the design of the system and has begun coding.

1. Danielle, the development team leader for the GSCS, has decided to emphasize the use of corporate software guidelines. Which of the following statements best describe the benefits the team might expect from documenting the code and making it readable?
    a. The documentation improves the efficiency of the code.
    b. The documentation provides traceability to design components.
    c. The documentation improves the organization of the code.
    d. a, b, and c
    e. a and b only
    f. b and c only

2. Which of the following statements does NOT describe a reasonable rationale for passing a variable by reference to a function?
    a. The changes to the variable values are needed after the function terminates and the variable size is small.
    b. The changes to the variable values are not needed after the function terminates and the variable size is small.
    c. The changes to the variable values are needed after the function terminates and the variable size is large.
    d. The changes to the variable values are not needed after the function terminates and the variable size is large.

3. A function with an input domain of the set of all real numbers is tested with sets of positive integers, negative integers and 0. In all of the tests, the function performs properly. It is safe to assume that the function has been tested thoroughly and will perform properly. (TRUE/FALSE)

In the following program fragments from the GSCS, identify violations (if any) of good programming style. Use the following choices in your response:
(a) Generality
(b) Efficiency
(c) Formatting
(d) Documentation
(e) No violations

4.
```
void PrintPartFile(){
/* Open the parts.dat file.  Print each line to standard output. */
/* Close the file. */
ifstream PartFile ("parts.dat");
char line[100];

while (PartFile.getline(line,100))
cout << line << "\n";

PartFile.close();
}
```

5.
```
int ValidateParts (PartList &parts, PartList &master){
/* Validate and count the parts in the part list (parts).          */
/* If a part in the list (parts) does not exist in the master list,   */
/*    return -1.                                   */
/* If all parts in the list (parts) exist in the master list,         */
/*    return the sum of the quantities of each part in the list (parts). */

int total = 0;

for (int i=0; i < parts.getcount(); i++)
if (!master.Exists(parts[i])) return -1;
for (int j=0; j < parts.getcount(); j++)
total += parts[i].getquantity();
return total;
}
```

6.
```
const int MAXSALES=100000; /* maximum number of sales stored */
const int MAXNAME=100; /* maximum name size */

struct CashierRecord{
char name[MAXNAME]; /* cashier's name */
float sales[MAXSALES]; /* sales made by the cashier */
int count; /* number of sales stored in the sales array */
} Cashier;

Cashier cashier1;

/* SumSales sums the sales transactions for the cashier. */
/* The return value is the sum of all transactions. */
float SumSales(Cashier c){
```

```
float total; /* variable that will store return value */
int i; /* loop counter */

total = 0;
/* sum the sales transactions */
for (i=0; i < c.count; i++)
total += c.sales[i];
return total;
}
.
.
.
int main(){
Cashier cashier1;
.
.
.
SumSales(cashier1);
.
.
.
}
```

7.  ```
    void Print(istream &is, ostream &os){
    /* Print each line of the input stream (is) to the output stream (os). */
    char line[MAXLINE];

    while (is.getline(line,MAXLINE))
    os << line << "\n";
    }
    ```

8.  ```
    /* Print each value of the values array on a separate line. */
    /* Print the total on a separate line after the values. */
    for (int i=0; i<count; i++)
    total += values[i];
    cout << values[i] << "\n";
    cout << "Total = " << total << "\n";
    ```

During code reviews of the GSCS, the following faults were identified.
Classify the type of fault in each code fragment.

9.  ```
    int n;
    float x[1000];

    x[i] = (1 - 2/(n-1)) * x[i - 1] + 2/(n-1) * x[i];
    ```

In this fragment, since n is an integer, the division of 2/(n-1) returns an
integer value.
    a. boundary fault
    b. initialization fault
    c. computation/precision fault
    d. b and c only
    e. a and b only
    f. none of the above
    ```

10. List::~List(){
    /* delete all of the elements in the list */
    for (int i=1; i < count; i++)
    delete list[i];
    }

In this fragment, the first item of the list (list[0]) is not deleted.
    a. initialization fault
    b. documentation fault
    c. precision fault
    d. b and c only
    e. a and b only
    f. none of the above

11. int list[10];
    for (int i=0; i<=10; i++) list[i] = i;

In this fragment, the loop includes an operation on list[10] which is not part of the array.
    a. initialization fault
    b. precision fault
    c. capacity or overload fault
    d. a, b, and c
    e. none of the above

12. float list[100];
    float xrange=list[99]-list[0];

    for (int i=0; i<100; i++)
    list[i] = (list[i]-list[0])/xrange;

In this fragment, list[0] is changed after the first iteration. All items of the array will be 0 after the array is executed. Also, there is no check on xrange. It may evaluate to 0 causing a division by zero.
    a. computation/precision fault
    b. initialization fault
    c. capacity or overload fault
    d. a, b, and c
    e. none of the above

13. Given the following assertions:
A_1: (T is an array) & (T is of size N) & (S is an array) & (S is of size N)

A_{end}: (T' is an array) & (T' is of size N) & ($\forall i, 0 \le i \le N, T'(i) = S(i)$)

Choose the statement that best describes what is happening between the two assertions.
    a. The values of array S are being assigned to the array T'.
    b. The values of array T are being assigned to the array S.
    c. The values of array S are being added to the values of array T'.
    d. The values of array T are being added to the values of array S.
    e. None of the above

58

14. Suppose the main objective of the GSCS development is to get a working system to show the customer as soon as possible. The best testing approach to choose would be:
   a. Bottom-up testing
   b. Top-down testing
   c. Big-bang testing
   d. a or b
   e. a or c

Implementation of the GSCS is complete and the development has entered the testing phase.

The figure below shows the component hierarchy of the GSCS system. Use this figure to identify the testing strategy indicated by the sequences given. The ";" is used between test sets and each test set is represented as a comma-separated list. For example, the sequence {F,G};{B,F,G} means that components F and G were tested first. Then, components B, F and G were tested.

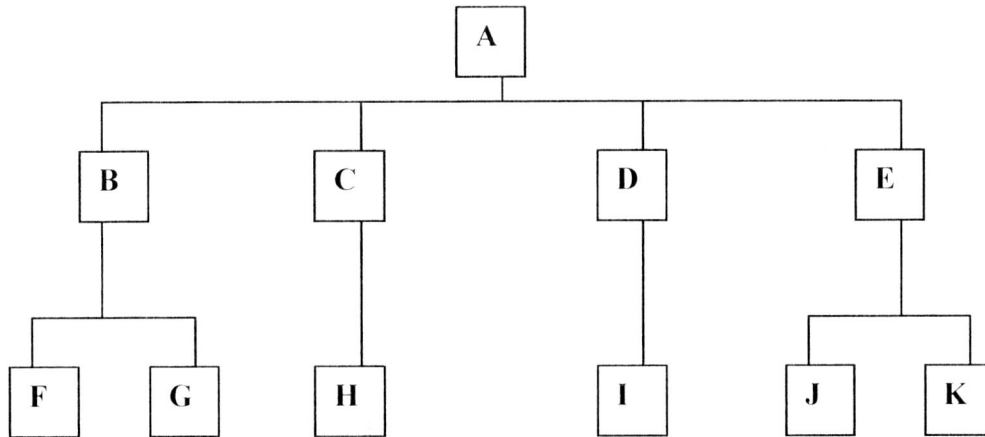

15. {J};{K};{I};{H};{G};{F};{B};{C};{D};{E};{A};{A,B,C,D,E,F,G,H,I,J,K}
   a. Top-down testing
   b. Bottom-up testing
   c. Sandwich testing
   d. Big-bang testing
   e. Modified top-down testing

16. {A};{A,B,C,D,E};{A,B,C,D,E,F,G,H,I,J,K}
   a. Top-down testing
   b. Bottom-up testing
   c. Sandwich testing
   d. Big-bang testing
   e. Modified top-down testing

17. {F};{G};{H};{I};{J};{K};{B,F,G};{C,H};{D,I};{E,J,K};{A,B,C,D,E,F,G,H,I,J,K}
   a. Top-down testing
   b. Bottom-up testing
   c. Sandwich testing
   d. Big-bang testing
   e. Modified top-down testing

18. {A};{B};{C};{D};{E};{A,B,C,D,E};{F};{G};{H};{I};{J};{K};{A,B,C,D,E,F,G,H,I,J,K}
    a. Top-down testing
    b. Bottom-up testing
    c. Sandwich testing
    d. Big-bang testing
    e. Modified top-down testing

19. {A};{F};{G};{H};{I};{J};{K};{B,F,G};{C,H};{D,I};{E,J,K};{A,B,C,D,E,F,G,H,I,J,K}
    a. Top-down testing
    b. Bottom-up testing
    c. Sandwich testing
    d. Big-bang testing
    e. Modified top-down testing

20. In a function of a component in the cashier subsystem of the GSCS, a variable does not get initialized properly. Which type of testing would most likely expose this defect?
    a. unit testing
    b. integration testing
    c. acceptance testing
    d. installation testing
    e. performance testing

21. A function X in component A requires a pointer to an integer to be passed as an argument, but a call to the function X in component B passes the value of an integer instead. Which type of testing would most likely expose this defect?
    a. unit testing of component A
    b. integration testing of components A and B
    c. performance testing
    d. installation testing
    e. acceptance testing

22. The gas pump subsystem is supposed to allow the user to choose whether or not a receipt is printed, but the print function has not been implemented. Which type of testing would most likely expose this defect?
    a. unit testing
    b. integration testing
    c. performance testing
    d. acceptance testing
    e. function testing

23. A configuration file used by the reporting subsystem is not placed in the correct directory in the customer's environment. Which type of testing would most likely expose this defect?
    a. integration testing
    b. installation testing
    c. performance testing
    d. acceptance testing
    e. function testing

24. A change is made to correct a fault. The fault has been fixed, but it has caused a fault in previously functioning code. Which type of testing would most likely expose this defect?
    a. unit testing
    b. acceptance testing
    c. regression testing
    d. performance testing
    e. installation testing

25. The customer is unhappy with the number of screens that must be traversed before getting to the parts list screen, a screen accessed frequently when using the system. Which type of testing would most likely expose this defect?
    a. integration testing
    b. installation testing
    c. performance testing
    d. acceptance testing
    e. function testing

26. The GSCS system includes reused components from a third-party vendor. The source code for the reused components is not available. Which type of testing is feasible?
    a. all-paths
    b. def-use
    c. branch testing
    d. black-box testing

Tom, the manager in charge of testing for the GSCS, is concerned about the reliability of the system. He decides to seed faults in the code to estimate the remaining faults. He has two teams testing the code. One team is led by David. The other test team is led by Daniel. Suppose 50 faults have been seeded in the code.

During testing by David's team, 70 faults are detected. Forty of the detected faults are seeded faults.

27. What is the Mills estimate for the percentage of remaining, non-seeded (indigenous) faults in the code?
    a. 10%
    b. 20%
    c. 50%
    d. 80%
    e. It is impossible to determine from the information given.

28. What is the Mills estimate of the total number of indigenous faults remaining?
    a. 7.5
    b. 10
    c. 17.5
    d. 30
    e. 37.5
    f. It is impossible to determine from the information given.

61

Suppose the same code is given to Daniel's test team. His team finds a total of 50 faults. Thirty-five of the faults found by Daniel's team were also found by David's team.

29. Using the numbers for Daniel's team, what is the Mills estimate for the total number of indigenous faults remaining?
    a. 17.5
    b. 30
    c. 50
    d. 71.5
    e. It is impossible to determine from the information given.

30. What is the effectiveness of David's group?
    a. 30%
    b. 50%
    c. 70%
    d. 85%
    e. It is impossible to determine from the information given.

31. What is the effectiveness of Daniel's group?
    a. 30%
    b. 50%
    c. 70%
    d. 85%
    e. It is impossible to determine from the information given.

32. Using the data from both test groups, what is the estimate for the total number of faults?
    a. 100
    b. 87.5
    c. 70
    d. 50
    e. It is impossible to determine from the information given.

33. Suppose 39 faults have been seeded into a component. Testing of the component has uncovered 32 of the seeded faults without uncovering any additional non-seeded faults. What is the level of confidence that the component is fault-free?
    a. 78%
    b. 80%
    c. 82%
    d. 86%
    e. None of the above

34. Using the data from the previous question, how many of the seeded faults would have to be found without uncovering additional indigenous faults to have a 90% confidence level?
    a. 32
    b. 35
    c. 36
    d. 37
    e. None of the above

35. Consider the following excerpts from problem reports filed for the GSCS. In which type of report, discrepancy or fault, does each item belong? Answer fault report or discrepancy report.
    a. "A segmentation violation occurred while viewing the part list. The part list array may not be big enough to hold all parts. Check the PartList class header."
    b. "In the requirements document, Section 2.1.5, a Print option should be included in all File menus. The File menu for the Part Configuration Screen does not include a Print option."
    c. "After submitting the Add Part form, it took 3 minutes before the results came back. Submitting the form should not take more than 1 minute."
    d. "When the cashier list is displayed, the newly added cashiers do not appear on the list. Check the Add method in the CashierList class. There was a similar problem with the part list. Theresa worked on the part list problem. See report number 201 for more details on the problem and her solution."

Review Exam 3 Answers

1. f; Readable code does not always improve efficiency. Sometimes, there is a tradeoff between readability and efficiency. [Sections 7.1, 7.2]
2. b; Passing a variable by reference means that the value of the variable will be changed. If the altered value is not needed after the function terminates and the variable size is small, the variable should be passed by value.
3. FALSE; It is not safe to assume that the function will work properly because it was tested only with integers. The function may produce the wrong output for non-integers, or fail due to round-off errors.
4. a; Only one file can be read and printed with this function. It could be written more generally.
5. b; The two loops can be combined to make this code more efficient.
6. b; Since the sales array of the Cashier structure is very large, the argument to SumSales should be passed by reference to improve efficiency.
7. e
8. c; Formatting of this code makes it misleading. It hides a fault in the code.
9. c; Because n is an integer, the expression 2/(n-1) will evaluate to an integer giving an incorrect answer. [Section 8.1]
10. e; The code doesn't do what the comment describes. The variable i is initialized incorrectly. [Section 8.1]
11. c; list[10] is out of the defined array boundary [Section 8.1]
12. a; The first element of the array (list[0]) is overwritten during the first iteration of the loop. The overwritten value is used in future iterations. When the loop terminates, each element of the array will be 0. The computation does not check for xrange = 0 which may lead to a division by zero error. Both of these faults are computation faults. [Section 8.1]
13. a; [Section 8.3]
14. b; With the bottom-up and big-bang approaches, the whole system has to be built before a working program can be shown to the customer. With top-down testing, stubs and drivers can be used to test the system before the entire system is built. [Section 8.4]
15. d; big-bang testing [Section 8.4]
16. a; top-down testing [Section 8.4]
17. b; bottom-up testing [Section 8.4]
18. e; Modified top-down testing [Section 8.4]
19. c; sandwich testing [Section 8.4]
20. a; unit testing; This defect can be isolated to a single function in a single component. Unit testing should uncover this type of defect. [Section 8.2]
21. b; Since this defect involves the interface between the two components, integration testing of components A and B should detect the defect. Unit testing of component A would not uncover the defect since the defect exists in component B. [Section 8.2]
22. e; Function testing is used to determine if the functions described in the requirements specification are actually implemented in the system. [Section 8.2]
23. b; The purpose of installation testing is to make sure that the system will function properly where it is installed. [Section 8.2]
24. c; The purpose of regression testing is to ensure that changes to the system have not negated the effects of previous tests. [Section 9.1]
25. d; Acceptance testing is where the system is checked against the customer's requirements. [Section 8.2]

26. d; Because the code is not available, the structure of the code is not available for testing. In this case, black-box testing is the only feasible option. [Section 8.2]
27. b; The percentage of indigenous faults remaining is equal to the percentage of seeded faults remaining. (1 - 40/50) = .2 [Section 8.8]
28. a;

$$\frac{seeded\_faults\_found}{seeded\_faults} = \frac{indigenous\_faults\_found}{indigenous\_faults}$$

$$indigenous\_faults = \frac{seeded\_faults \times indigenous\_faults\_found}{seeded\_faults\_found}$$

$$indigenous\_faults = \frac{50 \times 30}{40} = 37.5$$

```
indigenous_faults_remaining = 37.5 - 30 = 7.5
```
[Section 8.8]

29. e; The number of seeded faults for the second test group is not given. [Section 8.8]
30. c; effectiveness = overlapping faults/faults found by the second group
effectiveness = 35/50 = 70% [Section 8.8]
31. b; effectiveness = 35/70 = 50% [Section 8.8]
32. a; total faults = 35/(.7 * .5) = 100 [Section 8.8]
33. b;

$$C = \frac{\binom{39}{31}}{\binom{40}{32}} = 0.8$$

[Section 8.8]

34. c;

$$C = \frac{\binom{39}{31}}{\binom{40}{s}} = 0.9$$

$$0.9 = \frac{s}{40}$$

$$s = 36$$

[Section 8.8]

35.

   a. fault report; The description of the problem includes information from the developer's point of view. [Section 9.8]

   b. discrepancy report; This description describes a difference between the requirements and the implementation. [Section 9.8]

c. discrepancy report; This description describes a problem from the user's point of view. [Section 9.8]

d. fault report; The description of the problem includes information from the developer's point of view. [Section 9.8]

Chapter 11: Maintaining the System

Learning Objectives:
After studying this chapter, you should be able to:
- Define what is meant by system evolution, and understand how it affects the software development process.
- Define what is meant by a legacy system, and understand how its characteristics affect maintenance.
- Define impact analysis, and understand when, how, and why it is done.
- Describe software rejuvenation, and why it is necessary.

Summary:
Delivery of a system to the customer does not mark the end of the software developers' involvement with the system. Rather, many systems require continuous change, extending even past delivery. In general, the more closely a system is tied to the real world, the more likely it will be to require changes (and the more difficult those changes will be to make). Software maintenance deals with managing change in this part of the life cycle.

Performing maintenance requires its own set of skills, in addition to those required for software development. Maintainers interact continually with colleagues, customers, and users in order to effectively define problems and find their causes. Maintainers need to be good detectives, testing software thoroughly and hunting down the sources of failure. Maintainers also need to understand the "big picture" of how software systems, with many complex interactions among their components, interoperate with the environment. Impact analysis, which builds and tracks links among the requirements, design, code and test cases, is necessary to evaluate the effects of a change in one component on the rest of the system.

Another important technique is software rejuvenation, which involves the redocumenting, restructuring, reverse engineering and reengineering of an existing system. The overall goal is to make hidden information explicit, so that it can be used to improve the design and structure of the code. Although complete rejuvenation is unlikely in the near future, it is being used successfully in domains that are mature and well-understood, like information technology.

Measuring maintainability is difficult. A true measure of maintainability requires evaluating the external behavior of a system and tracking the mean time between failures. However, waiting until the system fails is too late to be of much use to developers and maintainers. Instead, internal attributes of the code, such as size and structure, are used to predict those parts of a software system that are likely to fail, based on past history. Static code analyzers are tools that aim to assist in this identification process.

Exercises:
1. The "Millenium Bug" or "Y2K problem" is perhaps the most infamous software maintenance problem. Many computer systems represent the year as only two digits and are expected to have problems in the year 2000, when the value for the new year ("00") is suddenly less rather than greater than the value for the previous year ("99"). Find a discussion of the Y2K problem written for nonscientists; for example, in a newspaper or popular magazine. How many of the maintenance problems listed in Section 11.3 are

accurately presented in the article? Are there issues in Section 11.3 that contribute to the Y2K problem but are not given in the article?

2. The Software Engineering Laboratory (SEL) at NASA's Goddard Space Flight Center collects data from all phases of its software development projects. When users fill out failure reports, they are asked to indicate the severity of the defect according to the following scale: major defect with no workaround; major defect, but workaround exists; cosmetic defect. How can this information be used to help the SEL understand its maintenance process better?

3. Maintenance is an area of great interest to software engineering researchers. Conferences and workshops such as ICSM (the International Conference on Software Maintenance) and WESS (the Workshop on Empirical Studies of Software maintenance) are devoted exclusively to maintenance issues, as is the *Journal of Software Maintenance*. Review a recent conference proceeding or journal issue and summarize the types of problems maintenance research addresses.

4. Researchers with the Institute for Information Technology of the National Research Council, Canada, study maintenance by observing the work practices of software engineers who are engaged in maintenance projects. A paper by Janice Singer and Timothy Lethbridge summarizes the methods they use to collect this type of data. (J. Singer, T. Lethbridge (1996). "Methods for Studying Maintenance Activities." In *Proceedings of the International Workshop on Empirical Studies of Software Maintenance*, Monterey, CA.) Summarize this paper from the viewpoint of a software maintainer. How disruptive are the data collection methods likely to be to the maintainer's work practices? What does the maintainer stand to gain by participating in such a study?

5. Revisit the program you wrote for Exercise 1, Chapter 7. Change the underlying data structure of the stack to a linked list rather than an array, and the data type of the stack elements to a string rather than an integer. How hard was this to do? On what types of activities did you spend your time? Critique your earlier program in terms of maintenance effort, paying attention to ideas such as comments, modularity, encapsulation, and others that affected the ease or difficulty of this task.

Answer Guidelines:

1. Many of the issues in Section 11.3 relate in some way to the Y2K problem. For example, the limits of human understanding are certainly applicable. There is a definite limit to how quickly maintainers can approach a system that is unfamiliar to them and understand enough about it to make the correct changes for a maintenance problem. That difficulty is compounded when the system being maintained is old and the chances of missing documentation or even source code have increased. Management priorities have been a major contribution to the problem. Since Y2K maintenance does not result in a new product but rather keeps an old product running, management in many cases did not assign a high priority to maintenance in general and Y2K maintenance in particular. As a result, Y2K was often not a high priority until very close to the year 2000, when the problem was no longer avoidable. Morale has been a problem in some cases, in which software practitioners were assigned part-time to handle the Y2K problem in addition to their other duties. This type of situation tends to reinforce the belief that Y2K maintenance is not an important or interesting task.

2. The severity scale helps the SEL understand better how its development process affects maintenance. It gives more information than simply collecting the number of changes that have to be made during maintenance; it allows some insight into whether most of the changes that have to be made are mostly small changes or large redesigns.

3. Common categories of software maintenance research include: program understanding, predicting effort, predicting components likely to require rework tool support.

4. By understanding the techniques that maintainers find useful in practice, this research hopes to provide a better idea of how software maintainers can benefit from tool support. That is, the point of this research is that tools should be created after the tool developers understand for which tasks maintainers really need support. The methods listed in this paper are at varying levels of intrusiveness; the authors understand that less intrusive means for collecting data will be more welcomed by maintainers. By participating in such a study, however, maintainers can expect that tools will be created that better address the requirements of the job they are undertaking.

5. Answers will vary depending on the quality of the original program. The exercise will be more useful if you have forgotten the details of the program since it was written, since then you will have to rely on reading the code, comments, and documentation. This situation is similar to what software maintainers face when working on code they themselves did not originally develop, or developed some time ago. It is hoped that you will find this exercise to be easy if you have made the code well documented, straightforward and easy to understand, and modular. However, some of these factors may be more important than others for your program, and other factors may also be a consideration.

Chapter 12: Evaluating Products, Processes, and Resources

Learning Objectives:
After studying this chapter, you should be able to:
- Discuss how feature analysis, case studies, surveys and controlled experiments differ, and the circumstances under which each is appropriate.
- Define measurement and validation, and understand how they are carried out in software development.
- Describe the Capability Maturity Model, ISO 9000 and other process models, and the differences and similarities between them.
- Describe what is meant by people maturity, and the role this may play in a software organization.
- Describe how and why development artifacts are evaluated.
- Define return on investment and its importance with respect to the software development process.

Summary:
Previous chapters have given an overview of the large variety of methods and tools that are available for use by software developers throughout the software life cycle. This chapter takes up the question of how developers can decide which method or tool is best to use. Answering this larger question requires accurate answers to a number of more specific questions:
- How can developers evaluate the effectiveness and efficiency of what they are already doing, so that they can tell if a change to the development process actually results in improvement?
- For a given situation, how can developers know which is the most appropriate method or tool to introduce into their development process?
- Once a change has been made, how can developers demonstrate that the products, processes and resources have the desired characteristics (such as quality)?

Evaluation of software development requires first choosing whether the most appropriate type of study is a feature analysis, survey, case study, or formal experiment. Models and frameworks are necessary to help developers understand the relationships being investigated; of course, the models and frameworks themselves must be evaluated in terms of how closely they match what is already known. Regardless of the type of study, measurement is essential for any evaluation. It is important to keep in mind that measures must be validated; that is, it must be shown that measures actually capture the concept of interest, and that the resulting predictions are accurate. A second important concept that is important to keep in mind is the difference between assessment and prediction. These common principles should be applied to the evaluation of software products, processes and resources.

Product evaluation is usually based on a model of the attribute of interest. This chapter introduced three quality models and discussed how each one addresses particular concerns about how specific attributes combine to form a picture of quality as a whole. Other considerations, such as software reuse, imply their own sets of product attributes that must be evaluated.

Process evaluation can be done in many ways. Postmortem analysis looks back at completed processes to assess the root causes of things that went wrong. Process models, such as the Capability Maturity Model (CMM), SPICE and ISO 9000, are useful for assessing the amount of insight into, and control over, the processes being used.

The CMM has inspired a host of other maturity models, including a people maturity model to assess the degree to which individuals and teams are given the resources and freedom they need to do their best. Software projects require other types of investment as well, including money and time. Return-on-investment strategies can indicate whether business is benefiting from investment in people, tools and technology.

Exercises:

1. In the key references section of this chapter, it is noted that the journal *Empirical Software Engineering* publishes not only descriptions of empirical studies, but data from these studies as well. What do you think are some of the benefits to other researchers having access to the data? Are there any benefits to practitioners?

2. Give an example from a previous programming project of when you engaged in black-box reuse. What are some of the benefits that can be expected from black-box reuse? What are some drawbacks? Give an example of a system for which black-box reuse would not have been appropriate.

3. Take a look at the latest issue of a journal that presents articles about software engineering. (*IEEE Transactions on Software Engineering*, the *Journal of Systems and Software*, and *IEEE Computer* are good examples.) Of the articles that present a new technique or tool for software development, how many actually present some kind of evidence that the proposed technique is an improvement over what is currently used? For those that do, classify the type of empirical study used, and identify the variables.

4. Select one of the studies that you identified in the answer to question 3. Analyze this study with respect to the common pitfalls in evaluation that are described in Table 12.2. For each pitfall, assess whether or not the study has successfully avoided the problem, and explain your reasoning. If the article contains sufficient information to allow you to judge whether the pitfall was avoided, that should also be noted. If there are pitfalls in this study, do the authors identify them and discuss their impact on the results?

5. A paper by Barbara Kitchenham, Lesley Pickard, and Shari Lawrence Pfleeger addresses in some detail common pitfalls of case studies in industrial environments (B. Kitchenham, L. Pickard, S. L. Pfleeger (1995). "Case studies in method and tool evaluation." *IEEE Software*, 12(4): 52-62). Use this paper to critique a case study of some software engineering technology. (The journals suggested in question 3 are good sources of case studies.) If there are problems with the study, do you think they can be corrected in such a way that the study will still be feasible to run?

Answer Guidelines:

1. Perhaps the most important benefit of published data is that they help researchers check each others' conclusions; they allow researchers to analyze the same data and see if their results match. Publishing data also assists in comparing data among studies since it allows researchers to understand any desired attributes of data sets (e.g. mean, median, amount of variation among the values). In the same way, publishing data also helps practitioners better understand the results of applying a technology, and may allow them to compare results in their own environment to data from outside.

2. Although you may report experiences with black-box code libraries or other forms of reuse, almost every programming language has the option to include functions from standard libraries, which may also be an example

of black-box reuse if the source code is not available. Benefits include being able to save effort by reusing functionality rather than implementing it from scratch; testing effort is also saved since presumably the reused component does not have to undergo unit testing. Drawbacks include the time required to find the component and figure out how to configure it for use in a particular system. A drawback unique to black-box testing is the fact that, since the internals of the component cannot be tested, it is more likely that defects in the code will be propagated unnoticed to other systems. Systems in which reliability or safety is an overriding concern may not be good candidates for black-box reuse for this reason.

3. Answers will vary. The point of the question is to determine whether you can differentiate articles describing empirical studies of the kind mentioned in this chapter (Section 12.1) from articles in which the claims are not substantiated, or are substantiated only with analytical reasoning. It is important to be clear as to which category each article you review falls into, and to back up your categorization with points from the article.

4. Answers will vary. The point of the question is to assess whether you understand the meaning of the nine pitfalls listed in Table 12.2, and the form they take in evaluation studies. Make sure you understand the definition of each pitfall, and can answer whether or not it appears in the study.

5. Answers will vary depending on the case study selected. There are many guidelines in the Kitchenham et al. paper that can be used to critique case studies; your paper should address questions such as whether a case study was an appropriate form for this study in the first place, and whether there are any problems of construct or internal or external validity. In many cases, correcting defects in empirical studies may require an infeasibly large amount of time or effort from the developers who serve as subjects; you should consider whether this is true for the study you have chosen.

Chapter 13: Improving Predictions, Products, Processes, and Resources

Learning Objectives:
After studying this chapter, you should be able to:
- Discuss strategies for improving predictions. Explain how reuse and inspections can be used to improve software products.
- Describe how cleanroom and maturity models can be used to improve software processes.
- Describe how investigating trade-offs is necessary to improve software resources.

Summary:
Chapter 12 provides an introduction to the methods used for evaluating software products, processes, and resources to determine their impact on development and maintenance. This chapter provides concrete examples of software evaluation and improvement by discussing actual instances of technology adoption in four areas: prediction, products, processes and resources.

Predictions can be improved by using u-plots, prequential likelihood and recalibration to reduce noise and bias. Products can be improved as part of a reuse program, or by instituting an inspection process. Processes can be improved by evaluating their effects and determining relationships that lead to increased quality or productivity. For example, models can be developed based on past history to predict when components will be faulty; this technique reduces the effort required to maintain a system, and ultimately leads to higher-quality software. Similarly, process maturity frameworks may assist organizations in implementing activities that are likely to improve software quality, although carefully controlled studies have not yet provided sufficient evidence as to their effectiveness. Finally, there is promise of improvement in resource allocation as we learn more about human variability and examine the trade-offs between effort and schedule.

One of the common threads in the technologies discussed in this chapter is the importance of human factors research. Many of the studies reported in this chapter emphasize the need for teams to check each other's work. Inspections, cleanroom, reuse and other quality-related processes involve the careful scrutiny of one person or organization's work by another. All of these approaches are largely dependent on people factors in order to be effective. In general, researchers admit that human variability is a key factor in determining whether quality and schedule goals will be met. Thus, an especially promising area of research in software engineering is into issues such as team size, collaboration styles, and good working environments, which determine how software engineers themselves can best be supported. A promising way to improve this type of research in software engineering is to learn from similar studies that have already been undertaken in the social sciences.

Research on improvement issues is growing, as developers increasingly ask for empirical proof that proposed technologies really work. This chapter illustrates the need for more surveys, case studies and experiments; the Basili and Green example shows how a collection of studies can be organized to build on each other. Of course, to be carried out effectively, such studies require that developers are willing to participate in case studies and experiments and to give feedback to those who are trying to determine what leads to improvement.

Exercises:

1. An organization currently uses informal, English-language requirements and requirements reviews in its software development process. A consultant has recommended that it switch to the more formal requirements language, Z. The organization decides to try out Z on a new project, to see whether or not it improves the software process. To evaluate Z with respect to the current process, what types of measurements should be collected on projects using English requirements? On the trial project? Justify your answers.

2. Describe an empirical study that could be used to assess whether Z represents an improvement for the organization. What type of empirical study would you select, and why? How much confidence could the organization have in the result? How much disruption would be necessary to the organization's usual software development process?

3. In a 1997 paper, Vic Basili describes a series of studies of a particular kind of software technology, called software reading. (V. Basili (1997). "Evolving and packaging reading techniques." *Journal of Systems and Software*, 38: 3-12.) Each study in the series contributed some knowledge about the use of this technology in a particular environment. A number of different types of studies were used: Some studies looked at whether or not the technology was feasible in the environment, other studies tested very specific hypotheses about the technology, and still other studies examined the use of the technology in detail. What kind of studies would you recommend for each of those goals? Sketch a series of studies for the organization interested in Z (discussed in questions 1 and 2) that incorporates all three goals.

4. Many studies in computer science compare different technologies and do not involve human factors. For example, a study of a new algorithm may seek to determine whether it runs faster than an older version on practical data sets. However, many empirical studies in software engineering involve human subjects, because they need to assess the usefulness of development techniques for the people who will use them. Find a recent journal article that describes an empirical software study using human subjects. Briefly summarize (two paragraphs) the study and its results. What are the things that make studies using human subjects different from studies that do not? Use specific examples from the journal article to illustrate your points.

5. Do a search of the literature in which you identify the relevant papers on two different approaches to process improvement. Use the references given in the textbook as a starting point. Compare and contrast the two approaches in a short report (less than five pages). Your report should be a summary of the two approaches, written for an organization thinking of investing in process improvement. You should answer questions such as: Where have the approaches already been applied? Have they been shown to work? What support is required from the organization? Identify other relevant criteria as you see fit.

Answer Guidelines:

1. The organization will need to collect measures of how effective its requirement process is; measures such as the time and effort required from developers would be good choices, as would some measure of the quality of the resulting requirements. (You should remember that "quality" is a difficult concept to measure directly, and propose a way it can be feasibly assessed. Measures of quality may vary depending on the interests of the organization, so you should be sure to justify your answer.) Other variables are required to describe the context in which the process is applied; for example, the type of project or experience of the developers using it. Collecting the same type of measures for both the Z and natural language requirements processes will enable comparisons between the two.

2. You may choose feature analysis, case studies or controlled experiments
    (surveys are excluded since there are no retrospective data). Because
    multiple answers are possible, you should be sure to justify your choice:
    What do you think are likely goals for the organization conducting the
    study? Which type of study stands the best chance of achieving those
    goals? You will also need to correctly answer the follow-up questions
    based on your choice of study type. Confidence and disruption are
    generally directly related; feature analyses would produce low confidence
    but minimal disruption, while controlled experiments would yield high
    confidence but place the most extra demands on developers' schedules.

3. A feature analysis or controlled experiment could provide a quick answer as to
    the feasibility of a technology. A controlled experiment is best for testing a
    particular hypothesis, since variables besides the one of interest can be
    controlled. A case study is probably the best choice for getting a more in-
    depth knowledge, since a project can be followed all the way to completion
    (and if a sister project can be found, compared to a similar project not using
    the technology to understand its effects). Answers as to the series of studies
    will vary, but here is one possibility: A feature analysis is undertaken to
    determine if Z looks promising. It seems to match the needs of the users, so
    volunteers are solicited who would be willing to try out the technology and
    report on the results. These volunteers are assigned to a new project, which
    is monitored as a case study. A comparison with a similar, previous study on
    which Z was not used seems to indicate that the use of the technology
    represents an improvement in the way requirements are specified. Finally, a
    larger controlled experiment is conducted to see if the improvement is noticed
    for a wide range of the developers in the organization.

4. Answers will vary depending on the studies selected. One acceptable answer
    could be sketched in the following way: Studies with human subjects have
    to contend with a wide variation among subjects, even those with similar
    backgrounds and experience levels. It is rare to find subjects who perform
    equally well on all tasks, even if they have had similar experience or
    training; humans have natural aptitudes and interests. Studies with human
    subjects also have to contend with variation within subjects; that is,
    humans do not perform the same task at a consistent level. They have bad
    days, or learn things as they go along; they can be distracted, or focus
    more intently on the task. Studies of computer technologies can be
    expected to produce much more deterministic results.

5. Answers will vary. In identifying the relevant literature on a particular
    approach to software improvement, you should focus first on finding the
    published work in which the approach is originally defined. If there have
    been major changes to the approach since it was first published, you should
    try to track down literature in which the changes are proposed and
    discussed as well. Also, you should look for publications that describe how
    the approach has been applied in practice--the most recent publications and
    most thorough descriptions are always among the most relevant. Use this
    list of publications to support the points you make as you compare and
    contrast the two approaches. Begin by summarizing the definitions of the
    approaches. Then, summarize the publications describing their application.
    Were you able to find many publications describing the use of the approach
    in practice? If not, has your search been less than thorough, or is the
    approach simply not used often? In what types of organizations have the
    approaches been applied? What kind of results have been obtained? Can you
    say anything about the factors that are present in each case that may have
    contributed to the good or bad results that were seen?

Chapter 14: The Future of Software Engineering

Learning Objectives:
After studying this chapter, you should be able to:

- Describe where the field of software engineering stands with respect to Wasserman's eight steps.
- Describe what is meant by "technology transfer," and why it is important.
- Understand what kinds of evidence can bear on technology adoption, and how researchers provide such evidence.
- Understand how decision making can (and should) occur in software project management.
- Describe some important areas for future work in software research and practice.
- Describe the issues involved in the professionalization of software engineering.

Summary:
Software engineering is a young field (the term itself was first used in 1968) but has already seen great changes. The field has progressed with the development of complex programming languages and more reusable products. Formal methods for problem description, tools for assisting software development, and useful design principles have been developed and helped software engineers tackle ever-larger problems. However, there is more accuracy in the large than in the small; the field tends to agree on broad principles but is less successful in pinning down the effects of specific decisions that project managers will need to make.

In the terms of Wasserman's eight principles, software engineering has experienced:

- The use of *abstraction,* to help focus on the core of the problem, most successfully applied in design and code. However, more work is needed in other areas such as software requirements, work habits, and user profiles.
- The development of a wide range of *analysis and design methods and notations* to suit personal preference and comfort. However, no common method or notation has been developed that the others can be mapped to, to simplify communication and understanding.
- The role of *user interface prototyping* has become more and more critical. Work needs to continue in this area to support the production of ever more responsive and useful products.
- The very beginning of the identification of *architectural styles and patterns* with their associated pros and cons.
- A growing understanding that *software process* affects product quality, but not exactly how that quality is affected by the visibility and controllability of the process. More work is needed in how specific process choices affect the development of the product.
- A focus on *reuse,* mainly of code. Reuse must be expanded to other work products throughout development and maintenance.
- The use of *measurement* to see if products meet quality criteria. Future work needs to expand to measure key characteristics of products, processes, and resources in ways that are unobtrusive, useful, and timely.
- Significant investment in *tools and integrated environments* that have not lived up to their promise. Current and ongoing efforts are looking at tools with more realistic expectations, for feasible tasks such as tracing connections among products, background measurement, and reuse support.

An important area where improvement is needed is technology transfer; that is, the transformation of a promising research idea into a technology that is useful and effective for practitioners. Technology transfer decisions have both a technical aspect (finding the right technology to solve a problem) and a commercial aspect (appealing to customers who need to have the problem solved). Widespread commercial adoption of promising technologies can take a decade or two, so given the time-to-market pressures of the industry today it is not surprising that software development organizations often rush to grab new technologies before there is clear evidence of benefit. Enabling decisions to be made on the basis of better and clearer evidence is a primary goal in the improvement of technology transfer practices.

Looking to the area of "diffusion research" in marketing helps us understand how decisions about technology adoption are made. Data across many organizations show that there are distinct types of technology adopters, who exhibit varying degrees of willingness to try out a new technology: innovators, early adopters, early majority, late majority, and laggards. Each group has different requirements for evidence of a technology's effectiveness and the level of support they need before they are willing to invest in using it. Knowing and being able to address these requirements is thus an important prerequisite to seeing new technologies effectively adopted in industry. However, studies have shown that software researchers have their own goals and preferences for the kinds of evidence they collect, which don't always address the needs of practitioners. This mismatch between the two communities diminishes the relevance of research work and results in technology decisions being made without the kinds of evidence that are really needed.

Conclusions about a technology have to be drawn from a collection of evidence, where each piece of evidence might count more or less than others based on what is known about it. The legal community has a long tradition of building conclusions in this way and can provide some guidance for addressing important issues. For example, we can place a particular piece of technology into one of five categories, based on what is known about its source and credibility: tangible evidence, testimonial evidence, equivocal testimonial evidence, missing evidence, or accepted facts. When various pieces of evidence conflict, decision makers need to decide whether some piece of evidence is flawed, or whether the information can be used to refine the conclusion by understanding how variations in the context from which the evidence was collected affected the results. In software technology adoption people generally look for evidence about a technology's relative advantage, compatibility, complexity, tailorability, and observability.

All of this information can be used to outline a general process for technology transfer. First, there should be a preliminary evaluation of a technology within an organization's culture. The results contribute to a growing body of evidence that can be evaluated itself to see if it contributes compelling evidence for adopting the technology. If the decision is made to invest in the technology, then effort must be spent to package and support it, to facilitate its adoption throughout the organization.

Of course, software development involves decision-making on a wide range of issues, not just technology adoption. Again, however, many other fields contribute both descriptive and predictive theories that help us understand the process. One such theory identifies four important elements that affect any decision: problem finding, problem context, problem solving, and legitimization. Group decision-making adds even more complexity, since issues of trust, communication, and cooperation are added to the mix. Group issues can be addressed by selecting an appropriate decision strategy (e.g., a dialectic process, third-party reconciliation, brainstorming, round robin). In an organization, the right choice of strategy can also depend on whether the decision is strategic, tactical, or routine.

Observational studies of decision-makers at work have led to a "recognition-primed" decision model, which suggests that people keep a mental repository of past experiences that can be compared to the current situation. In this model, people reason about which experience is closest to the current situation, and then use mental simulation to estimate whether the same solution can apply. However, the reasoning process is not always so straightforward. Bias can creep into decision-making in numerous ways: examples are contextual bias, stereotype threat, status-quo bias, and a reluctance to appear negative. People often tend to over-value evidence that is case-specific, recent, or particularly vivid.

The situation of group decision-making is similar. Techniques such as Delphi exist to help teams converge to a solution. However, bias can enter the process, often through issues of group dynamics.

Recently, there has been much discussion towards licensing software engineers, much as other engineering disciplines license their professionals. The goal is to improve the quality of software products by guaranteeing a minimum standard of knowledge and competency for all software developers. In order for this to be possible, several groups are attempting to define a body of knowledge for software engineering: a description of the knowledge, skills, and expertise that every software engineer should have.

Once established, the body of knowledge can be enforced either by requiring practitioners to be licensed or by introducing voluntary certification that practitioners can choose to obtain. Engineering societies in the United States and Canada argue that software engineers should be licensed as professional engineers, and that only licensed professionals should be permitted to develop certain types of software. The argument is that this would improve the quality of software products by raising the competence of practitioners and encouraging the use of best practices. However, many practitioners disagree, claiming that there is no evidence to support the claim that licensing would improve quality, and that this may afford false assurances to the public. Furthermore, these practitioners believe that it is better to attempt to certify software products than professionals. Certification, unlike licensing, is not required for a professional to practice software engineering. It is a document bestowed to the professional attesting that he or she is competent in software engineering, and may be used to provide assurances to the public. Non-certified professionals, however, are free to perform software-engineering activities. Certification is usually provided by professional societies.

Also required for the professionalization of software engineering is the establishment of a code of ethics. This is a description of the ethical and professional obligations of a software engineer. The code of ethics is meant to encourage ethical conduct, inspire public confidence in the profession, and provide a basis to evaluate the actions of professionals.

There are two major international organizations that offer resources for professional development of software engineers: the Institute for Electrical and Electronics Engineers (IEEE) and the Association for Computing Machinery (ACM). There are also numerous regional and national organizations.

At this time, the field of software engineering is grappling with not only technical issues, but also with questions about the field itself. One of the themes of this chapter (and of this book) has been that, to address such questions, we need to view software engineering in its broader setting, recognizing that software is the product of creative people working in teams. We must study the ways we are similar to other engineers but also embrace other disciplines, including the social sciences, so that our processes are effectively tailored to the human beings applying them, and our products are as useful as possible to our customers.

Exercises:

1. The "recognition-primed" decision model postulates that people make decisions by keeping a repository of past decisions and their results, against which the current situation is compared to suggest a likely strategy. Ongoing work is attempting to apply this theory at the level of whole organizations, by creating an organizational "experience base," describing the past work of all employees, which can be searched for answers to new problems. Can this model be applied directly to the organization? What are some complications that will have to be overcome before systems of this type could be effective?

2. Find a paper from the research literature describing a new technology. Remember in this context that "technology" can have a broad meaning, including software processes, tools, or specific techniques. Describe the particular technology being proposed. Does the paper describe who the anticipated users of the technology will be? Can you categorize those users according to the types of adopters in Figure 14.1? What arguments are made as to the technology's effectiveness? How could you classify those arguments according to the categories of evidence proposed by Schum (described in Section 14.2)?

3. Find a paper describing an organization's practical experience with a particular technology. If at all possible, find one describing experience with the same technology you chose in question 2. (Many conferences, including ICSE, now include tracks dedicated to industry reports, making these conference proceedings a good place to start your search.) How does the paper measure the success (or lack of success) with the technology? What kinds of evidence are presented to support the evaluation of effectiveness? How would you classify that evidence according to the categories of evidence proposed by Schum (described in Section 14.2)?

4. As a project manager, John has been using design inspections on his projects since he came to his current employer, even though his manager does not believe that the inspection personnel have the necessary background to be successful. Over the last five years, seven design inspections were undertaken and John considered all of them successful (i.e., they all found some significant issues, and no major defects caused by design were found in the product in later development or use). However, in this year three inspections were undertaken and all were unsuccessful (major problems slipped through). One of these instances was particularly embarrassing for John since a major defect was not found until after delivery to the customer, and the redesign that was necessary was particularly expensive. Now John is starting a new project (which is not very similar to his previous projects in this organization) and has to consider whether to spend the resources on a design inspection again. What sources of bias should he be aware of that might affect his decision?

5. Given the situation described in question 4, the body of evidence John is accumulating about design inspections has internal contradictions. What can John do to try to draw a meaningful and accurate conclusion?

6. Pick a country other than the United States and Canada and compare its rules for licensing engineers with those of these two countries.
7. Read the ACM/IEEE software engineering code of ethics (sidebar 14.2) and describe actual cases where the code was violated.

Answer Guidelines:
1. It is hard to apply the model directly, primarily for two reasons: first, the information at the organizational level comes from many employees, not just one person's past experience. Secondly, the information has to be made explicit, so that other people can share and understand, not just stored for personal use. From these differences, there are a number of difficulties that arise. Some of the most important are: Each item that is stored has to be classified in some meaningful way so that it can be found again, and the user can judge how close it is to the current situation. A related problem is that queries to the experience base have to satisfy two (often contradictory) requirements: they must make sense to the person doing the query, matching how he or she actually thinks of the problem trying to be addressed, and also be powerful and accurate enough to be used to find relevant information in the base. And, the information has to be stored in such a way that it is useful to the person doing the query when it is found. That means that somehow the context of the decision, the decision itself, and the results have to be described in a way that is understandable and meaningful.

2. Answers will vary depending on the paper chosen. It is important to note that research papers often fail to address the anticipated users of a proposed technology; the type of adopter for whom this technology is suitable may have to be inferred from the amount of existing evidence and support for the technology. The type of evidence cited to support the effectiveness of software technologies vary widely, although there is some evidence that the number of papers citing some empirical evidence (which would be categorized as testimonial evidence in Schum's taxonomy) has been increasing.

3. Answers will vary depending on the paper chosen. Ideally, measures of success would come from Rogers' list of technology attributes described in Section 14.2. The type of evidence cited to support the effectiveness of software technologies vary widely.

4. In this specific situation, a number of biases might come into play for John. Decision makers tend to be biased toward evidence that is recent and vivid, so John might over-value the evidence from this year, especially from the project that he found particularly embarrassing, and make an overly negative judgment about the inspections' value. Since people also tend to be biased toward case-specific evidence, John might be tempted to make a larger generalization about inspection effectiveness even before he examines how the new project differs from the old ones in ways that might impact the inspections. There is nothing in the question to lead us to believe that contextual bias would apply, although how John frames the question to himself would certainly play a role. If he asks himself whether he "wants to spend the resources" or "wants to actively pursue a higher-quality design" in the new project (two different ways of saying the same thing), his answer could certainly be influenced. There would not appear to be any status quo bias in this example since it is clear that the new project will not be a familiar environment. Although it probably wouldn't come into play in the decision, stereotype threat may be affecting the results; if the inspection personnel know that

others in the company believe they don't have the background to be effective, this could be influencing their performance.

5. Since all of the evidence comes from personal experience, John shouldn't weigh some of it less than others due to the source (for example, he might not have paid as much attention to some inspections if he had only heard about them second-hand). John should examine the evidence to make sure that what he knows is accurate. Were the previous inspections really as successful as he thinks? Did the ones this year really miss issues they should have been expected to catch? If the evidence is accurate then he should pursue contextual factors that might explain the discrepancy; for example, were the inspections this year on different types of systems, using different personnel, or using a different inspection process? These contextual factors might explain why some were successful and others not.

6. Try to consider the following issues in the country you are researching:
   - must the engineer obtain a degree from an accredited program or school?
   - must the engineer write an exam prepared by a licensing board after completing the degree?
   - is experience in the engineering field required for obtaining the license?
   - must the engineer be recommended by other engineers?

7. A few examples are: developing harmful viruses, hiding known software vulnerabilities, leaving hidden "backdoors" in developed systems, developing software that can be used only for illegal purposes.

Review Exam 4

The following questions are in reference to a hypothetical "Gas Station Control System" (or GSCS) that will be used to help manage an American-style gasoline or service station. Our hypothetical gas station basically provides two services:

- There is a small store that carries car parts. Inside the store is at least one cash register, operated by a cashier who is an employee of the gas station.
- There are a number of gas pumps, at which customers can park their cars, interact with the system to pay via credit card, and then pump their own gas. Alternatively, the customer can pay for his or her gas via cash or credit card by going into the store and paying directly to the cashier.

Thus, the GSCS has two main classes of users. The first is the cashier, who uses the GSCS to record purchases of car parts by customers. The GSCS must allow the cashier to enter the type and number of parts purchased, then compute the total purchase price and handle the payment. Customers purchasing gasoline are the second type of user. These customers interface with the system at the gas pump by specifying the amount and type of gas they will buy, paying either at the pump or to the cashier, and then pumping the gas themselves.

The system also has to interact with other automated systems to perform its tasks. For example, in order to accept credit card payments, the GSCS must interface with a system maintained by the credit card company. The credit card system is responsible for checking that the customer's account is in good standing and can accommodate the amount of the purchase, and for debiting the customer's account and eventually reimbursing the gas station. The operation of these external systems is beyond the scope of the GSCS, although the GSCS needs to know how the external systems will communicate the success or failure of their tasks.

The GSCS is divided into three subsystems:

- A gas purchase subsystem, that takes care of customer interaction with the gas pumps;
- A cashier subsystem, that interacts with the cashier to accept payment for the purchase of car parts and gasoline;
- A tracking subsystem, that logs all purchases and tracks the inventory remaining.

The questions in this section have to do with maintenance issues in the implementation of the system, and with the operation of the system once it reaches the maintenance phase of the life cycle.

1. While implementing the system, the development team has given some thought to the type of maintenance changes the system will require. The first step in doing this might be to:
   a. Classify the system as an S-type system.
   b. Classify the system as a P-type system.
   c. Classify the system as an E-type system.
   d. Recognize that this system is likely to require no maintenance activities.

2. The development team also recognizes that certain attributes of the system itself may make it easier or harder to maintain. Which of the following statements about the system are likely to affect the effort required to make changes?
   a. The GSCS must respond to customers in real time.
   b. The requirements and design are well-documented.
   c. The GSCS must interface with several different pieces of hardware, such as the cash register, the gas pumps, and the credit card systems.
   d. a and b
   e. a and c
   f. b and c
   g. a, b, and c

3. TRUE or FALSE: While implementing the system, the team tracks seven measures of software complexity, on the assumption that the most complex modules will be likely to require the most future maintenance. A reasonable way to minimize the data collection effort would be to select the one measure from this set that seems best correlated with maintenance effort and discard the rest.

4. On the past several projects, the team has tried to use a predictive model that estimates the amount of maintenance required by a system based on the code complexity measures, among other factors. However, the predictions seem to consistently underestimate the actual effort required by about 40%. Which of the following is a valid assessment of the model?
   a. It suffers from bias, which should be assessed with a u-plot.
   b. It suffers from noise, and should be assessed using the prequential likelihood function.
   c. It suffers from both bias and noise and should be discarded.

5. TRUE or FALSE: The prediction system described in question 4 is valid only if the acceptance range is greater than 40%.

6. TRUE or FALSE: If a measure (such as one of the complexity measures from question 3) were not valid for predicting effort, it could not be internally valid.

While implementing the system, the development team keeps in mind the Belady-Lehman equation of maintenance effort. They would like to use this equation as a guide that will hopefully allow them to save effort during the maintenance phase. According to this equation, are the following expectations of the development team TRUE or FALSE?

7. A system developed using good software engineering principles will be slightly easier to maintain than one that hasn't used these principles.
8. The best use of resources would be to require someone unfamiliar with the system to perform the maintenance, since that person is unlikely to make the same mistakes or assumptions as the original development team.
9. All else being equal, if the development team is equally familiar with two systems from different environments, and the systems are equally complex, the expected maintenance effort is roughly equal.

After the system is completely implemented and has been in operation for some time, a number of changes have been identified that should be made to the system.

10. As changes are made to the system, which of the following would be reasonable to expect?
    a. If enough new functionality is added, it will eventually be more cost-effective to rewrite the GSCS rather than continue modifying it.
    b. The number of modules in the code will increase and the connections among them will become more complicated.
    c. Measures of the programming process, such as productivity of the maintenance team, will vary greatly as the system changes over time.
    d. a and b
    e. a and c
    f. b and c
    g. a, b, and c

11. One of the credit card companies upgrades its system for handling credit card payments, and this requires a slight change to the type of data that the GSCS needs to send to it. This situation:
    a. Should lead to a corrective change.
    b. Should lead to an adaptive change.
    c. Should lead to a perfective change.
    d. Should lead to a preventive change.
    e. Should require no maintenance to be performed.

12. The gas station owner has stipulated that the GSCS should be able to handle additional gas pumps, if the station decides to invest in them in the future. However, the development team realizes that the way in which it handles concurrency will not scale up if more gas pumps are added at the gas station. This situation:
    a. Should lead to a corrective change.
    b. Should lead to an adaptive change.
    c. Should lead to a perfective change.
    d. Should lead to a preventive change.
    e. Should require no maintenance to be performed.

13. An additional service is added for customers at the gas station. (Customers can now rent parking spots.) This situation:
    a. Should lead to a corrective change.
    b. Should lead to an adaptive change.
    c. Should lead to a perfective change.
    d. Should lead to a preventive change.
    e. Should require no maintenance to be performed.

14. When receipts are printed, if the customer's name exceeds a certain length then the purchase price does not fit on the receipt and is not printed. This situation does not occur very frequently (at most, once a week). This situation:
    a. Should lead to a corrective change.
    b. Should lead to an adaptive change.
    c. Should lead to a perfective change.
    d. Should lead to a preventive change.
    e. Should require no maintenance to be performed.

15. The situation described in question 14 represents a problem with the quality of the system because it represents a reduction in
    a. Reliability
    b. Integrity
    c. Consistency
    d. a and b
    e. a and c
    f. b and c
    g. a, b, and c

16. After the problem discussed in question 14 is identified, one of the developers redesigns a small part of the design to fix the problem, and changes the code accordingly. She then updates the requirements document so that the functionality now in the system is explained correctly. This is an example of:
    a. Maintaining vertical traceability
    b. Maintaining horizontal traceability
    c. Both a and b
    d. Neither a nor b

17. Operation of the system also reveals problems with the way it handles concurrent users at different gas pumps. Upon investigation, it was discovered that this problem stems from a module that was specified correctly in the requirements and design, but was implemented incorrectly in the code. This problem might have been discovered earlier if the team had used an appropriate:
    a. Linker
    b. Debugging tool
    c. Cross-reference generator
    d. Static code analyzer

18. Suppose that we want to evaluate the quality of the GSCS using Boehm's quality model. From which of the following perspectives would we assess the utility of the system?
    a. The owner of the gas station
    b. The cashiers and customers at the gas pumps
    c. The maintainers of the system
    d. a and b
    e. a and c
    f. b and c
    g. a, b, and c

19. The team members who worked on the gas purchase subsystem used a new CASE tool, and they are claiming that it should be adopted by the entire team. The team leader decides to investigate whether team performance would really be improved in this way. As a basis for his evaluation, he interviews several team members and looks for trends and patterns in their responses. He asks members who used the tool questions such as: whether the use of the tool led to more frequent or characteristic kinds of problems, whether the tool was reliable, and what kinds of tasks the tool was used for. He also talks to team members who did not use the tool, in order to see if they experienced problems that using the tool might have avoided.

The team leader will then try to relate this information to any differences in productivity between team members who used the tool and those who did not. This type of investigation would best be described as a:

- a. Feature analysis
- b. Case study
- c. Survey
- d. Formal experiment

20. The type of investigation described in question 19 is probably a good choice for an initial answer to this question, because:

- a. The effects of potentially confounding factors can be easily eliminated during the analysis, so that any relationship between tool use and productivity will be easy to see.
- b. This type of investigation is well-suited to retrospective data, and thus good use can be made of data already collected for other purposes.
- c. It ensures that the data collected about the tool will be representative of all important types of users.
- d. a and b
- e. a and c
- f. b and c
- g. a, b, and c

21. Based on the initial investigation described in question 19, the tool looks promising for use by the development team. The team leader would like to run one more small study to confirm this indication. He decides that the most appropriate type of study will be a formal experiment. He constructs a small programming assignment that he feels should take only a few hours, and gives the assignment to two groups of developers who have agreed to participate. Members of one group are asked to program the solution as they normally would, while the second group is asked to come up with a solution using the tool. The first group has no access to the tool, and cannot use it; and the team leader can examine the files produced by the tool to make sure the second group actually did use it as expected. Because there is a learning curve involved in use of the tool, the second group consists of developers who used the tool on the last project. The team leader can then study the quality of the solutions produced, and the effort required, to assess how useful the tool would be. The above study suffers from which of the following pitfall(s)?

- a. Bias
- b. Homogeneity
- c. Misclassification
- d. a and b
- e. a and c
- f. b and c
- g. This study has none of these pitfalls.

22. TRUE or FALSE: Assume that any pitfalls identified in question 21 are fixed. The team leader can be very confident that the results seen from the study would apply if the team used the tool on a real project.

23. TRUE or FALSE: The study described in question 21 directly tests the following hypothesis: "Using the tool produces better quality software than using the normal development method in this environment."

24. After studying the issue carefully, the team leader is convinced that the tool would be useful to the group, and acquires it for the next project. To assess whether his decision was a good one, the team leader monitors

the number of hours developers actually spend using the tool. However, it turns out that, compared with the last project, developers on this project end up using it much less. The team leader can reasonably conclude:
- a. The developers would find the tool more useful, if only they would use it more.
- b. This project is different in some way from the last one, which makes the tool less applicable.
- c. This project is simply smaller than planned, and requires less development activity.
- d. a and b
- e. a and c
- f. b and c
- g. a, b, and c

Once the project is completed and some maintenance tasks are taken care of, the team leader decides to spend some time reviewing the team's software development process, in order to identify potential improvements that can be made for the next project.

25. TRUE or FALSE: The team leader's normal post-project activity is to schedule some time for a one-on-one interview with each member of the team. He asks each member how he or she felt about the last project. He allows them to talk about organization, process, or anything else they find important and does his best not to ask leading questions or to give his own opinion. This approach is an optimal way to conduct postmortem analyses.

26. TRUE or FALSE: The team leader decides to try something new for this project: A "Project History Day" designed to track down the root causes of problems experienced while developing the GSCS. He invites the entire development team to the full-day meeting, expecting each member to raise any important problems encountered and the entire team to participate in discussing how to avoid it in the future. This Project History Day should be expected to be a successful tool for process improvement.

27. TRUE or FALSE: The final step of the team leader's process improvement effort is to produce a report to share the team's process discoveries with managers and other developers in the organization. The team leader is careful to include positive as well as negative findings. The top three problems of the last project are discussed in detail, along with suggested ways of fixing them. This strategy is an optimal way of publishing postmortem analysis results.

28. The team has also considered CMM as a way to improve their software development process. Which of the following accurately describes the CMM?
- a. It is meant to be used by a software development organization, which can use the key process areas to determine which aspects of their development process to improve.
- b. It is meant to be used by software customers, who can use it to assess the strengths and weaknesses of the software developers with whom they contract.
- c. The highest CMM ranking corresponds to the situation in which the software development process is understood simply as a "black box" that converts the inputs to the process into quality software.
- d. a and b
- e. a and c
- f. b and c
- g. a, b, and c

29. TRUE or FALSE: The ability to change the software development process based on lessons learned from previous projects is achieved at an early level of the CMM ranking system, and allows an organization to progress to higher levels.

30. TRUE or FALSE: One criticism of the CMM is that it assesses only the technical quality of an organization and largely ignores business quality.

31. Which of the following statements best capture the difference between CMM and SPICE?
    a. CMM defines desirable practices, which serve as a benchmark for comparison.
    b. The method for performing a SPICE evaluation is prescribed so as to be as objective as possible.
    c. SPICE addresses processes, distinguishing between base and generic practices.
    d. a and b
    e. a and c
    f. b and c
    g. a, b, and c

32. In contrast to the CMM, the people capability maturity model:
    a. Is aimed at assessing the capability of the developers comprising the development organization.
    b. Focuses more on the software developers themselves as a resource of the software organization, and less on the technology used by the organization.
    c. Awards a high level of maturity to an organization that has a quantitative understanding of how its practices are increasing the critical skills of its staff.
    d. a and b
    e. a and c
    f. b and c
    g. a, b, and c

After the GSCS has been deployed and begun stable operation, the development team starts on their next project, building an inventory tracking system for a convenience store.

33. One of the first things the development team realizes is that the inventory system from the GSCS can be largely reused in the new system, with minor modifications. If they are able to reuse modified parts of the GSCS in the new system, this type of reuse could be described as:
    a. Producer, black-box reuse
    b. Producer, white-box reuse
    c. Consumer, black-box reuse
    d. Consumer, white-box reuse

34. Because of situations like the one described in the previous question, the development teams decides that they would like to look into creating a reuse library. Which of the following are reasonable expectations about investing in reuse?
    a. It will improve the speed at which prototypes can be constructed.
    b. It will produce concrete benefits in the short term.
    c. It will help reduce time spent on unit testing as well as on coding.
    d. a and b
    e. a and c
    f. b and c
    g. a, b, and c

35. TRUE or FALSE: Studies have shown that, under certain conditions, code reuse can actually lead to more fault-prone software than writing code from scratch.

36. TRUE or FALSE: To help decide whether or not investing in a reuse library would be worthwhile, the team looks for "testimonial evidence." This means they would like to base the decision on information from sources such as direct observation of code libraries in use and second-hand information from other developers who have experience with them.

37. TRUE or FALSE: The credibility of the evidence described in the previous question is related primarily to its accuracy.

38. If the team lead analyzed the team as being in the "mainstream market" in terms of adopting new technologies (as opposed to being in the class of "innovators" or "early adopters"), which of the following would be true?
    a. The team would be willing to invest some of its own time into figuring out for themselves how to install and use the library, if support was not available.
    b. The team would be willing to invest in a reuse library only after there was widespread evidence of its effectiveness.
    c. An important factor in the decision would be what other members of the organization's business community are doing.
    d. a and b
    e. a and c
    f. b and c
    g. a, b, and c

Review Exam 4 Answers

1. b; The GSCS is a P-type system, since the problem can be described directly and completely, and has an exact solution. Unlike an E-type system, the system is not embedded in the environment; that is, the practical abstraction of the problem is unlikely to change due to an improved understanding resulting from the solution. As a P-type system, incremental change is possible in order to improve the solution. [Section 11.1]

2. g; In general, a system with real-time requirements is more difficult to change than a system without such requirements. The existence of documentation affects maintenance effort since a system without well-documented code and design can be almost impossible to search through for a problem's solution. The need to interface with different types of hardware can also be expected to affect maintenance effort since it is possible that the code will require changes every time any piece of hardware is upgraded or replaced. [Section 11.3]

3. FALSE; Section 11.4 of the textbook describes how it is necessary to be cautious in using only one measure to represent complexity, since each measure captures only one attribute of the system, and there are many attributes that contribute to complexity.

4. a; The prediction is biased because it is consistently less than the actual value. However, because the predictions do not fluctuate as underestimates and overestimates of the actual value, we cannot say the prediction is noisy. [Section 13.1]

5. TRUE; A prediction system is said to be valid if it makes accurate predictions. The acceptance range specifies the accuracy required of the model. [Section 12.3]

6. FALSE; The internal validity of a measure (how well it measures the attribute it claims to) should not be rejected just because it is not a part of a valid predictive system. The textbook uses the example of lines of code, which is a valid measure of program size but which is not always useful as a predictor of faults. [Section 12.3]

7. FALSE; The variable 'c' is reduced by software engineering practices and is an exponential term in the equation. Thus, even small changes to 'c' have the potential to greatly affect the expected effort. [Section 11.3]

8. FALSE; The variable 'd,' the team's familiarity with the software, decreases the expected effort as it decreases. [Section 11.3]

9. FALSE; The relevant variable here is 'K,' which is an empirical constant that depends on the environment. [Section 11.3]

10. d; The fourth "Law of Software Evolution" states that there will be no significant fluctuations in organizational attributes, such as productivity. [Section 11.1]

11. b; This change is necessary for the system to adapt as it evolves over time. [Section 11.2]

12. d; This change involves modifying part of the system to prevent future faults. [Section 11.2]

13. b; This change is necessary for the system to adapt as its requirements evolve over time. [Section 11.2]

14. a; This change is necessary to directly correct a fault. [Section 11.2]

15. d; Since a given input will always result in the same behavior there is no reduction in consistency. (Whether the failure occurs or not depends entirely on name length.) However, this failure means that the system does not always produce the desired result (the customer may not receive a useful receipt of his or her purchase), which represents a reduction in integrity. The existence of this problem also reduces the amount of time the system can run between failures, representing a reduction in reliability. [Section 12.4]

16. b; Horizontal traceability addresses the relationships within a collection of work products, such as requirements, design, and code documents, which all describe the same system. Vertical traceability, in contrast, addresses relationships between the subcomponents of one such work product. [Section 11.5]

17. c; Cross-reference generators assist developers by representing the traceability between various system work documents. If the team had used a cross-reference generator, it would have been more likely to note that components of the requirements and design were not represented in the code. [Section 11.5]

18. g; Boehm's model assesses utility from the viewpoint of three types of users. First, the customer of the system (the gas station owner) who is pleased with the utility if the system performs according to his or her requirements. Second, the users of the system (cashiers and gas station customers) who will be assumed to be pleased with the utility if the system operation will not change as components are upgraded or replaced. Third, the maintainers of the system who will be pleased if the system is easy to understand and make changes to, as necessary. [Section 12.4]

19. c; A survey is a retrospective study that attempts to discover the effects of a method, tool, or technique on participants. [Section 12.1]

20. b; Surveys are well-suited to the use of retrospective data. However, because the experimenter cannot manipulate key variables in the environment, it is difficult to assess the impact of potentially confounding factors. For example, the experimenter cannot ensure that the data collected will be representative of different types of users, since the experimenter cannot determine the makeup of the population sampled. [Section 12.1]

21. a; This study suffers from bias because the assignment of developers to groups (those who use the tool versus those who don't) may affect the results. Because all of the developers who are in the "tool use" group have previously adopted the tool on their own, we might wonder whether the tool is somehow better suited to their preferred working style. That is, the results seen for this group may not be the same as those seen for a random group of developers. The study does not suffer from homogeneity or misclassification because the two groups will have different levels of the factor (tool use) and the experimenter can check whether or not the groups performed as instructed. [Section 12.2]

22. FALSE; There is an additional pitfall, namely that the study is too short to expect its results to scale up directly to a real project. It is possible that the study would underestimate the usefulness of the tool, since there may be a learning curve that cannot be overcome in the few hours allotted to the study. Conversely, the study may overestimate the usefulness, since the tool may work well for very simple problems but not apply well to something as complicated as a real project. [Section 12.2]

23. FALSE; The hypothesis given cannot be tested directly because "software quality" is not quantifiable. That is, the experimenter will have to select a way of measuring software quality that can then be tested in the experiment. [Section 12.2]

24. g; Section 13.2 discusses an analogous situation in which inspection effectiveness is studied. In interpreting results of this sort, it is always necessary to keep in mind alternative explanations for observations; for example, human subjects don't always use technologies in the way researchers expect them to, and there are usually large variations between projects.

25. FALSE; Ideally, the team leader would attempt to solicit this information while preserving the anonymity of the respondents, in order to be more certain that the information is not biased. Also, the unstructured nature of the interviews does not allow comparison across projects, because

there is no guarantee that the team members will focus on the same issues at each interview. [Section 12.5]

26. FALSE; A better approach would be to identify issues for discussion beforehand. This approach would help keep the discussion focused, and could help make sure only people with relevant experience are invited to participate in the discussion. [Section 12.5]

27. TRUE; This description matches the guidelines given in the textbook for successfully publishing the results. In particular, while much benefit can be gained from distributing such a report to peer developers, managers are also stakeholders in the software development process and can benefit from insight into the process. [Section 12.5]

28. d; The CMM identifies important "key process areas" against which organizations can be assessed by themselves and customers. At the highest CMM level, the organization is expected to have achieved greater insight into what goes on within its software development process; it should not be considered a "black box." [Section 12.5]

29. FALSE; The ability to change the software process based on previous lessons learned is achieved at the highest level of the CMM. [Section 12.5]

30. TRUE; The CMM focuses on improving detection of faults, time to market, and operational failures, but ignores such business quality measures as customer satisfaction or appropriateness of functionality. [Section 13.3]

31. c; In contrast to the CMM, which evaluates organizations, SPICE evaluates processes. Both CMM and SPICE define a set of "best" practices for comparison and attempt to perform the comparison as objectively as possible. [Section 12.5]

32. g; The people capability maturity model is focused on improving the skills of individual developers and teams, and does the by helping the organization build up a quantitative understanding of how it can contribute to improving the critical skills of its staff. This quantitative understanding occurs at the second-highest level of maturity, the "managed" level. The key process areas are concerned with the skills of individuals and teams, not the technology they use. [Section 12.6]

33. d; Since this situation deals with the use, not the construction, of reusable components it represents consumer reuse. Since the subsystem will have to be modified before being reused, this will be white-box reuse. [Section 12.4]

34. e; Because early prototypes may be constructed using some of the reusable functionality, these prototypes could be constructed more quickly with a reuse library. (Later versions of the system will presumably require the reusable components to be tailored more, so the time savings will not be as great.) Also, if components are unit tested before being placed in the library and then reused verbatim, they need not be tested again. However, creating a useful reuse library requires a large initial effort (necessary for identifying reusable components, making them as reusable as possible, and then testing them thoroughly) and so may not produce large concrete benefits in the short term. [Section 12.4]

35. TRUE; The Moeller and Paulish study described in section 13.2 shows that, in a particular environment, reused components that required some changes (about 25% of the lines of code) were more fault-prone than components written from scratch.

36. TRUE; "Testimonial evidence" includes direct observation, second-hand experience, and opinion. [Section 14.2]

37. FALSE; Credibility of evidence is also related to the credibility of the source. [Section 14.2]

38. f; Mainstream market adopters are generally only willing to invest in a new technology when widespread evidence of its effectiveness and adequate support and training are already available. [Section 14.2]

Final Exam

The following questions are in reference to a hypothetical "Loan Arranger" system. The Loan Arranger is meant to assist a "consolidating organization," a specific type of business in the financial domain.

Bank customers often borrow money from banks; they promise to repay the loan plus interest over a certain period of time. Each of these loans is an ultimately lucrative proposition for the bank, but usually a long period of time is required for the bank to collect its earnings. Also, there is always the chance that a borrower will be unable to repay the loan. Consolidating organizations make money by buying loans from banks and reselling them to investors. Loan analysts, employed by the consolidating organization, work with investors to select a set of loans that meet their requirements in terms of time, risk, and initial purchase price.

The Loan Arranger application has two main types of functionality. First, it tracks all of the loans that are owned by the consolidating organization. (The entire set of loans owned by the organization is known as its "portfolio.") In order to track loans correctly, the Loan Arranger must interface with the banks to find out about new loans that should be added to the portfolio, or updates to loans that are already in the portfolio. Second, the Loan Arranger allows a loan analyst to select a subset of loans from the portfolio that match an investor's desired investment characteristics (these subsets of loans are referred to as "bundles"). The loan analyst can either select the bundle manually, or ask the system to select an optimal bundle given the investor's constraints. The Loan Arranger then updates the portfolio when the bundle is purchased by the investor. There are numerous constraints on how this functionality is to be achieved; most importantly, the Loan Arranger must be usable by more than one analyst at a time.

As a first step in developing the Loan Arranger, the development team meets with a representative from the consolidating organization to formulate a set of requirements.

1. Which of the following statements best describe the benefits that the consolidating organization may expect?
   a. The requirements process can help the consolidating organization think more clearly about the performance issues that are necessary for the Loan Arranger (for example, the maximum amount of time allowable for a search through the portfolio).
   b. The requirements process can help the development team communicate with the representative from the consolidating organization about the system.
   c. The requirements process can help the development team specify the types of data structures that will be used in the Loan Arranger, in order to ensure that the performance requirements are met.
   d. a and b
   e. a and c
   f. b and c
   g. a, b, and c

2. The development team needs to pick a representation for the requirements. Which of the following are valid choices and rationales?
   a. Structured Analysis and Design Technique, because it may be useful to view the system at different levels of detail at different times (for example, it may be useful to specify the inputs and outputs of the system before proceeding to design the mechanisms by which loans are included in bundles to be sold).
   b. Warnier diagrams, because they will be helpful in understanding the different types of loans that must be handled by the system.
   c. Data flow diagrams, since these will help the development team understand how the functionality can be used by multiple users simultaneously.
   d. a and b
   e. a and c
   f. b and c
   g. a, b, and c

Mark items 3 through 6 TRUE if they belong in the requirements for the Loan Arranger, and FALSE if they do not.

3. A description of the skills and knowledge the development team assumes that the loan analysts already have.
4. A description of how the consolidating organization decides which loans to buy from banks for inclusion in the portfolio.
5. Constraints on the maximum allowable time for the system to automatically suggest an "optimal" bundle of loans for sale to investors.
6. The hardware on which the Loan Arranger will be designed to run.

A requirements review is undertaken to make sure that the requirements adequately describe the system to be built.

7. Which of the following excerpts should be considered valid functional requirements during the review?
   a. "Once the Loan Arranger has automatically generated a bundle, the loan analyst must be able to modify it manually. The loan analyst may modify a bundle by either removing loans which are already included, or adding additional loans."
   b. "A record should be kept for each bank from which loans are purchased, consisting of the name of the bank, the name of a contact person at the bank, and the phone number of the contact person. The loan analyst should be able to edit fields that are changeable."
   c. "The expected profit of a fixed-rate loan is the amount of interest that will be received over the remaining life of the loan. The formula for computing loan interest is included in Appendix A."
   d. a and b only
   e. a and c only
   f. b and c only
   g. a, b, and c

8. Which of the following can be considered examples of valid nonfunctional requirements?
    a. "If updates are made to any displayed information, the information is refreshed within five seconds."
    b. "The application must ensure that users are limited to authorized loan analysts."
    c. "The application must be available for use by a loan analyst during 97% of the business day."
    d. a and b only
    e. a and c only
    f. b and c only
    g. a, b, and c

In questions 9 through 12, review the given excerpt from the requirements and decide whether it is an adequate requirement or not. If the excerpt is adequate, mark choice 'e.' If it should be rewritten, mark all the reasons that apply.

9. "A borrower can be in one of three states: 'good,' 'late,' or 'default.' A borrower is considered to be in 'good' standing if all loans to that borrower are in good standing. A borrower is considered to be in 'default' standing if any of the loans to that borrower have default standing. A borrower is said to be in 'late' standing if any of the loans to that borrower have late standing."
    a. This requirement should be rewritten; it is incorrect.
    b. This requirement should be rewritten; it is ambiguous or inconsistent.
    c. This requirement should be rewritten; it is unrealistic.
    d. This requirement should be rewritten; it is unverifiable.
    e. This requirement is fine.

10. "The format of the reports is at the discretion of the individual banks. The Loan Arranger must be easily extensible, so that it can handle new file formats as necessary."
    a. This requirement should be rewritten; it is incorrect.
    b. This requirement should be rewritten; it is ambiguous or inconsistent.
    c. This requirement should be rewritten; it is unrealistic.
    d. This requirement should be rewritten; it is unverifiable.
    e. This requirement is fine.

11. "Each loan must have a loan amount of at least $1000 but not more than $500,000. There are two types of loans: regular and jumbo. A regular loan is for any amount less than or equal to $275,000. A jumbo loan is for any amount over $275,000."
    a. This requirement should be rewritten; it is incorrect.
    b. This requirement should be rewritten; it is ambiguous or inconsistent.
    c. This requirement should be rewritten; it is unrealistic.
    d. This requirement should be rewritten; it is unverifiable.
    e. This requirement is fine.

12. "The user must be advised when a search request is inappropriate or illegal."
    a. This requirement should be rewritten; it is incorrect.
    b. This requirement should be rewritten; it is ambiguous or inconsistent.
    c. This requirement should be rewritten; it is unrealistic.
    d. This requirement should be rewritten; it is unverifiable.
    e. This requirement is fine.

After the initial requirements have been defined, the team decides to develop an initial project plan. First, the risks are identified and assessed. Determine whether or not each of the statements 13 through 15 is describing a risk. Answer TRUE if the statement describes a risk, FALSE otherwise.

13. The developers of the Loan Arranger application do not have much experience in the financial domain.
14. The Loan Arranger application must interface with many external systems.
15. Prototyping is used on the Loan Arranger application to make sure that the team is implementing the correct functionality.

In addition to the risk management activities, cost, schedule and effort estimations are done. On the past several projects, the team has tried to use a predictive model to estimate the expected size of the project. The relative errors of the predictions on the last five projects are shown below. A relative error of 0 means that there was no difference between the predicted and actual values. A positive relative error means that the prediction was an overestimate, while a negative value indicates an underestimate.

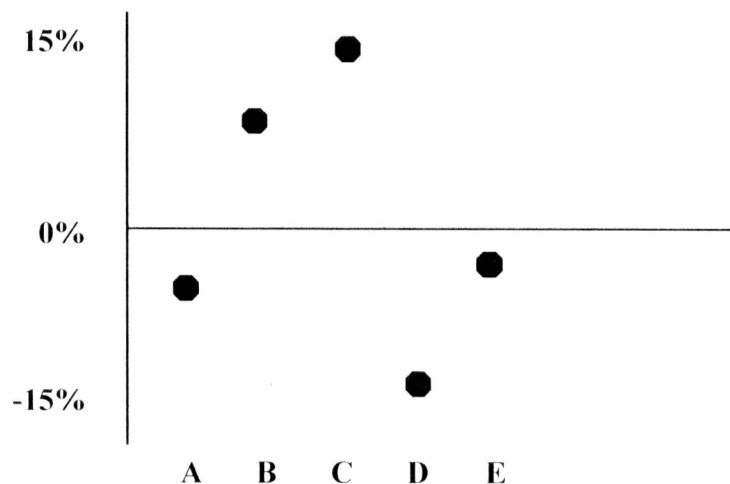

16. As can be seen from the graph, predictions are usually within 15% (plus or minus) of the actual effort. However, for a given prediction, it is impossible to say whether it is an underestimate or an overestimate of the actual value. Which of the following is a valid assessment of the model?
    a. It suffers from bias, which should be assessed with a u-plot.
    b. It suffers from noise, and should be assessed using the prequential likelihood function.
    c. It suffers from both bias and noise and should be discarded.

96

Suppose the COCOMO 2.0 estimation process has been chosen to estimate size and effort for part of the project.

17. The loan search and selection subsystem of the Loan Arranger application has 10 screens and 20 reports. Two screens are rated as difficult, 5 as medium and 3 as easy. Ten reports are rated as difficult, 6 as medium and 4 as easy. Using the COCOMO 2.0 stage 1 model, how many new object points does the subsystem have? Assume no 3GL components or reuse of existing components.
   a. 210
   b. 137
   c. 109
   d. 30
   e. None of the above

As part of an on-going investigation into the benefits of a new size estimation technique, the size of part of the Loan Arranger application will be estimated using the experimental technique. The technique has been used on several projects in the past. The estimates generated by the technique and the actual values for project size are shown below. The criteria for a good estimating technique are: 75% of the estimates should be within 25% of the actual value; and the mean magnitude of the relative estimated errors should be less than 25%. Use the table of project size estimates and the criteria given to answer the questions about the estimation technique.

Project	Estimate	Actual
A	5000	10000
B	25000	20000
C	50000	80000
D	70000	110000
E	40000	45000
F	45000	50000

18. Given the table of estimates and actuals, what is the MMRE? Round to the nearest 1/100.
   a. 0.04
   b. 0.14
   c. 0.28
   d. 0.34
   e. 0.43

19. What is the PRED(.25)?
   a. 0.25
   b. 0.28
   c. 0.33
   d. 0.50
   e. 0.75

20. Based on the criteria for a good estimation technique and the estimate data gathered so far, can this technique be used to create good estimates for the Loan Arranger project? (Yes/No)

21. Several estimators use various techniques to estimate the amount of effort required for the Loan Arranger project. Each estimator arrives at his or her estimate independently. The independent estimates are 600 person-months, 650 person-months, 800 person-months and 750 person months. Using these estimates, what is the Delphi estimate for this project? Round to the closest month.
    a. 700 person-months
    b. 684 person-months
    c. 648 person-months
    d. 600 person-months
    e. 523 person-months

22. TRUE or FALSE: When the Delphi method is used and participants are allowed to iterate through the process several times, group dynamics drives the group consensus to converge close to the median of the estimates.

23. If the Delphi estimate for effort is used and there are 20 team members working on the project, how many months will the project take? Assume all team members can work concurrently. Round to the closest month.
    a. 26
    b. 30
    c. 32
    d. 34
    e. 35

24. If there are 20 team members assigned to the project team, how many potential lines of communication exist?
    a. 20
    b. 45
    c. 190
    d. 400

To build a schedule, the critical path method is used. The activity graph (shown below) is used to depict the dependencies among the activities and milestones of the Loan Arranger project. The nodes of the graph represent the milestones of the project. The edges linking the nodes represent the activities. The numbers adjacent to the edges represent the number of days required for the activity. For example, it will take five days to complete the activity starting at milestone A and ending in milestone C. Use this activity graph to answer the following questions:

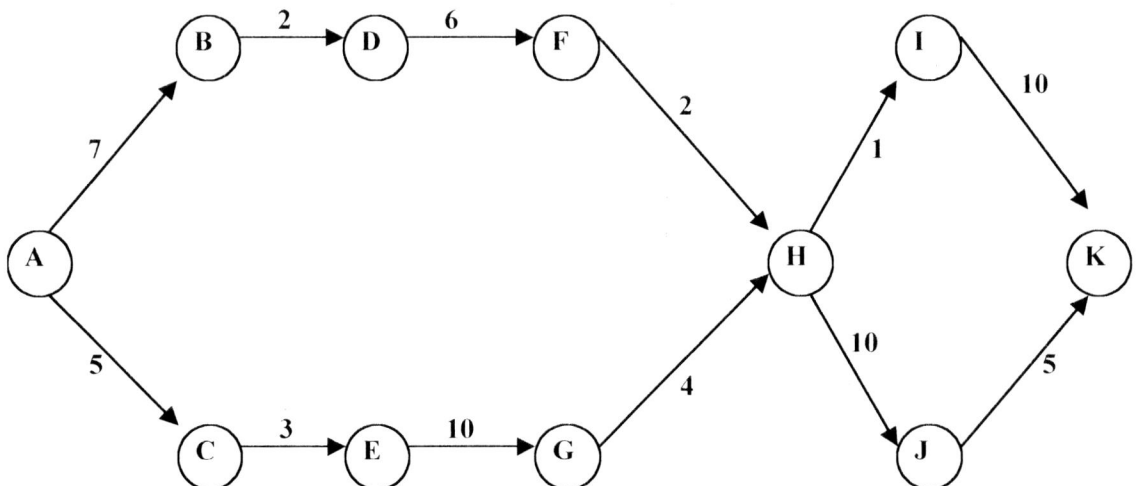

25. Which of the following is a critical path from milestone A to milestone K?
    a. ACEGHJK
    b. ACEGHIK
    c. ABDFHJK
    d. ABDFHIK

26. What is the slack time for the activity starting at milestone F?
    a. 4
    b. 5
    c. 16
    d. 21

27. What is the length of the critical path identified in question 25?
    a. 28
    b. 32
    c. 33
    d. 37

28. Which milestones are precursors to J?
    a. D
    b. E
    c. I
    d. D and E
    e. D and I
    f. All of the above

The development team decides that the next step is to create an architectural design and then a module design.

29. The architectural design is felt to be of value because it will allow the consolidating organization to check:
    a. How its policy of allowing banks to specify the format of their reports will affect the system.
    b. What functions the loan analysts can access at any given time.
    c. Whether the reports generated by the system will match the report format already used by the organization.
    d. a and b
    e. a and c
    f. b and c
    g. a, b, and c

30. Which of the following are valid rationales for creating a separate module design?
    a. The architectural design will be useful for communicating with the representative of the consolidating organization; it may contain financial jargon but not implementation details or programming jargon.
    b. The architectural design will not include detailed financial formulas so it will be independent of the implementation.
    c. The module design should contain more detail about what data structures will need to be used in order to meet the performance requirements.
    d. a and b
    e. a and c
    f. b and c
    g. a, b, and c

31. The team has to decide on a general approach to creating the design. Which are NOT valid choices and rationales?
    a. Data-oriented decomposition, because the data structures are central to the design of the system, and many aspects of the data structures are highly constrained by the requirements.
    b. Modular decomposition, because the system functions are highly interdependent, so the system is not easily divisible into separate subsystems.
    c. Event-oriented decomposition, because the type of functionality available to the loan analyst at any given time will depend on the current state of the system, as determined by the actions of all loan analysts using the system.
    d. a and b
    e. a and c
    f. b and c
    g. a, b, and c

32. The team leader decides that the logical next step is to decide on an architectural style for the system. Which of the following are valid choices and rationales?
    a. Peer-to-Peer, since this design style would allow changes to the portfolio of a peer to be disseminated to and propagated through other peers in the network.
    b. Client-Server, since this design style would be a convenient way to allow many different loan analysts to view the same data in different ways.
    c. Repository, since it will be convenient to view the system as a central data store (the portfolio of loans) with mechanisms for storing, retrieving, and updating the data.
    d. a and b
    e. a and c
    f. b and c
    g. a, b, and c

33. Since the development team has some experience with concurrency from a previous project, the technology involved in this system is well understood. The team has decided on an object-oriented design, which breaks the system into several components, and the team members are fairly confident they understand how each of the components will achieve the required functionality. On the other hand, it is not yet clear how the components will interact with each other and with external systems. A reasonable strategy for completing this design would therefore be:
    a. Prototyping
    b. Fault-tree analysis
    c. Design by contract

```
┌──────────────┐      ┌──────────────┐      ┌──────────────┐
│ Bank         │      │ Loan         │      │ Borrower     │
├──────────────┤      ├──────────────┤      ├──────────────┤
│              │──────│              │──────│              │
├──────────────┤      ├──────────────┤      ├──────────────┤
│              │      │              │      │              │
└──────────────┘      └──────┬──\────┘      └──────────────┘
                             │   \
                             │    \      ┌──────────────┐
                             │     \     │ Bundle       │
                             │      \    ├──────────────┤
                             │       \───│              │
                             │           ├──────────────┤
                             │          /│              │
                             │         / └──────────────┘
                      ┌──────┴────────/─┐
                      │ Loan Arranger    │
                      ├──────────────────┤
                      │                  │
                      ├──────────────────┤
                      │                  │
                      └──────────────────┘
```

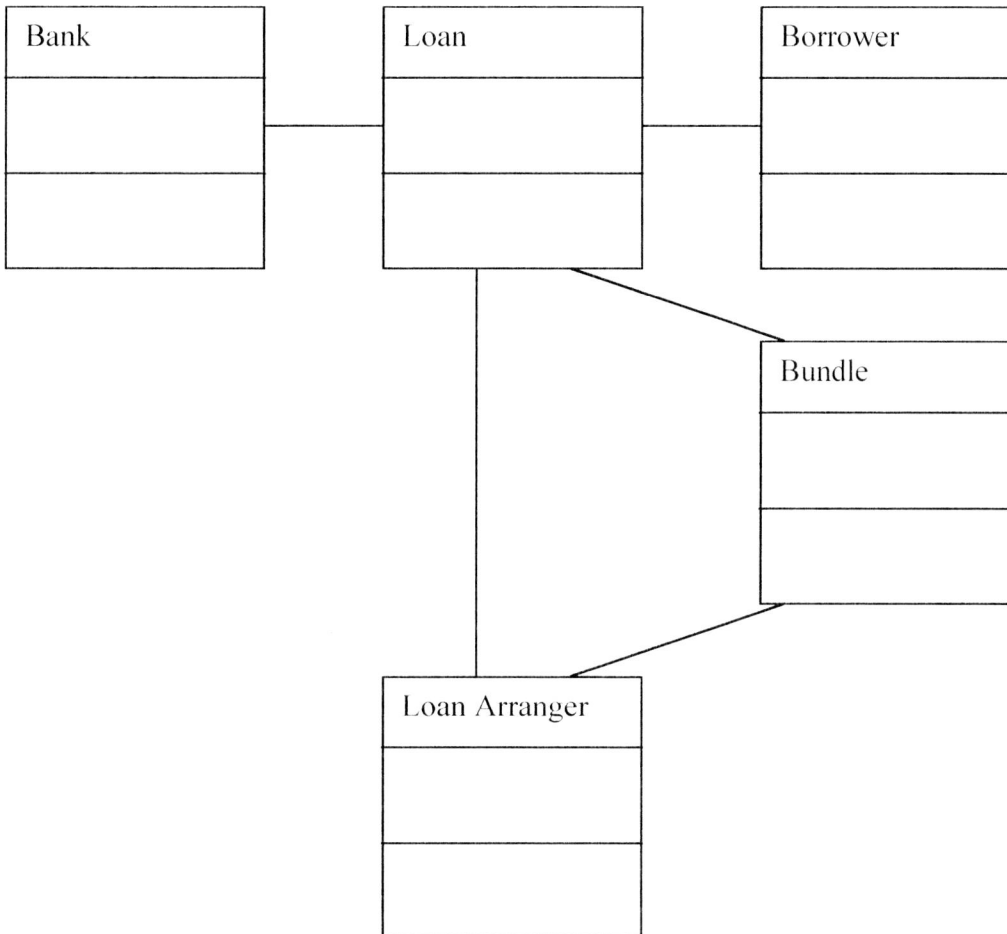

This is the class diagram for the initial high-level design of the Loan Arranger system.

34. Which of the following best describes the amount of coupling for class Loan, relative to the other classes in the high-level design shown above?
    a. High coupling
    b. Low coupling
    c. Can't tell

35. Which of the following best describes the amount of cohesion for class Loan, relative to the other classes in the high-level design shown above?
    a. High cohesion
    b. Low cohesion
    c. Can't tell

36. Based on what is known about the level of cohesion and coupling for class Loan, it is reasonable to assume that:
    a. It will probably be easier to modify than class Borrower.
    b. It will probably be harder to modify than class Borrower.
    c. No conclusions can be drawn about the ease of modification.

37. After an internal review, some of the designers want to add more classes to the high-level model. Which of the following are appropriate for a high-level design?
    a. Classes "Variable Rate Loan" and "Fixed Rate Loan," subclasses of "Loan," which are handled differently by the consolidating organization.
    b. Class "Acceptance Dialog," which controls the window that appears on the screen when a new loan can be purchased by the consolidating organization.
    c. Class "Identification Number," which consolidates the implementation for unique loan ID numbers in the system.
    d. a and b
    e. a and c
    f. b and c
    g. a, b, and c

38. To estimate the amount of effort that will be needed to construct the system, the team could look at which of the following metrics during system design?
    a. Lack of cohesion of methods
    b. Number of key classes
    c. Number of support classes
    d. a and b
    e. a and c
    f. b and c
    g. a, b, and c

39. TRUE or FALSE: The Weighted Methods per Class (WMC) metric is useful for identifying classes that are potentially reusable classes. These classes are likely to be the ones with the highest values of the metric.

40. TRUE or FALSE: Number of Children (NOC) is useful for identifying those classes on which greater testing effort should be spent. These are the classes with high values for the metric.

41. TRUE or FALSE: Response for a Class (RFC) is useful for identifying those classes on which greater testing effort should be spent. These are the classes with high values for the metric.

42. The following figure represents the state diagram created during design for class "Borrower." Which of the following statements are true?
    a. Regardless of the state of the borrower, if any loan is default, the borrower is considered in default status.
    b. Regardless of the state of the borrower, if any loan is late, the borrower is considered in late status.
    c. Regardless of the state of the borrower, if any loan is good, the borrower is considered in good status.
    d. a and b
    e. a and c
    f. b and c
    g. None of these

43. TRUE or FALSE: It cannot be determined what state an object of type Borrower will be in when it is created.

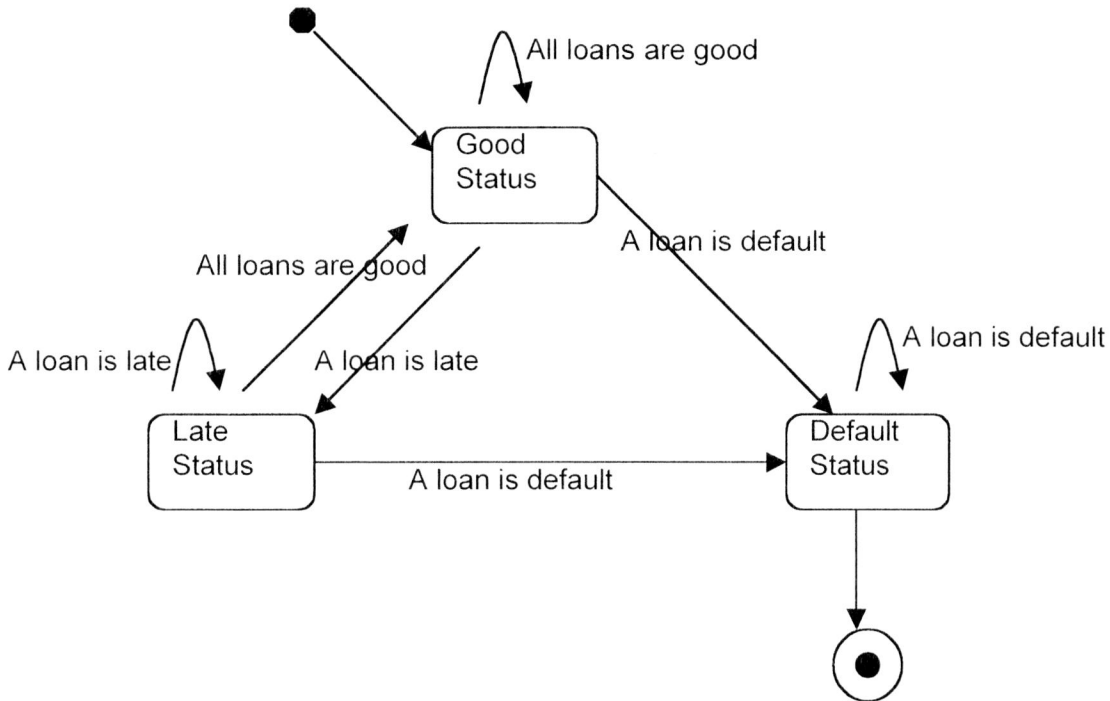

As a next step, the high-level design is expanded into a low-level design.

44. In the design, the portfolio is represented as a central data store. This data store is accessed (and potentially modified) by a number of other system components. For example, one component updates the data store when new information is received from a bank, while another component searches the data store for loans to create a bundle. The relationship between these components and the data store is best described as:
    a. Content coupled
    b. Common coupled
    c. Control coupled
    d. Stamp coupled
    e. Data coupled

45. Which of the following items of information are NOT appropriate for inclusion in the final design?
    a. The format of the screens that will be used by the loan analyst
    b. The format of the reports the system will generate for use by the loan analyst
    c. The format and storage specifications of archival reports
    d. None of the above (all are appropriate)
    e. a and b
    f. a and c
    g. b and c
    h. a, b, and c

From previous projects, the team leader has realized that the team typically experiences many problems in the implementation phase due to poor decisions made in the design phase. To address this problem, the team leader decides to make a process change: the addition of active design reviews to the team's software development process.

46. In preparing for the active design review, which of the following would be appropriate actions for the team leader?
    a. Invite program designers to the reviews, instructing them to gain a better understanding of the design.
    b. Invite program designers to the reviews, instructing them to critique the existing design.
    c. Require the design to be redone and schedule added reviews, if major problems are discovered during the review.
    d. a and b
    e. a and c
    f. b and c
    g. a, b, and c

47. The design reviews discussed in question 46 require a lot of extra time from the developers: planning, preparing for, and then actually holding the meetings. The team leader would like some empirical indication whether this additional investment in design time actually pays off. His idea is to introduce critical design reviews on the Loan Arranger project only, and to compare the results on this project to the results on the development team's previous projects. As much as possible, he intends to make sure that everything else about the Loan Arranger project is typical of the kinds of projects the team usually works on. If key factors on the Loan Arranger are not typical for other projects of this team, then he will at least document those key factors and reason about their possible influence on the results. This type of study would be best described as a:
    a. Feature analysis
    b. Case study, with sister projects
    c. Case study, with baseline
    d. Case study, with random selection
    e. Survey
    f. Formal experiment

48. A benefit of the type of study identified in question 47 is that:
    a. Any differences in the implementation phase can be directly attributed to the use of critical design reviews.
    b. The more typical both the Loan Arranger project and the comparison projects are, the more confidence there is that differences in the implementation phase are due to the use of critical design reviews.
    c. No conclusions can be drawn about the effects of critical design reviews, but it can be determined how software developers on this team will react to the new process.

Once the design of the system has passed the critical design review, the project moves into the implementation phase.

49. To best implement the system, the development team has to give some thought to the type of maintenance changes the Loan Arranger system will eventually require. Since few (if any) changes are expected in the way the consolidating organization tracks and bundles loans, the team should:
    a. Classify the system as an S-type system.
    b. Classify the system as a P-type system.
    c. Classify the system as an E-type system.
    d. Recognize that this system is likely to require no maintenance activities.

During implementation, several problems occur. Identify the problems as errors, faults or failures.

50. A developer implementing a component to keep track of loan updates thinks that the only modifications to loans will be additions and deletions of loans. The developer doesn't realize that interest rates on loans may change also.
51. A loan analyst notices that the loan total (original loan amount + interest) displayed on the screen is incorrect. The total value is less than the original loan amount.
52. In the code for computing loan profit, the initial purchase price is added to the profit. It should be subtracted.
53. When a loan analyst conducts three optimal bundle searches using different search criteria each time, the same set of loans is always returned. Not all of the loans returned match the criteria specified by the loan analyst.

While implementing the Loan Arranger, the development team finds out it is likely that they will be doing additional projects in the financial domain.

54. As part of the Loan Arranger, the team implements a module that calculates the interest that will be paid on a fixed-rate loan. Because it is likely that any future projects in the financial domain will also need to use this function, the module is designed to be reusable, with clearly defined and simple inputs and outputs. It is intended that any future projects can thus reuse the module directly, as long as they know the correct inputs to send and the correct output format to expect. This is an example of:
    a. Producer, black-box reuse
    b. Producer, white-box reuse
    c. Consumer, black-box reuse
    d. Consumer, white-box reuse

55. Suppose that a future project does in fact have need of a module to calculate fixed-rate interest. Which of the following problems may stand in the way of effectively reusing the module described in question 54?
    a. The developers of the future project will have to search through all of the components available for reuse, and may not find the module.
    b. The developers of the future project may not be properly trained, and may not even recognize the situation as a potential for reuse.
    c. The developers of the future project may not be motivated to reuse, and may end up re-implementing the functionality from scratch.
    d. a and b
    e. a and c
    f. b and c
    g. a, b, and c

When implementation of a module is complete, it undergoes code review. In the following program fragments from the Loan Arranger application, identify violations (if any) of good programming style that should be caught during review.

Use the following choices in your response:
(a) Generality
(b) Efficiency
(c) Formatting
(d) Documentation
(e) No violations

56. void PrintLoanList(LoanList *loans){
     LoanList *l = loans;

     while (l){
     cout << *l << "\n";
     l = loans->next;
     }
     }

57. float ValidateLoans (LoanList &bundle, LoanList &loans){
     /* Validate and calculate the total profit of the loans in the bundle. */
     /* If a loan in the bundle does not exist in the loans list,   */
     /*   return -1.   */
     /* If all loans in the bundle exist in the loans list,   */
     /*   return the total profit for all loans in the bundle.   */

     float total = 0;

     for (int i=0; i < bundle.getcount(); i++)
     if (!loans.Exists(bundle[i])) return -1;
     for (int j=0; j < bundle.getcount(); j++)
     total += bundle[i].getprofit();
     return total;
     }

58. /* if the loan amount is greater than 275K, it is a jumbo loan */
     if (l->getamount() > 275){
     type = JUMBO;
     if (l->getprofit() > 10)
     /* if the profit is greater than 10K, add the loan to the bundle */
     bundle->addloan(l);
     }
     else /* a regular loan */
     type = REGULAR;

106

During code reviews of the Loan Arranger, the following faults were
identified. Classify the type of fault in each code fragment.

59. float ComputeProfit(float initial, float rate){
     float profit;

     profit = (1+rate)*initial + initial;
     return profit;
     }

In this fragment, the function used to calculate the profit is incorrect.
        a. initialization fault
        b. computation fault
        c. precision fault
        d. b and c only
        e. a and b only
        f. none of the above

60. LoanList::~LoanList(){
     /* delete all of the elements in the list */
     for (int i=1; i < count; i++)
     delete list[i];
     }

In this fragment, the first item of the list (list[0]) is not deleted.
        a. initialization fault
        b. computation fault
        c. precision fault
        d. b and c only
        e. a and b only
        f. none of the above

61. Loan *loans[10];
     for (int i=0; i<=10; i++) loans[i]->setprofit(0);

In this fragment, the loop includes an operation on loans[10] which is not
part of the array.
        a. initialization fault
        b. precision fault
        c. capacity or overload fault
        d. a, b, and c
        e. none of the above

107

62. One module of the Loan Arranger describes its functionality by means of the following assertions:

A_1: (T is an array) & (T is of size N) & ($S' = 0$)

A_{end}: (T' is an array) & (T' is of size N) & $S' = \sum_{i=1}^{N} T(i)$

Choose the statement that best describes what is happening between the two assertions.

   a. The values of array T are being assigned to the array S'.
   b. The values of array S are being added to the values of array T'.
   c. The values of array T are being added to the values of array S'.
   d. The sum of the values of array T are being assigned to S'.
   e. None of the above

When implementation of the Loan Arranger is nearly complete, testing begins.

The figure below shows the component hierarchy of the Loan Arranger application. Use this figure to identify the testing strategy indicated by the sequences given. The ";" is used between test sets and each test set is represented as a comma-separated list. For example, the sequence {F,G};{B,F,G} means that components F and G were tested first. Then, components B, F and G were tested.

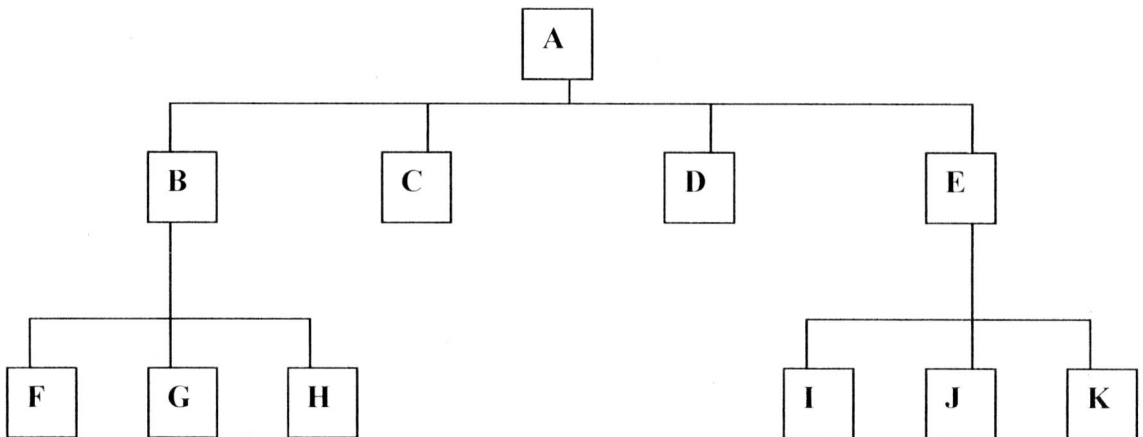

63. {A};{A,B,C,D,E};{A,B,C,D,E,F,G,H,I,J,K}
   a. Top-down testing
   b. Bottom-up testing
   c. Sandwich testing
   d. Big-bang testing
   e. Modified top-down testing

64. {F};{G};{H};{I};{J};{K};{B,F,G,H};{C};{D};{E,I,J,K};{A,B,C,D,E,F,G,H,I,J,K}
   a. Top-down testing
   b. Bottom-up testing
   c. Sandwich testing
   d. Big-bang testing
   e. Modified top-down testing

65. {A};{F};{G};{H};{I};{J};{K};{B,F,G,H};{C};{D};{E,I,J,K};{A,B,C,D,E,F,G,H,
    I,J,K}
    a. Top-down testing
    b. Bottom-up testing
    c. Sandwich testing
    d. Big-bang testing
    e. Modified top-down testing

The following issues were caught during testing. For questions 66 through
69, identify the type of testing most likely to have discovered the defect.

66. In the component that searches for the optimal loan bundle, the
    investor's desired loan characteristics are not initialized properly. The
    parameter containing these characteristics is ignored. Which type of
    testing would most likely have exposed this defect?
    a. unit testing
    b. integration testing
    c. acceptance testing
    d. installation testing
    e. performance testing

67. The getBundle method in the Bundle component requires a pointer to an
    array to be passed as an argument, but a call to the getBundle method in
    the Reports component passes the value of an array instead. Which type of
    testing would most likely have exposed this defect?
    a. performance testing of the Bundle and Reports components
    b. installation testing of the Reports component
    c. unit testing of the Bundle component
    d. integration testing of the Bundle and Reports components
    e. acceptance testing of the Bundle and Reports components

68. The bundle selector is supposed to allow the analyst to choose manually
    whether or not a loan should be included in the bundle, but the manual
    modification of bundle selection has not been implemented. Which type of
    testing would most likely have exposed this defect?
    a. unit testing
    b. integration testing
    c. performance testing
    d. acceptance testing
    e. function testing

69. The Loan Arranger has to interface with another external banking system.
    The interface to the external system has not been specified correctly.
    Which type of testing would most likely have exposed this defect?
    a. integration testing
    b. installation testing
    c. performance testing
    d. acceptance testing
    e. function testing

70. The missing functionality described in question 68 is a serious defect in the
    system. It will take a significant amount of effort to correct the problem by
    doing redesign, recoding, and retesting. The team leader is not sure how this
    can be accomplished in the time remaining before the due date, or even if it
    is still possible to make that date. In trying to decide how to address this
    problem he thinks immediately of a system that was under development last
    year and also had significant missing functionality. The solution used on

that system, of going straight to implementation of the new functionality without spending time on a redesign, might also work in this case, with some adaptations to take into account the fact that the current development team is much less experienced. Reasoning in this way is known as "anchoring and adjustment" and potential problems are that:

    a. The "anchoring" dominates and there is too little adjustment of the previous solution to the specific circumstances of the new problem.
    b. Arguing from analogy is always inherently dangerous.
    c. More suitable analogies might be overlooked because they are less recent.
    d. a and b
    e. a and c
    f. b and c
    g. a, b, and c

The bundle selection functionality is expected to be very complex, and there is concern about the reliability of this software. It is decided that faults will be seeded in the code to estimate the remaining faults. Two test teams will test the software.

Suppose 100 faults have been seeded in the code. During testing by the first team, 120 faults are detected. Sixty of the detected faults are seeded faults.

71. What is the Mills estimate for the percentage of remaining, non-seeded (indigenous) faults in the code?
    a. 10%
    b. 40%
    c. 50%
    d. 60%
    e. It is impossible to determine from the information given.

72. What is the Mills estimate of the total number of indigenous faults remaining?
    a. 7.5
    b. 10
    c. 40
    d. 50
    e. 60
    f. It is impossible to determine from the information given.

Suppose the same code is given to the second test team. This team finds 80 seeded faults and 70 non-seeded faults. 90 of the faults found by this team were also found by the other team.

73. Using the numbers for the second team, what is the Mills estimate for the total number of indigenous faults remaining?
    a. 0
    b. 17.5
    c. 20
    d. 87.5
    e. It is impossible to determine from the information given.

74. What is the effectiveness of the second test group?
    a. 30%
    b. 40%
    c. 60%
    d. 85%
    e. It is impossible to determine from the information given.

75. What is the effectiveness of the first test group?
    a. 25%
    b. 42%
    c. 64%
    d. 75%
    e. It is impossible to determine from the information given.

76. Based on the effectiveness of both test groups, what is the estimate for the total number of faults?
    a. 200
    b. 100
    c. 78
    d. 32
    e. It is impossible to determine from the information given.

77. Suppose 49 faults have been seeded into a component. Testing of the component has uncovered 45 of the seeded faults without uncovering any additional non-seeded faults. What is the level of confidence that the component is fault-free?
    a. 74%
    b. 80%
    c. 85%
    d. 92%
    e. None of the above.

After testing is complete, the system is delivered to the customer. Once it has been in operation for some time, a number of problem reports are returned.

78. Consider the following excerpts from problem reports filed for the Loan Arranger. In which type of report, discrepancy or fault, does each item belong? Answer fault report or discrepancy report.
    a. "The requirements document states that after the search for desirable loans returns a list of loans, the user should be able to remove or add loans from the list. The current software does not allow the user to modify the list after the search."
    b. "After submitting a search query for desirable loans, the results never came back. There should be a time out on the search and/or a message indicating the search is still in progress."
    c. "The search criteria are being ignored. There are two possible problems. The criteria may not be initialized correctly or the updates to the criteria may not be working properly. Check the constructor and the SetCriteria method of the Criteria class."

Other ideas for changes to the system are identified by the development team.

79. In order to deliver the system on time, the development team implemented a straightforward, brute force algorithm for creating bundles. This algorithm is sufficient for the consolidating organization's current needs but will not be able to meet the performance requirements if the volume of business increases. This situation:
    a. Should lead to a corrective change.
    b. Should lead to an adaptive change.
    c. Should lead to a perfective change.
    d. Should lead to a preventive change.
    e. Should require no maintenance to be performed.

80. If the brute force algorithm described in question 79 does cause the Loan Arranger system to not meet the performance requirements, this situation would be an example of:
    a. An exception
    b. An error
    c. A fault
    d. A failure
    e. None of the above

81. One of the banks has defects in its own software and sometimes sends data to the consolidating organization in which some of the records are not in the correct format. When this occurs the Loan Arranger alerts the loan analyst and none of the data from this bank is updated in the portfolio. This situation:
    a. Should lead to a corrective change.
    b. Should lead to an adaptive change.
    c. Should lead to a perfective change.
    d. Should lead to a preventive change.
    e. Should require no maintenance to be performed.

82. If the Loan Arranger receives bad data and reacts as described in question 81, this situation would be an example of:
    a. An exception
    b. An error
    c. A fault
    d. A failure
    e. None of the above

83. A mistake is noticed in the algorithm that computes the credit standing of loan recipients. That is, the value of a loan may be incorrectly computed because it is assumed to be a more or less risky proposition for investment than it actually is. This situation:
    a. Should lead to a corrective change.
    b. Should lead to an adaptive change.
    c. Should lead to a perfective change.
    d. Should lead to a preventive change.
    e. Should require no maintenance to be performed.

84. The erroneous module from question 83 (that computes credit standing) suffers from:
    a. An exception
    b. An error
    c. A fault
    d. A failure
    e. None of the above

85. Upon investigation, it is found that the problem described in question 83 results from a misconception in the original requirements. That is, the development team misunderstood the algorithm that the representative from the consolidating organization described. Then, this misunderstood algorithm was carried through the requirements, design, and implementation phases. This problem might have been discovered earlier if the team had used an appropriate:
    a. Linker
    b. Debugging tool
    c. Cross-reference generator
    d. Static code analyzer
    e. None of the above

Based on lessons learned during the Loan Arranger project, the team leader would like to invest further in process improvement.

86. Because he feels the need for continuing to improve the software development process, the team leader has decided to use CMM as a guide for process improvement. Which of the following represent potential problems that the team may encounter with CMM?
    a. It is not possible to customize the CMM to any special needs of the organization.
    b. The team might feel it necessary to invest in key process areas from a maturity level 2 or 3 levels higher than the organization's current ranking.
    c. The assumption behind the CMM is that every key process area is needed by the organization; in reality, this assumption might not be correct.
    d. None of the above represent real problems with the CMM.
    e. a and b
    f. a and c
    g. b and c
    h. a, b, and c

87. Which of the following are reasonable rationales for choosing CMM over another process maturity model?
    a. Unlike SPICE, CMM clearly defines a set of desirable practices and processes.
    b. Unlike in ISO9000, software measurement is a strong and explicit component of CMM.
    c. Unlike both SPICE and ISO9000, the goals of CMM can be easily mapped to concrete questions and metrics.
    d. a and b
    e. a and c
    f. b and c
    g. a, b, and c

Final Exam Answers

1. d; Choice C is false because the requirements cover only what functionality is to be implemented, not how. [Section 4.1]
2. d; Data flow diagrams describe how data are input, processed, and output by the system but do not contain any mechanism for describing concurrency. However, SADT does allow multiple views of the system at different levels of detail, and Warnier diagrams do help organize the relationships among data. [Section 4.5]
3. TRUE; The requirements specification should contain anything relevant to how the system will interact with its environment. [Section 4.2]
4. FALSE; The requirements specification should contain anything relevant to how the system will interact with its environment. The requirements should describe what data are input to the system; why those data are of interest to the organization is outside the scope of the requirements. [Section 4.2]
5. TRUE; The requirements specification should contain anything relevant to how the system will interact with its environment. [Section 4.2]
6. TRUE; The requirements specification should contain anything relevant to how the system will interact with its environment. [Section 4.2]
7. e; Choice B is ambiguous because it mentions that some fields are changeable but does not mention which ones. [Section 4.3]
8. g; Nonfunctional requirements describe constraints on the system; typically, these constraints limit developers' choices in constructing the system. [Section 4.1]
9. b; This requirement is ambiguous, because if a borrower has both default and late loans it is not clear whether the borrower is in 'default' or 'late' status. [Section 4.3]
10. d; The phrase 'easily extensible' is unverifiable. How can extensibility be measured? [Section 4.3]
11. e; The formula given can be easily verified for correctness, and is not ambiguous. [Section 4.3]
12. b and d; This requirement is ambiguous because there is no definition given of "inappropriate" and "illegal". As such, this condition cannot be tested, since it is unclear what set of inputs are intended to yield advice from the system. [Section 4.3]
13. TRUE; Lack of experience is a risk. [Section 3.4]
14. TRUE; Interfacing with externally developed systems is a risk. [Section 3.4]
15. FALSE; Prototyping is a risk control. [Section 3.4]
16. b; Predictions are noisy when they fluctuate more wildly than the actual measure. [Section 13.1]
17. b; (2*3) + (5*2) + (3*1) + (10*8) + (6*5) + (4*2) = 137 [Section 3.3]
18. c; $$MMRE = \frac{\frac{5000}{10000} + \frac{5000}{20000} + \frac{30000}{80000} + \frac{40000}{110000} + \frac{5000}{45000} + \frac{5000}{50000}}{6} = 0.2825$$
[Section 3.3]

19. d; Half of the estimates are within 25% of actual values. [Section 3.3]

20. No; using criteria $MMRE < 0.25$ and $PRED(0.25) > 0.75$. [Section 3.3]

21. a; 700 person-months is the average of the four estimates [Section 3.3]

22. FALSE; Although the method tends to produce convergence on the median estimate, a strong personality in the group (or other group dynamics issues) can push the group consensus toward another value. [Section 14.3]

23. e; 35 months [Section 3.3]

24. c; (n(n-1))/2)= 20(19)/2 = 190 lines of communication [Section 3.2]

The following table can be used to answer questions 25 to 28:

Activity	Earliest Start Time	Latest Start Time	Slack
A	1	1	0
B	8	13	5
C	6	6	0
D	10	15	5
E	9	9	0
F	16	21	5
G	19	19	0
H	23	23	0
I	24	28	4
J	33	33	0
K(finish)	37	37	0

An activity label in the table should be read, "the activity beginning at milestone $<label>$." For example, the activity beginning at milestone B has an earliest start time of 8.

25. a; ACEGHJK is the critical path. In the table above, it represents the path with 0 slack time from start (A) to finish (K). [Section 3.1]

26. b; 5 is the slack time for the activity starting at milestone F. [Section 3.1]

27. d; 37 is the length of the critical path. [Section 3.1]

28. d; I is not a precursor to J. [Section 3.1]

29. d; The architectural design addresses issues such as where the data comes from, and what happens to the data in the system. [Section 5.1]

30. e; The architectural design should be able to be understood by the customer; it should therefore contain financial information but not implementation details. (There is not necessarily any connection between financial formulas and implementation.) The module design should include more details about how the system is to be implemented. [Section 5.1]

31. b; If system functions are highly interrelated, it will be difficult to separate the system into components for which the internal organization and the relations to other components can be described. [Section 5.3]

32. f; In a Peer-to-Peer architecture, the peers are components that provide similar services with varying data. In our system loan analysts and institutions provide different services and cannot be considered peers (a loan analyst does not have portfolios). [Section 5.4]

33. c; Design by contract views a software system as a set of communicating components, which may be a useful way to think of the components in the object-oriented design. Design by contract also places the most emphasis on how components interact (specifying the preconditions, postconditions, and invariants that exist when one component calls another). Since the interaction of components is an area that will be important to address in this design, design by contract appears the best choice. [Section 6.8]

34. a; Coupling measures the amount of dependence among components. Since class Loan interacts with four other classes (at least double the number for any other class), class Loan has a high degree of coupling. [Section 6.2]

35. c; Cohesion measures how related the internal parts of a component are. Since this figure gives no details about the internal structure of components, no conclusions about cohesion can be drawn. [Section 6.2]

36. b; The high degree of coupling for class Loan leads to the possibility that a change to this class may require changes in many other parts of the system. A change to class Borrower, on the other hand, has the potential to affect only one other class. Additionally, components are often easier to understand if they are not intrinsically tied to others. Thus, for many types of changes it is reasonable to assume that modifications to class Loan will be more difficult. [Section 6.2]

37. a; The high-level design should describe real-world entities in the problem, not the details of the solution. [Section 5.3]

38. b; Number of key classes can be measured during system design to get an idea of the size of the system, while number of support classes cannot be accurately measured until program design. The "lack of cohesion of methods" metric is useful for finding complex classes that can benefit from additional care in construction, not for estimating system size. [Section 6.7]

39. FALSE. Classes with large numbers of methods are likely to be more application specific, limiting the possibility of reuse. [Section 6.7]

40. TRUE. The number of children gives an idea of the potential influence a class has on the design. If a class has a large number of children, it may require more testing of the methods in that class. [Section 6.7]

41. TRUE. If a large number of methods can be invoked in response to a message, the testing and debugging of the class become more complicated since the class requires a greater level of understanding on the part of the tester. [Section 6.7]

42. a; According to the diagram, once in default status, the borrower can never return to good or late status. [Section 6.4]

43. FALSE. The black dot representing the start state leads to the state marked "Good Status," meaning that it will be the default state for any new object of this type. [Section 6.4]

44. b; Common coupling exists when the design is organized such that data are accessible from a common data store, and potentially multiple components can access that data. [Section 6.2]

45. d; The design should describe the system in such a way that it can be validated whether or not the system will meet the needs of the organization. These needs should include not only day-to-day use but longer term needs such as archiving. [Section 5.8]

46. g; Program designers are present both to critique the design and to better understand it, so that they can then derive their more detailed program designs from it. If major problems are identified, the design is redone. [Section 5.9]

47. c; This study is a case study, since key factors that may affect the outcome are identified, documented, and controlled as much as possible. Since the study will be conducted on a single project that has real constraints and deadlines, we can assume that the level of control of key variables will not be high enough to make this a formal experiment. Since the project in which the new process is being evaluated will be compared to a set of past projects that are meant to be typical, the case study makes use of a baseline for comparison purposes. [Section 12.1]

48. b; The aim in this type of study is to select a subset of past projects for comparison that are as similar as possible to the one using the new

process. This selection process helps ensure that any differences are due to the new process and not other sources of variation. [Section 12.1]

49. b; The Loan Arranger is a P-type system, since the problem (tracking and bundling loans) can be described directly and completely, and has an exact solution. Unlike an E-type system, the system is not embedded in the environment; that is, the practical abstraction of the problem is unlikely to change due to an improved understanding resulting from the solution. As a P-type system, incremental change is possible in order to improve the solution. [Section 11.1]

50. error; These statements are describing a misconception on the part of the developer. [Sidebar 1.1]

51. failure; These statements describe a departure from the required behavior. [Sidebar 1.1]

52. fault; These statements describe a mistake that has been manifested in the code. [Sidebar 1.1]

53. failure; This is an example of the system performing incorrectly. [Sidebar 1.1]

54. a; This example is of producer reuse since reusable components are being created. The situation described also illustrates black-box reuse since the module is meant to be reused without modification. [Section 12.4]

55. g; The need to search through large repositories of components to find the best one for a particular reuse need is one of the biggest obstacles to effective reuse. Section 12.4 of the textbook describes some work in component classification that attempts to solve this problem. It also describes experiences at Raytheon and GTE, and how these organizations have designed their reuse programs to avoid the pitfalls described in choices b and c.

56. d; No documentation

57. b; The two loops can be combined to make this code more efficient.

58. c; The *else* clause matches with the first *if* clause. The formatting of this code makes it misleading.

59. b; Because the equation to calculate the profit is incorrect, the fault is a computation fault. [Section 8.1]

60. a; The variable *i* is initialized incorrectly. [Section 8.1]

61. c; list[10] is out of the defined array boundary. [Section 8.1]

62. d; [Section 8.3]

63. a; top-down testing [Section 8.4]

64. b; bottom-up testing [Section 8.4]

65. c; sandwich testing [Section 8.4]

66. a; unit testing; This defect can be isolated to a single function in a single component. Unit testing should uncover this type of defect. [Section 8.2]

67. d; Since this defect involves the interface between the two components, integration testing of the Bundle and Reports components should detect the

defect. Unit testing of the Bundle component alone would not uncover the defect since the defect exists in the Reports component. [Section 8.2]

68. e; Function testing is used to determine if the functions described in the requirements specification are actually implemented in the system. [Section 8.2]

69. a; Since the defect deals with interfaces, integration testing should detect the defect. [Section 8.2]

70. e; Arguing from analogy is a particularly useful way of learning from past experiences, but care must be taken not to "anchor" on the wrong past experience or to insufficiently "adjust" to the new circumstances. [Section 14.3]

71. b; The percentage of indigenous faults remaining is equal to the percentage of seeded faults remaining. (1 - 60/100) = .4 [Section 8.8]

72. c;

$$\frac{seeded\_faults\_found}{seeded\_faults} = \frac{indigenous\_faults\_found}{indigenous\_faults}$$

$$indigenous\_faults = \frac{seeded\_faults \times indigenous\_faults\_found}{seeded\_faults\_found}$$

$$indigenous\_faults = \frac{100 \times 60}{60} = 100$$

indigenous_faults_remaining = 100 - 60 = 40
[Section 8.8]

73. b;
indigenous faults = 100*70/80 = 87.5
indigenous faults remaining = 87.5 - 70 = 17.5
[Section 8.8]

74. c; effectiveness = overlapping faults/faults found by the second group
effectiveness = 90/150 = 60%
[Section 8.8]

75. d; effectiveness = 90/120 = 75% [Section 8.8]

76. a; total faults = 90/(.6 * .75) = 200 [Section 8.8]

77. e;

$$C = \frac{\binom{49}{44}}{\binom{50}{45}} = 0.9$$

[Section 8.8]

78.
    a) discrepancy report; This description describes a difference between the requirements and the implementation. [Section 9.8]
    b) discrepancy report; This description describes a problem from the user's point of view. [Section 9.8]
    c) fault report; The description of the problem includes information from the developer's point of view. [Section 9.8]

79. d; This change involves modifying part of the system to prevent future faults. [Section 11.2]

80. d; A failure is an instance during system operation in which system behavior deviates from expectations. [Section 5.5]

81. e; This type of response may or may not be the optimal way of handling such a situation (since discarding the entire report potentially discards valid records). However, since the response is consistent and reliable, it does not represent a defect in the system unless it somehow fails to meet the needs of the customer. [Section 11.2]

82. a; The description provided illustrates the Loan Arranger handling an exception; that is, responding to a situation that is counter to the intended operation of the system. [Section 5.5]

83. a; This change is necessary to directly correct a fault. [Section 11.2]

84. c; A fault is a defect in a software product, resulting from some human error. [Section 5.5]

85. e; Choices a through d are all tools that can help catch defects introduced after the requirements stage. To catch the faulty algorithm, a way of ensuring requirements correctness would have been necessary (for example, requirements reviews). [Section 11.5]

86. f; Both choices a and c are true statements about the CMM. The same key process areas are recommended for every organization. [Section 12.5]

87. b; Choice b is the only true statement. SPICE also defines a specific set of desirable practices, and both SPICE and CMM have goals that can be mapped to questions and metrics. [Section 12.5]

CL

005.
1
SHU

ANIMALS IN ARCHAEOLOGY

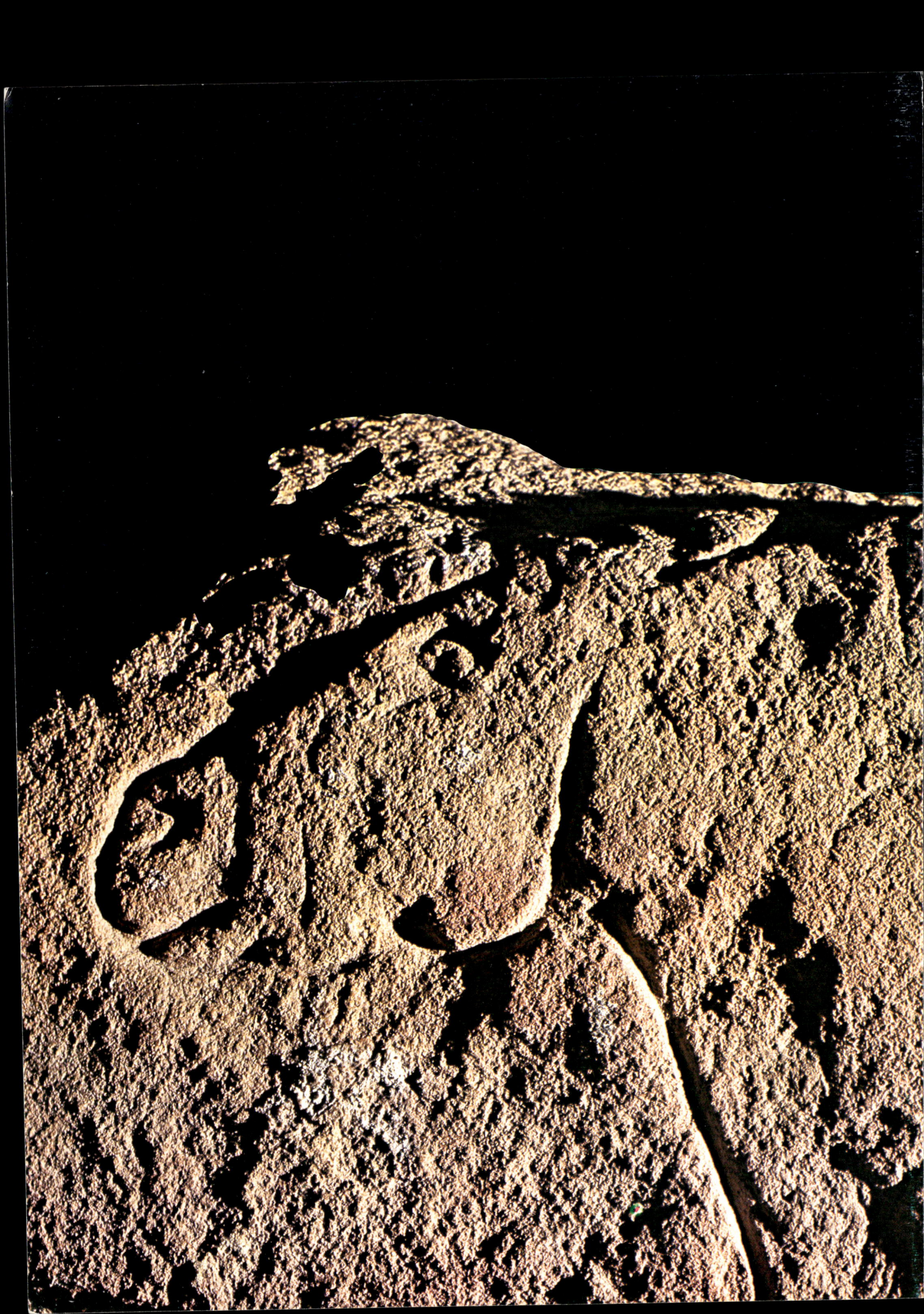

ANIMALS IN ARCHAEOLOGY

EDITED BY
A. HOUGHTON BRODRICK

BARRIE & JENKINS
LONDON

Acknowledgments

For permission to reproduce the
illustrations in this volume grateful
thanks are due to the many museums,
authors and publishers whose names
are given in the captions to the
illustrations
Also thanks are given to Barbara Vender
for help with editing and gathering
illustrations for this book

First published in Great Britain, 1972, by
Barrie & Jenkins Ltd
2 Clement's Inn, London W.C.2

Designed by Michael R. Carter

Printed in Great Britain by
Jarrold & Sons Ltd, Norwich

ISBN 0 214 65340 4

CORRIGENDUM

Line 8 of the Acknowledgments:
Barbara Vender should read Barbara Bender

CONTENTS

INTRODUCTION

A. HOUGHTON BRODRICK

In this book a number of archaeologists and art historians have collaborated to produce a symposium on man and other animals in the ancient world.* The material used derives from a wide variety of sources, with particular emphasis on art.

For countless ages man seems to have been a rather rare animal whose survival must at times have appeared doubtful. His relationship with other animals was that of hunter and hunted, and although he undoubtedly managed to kill many animals he always ran the attendant risk of being killed by them. Doubtless men's attitude towards at least the larger mammals was one of mingled fear and admiration plus an understanding, based on observation, that his fearsome enemies were in essentials of like nature to himself. They were born in the same way, they copulated in the same way and they died in the same way – 'so that a man hath no pre-eminence above a beast' – and both animals and men died mostly by accident, in fighting, of disease and very rarely of old age.

We are the only animals that have managed to exploit other animals. For us they have been furnishers of fur and hides to keep out the cold (and without such protection men would never have survived the cold of the last Ice Age in Europe), suppliers of threads and cords, of shovels and bludgeons. Much later, animals were domesticated and incorporated into a settled agricultural way of life, a development that made possible the beginnings of civilization.

The symbiosis, the linked lives, of men and animals is a constant factor in our history. The importance of animals, the fear and the awe felt towards them has frequently been expressed, in myth, in legend and in art.

For countless millennia man existed with many crafts but no art. When finally the first creative art appeared in parts of western Europe it centred round representations of animals. For the most part, they were engraved or painted on cave-walls but there was also, during the long time-span of the Old Stone Age, some production of sculpture and small female figurines as well as small carvings or engravings on pieces of bone or stone, again usually of animals.

* In this connection 'ancient' is taken to signify 'prehistory and . . . long-lasting civilizations which arose before our era'.

This Late Old Stone Age art lasted a very long time. It probably began between 35,000 and 25,000 years ago and it came to an end with the fade-out of the last Ice Age and the radical change of climate in Europe some 9,000 to 8,000 years before our era.

From the time, early in this century, that ancient cave-art was recognized as authentic, until now, discussion has flourished as to its 'meaning'. Some plausible interpretations have been suggested, and not a few wild ones (some have professed to see in the animal pictures clear proof of the 'primitive monotheism' of Palaeolithic man!). Professor Leroi-Gourhan gives us what is by far the most interesting and complex explanation. It is obviously highly instructive for us to learn as much as we can about why men some 200 centuries ago adorned the dark, remote recesses of subterranean caves with great frescoes of beasts, with strange symbols and with occasional enigmatic composite figures. If we understood why these things were done we should find out a good deal about man's mental and moral evolution and about how he conceptualized his relations with animals. But we must not try to force the evidence.*

It is, at any rate, clear that Late Old Stone Age man was intensely preoccupied with animals, observed them with great care and drew their pictures often with great skill (though the quality of much of Palaeolithic art is exaggerated by some enthusiasts). In fact, our remote ancestors studied animal behaviour and they began a long tradition of animal portraiture.

It is very probable that the painted rock-walls of dark, cavernous recesses formed the back-drop of a 'theatre' where some sort of rituals were performed. Perhaps chants formed an important part of such rituals – pictures have a life of their own, they encourage us to talk and they make myths and legends as much as they illustrate them. Perhaps when man became an artist and drew pictures of animals he took the first steps towards thinking in symbols. Although thousands of years elapsed between the time of the last cave-paintings of western Europe† and the first attempts of writing in Mesopotamia and Egypt representations of animals figured in the earliest scripts. In some measure, therefore, we may say that man's preoccupation with animals lies at the basis of literature and science.

Although we are not justified in talking about Old Stone Age man 'adoring his gods,' our human story is so filled with sacred beasts, animals in human form and men in animal form, of animals that talk and all the rich content of legend, myth, folklore and fairytale, that perhaps we are not being too daring in suggesting that even in Palaeolithic times animals were thought to be possessed of strange powers and that some beasts

* For instance, the prehistoric caves of Pech-Merle in the Lot *département* of south-west France contain a wealth of fine pictures mostly, of course, of animals. The problem of interpretation is not, however, much helped by the inscription over the entrance informing the visitor that 'here primitive Man adored his gods'. We may ask just what 'primitive Man' was – or is – how we know he had 'gods' and how was the 'adoration' performed?
† After the disappearance of western European cave-art at the end of the last Ice Age (about 8000 B.C.), there flourished in western Spain the so-called 'Levantine art' on rock-faces. It is of doubtful dating but does not at all resemble the naturalistic animal art of earlier times. The Levantine pictures represent domestic scenes, hunting, warfare and there is an abundance of human figures. The connection, if any, of this art with that of the Neolithic Near East and of Africa is not clear.

were held to be the authors of some of the dangers and disasters that plague men. Such creatures must be propitiated. 'Religion' it has been said, in its crudest form is a 'technique for success' that is for attracting good luck here and now.

Until quite recently, we had little or nothing to link the art traditions of Palaeolithic western Europe with the earliest representational art of the Near East. But as Sonia Cole points out in her article on the Neolithic, it is clear that the change-over from a food-gathering and hunting way of life to one of permanent settlements, agriculture and domestic animals had already begun as early as 7000 B.C. in the Near East where at the now-famous site of Çatal Hüyük we have not only well-built dwelling complexes but also what must be called 'shrines' with paintings of animals on the walls, and rams' and bulls' heads, horned 'altars' and in one case an enigmatic wall-painting of human-headed vultures or human beings (possibly women) disguised as birds.

The evidence indeed is for a culture very much richer than anything we can attribute to Old Stone Age man, but certain resemblances do suggest that there may have been some tenuous link between the traditions of, say, Lascaux and Altamira and of the Neolithic sites in Anatolia, though it must be admitted that the time that elapsed between the last Magdalenian (i.e. Late Old Stone Age) pictures and the earliest in the Near East is considerable, maybe 2,000 years. What is perhaps most striking is the prominent place occupied by bulls in the Palaeolithic cave-paintings and also in the Neolithic of the Near East. Bulls loom large in the French and Spanish caves, bulls were obviously of great significance to the people of Çatal Hüyük 8,000 years ago. A bull 'deity' may well be one of the earliest known to man. Certainly the protecting horns, real or imitated, figured in sanctuaries for a very long time.

In Egypt the classical land of sacred animals and of animal divinities, as Richard Carrington brings out clearly in his article, the bull Apis survived as an object of a special cult until Ptolemaic times (i.e. until towards the beginning of our era) and as far back as the First Dynasty a bench of about 300 bulls' heads modelled in clay and set with real horns surrounded the tomb of King Uadji at Sakkara. 'Horned' altars appear all over the Near East from ancient Palestine to Crete.*

In Mesopotamia, the land of great empires and powerful war-like monarchs, there is an abundance of material regarding animals; there are imposing bas-reliefs of lion-hunts, the bull-complex appears as represented by the huge winged man-bulls, the Mesopotamian 'cherubim', and animals were kept as pets, or at least were the inmates of parks and zoos. Mlle Aynard also draws on ancient literature to illustrate the part played by animals in the life of the men who contributed so much to civilization.

The Aegean area is one very near to us. Not only did the first European civilization arise in Crete, but against the Cretan and Mycenaean background of myth and fable, of animal art and of Minotaur legends,

* The worship of the bull Apis was established by the time of the First Dynasty (before 3000 B.C.) and there is a curious example of the persistence of bull-sacrifice until modern times despite the all-embracing influence of Islam. A British archaeologist who was present at the obsequies of King Fuad (died 1936) in Cairo found the heat and the crush so great that he made his way out of the mosque by a side-door and walked into a scene of carnage. On all sides cattle were being slaughtered, the street ran with blood and echoed to the terrified bellowing of beasts and the shouts of excited men.

we are swept along towards the magnificence of Greek art and the heritage that dominates our own.

In India today some animals are still 'sacred'. One of the things that strikes the traveller most is the swarms of half-starved cows which wander unmolested in town and village or lie down on pavement or road. So deep-rooted is the belief in the cows' sacrosanct character that proposals for reducing the useless cow population are met by popular outcry. Mlle Auboyer reviews for us the whole pageant of animal and man, the great horse-sacrifices, animals as pets and presents a collection of illustrations which well indicate the life in common of man and beast in India. One of the most striking features of Indian animal art is the vein of empathy, or sympathy that is visible in it. No doubt neither in the case of India nor any other land do the ancient monuments tell the whole story. The full measure of man's beastliness to beasts is, of course, not fully recorded in art. But men have had pets from early times and often enough we are told of horses or hounds so beloved by their masters that monuments have been raised to the animals' memory. Even in what we are inclined to think of as the harsh society of medieval Europe, or at least of northern Europe, there are plenty of recumbent tomb-statues shown with a pet dog lying for all eternity at the feet of its mistress or master.

Dogs, indeed, were the first animals to be tamed and even domesticated and seem to have had a 'special relationship' with man. Strangely enough, they do not figure as much as we might expect in ancient art. In some countries they came to be abhorred as 'unclean' though in Zoroastrian Persia (the home of much artistic, social and religious tradition exported far and wide) bitches were regarded as sacrosanct.

And dogs are about the only animals we think of as petted by the Chinese, though in fact there were others. Still we may not be far wrong in thinking that in the past, as today, the reaction of most Chinese with regard to any animal is a query 'Is it good to eat?' None the less, the ancient monuments of China, the bas-reliefs, sculptures, figurines and paintings prove clearly enough that the Chinese have always liked and admired animals in good condition. The wildlife of China was impoverished a long time ago but as long as the Empire lasted, elephants (that once lived in Chinese forests and woodlands) still figured in the Imperial procession of the Sacrifice to Heaven. China is the classical land of mythological, imaginary beasts. The story of the dragon alone throws light upon a whole chapter of human invention and belief.*

Whatever may be the part man has made animals play for his convenience – animals as gods, as sacrificial victims, as food, as quarry for the chase, animals as slaves, creatures on which to vent frustrated spite or on which to lavish affection, they can, if treated with understanding, teach us more than we can teach them. As the late J. B. S. Haldane put it, the study of animal behaviour 'is likely to yield a much better account of the origin of human purpose and I think this possibility alone is quite sufficient to justify all the research which is being done upon it'.

* Human sacrifice lingered long in some provinces of ancient China and in the time of the Shang dynasty (before and after about 1200 B.C.) as in ancient Egypt, men and beasts shared a common fate at royal funerals: both were slaughtered to accompany dead kings on their last journey. Chariots, charioteers and animals were all sacrificed together.

But we must care to see that there are animals left to observe. We are heedlessly engaged in killing off so many species of animals and, what is as bad, in upsetting the natural interplay between ecology and evolution, that by the time we get round to realizing what is happening it may be too late. What happens to animals can also happen to us, perhaps that is one of the lessons to be drawn from animals in archaeology.

1
ANIMALS OF THE OLD STONE AGE

ANDRÉ LEROI-GOURHAN

The human story may be divided into two chapters: first, the Palaeo-lithic, or Old Stone Age, which lasted for more than 1,000,000 years, and then the 'modern' period, which, despite all that has happened within it, has only lasted some 7,000 or 8,000 years. Between the time when the predecessors of the human race chipped their first flint tools and the time when our close ancestors grew their first plants and domesticated their first sheep, tens of thousands of years went by. During this immense period of time both wild animals and hominids existed, the latter very, very slowly making their way up the evolu-tionary ladder.* Indeed, at the beginning of this evolution, the hominid still showed hardly any of the characteristics which later distinguish him from other animals. But those that he did show were vital. Whether ape, half-ape or half-man, he stood upright and developed the first tool by splitting pebbles to make knives. As a result, a particular relationship was established between animals, whose 'hands', except on rare occa-sions, were used only for walking, and hominids, whose hands, helped by a brain that became more and more complex, became a vital means of control. During Palaeolithic times this relationship was invariably that of hunter and quarry, but always with the attendant risk to the hunter that the roles could well be reversed.

There is little point in lingering over the details of the evolution of the hominids and of the Old Stone Age since this study is primarily about the animals. It is, however, useful to remember that, broadly speaking, the archaeologist recognizes three Palaeolithic periods and three types of hominids.

The earliest period is called the Lower Palaeolithic. Its slow evolution lasted an almost unimaginable length of time, probably more than 2,000,000 years, then merged, 200,000 or 300,000 years ago, into the Middle Palaeolithic. The most primitive Lower Palaeolithic hominids are called *Zinjanthropus*, *Telanthropus* and *Australopithecus*. More evolved ones, which, though still primitive, show considerable advances, are called *Pithecanthropus*, *Sinanthropus* and *Atlanthropus*.

* 'Hominid' is a term that covers all types of primates which are more man-like than ape-like. The French stress the ape heritage by calling them 'anthropiens'.

The Middle Palaeolithic is shorter. It ended about 40,000 years ago. The hominids of this period are much closer in type to us. Neandertal man, were it not for his prominent eyebrow ridges and rather receding chin, would hardly seem out of place in the modern world.

By geological reckoning, the Upper Palaeolithic only lasted a moment, from 40,000 to 10,000 years ago. But this is the period during which our species, *Homo sapiens*, evolved, and within 30,000 years emerged as a cereal-farmer, stock-breeder and maker of a highly efficient tool-kit.

There is much more information about the Upper Palaeolithic than about the earlier periods, and there are good reasons for this. First of all, the number of man-made objects increased enormously from one Palaeolithic period to the next. Art, for example, only appeared in the last period. Secondly, because of the natural processes of decay, fewer tools and bones are preserved from the beginning of the Palaeolithic than from the end. Moreover, excavations have taken place in Europe for over 100 years, in the rest of the world for, at most, only a few decades. It is understandable, therefore, that there is more to say about the European Upper Palaeolithic than about the Lower Palaeolithic of Kafiristan.

One must distinguish between 'animals in archaeology' and 'animals in palaeontology'. Even though the archaeologist and the palaeontologist may study the same rhinoceros's tibia they look at it from very different points of view. At the back of his mind, the archaeologist visualizes the hunt, vast meals and magical rites. The palaeontologist can usually decide what sort of animal it was, the archaeologist has a much more difficult time trying to decide what it was used for. For the palaeontologist all the bones are of interest, for the archaeologist they are only interesting within a particular context; he wants to know whether the bones were found on a sacrificial site or in a refuse-dump, whether the bones were scraped with flint knives or broken to get at the marrow, whether the skin could have been used for clothing or the teeth for pendants. In other words, what interests the archaeologist about an animal is the man behind it.

Man and Animal

The animal was undoubtedly important as a source of food, of raw material and of aesthetic inspiration. Just how important is hard to say. Flint and bone are the only substances which resist decay and one's picture of prehistoric life is undoubtedly falsified because of the disappearance of perishable objects. We have evidence that Upper Palaeolithic men killed game with weapons tipped with bone points, but we do not know how important the game was; was it only a side-line to plant-food? Since all that remains are the stone knives and the bones we tend to think of prehistoric man as essentially carnivorous. But, in fact, the concept of 'Man the Carnivore' may be just as false as the idea of 'Man the Cave-Dweller'. They *sometimes* lived in caves and they sometimes ate meat. In acknowledging the probable importance of plant-foods one is also acknowledging the importance of the women who had the thankless task of eking out with roots and wild fruits the undoubtedly often insufficient meat-supply brought home by the hunters.

2

Hunting and Fishing

LOWER AND MIDDLE PALAEOLITHIC   Relatively little is known about the methods used by Palaeolithic man for hunting both large and small game, but it is clear that already in the Lower Palaeolithic he was able to kill almost all kinds of animals. The oldest hominids, the Australopithicines, were able to kill panthers and large antelopes. At Torralba in Spain there is a Lower Palaeolithic site where there are great quantities of elephant bones broken up by hominids who left their clumsy knives on the site. It is difficult to believe that the hunters killed the elephants with bits of flint; perhaps they dug pits or stampeded the animals to their death over the edge of steep cliffs. One has to admit that from the earliest time until the appearance of Neandertal man, thus the whole of the Lower Palaeolithic, we have no evidence on this point other than the presence of the skulls and leg bones of very large animals on habitation sites, which simply presupposes that there was some means of killing them. When it comes to the smaller animals, the deer or horses or even smaller game, the hominids had a wide range of possible weapons: wooden clubs and spears, or heavy stags' antlers made into bludgeons by cutting off some of the tines. Evidence to show how early man constructed traps or prepared hunting-poisons will probably never come to light. From the beginning of the Lower Palaeolithic until the end of the Middle Palaeolithic, both in Africa and in Europe, more or less regular, rounded stones, roughly pecked and about 6 inches in diameter, are found on the sites. They have been called *bolas*, the Spanish word for ball – a term which does not commit the prehistorian

Fig. 1
Patagonian hunters using the *bolas* to bring down guanaco.
After a painting by M. Wilson in C. Burland, *Men without Machines*, Aldus Books Ltd., London, 1965.

3

in any way! It is quite probable that these balls were fixed to thongs and were used in the same way as the South American Indians' *boleadoras* which are thrown, in twos or threes, with the ends of the thongs tied together, between the legs of the animal, thus entangling it so that it can then be finished off with a spear or a club. Such a weapon, if it really existed, could only be used in open country. But if the early hominid had worked out the *bolas* attack he may well also have used a hanging noose and could have placed all sorts of snares suitable for different-sized animals in the woods.

UPPER PALAEOLITHIC With the appearance of *Homo sapiens* about 40,000 years ago there is more and increasingly detailed evidence. Between the Ural Mountains in Russia and the Atlantic seaboard are hundreds of Palaeolithic habitation sites: caves, rock-shelters, tent-floors and hut-floors. The debris that littered the floor or piled up round the habitation provides much information about the various activities. Obviously, we have only indirect evidence for hunting and fishing since these activities took place away from the habitation sites, but, by examining the bones and such weapons as have survived, and by studying the paintings and engravings which the men made on cave-walls, one can begin to ask a number of pertinent questions, even if we still cannot detail the hunting methods used.

The size of the game ranged from frogs to mammoths and woolly rhinoceros and included aurochs,* bison, horse, deer, reindeer, and a great variety of other mammals, birds, and fish. The relative and total quantity varied, depending on the time period, the climate and the region. One site might show evidence of twenty different mammals, whereas another might be highly specialized, showing a dependence, for example, on reindeer. Interesting insights can be obtained by considering the particular animals hunted and the relative proportions of the various species, especially if one uses this data in conjunction with an analysis of the fossilized pollen of plants from the same period. This is one of the ways in which one begins to have some idea of the different types of sites, some seasonal, some more or less permanent. It becomes increasingly clear that the Palaeolithic hunters, particularly those of the Upper Palaeolithic, did not spend their lives in continual and haphazard wanderings; the time when people believed in 'wandering hordes' is now long past. In fact, common sense would suggest that in order to exploit animal and edible plant resources one requires a detailed knowledge of a specific region and will move around within that region following the location of different seasonal resources. A good illustration of this is the Magdalenian encampment at Pincevent (Seine-et-Marne, France).† Here, about 10,000 B.C., within an area of several acres alongside a fording-place on the Seine, a considerable number of hunters coming from different parts of the region gathered and set up their tents. They concentrated on hunting reindeer, and thousands of bones are strewn round the tent-floors. The age at which the reindeer were killed can be worked out by analysing the degree of dental development and, on this site, such an analysis shows that the Magdalenians settled here about May and remained till July, then came back again in the autumn and stayed during parts of the winter. They

* Aurochs are enormous wild cattle, standing 6 feet 6 inches to the withers.
† Magdalenian groups lived in western and central Europe at the end of the Upper Palaeolithic, from about 17,000 to 9000 B.C.

Fig. 2
Reconstruction of a mammoth hunters'
dwelling based on finds at Pushkari, near
Novgorod–Seversky, Southern Russia.
After G. Clark. *The Stone Age hunters*,
Thames and Hudson, London, 1967.

obviously followed a regular cycle undoubtedly geared to the migration of the herds of reindeer, horse or bison, and arrived at a particular place at a particular time when they knew their quarry would be there. One finds similar 'villages' of tents in central Europe and Russia associated with vast numbers of mammoth bones.

The Upper Palaeolithic hunters' equipment included very fine points made from bone, mammoth ivory or reindeer antler. These points, some of which were probably poisoned, were mounted on spear- or arrow-shafts and must have been very effective, even against large game. Bone was an important element in Upper Palaeolithic equipment, both for making weapons and certain tools, such as punches, and for use in constructing dwellings. For example, in Russia, in central Europe and even in France (at Arcy-sur-Cure, Yonne), large bones or mammoth tusks were used as a framework or to anchor the tents.

Animals played an equally important role as a source of clothing and for making the inside of the dwellings more comfortable. Marks left on the bones when scraping off the hides suggest that reindeer, bear and wolf skins were frequently used.

Ornaments

The use of animal teeth, carved bone pendants and shells is evidence of the aesthetic and probably also the religious sensibility of Palaeolithic man. The first bone pendants and bears' and wolves' teeth perforated for suspension appear right at the beginning of the Upper Palaeolithic. The canine teeth of stags were particularly highly valued and from the beginning of the Upper Palaeolithic not only are there perforated examples used as pendants, but also copies made of carved bone. Costume jewellery thus has a pedigree of some 30,000 years!

5

The Animal in Man's Conception of the World

The technical and economic role of animals in the life of Palaeolithic man was so important that they were almost bound to have also had some religious significance. It is difficult enough trying to discover hunting methods or the ways in which game was prepared for eating, but it is still more difficult to comprehend, by archaeological means, the religious universe of prehistoric man The use of ethnographic comparisons, using the few primitive groups which have been studied, is not only uncertain but often dangerous since it leads to a reconstruction of prehistoric society from a hotch-potch of elements borrowed from the Australian aboriginal, the Eskimo, and the Red Indian. Archaeological information is very rarely definitive about metaphysical aspects of human life, and even under the most favourable conditions the evidence will show the existence of religious preoccupations without being able to explain their significance.

There is almost no material evidence until the Upper Palaeolithic and the appearance of *Homo sapiens*. *Pithecanthropus, Sinanthropus,* and Neandertal man were undoubtedly great hunters and it is quite possible that they incorporated animals into a vision of the world in which the boundaries between natural and supernatural were not clearly defined. But this is very hard to prove. For several decades it was thought that there was evidence of a cave-bear cult. The great cave-bear became extinct towards the end of the last Ice Age (about 8000 B.C.), but one finds, in the caves where they hibernated, great piles of bones from bears of all ages, who, for various reasons, died during their hibernation. The ossuaries in which these skeletons are jumbled together, often in deposits several metres thick, have attracted man's attention for a long time. In medieval times these 'unicorn bones' were used by apothecaries. In the nineteenth century they were worked as a source of phosphate manure. Then the archaeologists began to show an interest in the cave-bear bones. Hundreds of bears ambling through the caves over many centuries, trampling the remains of their kind among the stones and digging out shallow pits for hibernation, left a curiously ordered impression which is sometimes very puzzling. Only the skulls which slipped down into crannies or were protected by slabs remained intact, whereas the long bones piled up in heaps along the cave-walls. In digging their 'nests' the bears created a circular rim of bones. These 'arrangements', in fact the work of innumerable generations of ambling, digging, cave-bears continuing to occupy the same caves, gave rise to a sort of science-fiction in which prehistoric man, pursued the bears into their deep retreats and then paid homage to the skeletons of their victims by placing their skulls in crannies or in rough cists made of stone slabs, laying the long bones in heaps along the walls. This very attractive theory has, for some time past, been undermined by scientific research and there remains very little to support the story. All one can say is that the Magdalenians, between 15,000 and 9,000 years ago, at a time when the cave-bears were probably extinct, must have noticed, when they explored the depths of the caves, the enormous skulls of the great cave-bear. It may be that they sometimes moved them or collected the teeth to make them into pendants. In a cave in the *département* of Saône-et-Loire in France a cave-bear tooth which the Magdalenians had collected from the depths of the cave was found in a hearth near the entrance.

However, the main source of information for the attitudes of pre-historic man towards animals comes from the works of art.

Animals in Art

We shall probably never know in detail the psychological relationship between man and animal before the appearance of modern man about 40,000 years ago. It is only then, with the first attempts at art, that early man leaves us some evidence of his intellectual attitudes. The first attempts are very rough, a few scratched lines on stones, or lines traced with red ochre. But already in the Aurignacian culture* there are representations of animals associated with oval signs or series of dots or rows of short, vertical lines. From this time on, about 30,000 B.C., the painted or engraved figures on the walls of habitation sites become more and more numerous. From these representations, which are found in Spain, France, Italy, central and eastern Europe, and which continue from the Aurignacian until the end of the Magdalenian, about 9000 B.C., we begin to catch a glimpse of the thoughts of our early forebears.

The first prehistorians who discovered this early art form were struck, as one still is, by the extraordinary quality of the drawings of the mammoth, bison and horses that decorate both the small movable objects and the cave-walls. The perfection of some of these works gave rise to the idea of a prehistoric art solely inspired by a love of form, with no motive other than the painting of the shapes and movement of the animals that surrounded prehistoric man. However, since the end of the nineteenth century, as a result of ethnographic research which brought to light the totemism, magic rites and religion of modern primitive groups, prehistorians have begun to have some conception of the religious implications of prehistoric art. Since then, many theories have been put forward, based on a comparison with modern hunting and gathering groups. Though such comparisons may be helpful they do not really throw much light on the thoughts of prehistoric man, for all they do is to compare certain elements of prehistoric art with elements of Eskimo or Australian aboriginal art. In this connection the example of 'sympathetic magic' is very striking. Some of the bisons painted or engraved on the cave-walls have marks on their bodies representing wounds. By comparison with examples from various living groups it is often believed that the prehistoric hunter drew the bison in order to symbolically 'kill' the image and thus assure control over the real animal. Such a supposition is quite plausible and would be justified if all the pictures of animals had symbolic wounds but, in fact, these form a minority. One cannot, therefore, accept that the motivation of our ancestors has really been understood. Just as with modern primitives, their way of representing the natural and supernatural world may have been more complex than one supposed.

One cannot understand the religious concepts of the Australian aboriginal simply by looking at his art. It is only comprehensible because we know, from their own accounts, about the myths behind the pictures. If the Australian aboriginal had ceased to exist, his art would be almost silent. But perhaps not completely. One could, by analysis of the frequency of the subjects painted and by a study of the spatial

* The Aurignacian culture flourished in Europe from 30,000 to 22,000 B.C.

relationships discover the bare bones of the artists' concepts. One might thus discover that certain animals were drawn to the exclusion of many others and that these animals were drawn in specific relationships one to another or to other objects or people. Such a study leads to the construction of a framework for the myths, without, however, allowing one to reconstruct the religious concept. It is, none the less, the only way in which one can comprehend certain concrete features without adding explanations possibly quite foreign to the painters' thoughts. The author has used a similar approach in his study of the religious concepts of the Upper Palaeolithic artists.

The art on the walls of the rock-shelters and caves lends itself more readily to this study than that on the movable objects. For the pictures on the walls remain where the artist put them and if there was a relationship between the representations, even if unconscious, the study of a sufficient number should make it possible to discover whether the distribution was haphazard or predetermined. There are more than 100 decorated caves and rock-shelters in Spain and France. Some, such as Font-de-Gaume, Altamira or Lascaux, have dozens of representations covering the walls within a relatively small area. In others, for example at Niaux, the representations form separate groups several metres apart.

There are three categories of representations: animals, people and symbols of various types but generally more or less geometric. Human figures are rare and, except in three cases, they do not seem to have any narrative connection with the animals round them. The three exceptions all show a man being attacked by a bison.

There are two distinct types of symbols: solid forms such as triangles, ovals, rectangles and circles, and linear forms such as lines of dots, dashes or branches. The human figures and the signs seem to correspond to the same symbolism and also have similar spatial relationships. One finds the human male and female and the symbolic male and female; the symbolic male represented by linear signs like the dashes, and the symbolic female represented by the solid signs like the oval (fig. 3). Some symbols are less stylized than others.

The animals, often very finely executed, appear in very varying numbers. Horses are the most numerous and are found in all the caves. Next come the bison, though in some cases, like Lascaux, its place is taken by the aurochs (figs. 4, 5). This first group makes up more than two-thirds of the total. Then come the ibex, stag, hind and mammoth (figs. 6, 7). Then, far rarer, the rhinoceros, bear and lion. The animals of the first group (horse, bison, auroch) are usually in groups (fig. 8). The ibex, hind, lion or bear are either single or in pairs, the rhinoceros is alone, except at Rouffignac, and the mammoths are usually represented by a few individuals.

The most striking thing is that the spatial distribution of the animals, both in terms of numbers and position, does not seem to be random. Within the caves there are places where the walls narrow in, places where they widen out into chambers, there are side chambers and often culs-de-sac. The animal representations can be divided into three topographic groups: central representations (horse, bison, aurochs), lateral representations (ibex, hind, mammoth) and representations at the back of the cave (bear, lion, rhinoceros). The caves have very different shapes and, in each case, prehistoric man had to adapt his work to a different setting, sometimes grouping all the representations on one wall, sometimes along the length of a passage, or sometimes dividing them

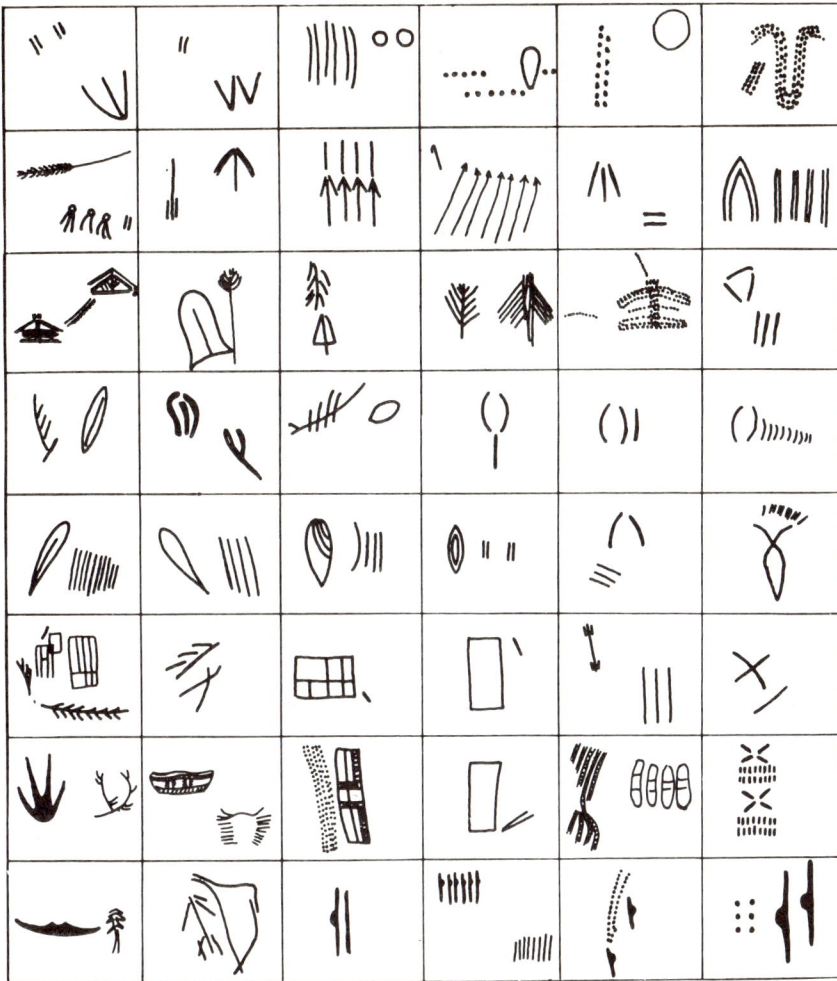

Fig. 3
Representations of male and female symbols in French cave art.
After A. Leroi Gourhan, *Prehistoire de l'Art Occidental*, Editions d'Art Lucien Mazenod, Paris, 1965.

between several chambers separated by narrow passages. Moreover, the arrangements of the tableau of figures did not take into account perspective as we know it, nor our conventions for representing movement. With rare exceptions, the animals are drawn stock-still and as though suspended in air so that there is very little similarity between the decoration of our religious buildings and the caves. Taken separately each cave-tableau leaves an impression of confusion but the repetition of the same distribution patterns in many caves allows one to comprehend the over-all organization.

In the most straightforward case, where all the figures are on one surface, one finds the bison and horse in the centre, then, as one moves outwards, an ibex, a deer, or a mammoth. There may even be only a bison and a horse (as at Marcenac, Lot). Here the theme has been reduced to its simplest expression. In other cases, an elaboration of the concept may be expressed both in the actual number of figures and in their topographic distribution. In the centre the number of bison may be increased to as many as thirty (as at Altamira, pl. 1 (colour)), the lateral figures may be ousted from the central panel and appear in the narrower passages to one or other side. In a cave like Lascaux, where there is a passage with successive chambers, the same theme of aurochses and horses may be repeated several times, separated by pictures of ibex or hinds in the passages. It may end at the back with a rhinoceros or a feline.

9

The distribution of the animals is not in itself enough to explain the significance of the cave art. One can simply make out that the horse and the bison have a role of primary importance in prehistoric thought, which is hardly surprising in view of the importance of these animals as game. None the less, it is also clear that the art does not simply represent the game hunted, for the reindeer, whose remains are abundant in the kitchen refuse throughout the Upper Palaeolithic, is very rarely represented on the cave-walls. On the other hand, the deer and sometimes the mammoth, systematically found in a marginal position, seem to be an element that forms a triad with the bison and horse, rather than a game-animal found there by chance. There is something even more strange; in some caves like Niaux and Rouffignac where the three-animal theme is repeated several times, each group seems to accord a privileged position to one or other of the three species. Thus on one panel at Niaux there is a large horse associated with a small bison and a small ibex, a large bison flanked by two small figures corresponding to the two other animals, and a large ibex with small bisons and horses.

Even if one cannot reconstruct myths and beliefs dead for thousands of years, at least the analysis of the framework of the themes makes it clear that Magdalenian concepts must have been very complex.

For a still more complete idea of the concepts of our ancestors one must also consider the symbols and the human figures. We have seen that the male and female human figures and the linear and solid symbols

Fig. 4
Wild auroch in the axial gallery at Lascaux.
By permission A. Houghton Brodrick.

were probably equivalent. The linear symbols are found in two contexts: they are either associated with the solid symbols in the central group with the horse and bison or aurochs, or else they are found alone near to narrow passages, on the lip of oval niches or at the entrance of a cul-de-sac. In some cases, for example at Gargas (Hautes-Pyrénées) or at Font-de-Gaume (Dordogne), some of these oval hollows in the cave-walls are coloured with red ochre and it can hardly be doubted that they were regarded by Palaeolithic men as female symbols. Thus the linear symbol/solid symbol and linear symbol/narrow opening are equivalent and the cave itself must have represented the feminine entity or the female. The position of the animals in this sexual system suggests a very complex metaphysical framework.

As well as these factors there are others, no less extraordinary. The solid sign is usually associated with the linear sign, thus forming a symbolic couple. In a fair number of cases a clump of dots is placed to the side of these two signs, in the same way as the animals, for example the bison/horse + ibex. Thus a similar triple arrangement with two more important elements and a third complementary element is associated with both the animals and the human symbols. The way in which the two categories are articulated is still not entirely clear; however, there is a certain amount of evidence which may help. As we have already seen, the linear symbol is associated with either a solid symbol or with a natural oval concavity. It may also be associated with

Fig. 5
Aurochs and stag in the main hall at Lascaux.
By permission A. Houghton Brodrick.

the marks representing wounds on the animals, the same 'wounds'
which led to the concept of 'sympathetic magic'. In some cases, at Niaux
or Pech-Merle, the 'wounds' undoutedly play the same role as the full
symbols. Perhaps, therefore, the wound symbol is a sexual symbol,
which leads on to the idea of the act of hunting being identified with
the art of reproduction.

The ideological fabric must certainly have varied considerably during
the 20,000 years in which prehistoric art evolved. In different regions
the mythological traditions may have taken very different forms, but the
fundamental concept of the representations remained the same. It
is clear that from the earliest Aurignacian representations, more than
40,000 years ago, when artistic mastery was still far from having been
achieved, the animals were associated with explicitly sexual symbols.
With many variations the same symbolic theme survived up until the
end of the Magdalenian, some 9,000 years ago, in Spain, France and
Italy. The same theme appears in central and eastern Europe in other
forms. Thus in Czechoslovakia as in Russia and the Ukraine there are
no wall-paintings, but clay or soft-stone figures represent the same
animals and the same symbols. A few years ago, in the cave of Kapova,
in the foothills of the Ural Mountains, some Palaeolithic paintings were
discovered, the most easterly yet found. Not without a certain surprise

Fig. 6
Deer in the main hall at Lascaux.
By permission A. Houghton Brodrick.

(Previous page)
Fig. 7
A young mammoth at Peche-Merle (Lot).
By permission A. Houghton Brodrick.

Fig. 8
Goats, wild horses and signs on the walls
of the axial gallery at Lascaux.
By permission A. Houghton Brodrick.

the bison, the horse and the mammoth were found yet again associated with triangular symbols and strokes.

One has to admit that the prehistoric mythology and rites are lost for ever, but, none the less, the analysis of the framework of prehistoric art makes its possible to discover a little of the lost past. We can discover the skeleton of the metaphysical preoccupations of Palaeolithic man just as we can recover his real skeletons and those of the animals which represented both his quarry and the substance of his thoughts on the secret organization of the world around him.

2
ANIMALS OF THE NEW STONE AGE

SONIA COLE

The Neolithic – Revolution and Evolution

For over a million years man had pursued wild animals for food and raw materials before he began to domesticate them. This new relationship did not diminish the respect which man felt towards animals, emotions which are shown so unmistakably in Upper Palaeolithic art. So long as hunting continued to be important – and there is plenty of evidence to show that it did long after the beginning of the Neolithic way of life – the spirits of the animals killed had to be propitiated to ensure a supply of game in the future. It was equally vital to encourage the increase of domestic stock and so we find that preoccupation with fertility was as great with farmers as it had been with hunters. Animal cults and symbolism were certainly no less elaborate during the Neolithic than they had been in Upper Palaeolithic times.

The Neolithic, with an economy based on the cultivation of crops and the keeping of domestic animals, developed gradually and was not confined to a particular period of time, but its duration varied in different areas. The first glimmerings of this new way of life appeared just before the end of the Pleistocene which, according to geological convention, ended about 8300 B.C. in Europe. This chapter is concerned mainly with a mere 5,000 years or so, from about 10,000 to 5000 B.C. when metal-using cultures began in western Asia. The area in question is equally restricted, lying mostly between the 30° and 40° parallels north and stretching from Iran to Greece. We shall make a few excursions in both time and space outside these narrow limits, but this is the key period and the nuclear area for our purpose.

During the long 'object-collecting' period of prehistoric research, the Neolithic was rather neglected. Pottery styles were studied and classified but that was almost as far as it went. In the late 1950s the discovery of the town-walls of Neolithic Jericho caused considerable excitement, but the spectacular art of earlier and later periods seemed to be lacking. Much of our knowledge of the Neolithic has been acquired within the past few years and it is revealing the striking continuity between the art and beliefs of Stone Age hunters and Bronze Age civilizations.

The late Professor V. Gordon Childe's concept of a 'Neolithic

Revolution' is sometimes criticized on the grounds that it is more of an 'evolution' than a 'revolution'. There is something in this, for archaeologists are accumulating more and more evidence to show that crop-raising and stock-keeping were very gradual processes and that for a long time pioneer farmers continued to be part-time or even nearly full-time hunters. It has been found that the initial steps leading towards the new economy took place much earlier than was suspected only a few years ago and it is significant that archaeologists working in western Asia now tend to use the term 'proto-Neolithic' instead of 'Mesolithic' for cultures like the Natufian of Palestine and its regional equivalents, lasting from about 9000 to 7000 B.C., which show evidence of a more settled way of life. Although it is becoming increasingly obvious that the change-over from hunting and gathering to full food production was more of an evolution than a sudden revolution, in its broader aspects Childe's definition still holds good. When we consider the long-term consequences of agriculture and animal husbandry there is no doubt whatever that 'revolution' is the right word. It was indeed an economic, cultural and social revolution and without it civilization would have been impossible.

The centre for this revolution was in the region known rather vaguely as the Middle East, comprising parts of western Iran, northern Iraq, Syria, Lebanon and Jordan. The reason for its location here is that this area is the natural home of wild wheat and barley, wild sheep and goats – the ancestors of the first domesticates. The area stretches for over a thousand miles and one of the chief centres for the 'Neolithic Revolution' seems to have been in the well-watered foothills of the Zagros Mountains, fringing the desert. It was not until about 5500 B.C. that farmers spread into the alluvial lowlands of the Tigris and Euphrates, more than a thousand years after agriculture was well established in the uplands.

This very broad generalization already needs to be amplified as a result of recent research and will certainly need even more elaboration in the future. Apart from the proto-Neolithic and Early Neolithic sites in the 'nuclear area' of the Zagros foothills, such as Qalat Jarmo (Iraq), Zawi Chemi Shanidar (Iraq) and Tepe Guran (Iran), there is the exceptional site of Tell es-Sultan at Jericho lying 900 feet below sea-level and based on a permanent spring (fig. 9). Very recently it has been found that at least two other entirely different environments seem to be involved in Early Neolithic settlements. One is on the Anatolian Plateau, where already by 6500 B.C. there was a large town at Çatal Hüyük based on trade and agriculture. In all the levels excavated so far pottery was present; certainly much earlier aceramic settlements must exist in Anatolia, but, apart from the lowest levels at Hacilar, very little is known about this phase as yet. Anatolia was the gateway to Europe via the Balkans and it has been found recently that a Neolithic economy was practised at Nea Nikomedeia in Greece much earlier than had been suspected.

The other environment which has extended our knowledge of Neolithic origins recently is more surprising. It is on the now-barren alluvial plain of Khuzistan in western Iran, which today has an annual rainfall of only 12 inches and is outside the natural habitat of wild wheat and barley. In the Deh Luran Valley, the settlement of Ali Kosh dates back to 6000 B.C. or even earlier. At first hunting and goat-herding were far more important than agriculture, but in the later stages cereals were cultivated.

16

If agriculture and stock-keeping did start in the Zagros area, they must have spread through Anatolia on the one hand and into southern Mesopotamia by way of the steppe-lands of Khuzistan on the other. Whether this simple idea of diffusion is the whole answer we do not yet know. There is plenty of evidence to show that there was a wide network of trade, particularly in obsidian from Anatolia, and so the idea of cultivating cereals and keeping domestic animals would have spread rapidly. But some areas would have been more suitable for herding, while in others the reaping of wild grasses may have led to their cultivation before domestic stock were kept; in fact, there may have been several separate centres for the origin of different forms of Neolithic economy rather than just one.

Clearly, domestication and agriculture could have started only in areas where cereals suitable for cultivation and socially inclined animals already lived wild; but this is not the whole story. There were other kinds of suitable wild plants in other parts of the world, notably rice in the Far East and maize in America, yet, as far as we know, these were not cultivated until much later. There were vast herds of docile antelopes in Africa, yet, apart from some short-lived experiments by the Egyptians, the people who lived among these animals made no attempt to domesticate them. To the basic ingredients of appropriate plants and animals must be added people of the right mental calibre with a

Fig. 9
Early Neolithic sites of the Middle East.

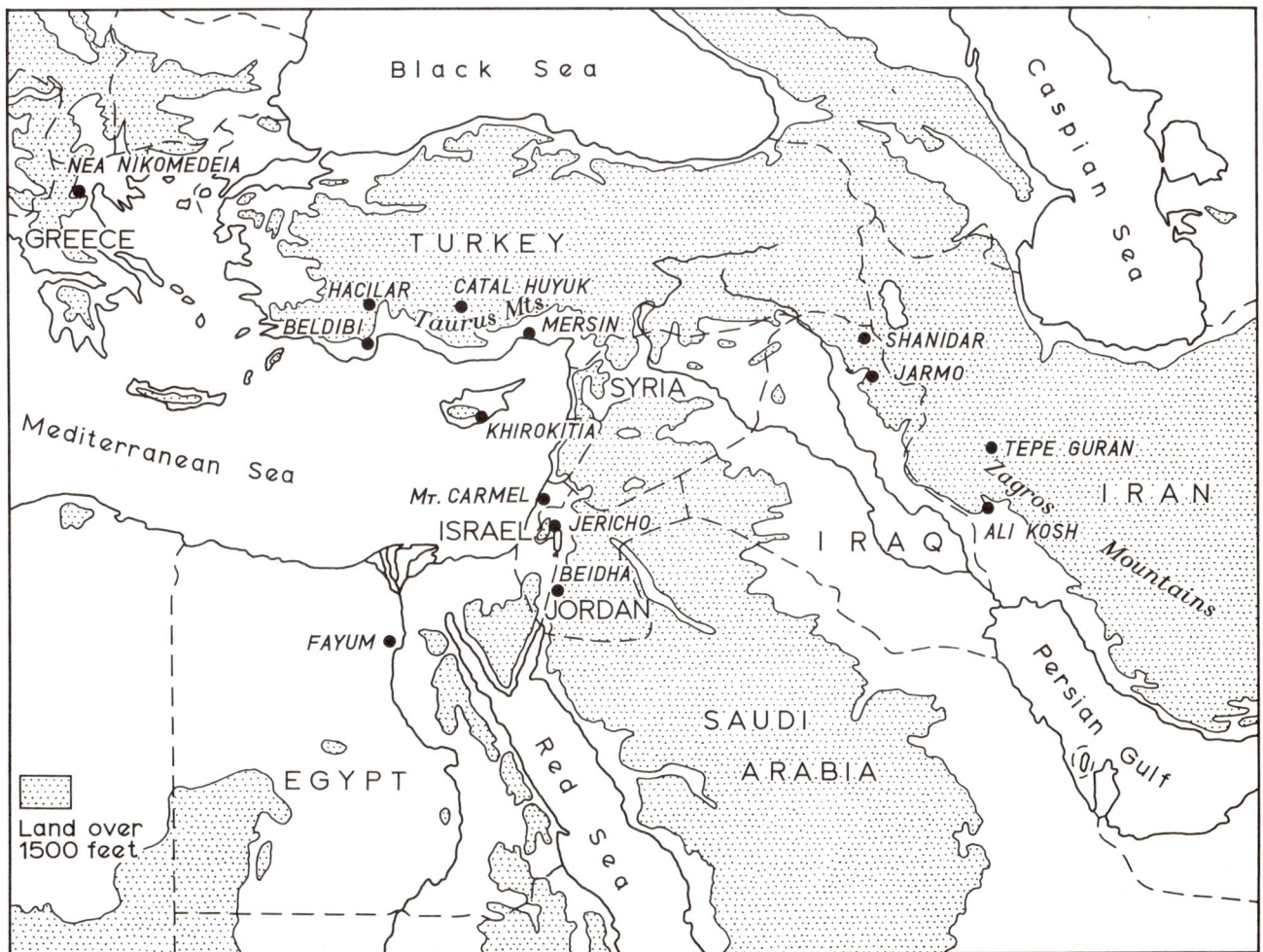

relatively sophisticated culture, people capable of seizing the available opportunities.

Here we are concerned with animals and not with plants, although, of course, the two are closely linked. Man had always lived on intimate terms with wild animals; that they had to be eaten was irrelevant; they were part of the surroundings, as familiar as members of one's own hunting-group. It was only after man became a farmer and certain animals were a menace to his crops that they were looked on as enemies and deliberately exterminated. Domestication was a natural and inevitable outcome of such a relationship and the only surprising thing is that it did not happen much sooner.

The most obvious answer is that nomadic hunters and food-gatherers could not drive herds of domestic animals from one camp to the next and that it was not until there were settled villages, based on agriculture, that stock-keeping would have been a practical proposition. Yet here again this does not seem to be the whole story. Semi-permanent settlements were evidently established in areas where the hunting was particularly good, but there is no evidence for them in the Near East before the end of the Pleistocene. At Zawi Chemi Shanidar, where the game was abundant, domestic sheep were apparently kept 2,000 years before there is any *certain* evidence of cultivated crops anywhere; and at Ali Kosh, where there was an overwhelming emphasis on hunting, goat-herding seems to have taken place before agriculture became at all important.

Why were animals domesticated at this particular period? It could not have been solely in order to have a permanent supply of meat, hides and bone on hand, for there was no lack of game in western Asia towards the end of the Pleistocene and hunters would have had no difficulty in catching their dinner on the hoof. Climatic changes in this area at this time are not too well known, but it is unlikely that they were very great. To a certain extent they must have caused changes in the local fauna as vegetation zones shifted a little both in latitude and altitude, but it is most improbable that there was a significant decline in the numbers of animals available. There would have been great herds of gazelles and onagers on the plains, deer and aurochs in the woodlands, sheep in the hills and goats in the mountains. The numbers of bones of wild animals in Early Neolithic levels show clearly that they were not in short supply. But though the climate may not have altered radically slight changes may have been a factor in the gradual domestication of animals.

There is a certain amount of evidence to show that in the period which concerns us here, from about 10,000 to 5000 B.C., western Asia had a rather more arid climate than during the later part of the Pleistocene. In the cave-deposits of the Wadi el-Mughara, Mount Carmel, for instance, a preponderance of bones of fallow deer is replaced in the Natufian levels by a sudden abundance of gazelle bones. This suggests drier conditions and more grasslands, though it has been argued that it may only reflect man's dietary preferences at that particular time. Although a fairly wide range of environments was within easy reach of Mount Carmel, it seems more likely that hunters would bring back to the caves the animals which were commonest in the vicinity. From about 10,000 B.C. when the Pleistocene ice-sheets were waning in Europe, the snow-line on mountains like the Taurus and Zagros also began to recede. This fact, like the increase of gazelles, suggests increased aridity. It is also significant that the gazelles of Natufian times were new arrivals in the area, species quite unknown before and apparently more closely related to forms now living on the African savannas than to any Asiatic species. Soon after, they became extinct, perhaps at a time when the climate became more humid once again.*[1]

In the later part of the Pleistocene, from about 26,000 to 10,000 B.C., there is a cultural hiatus at many sites at higher altitudes, for instance at Shanidar.[2] Presumably the climate at that time was too cold in the mountains and the people moved down to lower altitudes. Then suddenly, with a slight rise in temperature, they came back. In the meantime they may have come into contact with other groups, who perhaps hunted different animals and used different hunting methods and weapons. Such contacts, indirectly due to climatic change, may have stimulated new ideas and new experiments in the menu. When they were driven out of the higher country by the cold these people were almost exclusively hunters; when they returned they were also intensive food-collectors. There is an abundance of snail-shells at sites where they had not appeared before and soon after, more significantly, grindstones and mortars show that there was an increasing dependence on vegetable foods. By 8900 B.C. at Zawi Chemi Shanidar we find the first evidence of domesticated animals.

Looked at in this light, domestication seems to have been part of one great movement, a spurt of cultural and economic evolution. Apparently domestication just happened, without forethought and certainly with no inkling of its tremendous implications. A few groups began to settle for at least a good part of the year in one place, either because game was abundant in the neighbourhood, or because there were plenty of wild plants to be harvested, sometimes because the fishing was good – or sometimes perhaps a combination of all three. There would have to be a permanent water-supply, perhaps a vantage-point from where the country could be surveyed for game, or a gorge where animals could be ambushed. One example is the Lower Natufian settlement at Eynan, on the shores of Lake Huleh in Israel, where the people lived in round stone houses, and reaped cereals (probably wild) but depended mainly on hunting and especially fishing.[3] Another example, in an entirely different environment, is Ali Kosh, where the abundance of gazelles, onagers, wild goats and aurochs led to the establishment of a settlement of pit-houses. Other important elements in the diet were catfish and freshwater clams. Today these no longer exist in the shallow, brackish streams near the site, but this does not necessarily imply a significant change in the local climate, since shifts in the base-levels and courses of rivers in Mesopotamia would have affected those of Khuzistan.[4] The presence of the aurochs, however, as well as cereal grains does suggest a rainfall rather greater than at the present time.

To settlements such as these, hunters may have brought back young animals to please their wives and amuse their children. No doubt they had done this for thousands of years; but whereas formerly these animals must have been abandoned when the camp moved on, in the relative security of a village it would be possible to rear them. And so, with no particular motive, animals may have been domesticated simply as one result of general economic change.

In some cases selective hunting of certain animals may have led to

* Source references, signalled by superior figures, are at the end of the book.

their subsequent domestication. Obviously, hunters would be more likely to collect the young of animals they habitually killed. Where there is a wide choice of game available, dietary preferences may be quite important and also perhaps the habits of the animals themselves, some being easier to hunt than others.

One of the biggest surprises in Neolithic research to emerge in recent years is the very early date, about 8900 B.C., for the presence of domestic sheep at Zawi Chemi Shanidar. This proto-Neolithic village in Iraqi Kurdistan lies below the famous Shanidar cave, where Dr Ralph Solecki found the remains of six Neanderthalers.[5] Kurdish shepherds still live in the cave during the winter and probably the proto-Neolithic people did the same, moving into the open in the summer months. Throughout the pre-Neolithic cave-deposits, which go back some 70,000 years, bones of wild goats outnumber those of sheep by three to one. The situation is very different at the time of the proto-Neolithic village with its Karim Shahiran culture (named after an open-air site a mile from Shanidar and the local equivalent of the Natufian). Both here and in contemporaneous levels in the cave the hunting of goats had become unimportant and the proportion of sheep bones rises sharply. From the large numbers of yearlings, it is believed that these sheep were domesticated. In view of the former prevalence of goats, one would have expected them to be domesticated before sheep. In this case specialization in hunting goats for thousands of years apparently did not lead to their subsequent domestication. The answer may lie in the cultural hiatus in the later part of the Pleistocene which has already been mentioned. During their absence from the mountains, the people presumably no longer met goats but may have got used to hunting sheep; when they returned, they domesticated these animals and neglected the unfamiliar goat.

We find rather the same situation at Ali Kosh, though in this case we cannot account for it by a long absence from the site. In the earlier proto-Neolithic levels there are plenty of bones of goats but no sheep have been identified and, in fact, according to Hole, there is no country suitable for wild sheep near the site.[6] Gazelles and onagers would have abounded on the plains, but the hunting of wild goats would have necessitated a climb up the steep rock cliffs several kilometres to the north. That these animals were killed in such numbers does suggest that they were especially esteemed and the increase in proportions in later levels probably means that they were domesticated. Sheep bones are found only in the upper zones, both in the aceramic and the pottery levels, and almost certainly they were domesticated. Why, when wild goats were available in the neighbourhood and wild sheep probably were not, should sheep have been imported and domesticated? Were they easier to keep, or did the people learn to appreciate the taste of lamb?

There are even more puzzling questions in connection with pigs, which never appear in domesticated form before the later (pottery) levels. Today, of course, wild boars are never hunted in Muslim countries, whereas most other wild ungulates have been exterminated. This prohibition seems also to have applied in many areas in Neolithic times. At Zawi Chemi Shanidar and contemporaneous levels in the cave, no pig bones were found although these animals must have been plentiful near the site. At Ali Kosh, pig bones are fairly rare in the earlier levels and disappear altogether in the pottery levels. In these circumstances, where wild boars were seldom or never hunted, one would not expect to find domesticated pigs. Yet at Tepe Asiab near Kermanshah in Iranian Kurdistan the commonest bones in proto-Neolithic levels were those of wild pigs and at Tepe Sarab the pottery Neolithic includes some remarkable clay figurines of boars which suggest that these animals were held in high esteem (fig. 10).[7] In the upper (pottery) levels at Jarmo, domesticated pigs were also important.

In western Iran and northern Iraq, therefore, we find different local customs with regard to pigs. The simplest explanation might be that pigs would be unsuitable for herders moving to new pastures seasonally. Yet at Çatal Hüyük, a large town where there is no question of seasonal movements, although there were domestic dogs, sheep, goats and cattle, and although wall-paintings leave no doubt that wild boars were hunted, there is no evidence of domesticated pigs. What are we to make of all this? Later we shall discuss the evidence further. One cannot be too happy with the explanation that pigs were eaten only where taboos were not in force, since it seems very unlikely that such fundamental beliefs would be merely local.

The whole question of why certain animals were hunted and others neglected, and why certain animals were domesticated in some areas and not in others, is fascinating and we can only speculate about the reasons. Usually there seems to be a strong conservatism attached to animal symbolism, which was important in connection with fertility at least from Upper Palaeolithic times onwards. The persistence of bear cults and especially cattle cults until the present day, possibly also the abhorrence of the pig, are examples of such deep-rooted traditions. The case of goats versus sheep is less clear-cut. We have seen that the Neanderthalers of Shanidar specialized in hunting goats. At Teshik Tash in Uzbekistan, which is in a similar mountain environment, a Neanderthal youth's burial surrounded by goat horns shows that these animals were held in high regard. Was the switch to sheep in Early Neolithic times due to the arrival of new people who had forgotten these traditions? Or were the reasons simply economic and ecological?

Selective hunting was certainly no less widespread during the Early Neolithic than it had been in Upper Palaeolithic times, though after the extinction of the mammoth and the decline of reindeer herds this is less obvious and less dramatic. During the time of the aceramic village at Ali Kosh, for instance, although two varieties each of wheat and barley were grown and domestic goats were kept, at least some of the people were evidently far more interested in hunting. Butchers used stone meat-choppers and slicing-slabs and the meat was cooked in brick-lined roasting-pits. Very interesting evidence was found of the use of particular tools and techniques for butchering different-sized animals. The limb bones of the aurochs and onager were split with heavy choppers, whereas the bones of smaller animals like gazelles and goats were notched with a flint blade and then snapped. An aurochs' tibia and a hind-leg bone of an onager were found split along almost the entire length, thus neatly exposing the marrow; this had been achieved by using a chopper in the manner of a wedge driven into wood. Slice-marks on the lower limb bones of many animals showed where the tendons had been cut, probably on the slicing-slabs, and hundreds of flint blades had been used for this purpose and for notching the bones. Although there is not much meat on an ungulate's foot, many first

Fig. 10
Clay figurine of a boar from Tepe Sarab.
½ natural size.
After R. Braidwood, *Scientific American*, Sept. 1960, courtesy of the Oriental Institute, University of Chicago.

phalanges showed signs of extensive roasting; the gourmets of the time evidently particularly appreciated the marrow of this particular portion and they went to a good deal of trouble to extract it.[8]

A 'butcher's shop' was also found at the Early Neolithic village of Beidha, near Petra in Jordan. One room was full of articulated joints and horned heads, while another contained many heavy stone choppers, hammers and grinders.[9] Although these villagers cultivated crops and their prosperity was derived mainly from trade, as at Ali Kosh hunting continued to be a major occupation. There is also some evidence of ritual in connection with the ibex, an animal that never seems to have been domesticated. A magnificent pair of ibex horns was found in a bone-tool maker's workshop and near by were frontals from which the horns had been sawn off; a complete pair of horns lay close by, apparently to be used next.

The continued dependence on hunting for meat and also for the raw materials for tools of bone, horn and antler is typical of Early Neolithic sites. The theory that animals were domesticated in order to have a permanent supply of meat and raw materials at the settlement is clearly not entirely satisfactory.

So far we have discussed evidence which seems to support at least four main conclusions about the origins of domestication. First, the initial stages must have been confined to the area where wild ancestors were already living, though not necessarily confined to one particular kind of environment within the 'nuclear area'. Second, there seem to be certain reasons, perhaps indirectly connected with a change of climate, why the 'Neolithic Revolution' took place at a particular time. Third, as far as we can tell there may have been no particular motive for domesticating animals, but probably it grew up as one effect of a general evolutionary change involving more permanent settlement in one place. Fourth, that at first the keeping of domestic animals did not cause any decrease in hunting.

We must now broaden the picture and see how and when the new economy spread, taking into account the many new discoveries made since 1960 which in many ways is a landmark in our knowledge of the Neolithic. The 1960–70 decade saw the discovery and excavation of many important new sites: Ali Kosh, Tepe Guran, Nea Nikomedeia and above all Çatal Hüyük, which without doubt is the most exciting Neolithic settlement yet discovered. Prehistoric investigations in Anatolia are so new that future excavations may well show that the 'Neolithic Revolution' began in that area just as early as in the Zagros Mountains.

The past few years have also been important in other ways. They have produced many radiocarbon dates, enabling us to establish a firm chronology. They have also seen a revolution in our knowledge of the recognition of domestic animals at early sites. This is due very largely to the work of Dr C. A. Reed of the University of Illinois, Chicago, who has collected all reliable evidence on the subject and disposed of many misleading statements about so-called 'domestic' animals which had cluttered up the archaeological literature without any foundation on fact. Since Reed's paper of 1960, giving dates for the earliest known domestication of various animals, many of these dates have been pushed back by several thousand years.[10] This shows the tremendous progress in recent research. Sheep were domesticated 3,000 years earlier than was known in 1960; pigs about 2,000 years earlier; cattle at least 1,000 years earlier. Fig. 11 summarizes this new information.

Proto-Neolithic people, as we have seen, began to keep domestic animals before the end of the Pleistocene (judging by the evidence from Zawi Chemi Shanidar). Soon after 7000 B.C. there were true Neolithic settlements, without pottery, with cultivated cereals and domesticated goats in the Zagros area (Jarmo) and at favourable sites based on springs in Palestine (Jericho). By 6500 B.C. the first known pottery appears at the large town of Çatal Hüyük in Anatolia, suggesting a long previous history of Neolithic economy as yet little known. By 6000 B.C. the pottery Neolithic was well established in many different areas (fig. 12). Agriculture based on irrigation had spread to the lowlands of southern Mesopotamia by 5500 B.C. and at about the same time the Neolithic way of life penetrated into eastern Europe north of the Balkans.

This new economy spread in two main directions: over the loess-lands of the Danube Basin (the Linear Pottery culture); and along the shores and islands of the Mediterranean to Spain (the Impressed Ware cultures) and then northwards up the Atlantic coast (the Western Neolithic). Recent radiocarbon dates show that Linear Pottery farmers, with their cattle, pigs and sheep, had reached Germany and the Netherlands by 4500 B.C.; but in spite of a well-developed agricultural economy these peasant farmers still hunted red deer, aurochs, bison and wild boar on a considerable scale. The Western Neolithic people reached

Years B.C.

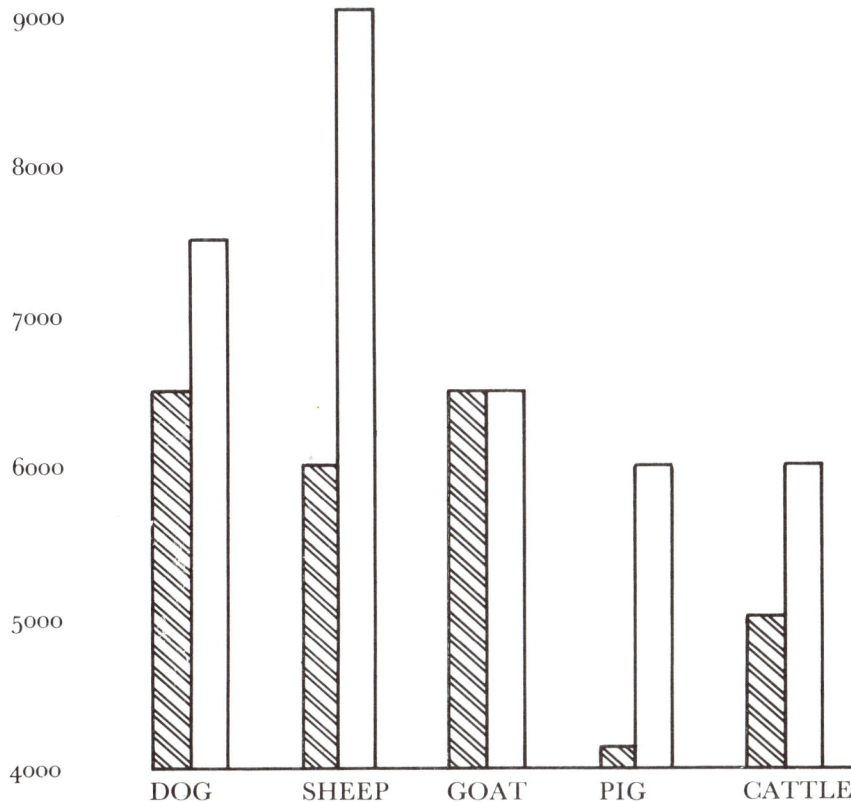

Earliest dates for domestic animals as known in
1960
1970

Fig. 11
Earliest dates for domestic animals as known in 1960 and 1970.

23

	Site	9000	8000	7000	6000	B.C.
ZAGROS FOOT-HILLS	ZAWI CHEMI SHANIDAR (IRAQ)	▨ Proto-Neolithic				
	QALAT JARMO (IRAQ)				Aceramic / Pottery Neolithic	Pottery
	TEPE GURAN (IRAN)				Pottery Neolithic	
IRANIAN PLAIN	ALI KOSH (IRAN)				Aceramic / Pottery Neolithic	
JORDAN RIFT	TELL ES SULTAN, JERICHO		Proto-Neolithic	Aceramic (A)	Pottery (B)	
ANATOLIAN PLATEAU	GATAL HÜYÜK				Pottery Neolithic	
	HACILAR			Aceramic	Pottery	
MACEDONIAN PLAIN	NEA NIKOMEDEIA					Pottery Neolithic

▨ Proto-Neolithic   ⋁⋀⋁ Aceramic Neolithic   ⫽ Pottery Neolithic

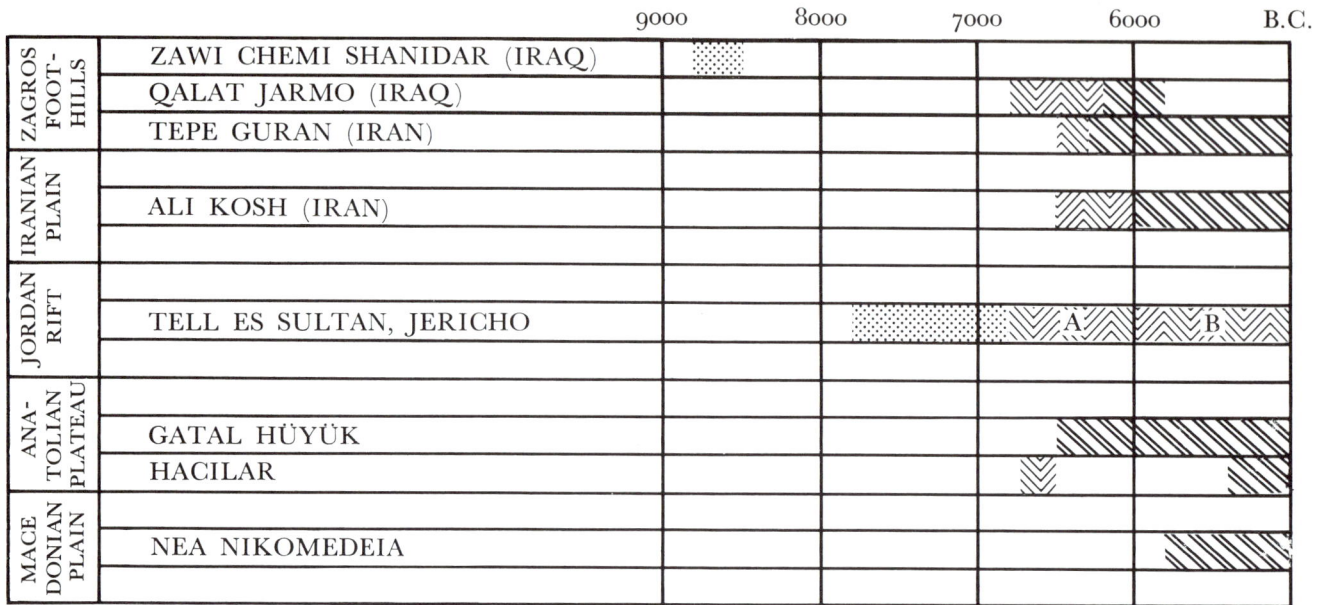

Fig. 12
Time-ranges of some Proto-Neolithic and Neolithic sites in five environmental areas.

Ireland and England by 3200 B.C., a thousand years earlier than was supposed only a few years ago. The fact that they were able to bring cattle with them speaks much for their skill in boat-building.

In northern Europe the effects of the beginnings of agriculture can be traced in the pollen spectrum at the time of transition from the Atlantic to the sub-Boreal climate about 3000 B.C. Curiously enough, signs of the keeping of domestic animals have also been traced in pollen diagrams. It has been suggested that a decline in elm and ivy pollen may mean that the leaves were collected for cattle-fodder to overcome what must have been a very real problem: winter feeding.[11] Evidence has been found both in the Ertebølle culture of Denmark and also in Switzerland, where heaps of elm and ash leaves occur in Neolithic settlements. Layers apparently composed of manure suggest that cattle were also fed on flowering ivy during the winter (in the Swiss lake-side settlements, cattle and pigs were far more important than sheep and goats).

South of the Mediterranean the earliest dated agricultural settlement is in the Fayum, Egypt, about 4500 B.C. The domestic goats of the Fayum were almost certainly introduced from western Asia, since there were no wild goats in Africa. Earlier Neolithic sites may well have existed in the Nile Valley, but they have been buried irretrievably beneath many feet of silt. Nomadic pastoralists spread over the Sahara from about 3000 B.C., during a period of considerably increased rainfall, and recorded their presence in magnificent rock paintings and engravings. Probably their cattle, which they depicted so often and in such individual detail, were domesticated from the local aurochs of North Africa.

It is more difficult to trace the spread of Neolithic economy – or possible independent centres of domestication – in the Far East because of the lack of dated sites. Domestic sheep and humped cattle were kept in Baluchistan and Pakistan at the time of the Indus Valley civilizations

24

about 3000 B.C.; humped cattle also appear on seals in Mesopotamia even earlier and presumably these animals were derived from India. The Neolithic of China is still undated, but the Yangshao culture centred on the Hwang Ho Basin had a well-developed agricultural economy possibly before 3000 B.C. and domestic pigs, cattle, sheep and/or goats were kept.[12]

Compared with the dates for Europe, then, the beginning of the Neolithic in Africa and the Far East seems retarded, but this may be partly due to our ignorance.

The Processes of Domestication

Whenever it was that the first experiments in domestication were made, we may be quite sure that it was much earlier than the dates when we find the first indisputable evidence. The reason is that the bones of the first domesticated animals are indistinguishable from their wild ancestors. As various mutations appeared among their stock early farmers would not at first have deliberately selected those animals for breeding; but the important point is that neither was there selection *against* such mutations as there probably would have been in the wild.[13] Eventually, because of isolation, variation arose among domesticated animals which thus differed considerably from their wild ancestors. Probably this happened long before deliberate breeding policies by man exaggerated such changes.

Even in the very early stages, however, there are certain ways of distinguishing between wild and domesticated animals. When Reed began his studies on this problem he had to collect skeletal material for comparison, for very little was available in museums. Before accepting bones from archaeological sites as being those of domestic animals he demanded proof that they were not of wild species; this was the exact opposite of the point of view of many a hopeful excavator, who had assumed that all goats, sheep, cattle and pigs were domesticated if they came from levels of a period that might be *expected* to contain domestic animals. As we have seen, hunting continued to be important long after domestic stock was kept and so this conclusion was by no means necessarily true.

Very often animal bones from Neolithic and later sites were not collected at all. A quotation from Reed illustrates well the deplorable lack of attention given to animal bones in archaeological sites until quite recently (there was, in fact, some excuse since there were very few osteologists competent and willing to study the bones). In spite of the obvious importance of cattle in the Halafian culture of Iraq from about 5500 B.C., as shown in the art of these people, no evidence had been produced to show that these animals were domesticated. 'Only a cow's horn (undescribed, unmeasured, unfigured and obviously unwanted) and unnamed, uncounted pig bones were found in the Halafian layers at Nineveh.'[14]

In general, the bones of domesticated animals compared with their wild relatives are smaller – because of inadequate feeding – and lighter, with weaker muscle ridges. The face is sometimes shorter, particularly in the case of pigs, and the teeth are smaller and overcrowded (this, of course, happens also in the case of domesticated man as a result of his diet).

In very early Neolithic or proto-Neolithic sites a more reliable sign of domestication may lie in the proportion of bones of animals of different ages. An unusually high percentage of bones of immature animals suggests that they were killed regularly once a year, either to provide food for their owners at a time when other food was scarce, or to avoid the problem of keeping the animals alive when pasture was in short supply.

The reason for believing the sheep at Zawi Chemi Shanidar to be domesticated lies in the large numbers of young animals. Throughout the earlier cave-deposits, the proportion of individuals one year old or less is not more than 25 per cent and this is about the average for kills of wild animals by hunters. Then suddenly, at the time of the village site, about 8900 B.C. the percentage of yearlings rises to 60.[15, 16] At the time of the earliest village of Ali Kosh no skeletal changes are apparent in the goats but the abundance of yearlings suggests domestication.[17] There is also a significant shift in the proportions of ungulate bones in the three main levels: in the lowest (proto-Neolithic), goat bones form 28 per cent; in the second (aceramic) phase goat/sheep bones are 44 per cent; and in the upper (pottery) levels goat/sheep bones are 55 per cent, while aurochs and onager diminish considerably and there are no pigs.[18]

At Nea Nikomedeia in Macedonia 47 per cent of the goat and sheep bones and 50 per cent of the cattle bones were of immature animals. Evidence for domestic pigs is even more convincing: more than 90 per cent of the bones came from animals about a year old.[19]

Nea Nikomedeia has provided some of the earliest evidence in Europe for domesticated sheep, goats, pigs and cattle. Radiocarbon dates between 6000 and 5600 B.C. make it approximately contemporaneous with Levels VI to VIII at Çatal Hüyük (by a coincidence excavations at both sites started in 1961). By this time domesticated cattle were probably kept at Çatal Hüyük but sheep were kept even earlier, at least below Level X. Among the bones of adult sheep and goats at Nea Nikomedeia, some were considerably larger than others; there would, of course, be differences in size between the sexes even though these differences are generally far less among domesticated animals than wild, but in this case the variations were considered to be more than merely sexual. It might mean that the larger animals were wild and the smaller domesticated, or possibly that the larger animals were in the course of domestication when one would expect considerable variation in size. In the case of the cattle from this site, the teeth are smaller than those characteristic of the European aurochs.

From their bones and teeth it is difficult enough to distinguish goats from sheep and even more difficult to separate wild from domestic goats and wild from domestic sheep. The few parts of the skull and skeleton that are diagnostic, particularly the horn cores, are not always to be found in the archaeological levels where we should most like to find them.

Quite early on, mutations affected the shape of the horn cores of goats (the horns, of course, would also have been affected but they are almost never preserved). The bezoar, *Capra hircus aegagrus*, wild ancestor of domestic goats, has straight, scimitar-shaped horns and the horn cores have a roughly quadrangular cross-section. Domestic goats from Early Neolithic sites such as the aceramic levels of Jarmo (where 80 per cent of all the animal bones were of goats) and Jericho are very similar to their wild ancestors but the horn core is flatter in cross-section. By later Neolithic and Bronze Age times the cross-section had become almond-shaped and the horns were twisted or screw-shaped, as depicted in the famous 'ram' – actually goat – caught in a thicket from Ur.[20]

During the second phase at Ali Kosh, from about 6500 to 6000 B.C., the goats had medially flattened horn cores and by the time of the third phase, from about 6000 to 5700 B.C., the goats had twisted horns, as was also the case in the upper (pottery) levels at Jarmo.[21]

Sheep and goats, as we have seen, were apparently the earliest food-producing animals to be domesticated. The proto-Neolithic settlement at Zawi Chemi Shanidar with domestic sheep soon after 9000 B.C. seems to be exceptional at present and there is no certain evidence of similar developments for instance with the contemporaneous Natufians of Palestine. There is then something of a hiatus until about 6500 B.C., when we find evidence of domesticated goats at numerous sites such as Jericho, Jarmo, Tepe Guran and Ali Kosh. No doubt future excavations will supply us with information about the transitional period of some 2,500 years and remedy this apparent lack of continuity.

The question of sheep versus goats in connection with selective hunting and possible dietary preferences has already been discussed. Apart from Zawi Chemi Shanidar in the earlier period, goats do seem to have been preferred to sheep among the village-farming communities of about 6500 B.C. and in some cases, such as at Ali Kosh and Tepe Guran, agriculture seems to have been secondary to goat-herding in the earliest phases. At Tepe Guran in Luristan it has been suggested that the first occupants, who lived in wooden huts, were primarily herdsmen, and it was only later that agriculture became important, testified by the increase in sickle-blades, querns and so on. This change was accompanied by a growth of the village and the construction of more solid, mud-walled houses.[22] The situation at Ali Kosh in Khuzistan further south was almost exactly the same: at first an emphasis on goats, later an increase in agriculture accompanied by better-made houses and then, curiously enough, in the third phase, after 6000 B.C., an emphasis once more on pastoralism at the expense of agriculture, associated with a great increase in both goats and sheep and a decline in cultivated grains.[23]

In the aceramic levels of Jarmo and Jericho there are goats but no sheep. At the Belt Cave in northern Iran, on the shores of the Caspian, sheep appear much later than goats. In the aceramic levels at Khirokitia in Cyprus, about 5700 B.C., there are goats with scimitar-shaped horns which nevertheless are thought to have been domesticated, but the evidence for domestic sheep is more doubtful. In the earliest agricultural settlements of Thessaly in Greece, no less than 83 per cent of the bones of domesticated animals are of goats, with only a few sheep and pigs.[24]

Apart from the dietary preferences of humans, there are the preferences of the animals themselves to be considered. The goat, being a browser, can thrive on small shrubs on mountain heights or in semi-desert country whereas sheep, being grazers, are less adaptable. Early Neolithic herdsmen had plenty of choice of land and it is unlikely that they would have spent much time on mountain-tops or desert fringes, though in certain cases perhaps the adaptability of the goat might have tipped the balance in its favour. It may be, for instance, that goats would do better than sheep at least during the dry summer months on the steppes of Khuzistan and this might explain the choice of these animals at Ali Kosh. We do not know enough about climate and vegetation zones in western Asia during this period to speculate very far on these lines but in general it seems likely that most of the country inhabited by the first herdsmen would have been equally suitable for goats or sheep. Both the bezoar and the Asiatic moufflon, *Ovis orientalis*, ancestors of domestic goats and sheep respectively, can still be found in hilly country in western Asia, though they may soon become extinct.

Apart from their meat, which most people consider to be inferior to mutton, goats may have been kept for the sake of their milk long before cattle were domesticated. It is often stated that milking was not practised during the early stages of domestication, presumably because the yield would have been very small until selection for it had been made. All the same, it seems unlikely that anyone living in close contact with animals would fail to appreciate the nutritive value of milk and it could not have been long before the yield improved. Very likely the process would have been reciprocal, the women giving suck to motherless kids and lambs and claiming a return of the favour when the animals reached maturity.

Probably we tend to underestimate the intelligence of early stockkeepers. As with milking, so it is often said that sheep were not domesticated for the sake of their wool. Reed, for instance, points out that only after the natural and random appearance of an increase in woolliness could selection have been made for that character.[25] Zeuner, however, draws attention to the fact that wads of wool are very noticeable when mouflons are in moult and the possibilities of felt, which is still made in central Asia, would surely not escape the attention of people forced to endure cold winters and cold nights.[26] From time immemorial goat skins must have been used for cloaks (and also for carrying water), but for warmth and comfort, as the advertisements tell us, there is no substitute for wool.

Early domestic sheep must have looked very like the feral Soay sheep of the island of that name in the St Kilda group, which may have been taken there in pre-Roman times. These animals are lightly built, with long legs, and the rams' horns are heavy, curving outward and downward in a single plane, while the ewes also sometimes have horns. Whereas in the wild mouflon the woolly undercoat consists of secondary fibres, the Soay sheep have a short, brown woolly fleece and the primary hair fibres are so reduced that they can hardly be seen.[27]

Until 1961, when excavations were begun at Çatal Hüyük, the earliest evidence for wool-bearing sheep was about 3500 B.C. both in Egypt and among the protoliterate civilizations of Mesopotamia. We know now that woollen garments were worn at Çatal Hüyük 3,000 years before this – at least we suspect it, for it is difficult to tell how much woolliness there was from carbonized fragments of textiles, preserved as the result of a great fire that destroyed the town about 6500 B.C. Some of the wall-paintings also give evidence of textiles, showing designs almost identical with those used in modern Anatolian rugs or *kilims*. In view of the number of rams' heads modelled on the walls of shrines and the absence of representations of goats, it seems more likely that the textiles were woven from sheep's wool rather than goats' hair; rams were obviously important in connection with fertility cults, as we shall see later, and it may be that they were particularly valued on account of their wool.

Having disposed of goats and sheep, we come now to the animal which must have helped to round up and control these animals, namely the dog. Until the discovery of the Zawi Chemi Shanidar sheep of about 8900 B.C. it seemed that the dog was the first animal to be domesticated. This may have been so, but we have no evidence before 7500 B.C. in Mesolithic Britain and possibly, though less certainly, at about the same time or a little earlier among the proto-Neolithic Natufians of Palestine. Since the dog is primarily an aid to catching food rather than a meat-supply in itself, in theory it might have been used by pre-agricultural hunters (there were – and still are – some peoples who did eat dogs: probably the Maglemosians of Denmark did so and certainly various American Indian tribes and Asiatic peoples did and still do). It has been said that modern hunting people do not use dogs to help in hunting (though there are exceptions) and that 'it is certain that the dog only became a hunting companion in fairly recent times'.[28] Once again evidence from Çatal Hüyük refutes this statement. A wall-painting in Level III of about 5800 B.C. shows an archer shooting at a stag and he is accompanied by what is clearly a domesticated dog.

The long controversy as to whether the ancestors of *Canis familiaris* were wolves, jackals, or a hypothetical wild dog of the pariah or dingo type seems to be settled in favour of the wolf. Wolves interbreed with domestic dogs to produce fertile offspring: their chromosome numbers are the same, whereas those of jackals are different; this is one argument in favour of wolf ancestry for the dog. Also, the 'dogs' from Natufian sites such as the Mount Carmel caves were found not to resemble the golden jackal, as originally suggested, but were almost indistinguishable from the small Arabian wolf, *Canis lupus arabs*.[29, 30] Whether in fact they were wolves or dogs is not certain, though Miss Clutton-Brock considers that the relatively wide muzzles do suggest the effects of domestication. In the aceramic levels of Jericho, which follow immediately after the Natufian at that site, the size variation shows that at least two breeds of dogs existed and this strengthens the argument for domestication in the proto-Neolithic stage. At Jarmo, although there is little in the way of osteological evidence, some of the clay figurines from the aceramic levels are surely conclusive. One short-legged little animal with a jaunty curled-up tail, fig. 13, is a charming caricature of the original Fido.

Whereas there is no certain evidence of domestic dogs in western Asia before about 6500 B.C., they have been identified at the Mesolithic site of Star Carr in Yorkshire dated by radiocarbon to 7538 ± 350 B.C. Although the margin of possible error in this date is large, there is no doubt that there were domestic dogs about 6500 B.C. in the Maglemosian of Denmark. At these sites two varieties have been distinguished, some of them so large that they must have been derived from European wolves. The identification of domestic dogs was based on the fact that the teeth are crowded and displaced, one of the usual signs of domestication.[31] It has been pointed out, however, that such abnormalities may occasionally occur in wolves.[32]

The first effect of domestication in dogs is a reduction in the size of the skull and a shortening of the jaw bones without a corresponding reduction in width, producing a relatively wide muzzle. As a result the teeth become compacted and may be much displaced. The next stage is a reduction in the size of the teeth themselves, especially the canines and carnassials.[33] The reason for all this is an unnatural diet of scraps and slops rather than good red meat which the dogs' owners would naturally keep for themselves.

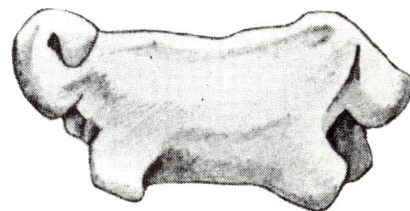

Fig. 13
Clay figurine of a dog from Jarmo.
Actual size.
After R. Braidwood, *Prehistoric Investigations in Iraqi Kurdistan*, Oriental Institute, University of Chicago, 1960.

A study of the animal skeletons associated with human burials in the Neolithic and early metal ages showed that out of 459 individual animals nearly half were dogs; cattle were the second most frequent, followed by sheep and goats.[34] There are several possible explanations of the popularity of dogs in funerary ceremonies. Least likely, perhaps, is that a favourite pet was chosen to accompany its master to the grave. On a more mundane level, dogs might have been regarded as a cheap offering in place of more valuable domestic animals. There is also a possibility that already in Neolithic times dogs were provided as guides for the dead, a belief that was widespread later on.

It seems likely, as we have seen, that dogs were domesticated independently from European and Arabian wolves. Apparently others were derived from the Indian wolf, *Canis lupus pallipes*, which seems to be the ancestor of the pariah dogs of India and other parts of Asia and also of the dingo, which was taken to Australia by people still in a hunting stage of economy. There is nothing particularly unusual in such independent centres of domestication – the llama and alpaca, for instance, were domesticated from the guanaco in South America without any contact with older centres of domestication. Probably cattle and pigs were also domesticated in several separate areas.

Just as the scavenging habits of wolves may have led them to prehistoric camps, so pigs and cattle, which have been called the 'crop-robbers', may have come into contact with man as a result of raiding his cornfields. Certainly they seem to have been domesticated later than sheep and goats; their bones are never found in the aceramic levels of Neolithic settlements but only in the later pottery levels, after the establishment of more permanent villages based mainly on agriculture.

Both the ancestors of pigs and cattle, the wild boar, *Sus scrofa*, and the aurochs, *Bos primigenius*, were distributed far more widely than the ancestors of sheep and goats. That versatile and omnivorous animal the boar was able to live in a great variety of environments – forests, swamps and open plains – throughout most of Europe, Asia and North Africa. The aurochs was also spread over the three continents, though it was more restricted to woodlands (which were then far more extensive than they are today after thousands of years of depredation by goats and woodcutters).

Pigs are particularly unco-operative over the matter of being driven, and it is difficult to imagine that they could have spread from only one centre of domestication in the time indicated by the archaeological evidence. It is far more likely that they were domesticated independently in several different areas. In Egypt, both pigs and cattle may have been domesticated from the local races of wild pigs and aurochs. The humped cattle depicted on cylinder-seals of the Mesopotamian and Indus Valley civilizations must be descended from the Indian aurochs, *Bos primigenius namadicus*. And in China, where pigs have been the most important domestic animal ever since Neolithic times, very likely they were derived from the local race of wild boar.

The surest sign of domestication in pigs is a reduction of the tooth row, particularly in the length of the third molar. Reduced third molars appear in the pigs of pottery levels at Jarmo and Jericho, though not in the aceramic levels; and at Nea Nikomedeia, where 90 per cent of the pig bones were those of yearlings, the third molar was slightly smaller than the average for wild boars.

Once early farmers needed to clear new land, they must have encouraged their pigs to grub about in the undergrowth, for apart from mechanical aids there is no more efficient machine than a pig for preparing the soil for agriculture. The pig is also a most economical animal to keep, since it can be fed on almost anything. Why, then, did so many taboos against pigs arise? It may have been because pigs are inclined to harbour tapeworms and other parasites and that pork may become dangerous for human consumption in hot climates. Zeuner suggested that because nomads could not keep pigs they despised them and showed their sense of superiority over settled pig-keepers by inventing prohibitions.[35]

The very fact that pig-keepers had to be *settled* presumably explains why domestic pigs are not found in the earliest aceramic levels. These animals could be kept only in permanent villages, thriving on agriculture and trade; they were out of the question for nomadic pastoralists or for those who depended to a large extent on hunting. But this does not explain the rather patchy distribution of pigs at later Neolithic sites. It is possible that the association of pigs with scavenging and death might have been significant and evidence for this is discussed later in connection with Çatal Hüyük. An aversion to pigs does seem to have existed from very early times in certain parts of western Asia, though not apparently to the same extent in Neolithic contexts in Europe. Among the animal skeletons associated with human burials it is significant that all the pig remains came from Europe, none at all from Asia.[36]

Whether or not religious considerations played a part in the keeping of pigs, there can be no doubt that they did so in the case of cattle. Probably more emotional factors were, and still are, attached to cattle than to any other animal and the sacrifice of bulls played a most important part in the fertility cults of nearly all ancient civilizations. Whether such reasons were significant in the domestication of cattle in the first place is a much-debated point and evidence from Çatal Hüyük does strengthen the argument in favour of these motives.

Wild ancestors of domestic sheep, goats and pigs still survive but the aurochs, unfortunately, is extinct; the last one was killed in Poland in A.D. 1627. Heinz and Lutz Heck, Directors of the Munich and Berlin Zoos, managed to 'reconstruct' the aurochs by cross-breeding from various strains of modern cattle which had certain characteristics of *Bos primigenius*. We also know its appearance very well from illustrations going right back to the Lascaux paintings. These show that the bulls were black, with a white stripe along the back and a white patch between the horns. The cows were reddish brown, with darker head and legs. The bulls stood about 6 feet at the shoulder and had immensely long horns. Sex differences were very marked both in colour and size (a fine engraving of a bull following a cow on a rock-face on the island of Levanzo, Sicily, illustrates the size difference very well).

This considerable difference in size between bulls and cows probably caused a certain amount of confusion in the past, when skulls and long bones of cow aurochses may have been wrongly described as belonging to a smaller domesticated breed. To add to the difficulties, it is almost impossible to distinguish between many parts of the skeletons of aurochs, European bison and Asiatic water-buffalo. Later on, as cattle were selected for docility and also probably were kept on short rations they became much smaller than their wild ancestors. Eventually a new breed developed, known as *Bos taurus longifrons* on account of the height of the forehead and characterized also by very short horns. Since cattle were no doubt difficult to control by farmers practising a shifting agriculture, and since bulls are persistent suitors, crosses between domestic cows and wild aurochs bulls must have occurred quite often; and so, after the *longifrons* type was well established, a *primigenius* strain of domestic cattle also emerged. From time to time such crosses may have been encouraged deliberately, for instance to provide suitable sacrificial animals for religious purposes. The *primigenius* strain still survives in Spanish fighting bulls, Hungarian steppe cattle, Highland cattle and English Park cattle (the Chillingham and Cadzow herds).

Symbols of Life and Death

It has already been mentioned that the 1960s saw a 'revolution' in our knowledge of the Neolithic and one further aspect of this new knowledge remains to be discussed. This is the tremendous progress that has been made in our understanding of Neolithic cults and religious beliefs. Much has been made of the ritual and 'magic' revealed in Upper Palaeolithic art and of the elaborate religions of Bronze Age civilizations, but very little was known about the intervening period. This apparent hiatus has now been filled in by the amazing wall-paintings and reliefs of Çatal Hüyük. If ever there was a revolution in our knowledge of the Neolithic, this is it.

For one thing, Çatal Hüyük is by far the largest Neolithic settlement known. The mound (*hüyük* is Turkish for 'mound') covers 32 acres, making it nearly four times as big as the earliest town at Jericho. Çatal Hüyük was a flourishing town by 6500 B.C. and nobody knows how long before that. By the end of the fourth season of excavations in 1965, Mr James Mellaart had probed 1,000 years of continuous settlement and was nowhere near the beginning. This 1,000 years is particularly important as it covers what had previously been a blank in Anatolian prehistory. The only excavated site extending back to the Neolithic was Mersin, on the southern coast of Anatolia, where the basal layer dates from about 5900 B.C. Then in 1957 Mellaart began to dig at Hacilar, west of Çatal Hüyük on the Anatolian Plateau. Here an aceramic, Neolithic was separated by a gap of many centuries from a sophisticated Late Neolithic lasting from 5700 to 5400 B.C. His search for a site to cover that gap led him to Çatal Hüyük, where he found all he had hoped for and far more.

The Neolithic inhabitants of Çatal Hüyük grew an astonishing variety of crops, but the town's wealth was above all founded on trade. The people travelled far and wide, to the mountains and to the shores of the Mediterranean, to obtain obsidian and semi-precious stones, leopard skins and sea-shells, even coal and copper. Their craftsmen manufactured superb weapons and ornaments; there were expert carpenters and weavers; and artists produced extraordinary wall-paintings and sculpture which have given us unique details of the religious rites of these people. In the forty or so shrines uncovered by 1965, the 'fertility goddess' is depicted over and over again. Often she is shown in the attitude of giving birth, associated with bulls, rams and human breasts. Sometimes she is the goddess of death, represented by scavengers such as vultures and wild boars. In her portrayals with leopards her dominance over animals is shown. But most fascinating of all, particularly in connection with its subsequent development, is the bull symbolism at Çatal Hüyük which is unique for this period. It is strange that no parallels for such cults have been found at other Early Neolithic sites; almost the only evidence of religious beliefs is found in figurines and occasionally in collections of human skulls (particularly at Jericho, where they are plastered).

An obvious symbol of power and virility, the bull must always have inspired feelings of awe and terror. It was inevitable that such an animal should come to be associated with life and fertility and in most of the ancient civilizations bull-gods were responsible for the procreation of human beings, animals and crops. Sometimes they were also linked with the sun or the moon, or with thunder and rain upon which the growth of crops depended. Temples were built for them; they were constantly depicted in stone and metal-work, and they were commemorated in famous myths like the Gilgamesh Epic and the Rig-Veda. The Egyptian Apis, the Indian Shiva, the Phoenician Baal, the Cretan Minotaur, Zeus abducting Europa, the bull-sacrifices of Mithraism – the examples are endless. The continuity of the bull cult from Bronze Age times right up to the ritual killing of the bull in modern Spain is obvious enough. What had not been obvious before the discovery of Çatal Hüyük was its ancestry.

Even the gap between the Magdalenian cave-paintings and the wall-paintings and plaster models of Neolithic Çatal Hüyük has narrowed. In 1961 a superb engraving of a bull nearly 4 feet long was discovered on a fallen rock in the shelter of del Romita in Calabria. Owing to the similarity of style with the engravings on the island of Levanzo (page 31) where a radiocarbon date of about 10,000 B.C. was obtained, this bull is also thought to date from the Epipalaeolithic.[37] Both in time and in geographical locality, these engravings lie between Lascaux and Çatal Hüyük. But there are other links in Anatolia itself. Rock-paintings and engravings of bulls and other animals at Beldibi, in the Antalya region of southern Anatolia, are attributed to a proto-Neolithic people with a culture similar to the Natufian of Palestine.[38] These new finds, as well as Çatal Hüyük itself, show both that Upper Palaeolithic traditions were not entirely lost and that the art of the Bronze Age had roots in the Neolithic. It would indeed be strange if this were not so, but only recently has it been possible to prove it.

As Mellaart points out, the name given to the Taurus Mountains is surely no coincidence.[39] The huge painted bulls of Çatal Hüyük are always on the north walls of the shrines, facing these mountains. The fertility goddess, modelled in plaster, appears on the west walls often in an attitude of giving birth and generally accompanied by bulls' heads. These appear either beside her or between her upraised legs. Sometimes there is a combination of a bull's horn and a modelled woman's breast. We are reminded of Professor A. Leroi-Gourhan's interpretations of the male and female symbolism in Upper Palaeolithic art: he found that the bison and the aurochs are nearly always associated with feminine signs.[40]

In the unfortunately named 'Venuses' of the Upper Palaeolithic, the emphasis was on breasts, stomach and thighs. At Çatal Hüyük we find a new feature: attention is focused on the navel, an obvious symbol of the continuity of life. In one shrine (E VI, 8) a plaster goddess nearly 4 feet high is shown giving birth to a huge bull's head; the only part of her which is carefully modelled is the navel. Facing her, on the east wall, were three bulls' heads above two rows of human breasts. The bulls' heads were originally painted with red muzzles and schematized hand impressions on the nose. Other bulls' heads (in shrine E VI, 7) also bore paintings of hands and it seems likely that the participants in the ceremonies touched the animals' faces with hands smeared in red ochre.

Built as one structure with this shrine was another (E VI, 14) in which was a huge plaster relief of twin goddesses with two heads and bodies but only one pair of arms and legs. Protruding from the lower part of the body of one of the 'twins' was a magnificent bulls' head, with muzzle, ears and a ring round the horns painted in red. A smaller bull's head had been modelled on its brow.

In one case (E VI, 10) the goddess gives birth to a ram's head, though as usual she is also accompanied by three bulls' heads. Originally this composition must have been 10 feet high.

As well as the innumerable plaster heads of bulls, there are many brick pillars incorporating the horn cores of aurochses (in a single case, a pillar contained the horn cores of rams rather than bulls). From the position of the pillars they seem to protect the platform which was used as a bed and beneath which the dead were buried. Their purpose was presumably to ward off evil spirits and bulls thus seemed to fill the role of protectors as well as being symbols of fertility and the continuity of life.[41]

In the earlier levels the bulls' horns, like their heads, are modelled in plaster. But from the time of Level VI A onwards, actual horns were usually incorporated. The horns themselves have perished and only the horn cores remain. In modern cattle the cores are about half the length of the horns. In one shrine at Çatal Hüyük the horn cores were about 3 feet long, indicating that in life this aurochs must have had horns 6 feet in length; it must have been specially selected for ritual purposes on account of its tremendous horns. Set in a plastered bench in another shrine were the horn cores of six bulls, with a seventh placed in a projection at the end of the bench (fig. 14). Mellaart does not consider that these 'benches' were altars, since he found no sign of sacrifice.

There is no need to stress the significance of bulls' horns, which were regarded as an outward sign of inner power and fertility. 'Horns of consecration', 'horns of plenty', horned head-dresses and so on were common in most early civilizations. One of the earliest representations of a woman associated with a horn (in this case a bison's horn) is the Upper Palaeolithic 'Venus' of Laussel. Apart from Çatal Hüyük, this

Fig. 14
A bench in shrine A VI, I, at Çatal Hüyük, incorporating the horn cores of seven bulls and brick pillars with horn cores.
After J. Mellaart, *Civilizations of the Near East*, Thames and Hudson, London, 1965.

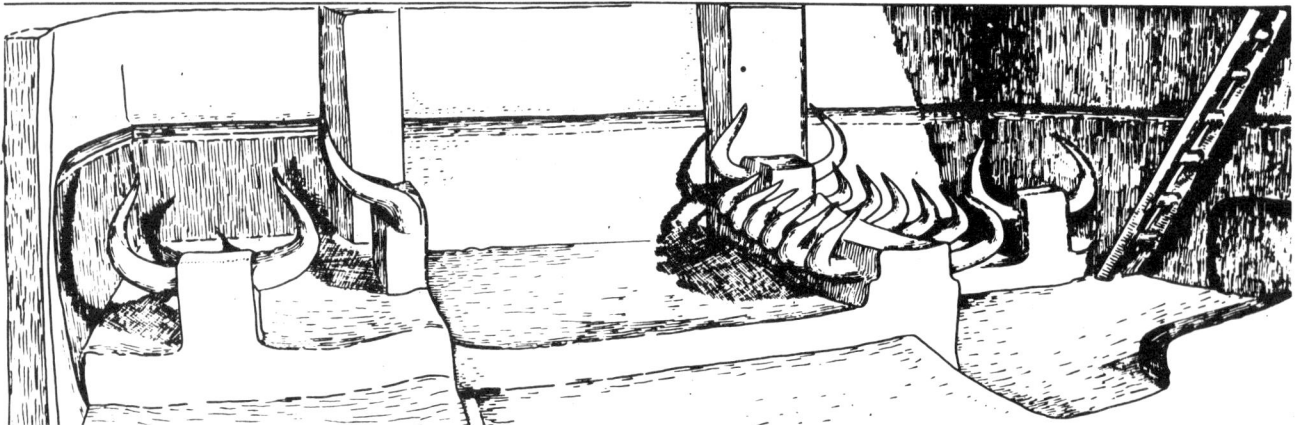

theme is rare in Neolithic contexts, though in the Late Neolithic of Hacilar the handle of a bone tool was carved in the form of a human figure wearing a horned head-dress and at Yümük Tepe near Mersin a Neolithic burial was accompanied by a horn-shaped emblem made of clay.[42]

It has been suggested that touching the bulls' horns, in order to obtain some of their power, was an important part of the famous bull-vaulting sports of Minoan Crete. Interesting parallels have been discovered recently in some of the wall-paintings of Çatal Hüyük. There is no doubt about the roots of some of these paintings in the Upper Palaeolithic. In the 'hunting shrine' of Level V, discovered in 1965, human figures are dressed in leopard skins and (probably) cattle hides, some wearing feathered tails; the animals are painted in a flat wash with contours, hoofs and other details added in black, in almost exactly the same style as that of many of the Magdalenian paintings (fig. 15). The animals include bulls, boars, bears and stags, onagers with black manes, and a superb pair of black cranes. A constantly recurring theme

Fig. 15
A red bull surrounded by a crowd of hunters. From Level V, Çatal Hüyük. After J. Mellaart, *The Illustrated London News*, June 1966.

35

shows men pulling or touching the animals' tongue or tail. Mellaart suggests that this is not a form of 'bear-baiting' but that the scenes represent man's control over animals: as he put it, 'if you pull a bull's tongue he will eat out of your hand'.[43] Even more interesting is the figure of a man jumping on the back of an enormous bull 6 feet long; part of his loin-cloth is caught on the bull's horns. This seems to be a direct forerunner of the bull-vaulting scenes of Minoan Crete.

There is another curious feature in this shrine. In general at Çatal Hüyük the men were buried under the corner platform and the women and children beneath the larger central platform. But in this 'hunting shrine', which one would have thought would be particularly dedicated to men, there were no male burials at all. Seventeen women were buried in this shrine (and no children); in the wall-paintings, on the other hand, there were about seventy male figures, but only three women.

One of the most prized animals hunted by the inhabitants of Çatal Hüyük was evidently the leopard. Not only was its skin worn – as shown in the wall-paintings – but also, as the most dangerous animal encountered it was associated with the goddess in her role of 'mistress of animals'. The importance attached to leopards may be gauged by the fact that one pair of these animals, modelled in clay mixed with straw (in shrine VI B, 44) had been painted over at least forty times, presumably each year at special ceremonies (fig. 16). As Mellaart observed, 'at Çatal Hüyük the leopard *always* changes its spots'. On peeling off the paint layer by layer, it was found that the later animals were yellow, with black spots and pink claws, mouth and tip of the tail, but earlier on they had been white, with black and white rosettes and red claws. One of the pair is rather stouter and is thought to be a female. A black stone statuette of a woman, coated with carbonized grain, lay on a platform in front of the she-leopard and other figurines, including one of a bearded man riding a bull, lay in a pile in the middle of the room.

Directly below the Level VI shrine just described lay another 'leopard shrine', in Level VII, showing that the same cult persisted for some time. It also contained a pair of leopards, but in this case the later layers were decorated with 'St Andrew's crosses' while the earlier layers had rosettes with dotted outlines. Yet another pair of leopards was discovered in 1965, in Level X; they are shown with their tails up as though fighting and the whole composition is 6 feet long. In the next building are paintings which seem to represent nets, which perhaps were used for catching leopards? If it seems unlikely that such powerful beasts could be caught in this way, we should remember the Minoan gold cup from Vapheio in Greece which shows bulls caught in nets. A painting in Level III at Çatal Hüyük shows men disguised as leopards; they are dancing, perhaps to ensure success in a forthcoming leopard-hunt?

Several figurines from Çatal Hüyük show men and women with leopards. A youth riding on a leopard, carved in limestone, originally formed a group with two women. Another limestone figurine shows a mature woman standing behind a leopard and in another case a girl wearing a leopard-skin scarf stands behind a leopard. In each case the spots were drilled into the limestone. One of the most delightful of the statuettes shows a plump woman wearing a leopard-skin top and a short fringed skirt, which looks rather like a woollen vest which has shrunk in the wash. Most imposing of all is the clay figure of a woman giving

36

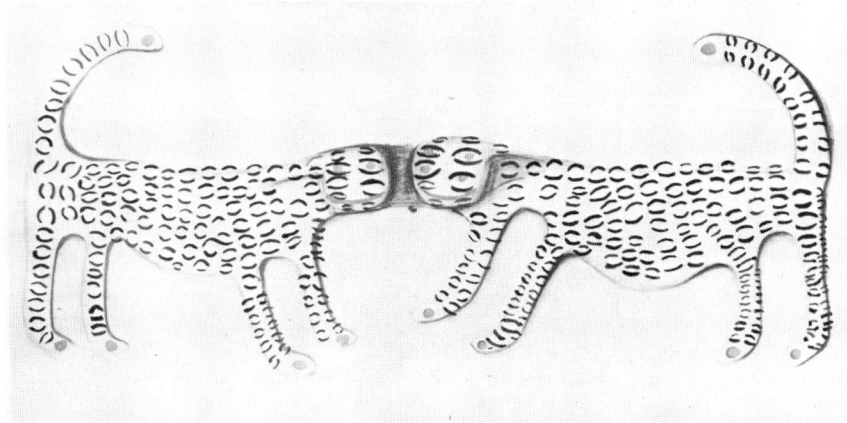

Fig. 16
Two leopards in relief from shrine E VII
44 at Çatal Hüyük.
After J. Mellaart, *The Illustrated London
News*, June 1966.

37

birth to a child; she is seated on a throne with felines on either side – no spots are indicated and it is possible that these animals are lions rather than leopards (pl. 2 (colour)). The animals' tails curve up the woman's back and over her shoulders. This figurine was found in a grain-bin and probably was placed there to increase the fertility of the crops.

Female figurines associated with leopards were also found at Hacilar in Level VI (c. 5550 B.C., about a thousand years later than those of Çatal Hüyük). From three houses came a collection of about forty magnificently modelled clay statuettes, all representing the 'fertility goddess' at different ages, sometimes as a young girl, sometimes as a mature woman. In one case she is seated on a throne in the form of a leopard whose tail curves up her back; another seated figure has two animal tails on her back but the throne is missing.[44]

From symbols of life and fertility we turn now to symbols of death. At Çatal Hüyük these are mostly confined to the east walls of the shrines, and it was below these walls that the dead were buried. The west walls on the other hand, were concerned with birth. The huge plaster goddess giving birth to a bull's head on the west wall of shrine E VI, 8 has already been described; on the opposite wall there were three more bulls' heads and thirteen modelled breasts. These, at first sight, seem to be symbols of life rather than death; but on peeling the plaster off the breasts it was found that each contained the lower jaw of a wild boar. This theme of 'death within life' is repeated in other shrines. In shrine VII, 21, a combination of horn and breast above a painted ram's head had been modelled round the lower jaw of a huge boar. A variation appears in shrine VII, 35, where two breasts placed vertically above a ram's head contained the skull of a fox and a weasel; these animals, like wild pigs, are scavengers and hence, presumably, chosen to represent death.

At Çatal Hüyük pigs do not seem to have been eaten, for their bones were not found among the food debris. It is possible that the association of these animals with death may have a very early origin. One of the Neanderthalers at Mount Carmel, the tall male known as Skhul V, was buried with the lower jaw of a very large boar. Miss Garrod wrote: 'There can be no doubt, from its position, and from the fact that the left forearm rests upon the broken, hinder ends of the mandible, that its inclusion in the grave was deliberate. Its presence is a subject for speculation rather than explanation.'[45] Here, perhaps, at Çatal Hüyük, is the explanation. From the position of the boars' jaws inside human breasts there can be no other possible interpretation than that they had magical or religious significance. The strong conservatism often attached to such beliefs makes it not at all impossible to imagine that the same symbols should have been used for at least 30,000 years.

Inside a pair of breasts in shrine E VI, 10, other strange objects appear. From apertures in place of the nipples protruded two birds' beaks and on opening the breasts, each was found to contain the skull of a griffin-vulture (*Gyps fulvus*, the largest vulture found in Anatolia) A collection of human bones was scattered in a hole below the platform in front of the breasts; this is unusual, for the burials below the platforms in the Çatal Hüyük shrines were generally tidy and complete.

The association of vultures with death is obvious and these birds are depicted in a spectacular series of wall-paintings. In shrine VII, 21, vultures *with human legs* hover over a headless corpse. Two human skulls

Plate 2
Figurine flanked by two felines from Çatal Hüyük.
After J. Mellaart, *Anatolian Studies*, XIII, 1963.

lay on the edge of the platform below this scene and another had been placed in front of a niche. On the west wall of the same shrine was a bull's head with vast horns and below it lay yet another human skull, with the imprint of a basket in which it must have been placed (fig. 17).

Even more impressive are the vulture paintings in shrine VII, 8, which were covered with at least 100 layers of plaster, 4 centimetres thick. The paintings stretch over the whole of the east wall, overlapping on to parts of the north and south walls. Seven vultures are swooping on six headless human corpses and in this case the human skeletons buried below these paintings were intact, with no heads missing. Mellaart suggests that the absence of heads in the paintings was a convention to indicate the dead, since in general the burial customs do not include removal of the head.

The birds with human legs suggest priests in disguise for the performance of burial rites. It seems that the flesh was removed from the corpses before they were given secondary burial under the sleeping-platforms. Probably the dead were first laid out in mortuaries outside the settlement and it may be that they were there picked clean by vultures. But if that was so, why, in another painting (in Level VIII), is a man with a sling apparently protecting a headless corpse from the attacks of two vultures?

Before leaving Çatal Hüyük and its extraordinary animal symbolism,

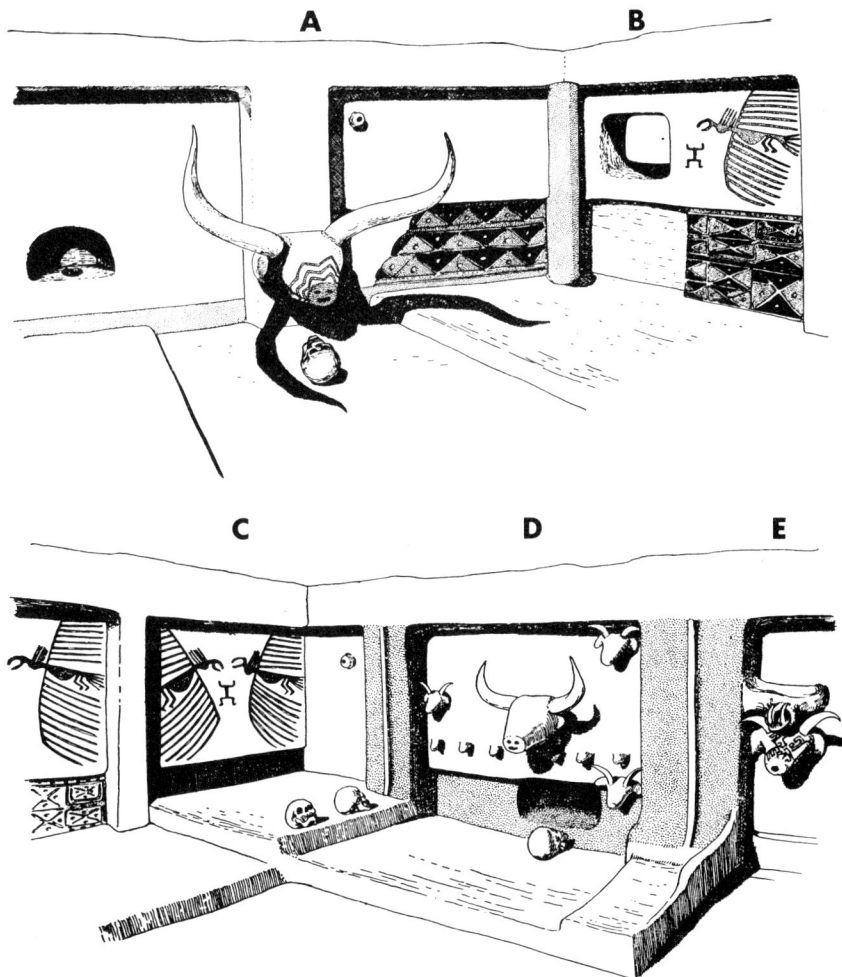

Fig. 17
Shrine VII, 21 at Çatal Hüyük:
A (west wall)—bull's head above human skull and remains of basket. Textile pattern, with breast above. Semi-circular niche to left, for libations?
B (part of north wall)—vulture with human legs hovering over headless corpse.
C (part of north wall)—two human skulls on edge of platform.
D (east wall)—bull's head above 6 breasts and accompanied by 3 rams. Niche below and human skull.
E (east wall)—ram's head with meander patterns in red, supporting horn and breast containing boar's jaw.
After J. Mellaart, *Anatolian Studies*, XIV, 1964.

one other strange occurrence must be mentioned. A shrine in Level X may have been built to commemorate an important woman whose body, covered with red ochre, was buried under the main platform. She had a mace, bone rings and necklaces of deers' teeth, detalium shells and other materials. Buried with her were the skulls, jaws and leg bones of several mice. It would be fascinating to know the reason for these unusual 'grave goods'.

There are, of course, many things about man's relationship with animals in ancient times that we can never hope to know or understand.

Fig. 18
Bear from Samus, Siberia. Height. 15 cm.
After Profs. Okladnikov and Gryasnov,
Antiquity, XXXVII, 1963.

We can make guesses about hunting magic, fertility cults, burial rites and so on, and sometimes we may be right. But we should not stretch the imagination too far and in some cases there may be quite prosaic explanations. The woman with the mice, for instance, might have had a nickname meaning 'mouse'; she might have kept pet mice, which her family buried with her; or she might even have enjoyed eating mice and so was provided with her favourite dinner.

It is possible that prehistoric people portrayed certain animals for no other reason than that they were fond of them, or were amused by them. This may have applied, for instance, in the case of clay figurines made simply as children's toys. Usually, however, when we probe deeply we find that other explanations suggest themselves. In a Neo-lithic grave at Samus in Siberia, for instance, there was a charming 'teddy bear' (fig. 18), which to our eyes looks like a toy. But when we remember the bear cults of circumpolar peoples and of the Ainu today, which include the rearing of a bear cub for ritual sacrifice, it is more likely that the Samus figurine had some deeper significance. At Nea Nikomedeia, although there were clay figurines of sheep, goats and other animals, the only ones carved in stone were some very fine frogs. Made in speckled green and blue serpentine, they look most naturalistic (fig. 19). One had a perforation, suggesting that it was worn as an amulet.[46] The site lies at the edge of what was evidently a marshy lake in Neolithic times and no doubt it was full of frogs. We might think that the villagers portrayed these creatures merely because they were amused by their bizarre appearance and by their incessant croaking were it not for the fact that stone frogs from Predynastic contexts in Egypt seem to have magical or religious significance.

Perhaps the most interesting fact we have learned from newly dis-covered Neolithic sites is that these people were far more sophisticated than we had suspected. These discoveries, particularly Çatal Hüyük, show the long continuity of artistic traditions and of cults and beliefs They emphasize man's preoccupation with fertility and the importance of his relationship with animals, above all with cattle.

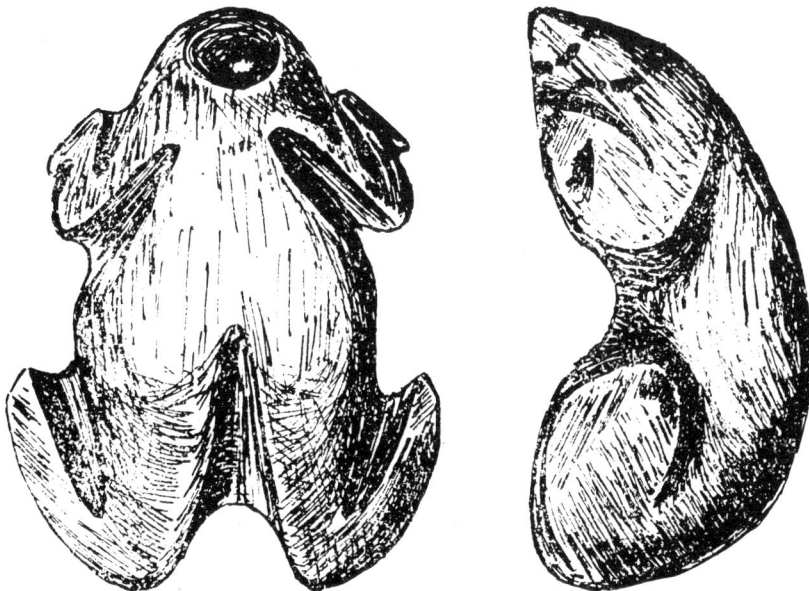

Fig. 19
Frog figurine, Nea Nicomedeia. $\frac{2}{3}$ natural size.
After R. J. Rodden, *Antiquity*, xxxviii, 1964.

3
ANIMALS IN MESOPOTAMIA

J. M. AYNARD

Mesopotamia, the Land of the Two Rivers, a vast plain watered by the Tigris and the Euphrates, stretches from the mountains of Armenia in the north to the Persian Gulf in the south, and is bordered on the east by the Iranian Plateau and on the west by Syria and Palestine, lands of the Mediterranean Littoral. Although the north of Mesopotamia is rather mountainous and its climate is somewhat severe, the south, that is the Delta of the Two Rivers, is warm and marshy. Sumerians and Semites (Assyrians and Babylonians) successively peopled the region, and their civilizations can be traced from their origins in the fourth millennium B.C. until the fall of Babylon in 539 B.C. The evidence comes from excavations carried out since the mid nineteenth century by archaeologists from many countries.

The names of the sites that have been brought to light are well known – in the north there is Nineveh, Kalah, Dur-Sharrukin and Assur, the capitals of the Assyrian rulers. In the central area, Babylon, with Mari to the north-west; in the south Ur, Eridu, Nippur, Lagash – the ancient cities of the Sumerians. On the slopes of the Iranian Plateau is Susa. These are but a few of the ancient cities whose palaces, temples, houses and tombs have emerged from the earth.

Our knowledge of the fauna of ancient Mesopotamia comes from a variety of sources. First of all, of course, there is the existing fauna, for most of the species found in these regions today were already there in remote times. Then there are the animal bones found during excavations. These bones are often in a very bad state of preservation, so that it is often difficult to identify them. The two sources that we shall concentrate on in this inquiry are the cuneiform texts and the sculptured monuments: documents in which the Mesopotamians themselves give us information about the animals of their country.

The variety of cuneiform texts, written in Sumerian or in Akkadian on clay tablets, is astonishing. There are religious, historical, magical, oracular, medical, legal and economic writings, there are letters and books of wisdom, proverbs and fables. In fact, a whole and rich literature has come out of the earth. Numerous texts give us valuable information about animals. Thus, for instance, the temple registers of the southern cities, particularly in Sumerian times, contain detailed accounts concerning the animals entering and leaving the farms of the vast temple domains. These accounts throw light on the composition of the livestock. A legal code gives us information about the theft of cattle and other beasts. A letter issued by a royal chancellery mentions the purchase of horses and mules for the king's stables. An oracular text tells us of the animals a man might see in his house or in the street. One of the most valuable sources for knowledge of the fauna are the word-lists, similar to dictionaries in which different chapters distinguish particular groups of animals or objects with all their different varieties. There are sections on snakes, birds, fish, sheep, goats, cattle, etc.[1] However, it must be admitted that in many cases we do not know exactly what species is meant by the term employed by the ancient scribes.

Additional information may be culled from the monuments with figures – bas-reliefs, statues, terracotta figurines and from the carved flat or cylindrical seals.* These carved stones are very numerous, often magnificent and of an exceptionally high artistic quality. The Mesopotamians were remarkable animal-artists. Whereas the representations of the human form are often clumsy, stiff and lifeless, the animals are splendid in their vitality, the accuracy with which attitudes and play of muscles are reproduced denote close observation as well as great artistry. It is rare that a monument, whether great or small, early or late, does not have some representation of animals. Often, when the animal forms serve as decorative motifs, they can be extremely schematic and difficult to recognize, notably on the very early pottery where a bull may be reduced to a bucranium and an ibex to the spiral of his great horns. The same is true when an animal forms part of a scene, either actively as, for instance, in hunting or pastoral compositions, or as a divine symbol on, for example, the *kudurrus* – the boundary-markers set up in the Kassite epoch at the end of the second millennium B.C.

As in the case of the written documents, the animal representations, particularly as regards small objects such as the cylinders, may present problems and precise identification of the animal is sometimes difficult or even impossible. Thus, fish, birds or snakes are often schematic in the extreme as also the innumerable horned beasts which are so often represented.

In a work published in 1939, an excellent archaeologist, Mrs Douglas van Buren, gave an inventory of all the species of animals represented on Mesopotamian monuments.[2] This list is still valid although, of course, new monuments have been discovered since the book appeared. The summary comprises forty-eight sections. First of all come the predatory beasts – lion, panther, wild cat, cheetah, wolf and jackal. After that there are the dog, fox, polecat, marten, bear, monkey, bat, hedgehog and porcupine, jerboa, mouse and hare. Among the equines we have horses, asses and mules followed by camels and dromedaries. Then we have cervines – fallow-deer, stag, roe-deer; the caprines – antelope, gazelle, oryx, ibex, wild goat, goat and he-goat; the ovids and the bovids – *Bos primigenius*, buffalo, zebu, bison. Both pig and wild boar are often represented. Whereas elephants, rhinoceroses as well as seals, cachalots and dolphins are rare and indeed, as regards the last three, identification is rather doubtful. Birds are numerous: eagle, vulture,

* The seals are engraved on hard stones and are rolled out on wet clay tablets.

falcon, crow, rook, starling, black partridge, owl, swallow, ostrich, dove, poultry, small birds, crane, heron, swan, goose, duck. Lastly, after the crocodile, the lizard, serpent, frog and tortoise, we pass on to fish, then to arthropods – flies, the *Orthoptera*, scorpions, spiders, centipedes and cockroaches.

This detailed list shows the wide range of the fauna represented on the Mesopotamian monuments. However, our aim is not to offer an exhaustive study, but rather to concentrate on certain of these animals, first the wild beasts and then the domestic ones. After that we will show briefly the role they played in the life of the inhabitants of the Valley of the Two Rivers.

Wild Animals. The Hunt

Hunting was certainly one of the earliest activities of the Mesopotamian people. They hunted for food, for clothing and also to protect themselves from beasts of prey that lived on the steppes and in the thickets bordering the river banks. Hunting scenes are represented in all epochs. It would appear that the earliest one known is painted on the sides of a jar from the Tepe Gawra site in northern Mesopotamia. It dates from the 'Ubaid period (mid fourth millennium B.C.). It has a very schematic representation of mountains enclosing a valley through which a river winds. There is a small human figure threatening, with an unidentifiable weapon, a large animal with long horns that is on the far side of the river and is pursued by a small animal, probably a dog.

More explicit, and of about the same date, is the hunter figured on the bottom of a bowl from Susa. There appears to be a tuft of feathers on his head, or is it a long lock of hair? He is bending his bow and aiming at a caprine. Circles ornamented with a chequered pattern probably represent water-holes round which the scene is being enacted.

Already at the end of the fifth millennium B.C. animals are represented on painted Samarra ware. Here the animals are shown alone with no hunters. But these wild, swift-footed but by no means ferocious beasts were certainly frequently hunted by all and sundry, whereas the lion was for the sport of kings. Indeed, goats' meat provided sustenance, their fur was warm and their skins could be used to make household utensils and vessels.

Although we can easily distinguish the caprine animals from some of the deer family and especially from the stag, characterized by the antlers whose tines are carefully indicated, it is often very difficult to identify the precise caprine species. Attempts have been made to distinguish between the ibex, living in high mountains, among rocks and snow, and the wild goat, which readily goes down into the thickets of the plain and is, perhaps, the ancestor of the domestic goat. The two animals, ibex and wild goat, are, however, distinguished above all by the shape and the protuberances of their horns, which in the case of the ibex are closer together and more prominent. But very often the artist does not show them, or at least not in a sufficiently exact fashion, and it is preferable in many cases to use the general term 'caprine'. It is also significant that some of the animals depicted by the Sumerians, who inhabited the plains of Lower Mesopotamia, are mountain animals –

such as the ibex, wolf, bison – which suggests we should be very cautious in our identifications, since it is possible that the artists sometimes represented animals they had never seen, but which they knew of either from descriptions or from imported representations. The same applies to some exotic animals which we shall mention later on.

Antelopes and gazelles – which are distinguished from the caprines by the absence of a beard and also by their long horns of varied and graceful shapes – are often depicted on the cylinders and shown bounding along one behind the other (fig. 20). The wild sheep, the moufflon with curved horns, were also much favoured by the proto-historic Mesopotamian artists, who derived decorative motifs from them. André Parrot describes how this was done: 'These animals were to provide them with an ideal repertoire. Among these animals those whose long horns helped to convey an impression of movement were particularly favoured. Perhaps, originally, the aim was to show animals coming to drink at a pool. But the only part shown of the animal is the body which is retained and this was compressed into the form of a triangle. Or the animals may take the form of circles jostling round a chequered lozenge while the head, tail and horns have been suppressed and all that remains is a Maltese cross with, in the background, four undulating segments – reminiscent of what was originally an animal representation. From naturalism, by way of schematization a return was made to geometry, to an abstraction, but to an abstraction which possesses its own language if one knows the stages by which it was arrived at.'[3]

The same process of evolution can be found at Susa where the long horns of caprine animals provided the potter with a motif he plays with in ornamenting the sides of his vases and the bottom of his cups (fig. 21).

In addition to these small and graceful animals, the various wild cattle provided a more formidable quarry. The *Bos primigenius*, the probable ancestor of our domestic cattle, is the most often represented from the earliest times onwards. Depictions of the buffalo with long, scimitar-like horns are more or less limited to the period of the Agade

Fig. 20
Medio-Assyrian cylinder seal impression showing hunting scene in mountainous area. Second half of second millennium B.C. Museum of Fine Arts, Boston.

45

Fig. 21
Bowl from Susa. Mid-fourth millennium B.C.
Louvre Museum.

Fig. 22
Gilgamesh-Agade cylinder seal impression.
Second half of third millennium B.C.
Louvre Museum.

46

dynasty (second half of the third millennium B.C.) and it is generally associated with the hero known as Gilgamesh, or with another hunter, perhaps his friend Enkidu, who master the beast by crushing it with their arms (fig. 22). The Gilgamesh Epic recounts this struggle. The goddess Ishtar, offended by the hero, prayed her father Anu, the king of the gods, to create a bull which she could take down to earth to avenge herself. 'When it arrived in the land of Uruk, it changed the pasture-land into a desert. It went down to the river and in seven gulps drained it dry. One hundred men of Uruk fell therein. Enkidu seized the bull by its horns. The bull shot out slaver in front and from the root of its tail scattered its excrement.' The two friends then put their heads together and devised a way of capturing the beast. 'Having chased it away, Enkidu then caught up with the bull and seizing it by the tail held it firmly with his two hands. Then Gilgamesh, like a gladiator, courageous and nimble, faced it, and struck it with his sword between the shoulder-blade and horns. When they had killed the bull they tore out its heart and placed it before the Sun.'[4] This scene is thus in part a bull-fight and in part a hunt.

There are also some representations of the humped bull (zebu), especially on seals from the Indus Valley, while the bison with its thick shock of hair and powerful forequarters is very clearly indicated on a stone bowl in the British Museum (fig. 23).

The chief enemy seems to have been the lion which attacked man himself as readily as it did his flocks and herds. Assurbanipal, King of Assyria (668–627 B.C.), tells how when the rains had caused the forest and reed-brakes to flourish, the lions began to swarm: 'They became fierce and terrible through their devouring of herds, flocks and people. With their roaring the hills resound, the beasts of the plain are terrified. They keep bringing down the cattle of the plain, they [keep] shedding the blood of men. As if the plague had broken loose, there were heaped up the corpses of dead men, cattle and sheep. . . . The villages are in mourning day and night. Of the deeds of the lions they told me. In the course of my march . . . their lairs (literally nests) I broke up. . . .'[5]

Lions are represented at all epochs and on all sorts of objects from amulets and seals in the form of recumbent lions (Uruk culture, end of the fourth millennium B.C.) to the monumental sculptures in Assyrian palaces (first half of the first millennium B.C.). Often they are portrayed leaping on to another animal – bull or deer – clinging to their hind quarters and devouring them. This is a very common motif that occurs as late as the Achaemenian period when lions were used to ornament the staircases of the palace in Persepolis. We can also see lions attacking men, as, for instance, on a very beautiful ivory from Kalah where a lion is shown savaging the victim it has overwhelmed. But the lion's ferocity could also make it a suitable guardian. The gates of certain temples (Lagash, Al 'Ubaid, Mari) were protected by statues of roaring lions.

Lion-hunting is represented from the beginning of the third millennium B.C. There is a basalt stele found in the town of Uruk that shows in the upper register a human figure – probably that of a king – armed with a hunting-spear which he is thrusting into the throat of the animal. Lower down the same personage is represented but this time shooting arrows into several beasts already pierced with arrows. On cylinders of the Agade period we can also see heroes fighting lions. But the finest lion-hunts – and the lion was *par excellence* the royal quarry – are figured on the bas-reliefs which adorned Assyrian palace walls, and especially

those of Assurnasirpal at Kalah and of Assurbanipal at Nineveh. These are among the finest works of art to have been discovered in Mesopotamia. Assurbanipal, standing in his chariot with his bow bent, is making a massacre of the lions and lionesses that are shown leaping on to the royal chariot or lying on the ground riddled with arrows (fig. 24). Attention has often been drawn to the anatomical accuracy of the representations, the best example of which is the wounded lioness struck by an arrow in the spinal cord. Though her hind quarters are paralysed the beast nevertheless rises on her front legs to face the enemy. Other bas-reliefs show servants carrying off dead lions and depict the King pouring a libation on to the pile of his victims. On the stone slabs inscriptions comment on the pictures: 'In an open space in the plain, fierce lions, dreadful children of the mountains came out. They surrounded the chariot, my royal vehicle. At the command of Assur and Ishtar . . . I shattered the might of those lions.' On a bas-relief on which the King is shown seizing a lion by the ear and piercing it through with his lance: 'In my might, on foot I seized a fierce lion of the plain by his ear. With the aid of Assur and Ishtar, lady of battle, I pierced his body with my lance.' Elsewhere the King seizes the animal by its tail and it rears on its hind legs and turns, roaring, to face its royal adversary.

In the parks of Assyrian palaces were menageries which the people might visit and where lions were bred for the royal chase. In the texts dealing with economic matters there are accounts relating to the arrival and departure of merchandise to and from the palace storerooms and mention is made of deliveries of sheep 'for the lion cubs'. An entertaining story of a lion's capture is recounted in a letter addressed to the King of Mari by one of his servants.[6] 'I have written to my Lord in these terms "a lion was caught in the barn of a house at Akkakâ. If this lion should remain in the barn until my Lord arrives, let my Lord write to me; or if I should bring it to my Lord, let my Lord write to me."' But the King did not reply to the letter, so the letter continued: 'The lion has been five days in the barn and although I threw it a dog and a pig, it will not eat. I said to myself "Let us hope it does not waste away." I was afraid. I made this lion get into a wooden cage and I have placed it on a boat and I am bringing it to my Lord.'

There is an Assyrian bas-relief showing a roaring lion coming out of a big cage whose flap-door is being manœuvred by a keeper prudently perched on the roof. On another bas-relief we can read: '. . . they let a fierce lion of the plain out of his cage and I on foot, with my spear-shaft . . . but did not end his life . . . I stabbed him later with my iron girdle dagger and he died.'

Such single combats between men and wild beasts, which are depicted on cylinders dating as far back as the Agade period (fig. 22), are somewhat reminiscent of the gladiatorial games in the Roman arenas, although one has to make allowance for the hyperbole so common in Assyrian texts.

Though lion-hunting scenes were a favourite motif of the neo-Assyrian artists, they also depicted wild bull and horse (or ass) hunts with the same skill and accuracy. One finds again, in the horse- or ass-hunting scenes, animals pierced by an arrow and attacked by a dog. a huge mastiff specially trained for such sport, while another horse turns round towards a young colt also being closely followed by the dogs (fig. 25). With regard to wild asses we may mention that one of the curses pronounced against anyone who violated the clauses of a *kudurru*

Fig. 23
Stone bowl with bison.
British Museum.

Fig. 24
Lion hunting scene on a bas-relief from the palace of Assurbanipal at Nineveh. 669–631 ? B.C.
British Museum.

49

is this: 'May the god Sin . . . cover his body as with leprosy, and may he then, like a wild ass of the plain, roam about outside the walls.' This gives us some idea of the herds of wild onagers and equine animals which must have roamed the plains in the neighbourhood of the towns.

The wild boar was represented from the earliest time onwards. In one Assyrian bas-relief a hare and a gazelle are being carried by servants. The bear, a denizen of the mountains, is not often represented but one may be seen on an attractive Mid-Assyrian cylinder, perhaps at the entrance to a cavern, along with other wild animals which are being pursued by hunters (fig. 20). Representations of panthers are very rare (they can easily be recognized by their spotted coats), but a panther may be seen on a large crater from Tepe Sialk (northern Iran) dating from the fourth millennium B.C.

Birds were shot with bows and arrows but also snared in nets, especially certain water-fowl (wild geese, ducks, cranes and herons). The ostrich, which is now extinct in Mesopotamia, lived formerly on the banks of the Euphrates. The great bird is represented, always with much elegance and accuracy, on several monuments and also on the embroideries which, in the bas-reliefs, adorn the sumptuous robes of Assyrian kings. Ostrich eggs were much in demand, treasured as art-objects and often ornamented with precious motifs such as those found in the Royal Tombs of Ur. Ostrich egg-shells were also magical material and they are an ingredient in the concoctions prescribed in the books of ritual.

Fig. 25
Wild horse hunting scene from the palace of Assurbanipal, King of Assyria, at Nineveh. 669–631 ? B.C.
British Museum.

To close this section on wild animals we cannot do better than to listen to the Assyrian monarchs presenting their bag to us: here is what Teglatphalasar I (1115–1077 B.C.) tells us in an inscription engraved on a clay prism: 'At the bidding of Ninurta, who loves me, four wild bulls which were mighty and of monstrous size, in the desert . . . with my mighty bow, with my iron spear, and with my sharp darts, I killed. Their hides and their horns I brought unto my city Assur. Ten mighty bull-elephants I slew. . . . Four elephants I caught alive. Their hides and their tusks together with the live elephants, I brought unto my city Assur. . . . I have slain one hundred and twenty lions by my bold courage and my strong attack, on foot, and eight hundred lions I have laid low from my chariot with javelins [?]. I have brought down all kinds of beasts of the field, and birds of the heavens that fly, among my hunting spoils. . . . Herds of deer, stags, ibex, and wild goats which Assur and Ninurta, the gods who love me, have given me for the chase, I have taken in the midst of the lofty hills.'

And here is the account of King Assurnasirpal II (883–859 B.C.) inscribed on the huge bulls and lions at his palace at Kalah: 'By my outstretched hand and impetuous courage, fifteen mighty lions from the mountains and forests I seized with my hand, and fifty lion-cubs I carried away, and in the city of Kalah and the palaces of my land, put them in cages, and I caused them to bring forth their cubs in abundance. Tigers [?] I captured alive with my hands, and herds of wild oxen, elephants and lions, and ostriches, male and female baboons [?], wild asses, gazelles, stags, bears, panthers and cheetahs [?], all the beasts of plain and mountain, I collected in my city of Kalah, letting all the people of my land behold them. O future prince among the kings, my sons, whom Assur shall call by name, or future peoples, or servants of the King [=royal viziers], or noble, or high official: thou shalt not abuse these creatures before Assur, Ninurta and Nergal, who love my priesthood, entrusted to me the wild creatures of the field, commanding me to follow the chase. Thirty elephants from ambush I slew, and 257 mighty wild oxen in my hunting-chariots. . . .'

These documents inform us that the Assyrian kings not only trained dogs for the chase but also falcons and cheetahs.

Domestic Animals. Flocks and Herds

If we can believe the geographers the ancient Valley of the Tigris and Euphrates was a vast steppe: 'before the third millennium hunting and gathering were easy. The great valleys of the Nile and the Euphrates formed natural oases, verdant forest-galleries with a tropical vegetation which must have been like that found today at Zor in the Jordan Valley. Gathering, hunting and fishing complemented the resources of the surrounding steppes.' On these steppes grew wild cereals: 'One can thus envisage that the earliest stages of the transition from a hunting-gathering economy to an agricultural economy took place in the semi-tropical forest-galleries of the Nile and Mesopotamia, perhaps at a time when the surrounding "steppe" was becoming more arid and was giving way to desert. It is also quite possible that the primitive plough was invented in these same areas and that as a result the ox, buffalo or ass, among other animals, were domesticated, or at least used for farming purposes. At first they would be used to break up the soil, to trample in the seed or to husk the grain by treading it out. Later on they would begin to be yoked. Thus in these regions the discovery of agriculture would, at least partially, explain the origin of stock-farming. This development although likely, remains hypothetical.'[7]

With this hypothesis in mind we can begin our study of domestic animals in ancient Mesopotamia. The ox was domesticated very early on and was, at all periods, a draught-animal. We find it harnessed to the King's chariots in the Royal Tombs of Ur (beginning of the third millennium B.C.) and to the chariots of the tributaries and prisoners whose long processions decorate the bas-reliefs of Assyrian palaces in the first millennium B.C. The ox was valued both for its meat and its hide. The possession of such an animal was certainly a sign of prosperity. We can see some of these well-nourished beasts on the Uruk cylinders and they are often shown, especially in the very early period, with an ear of wheat – symbols of fertility.

In southern Mesopotamia the cattle-sheds were made of big bundles of reeds set side by side to form walls while the inclined ends were tied together to form a sort of roof. On archaic cylinders and stone bowls one can often see schematic representations of such rustic shelters notably on a cylinder in the Ashmolean Museum at Oxford (fig. 26). Owing to the adoption of a fairly widespread artistic convention one looks into the shed, inside some of which there are calves, in others there are jars with handles – either for milk or for drinking-water for the animals. From the sheds emerge the forequarters of young beasts that are eating from the feeding-troughs. Above there is a frieze of adult animals in serried ranks. Milk was one of the Mesopotamians' basic foodstuffs and was especially used for cheese-making.

Dairy scenes are fairly common. The most famous is a bas-relief from the Temple of Al 'Ubaid (beginning of the third millennium B.C.). In the centre is the reed shed from which emerge the animals' forequarters. To the right, men, seated on low stools placed behind the animals, are milking two cows. A young calf licks its mother. To the left servants are engaged in pursuits thus described by Dr Contenau: '. . . one man swings a large jar backwards and forwards to churn the milk. The curd is being separated from the whey by filtering. A third person pats the butter down into a jar, something which is still done today in Syrian villages.'[8] Perhaps one could see a goatskin bottle instead of the jar shaken by the first person and this might suggest the making of cheese or yoghourt. Before we leave the dairy we must mention Phoenician ivory plaques that have been found in Assyrian palaces. These carvings show a cow turning her head to lick the calf she is suckling.

Mesopotamian flocks and herds were composed not only of bovids but also, and mostly of sheep and goats which were, of course, much less valuable than oxen. Several cylinders show small livestock watched over by shepherds and their dogs. On one such cylinder the shepherd holds a long-thonged whip while a servant milks the goats. In the upper part of this scene there are small discs which may well be cheeses drying out. Sheep's wool served for weaving cloth and blankets and sheep-shearing must have been an important operation. A servant of the King of Mari keeps his master informed of the difficulties he has to cope with: 'As soon as I began the shearing I wrote to my Lord, for on that day a dreadful rain fell and a hundred sheep remained unshorn.

Fig. 26
Cylinder seal, southern Iraq. Early third millennium B.C.
Ashmolean Museum.

It took me ten days to finish the shearing because of the rains and the lack of shearers.' He then asks for more help to be sent him and ends up thus: 'However, two sheep, two kids, the best of the flock, choice wool for the tailors and milk I have sent to my Lord.'

The Mesopotamian 'encyclopaedias' devote several chapters to the smaller livestock. For example, in the sections devoted to sheep, there are, in addition to fat sheep, plump sheep, young and old beasts, some picturesque items such as 'sheep marked with a red-hot iron' which indicates that the practice of branding sheep existed in those regions – and also 'sheep sheared with clippers' and 'sheep with a belt' – perhaps to support the huge, heavy tails of some animals, unless it refers to a device for preventing the rams from mounting ewes. Then there are 'sheep for the lions' and 'sheep for the wolves', probably to be used as bait for these beasts of prey. There were also sick animals and ewes which had, or had not, lambed.

The meat was not only for feeding the population but also for the Table of the Gods to whom it was offered up in sacrifice. If we return to the Third Dynasty of Ur (about 2000 B.C.) when the temples were great landed proprietors possessing not only estates but also flocks and herds, we find in the temples' accounts long lists of bulls, oxen, cows, sheep, ewes, lambs, he-goats and she-goats, kids and also gazelles. Each animal has a descriptive note relating to its fatness, its origin, its fecundity. There were also hybrids, goat crossed with ibex, lamb crossed with moufflon. Many of these animals were destined for the temples, as regular offerings or for special festivals, but some were also for the kitchen since the temples had to feed a numerous staff. Sometimes the animals were delivered dead, thus: 'a goat, dead stock, for the dogs, received by Ilibani the keeper of the dogs'. Some supplies went to the Royal Palace: 'One young sow from the cane-brake for roasting, a duck, three fat doves, dead, taken to the palace on the thirtieth of the month.' Often the animals offered up to the gods were given by devotees desirous of attracting the favour of a particular divinity. And so that their action should not be forgotten these pious people had themselves pictured, generally on an engraved cylinder which they carried with them and used as a seal, holding the animal they had offered in their arms. These 'offering scenes' were numerous in all epochs. The animal is generally a kid, which for an ordinary citizen was a less expensive sacrifice than a sheep or, of course, an ox.

Pig-breeding (there is a terracotta plaque of a sow suckling her piglets), and farmyards full of geese and ducks were also elements of farming. It seems that cocks and hens were not known until comparatively recent times. Many stone weights in the form of ducks have been found. The birds have their legs folded under their bodies and their heads stretched out along their backs and so form a smooth, oblong object. The weight is sometimes engraved on the piece and some are very small (one-eighth of a shekel, roughly a gramme) while some are bulky (twenty minas, nearly ten kilograms). We have mentioned that doves were provided for the royal table and there are small terracottas of these birds as well as a fine lapis-lazuli figure studded with gold which came from Susa. On certain offering-tables there are representations, especially during Assyrian times, of large birds which may have been swans. And lastly, it seems that the great domains were provided with ponds in which fish were kept for festivals. There is a representation of such a fish-pond on an Assyrian bas-relief from Nineveh.

We mentioned that, as well as oxen, asses were harnessed to the earliest ploughs, but the ass was also frequently ridden and in later times was mainly used as a beast of burden. The heavily laden donkey which one still finds on the Near Eastern roads had ancient forerunners, but these, as we shall see, were neither despised nor mocked. Other equids were also used as draught- or saddle-animals. But the problem is to know which ones. The date of the first appearance of the horse in Mesopotamia has been much discussed, without, however, any definite conclusion being reached. In the texts, where the equid is represented by an ideogram that means 'mountain ass' or 'eastern ass', horses are not mentioned much before the end of the third millennium B.C. There are references to horses in letters dating from the time of the First Babylonian Dynasty, the beginning of the second millennium B.C. Thus, part of a letter addressed by the King of Mari to his envoy at Carchemish in Hittite country, reads: 'I have spoken to him [the King of Carchemish] about white horses. This is his reply: "There are no white carriage horses. I will write so that white horses may be brought from the region where they are to be found. In the meantime I will get him to send Harsamnite bay horses."'

At any rate, it looks as though the horse was not at all common until the middle of the second millennium B.C., when treatises on 'hippology' are found. The horse is often mentioned in neo-Assyrian texts and frequently represented on contemporary royal palace bas-reliefs. The Assyrians did not represent galloping horses in the positions that we know from photography. However, the 'Assyrian gallop', though in a sense false, makes a very fine impression and has been termed *cabré allongé* ('the elongated rear').[9] When harnessed to chariots, and above all to royal chariots, the horse was used for travelling, for hunting and for warfare. Horses were owned by kings and great men. Lesser people had to make do with mules and asses. The Bible preserves a memory of the terror inspired by the Assyrian cavalry: 'They shall lay hold on bow and spear; they are cruel, and have no mercy; their voice roareth like the sea; and they ride upon horses, set in array as men for war against thee, O daughter of Sion.' (Jeremiah, 6: 23.)

The horse came from the north, from the Anatolian Plateau, and from the east, the Zagros Mountains. It seems indeed very probable that horses were known in Elam before they were known in Mesopotamia. There is a shell plaque (dating from about 2500 B.C.) from Susa, and on this a species of horse known as the 'Przevalsky horse' – a small, stocky animal with a long tail – is represented. Later on, under the Assyrian Empire, horses were imported not only from Elam, Persia and Asia Minor, but also from the region of Lake Van and Urmiah (present-day Armenia) as well as from Arabia and perhaps from Ethiopia. They were black, white or piebald in colour. White horses are sometimes mentioned as being offered up in sacrifice to the gods.

Before horses became common in Mesopotamia, vehicles were drawn by onagers. It seems to be these animals that were harnessed to the chariot of Queen Pu-Abi (whose name was formerly read as 'Shub-ad') found in the Royal Tombs of Ur. The onager differed from the horse by having longer ears, a short, straight mane and a tail ending in a tuft of hair. A very lifelike and elegant little model of an onager adorns the rein-ring of the Queen's chariot (pl. 3), whereas the King's chariot to which oxen were harnessed, has models of bovids. The animals drawing the Queen's chariot were at first identified as asses and lately someone has

questioned whether the 'onagers' might not be small oxen, but the animal bones are in too poor a condition to allow definite identification.[10] This is an example of how difficult it sometimes is to identify the animals represented on the monuments and how questionable identifications may be in certain cases.

The Mesopotamians had mules but these are not often represented until Assyrian times and were mainly used as beasts of burden. Camels and dromedaries might be used either for riding or as beasts of burden. Dromedaries were known from the beginning of the second millennium B.C., and the scribes differentiated between the dromedary from Arabia – the 'ass of the sea' and the camel which originally came from Bactria – 'the wild bull of the mountains' or 'from abroad'. The latter seems to have already been known to the Sumerians if one can rely on a text which reads: 'O Tammuz give me camel's milk, camel's milk is sweet, the cream [?] of the camel is sweet.' The Assyrian kings bought Bactrian camels or received them as tribute from conquered peoples (fig. 27), notably the Arabs, except when the camels were part of the war booty.

Domestic animals were very important and there were laws concerning them. Thus the Hammurabi Code from the beginning of the second millennium B.C. devotes several paragraphs to them. Paragraph 8

Fig. 27
Obelisk of Salmanasar III, King of Assyria (853–824 B.C.). British Museum.

concerns the theft of livestock: 'If a man has stolen an ox or a sheep or an ass or swine or a goat if [it is property] of a god [or] if [it is property] of a palace, he shall pay thirty-fold; if [it is the property] of a villein, he shall replace it ten-fold. If the thief has not the means of payment, he shall be put to death.' Paragraphs 224 and 225 stipulate: 'If a veterinary surgeon has made a deep incision in [the body of] an ox, or an ass and saves [its life], the owner of the ox or the ass shall give the surgeon a sixth of [a piece of] silver as his hire. If he has made a deep incision in [the body of] an ox or an ass and causes its death, he shall give a fifth of its price to the owner of the ox or the ass.' Paragraphs 242–9 relate to various cases when a hired ox dies or is hurt: 'If a man has hired an ox or an ass and a lion kills it in the open country it is the owner's [risk].' But if the death of a hired ox is due to the negligence or the blows of the hirer, he must replace the animal. Paragraph 150 refers to the case where an ox gores a man and kills him in the street. If the owner, knowing his animal was bad-tempered had not tied it up or fixed pads on its horns, he was subject to a fine The fee for hiring animals was fixed and especially that for an ox or an ass to tread out the corn after the harvest. These are but some examples of the laws.

To stress just how attached the Mesopotamians were to their domestic animals one may note that these were sometimes given names that have survived. We have names for horses, cows and dogs. Some are derived from divine names as are those of the people. Others are derived from the animal's country of origin, or from its physical peculiarities. Thus a horse might be called 'Red' or 'The Split-Eared One' or the 'Spotted One'. Conversely, but indicating similar sentiments, women were sometimes given the names of animals, often in the form of friendly diminutives such as 'Little Ewe', 'Lambkin', 'Little Bear' or 'Gazelle'.

No mention of domestic animals would be complete without referring to dogs, which were very common and are often represented, unlike domestic cats which seem to have been very rare, if not unknown. We have already noted that on Assyrian bas-reliefs showing hunting scenes there are ferocious mastiffs held on leashes by servants and trained specially for the hunt (fig. 25). These enormous dogs are to be seen on monuments of all periods. They can be recognized pursuing the wild boar on cylinder-impressions from Susa as early as the beginning of the third millennium B.C. The most celebrated piece is a steatite statuette known as 'The Dog of Sumu-Ilum' since an inscription by this King of Larsa is engraved on the dog's back (fig. 28). The animal, with a thick snout and drooping ears, is lying down but is ready to leap. It is one of the masterpieces of animal representation.

Mastiffs can also be seen on terracotta plaques dating from the beginning of the second millennium B.C. The animals are held on leashes by a man. A strap runs round their bodies and a chain passed twice round the neck forms a sort of collar.

King Nebuchadnezzar of the neo-Babylonian dynasty informs us that he buried, under the threshold of the Temple of Gula: 'two dogs of gold, two of silver and two of bronze with powerful limbs and massive bodies' – which is quite a good description of our mastiffs. The dog we may note was the symbol of the goddess Gula.

Other races of dogs are represented. There is a terracotta plaque, of approximately the same date as the previous one, showing a child astride an Alsatian-type dog with a sharp muzzle, pointed ears, thick mane and bushy tail. In outdoor scenes large sheep-dogs are shown

56

Fig. 28
'The dog of Sumu-Ilum'. End of third millennium B.C.
Louvre Museum.

with flocks. The dogs were there as much to watch over the animals as to defend them against beasts of prey and thieves. There are also small amulets in the form of dogs with short legs and with either long or short tails. And there are the great greyhounds bounding round the goblets from Susa (fig. 21), but which are almost unknown later on.

OTHER ANIMALS   Monkeys do not live in Mesopotamia and they do not seem to have ever existed there in the wild state. But there are representations of these animals from early times onward, on amulets, terracotta plaques, statuettes and bas-reliefs. Mrs van Buren thinks that the artists copied objects imported from abroad, from the Indus Valley or Egypt. But it is probable that merchants imported monkeys as curiosities and they also figured among the exotic animals brought by tributaries to Assyrian monarchs. It is as such that they are shown on the black obelisk of King Salmanasar (fig. 27). In statuettes from Susa the animal is represented in a very precise and realistic fashion, sitting on its haunches, with its hands on its knees. It has no tail and the limbs are long and slender. Though the ancient representations are very lifelike, the artists of the Assyrian epoch sometimes gave their monkeys almost human attitudes and faces (fig. 29).

On the black obelisk, in addition to monkeys, the tributaries brought the King an elephant, which, although it was hunted, was practically never represented, and a rhinoceros, which again was an animal foreign to Mesopotamia. The same is true of the crocodile of which only two representations are known, both clearly influenced by – or imported from – the Indus Valley. Such animals populated the zoological gardens.

We have seen something of domestic birds and of bird-hunting. Mesopotamia has numerous species of small birds but, unfortunately they are depicted on the monuments in too schematic a fashion for us to be able to identify them. But the Babylonians described the early

Fig. 29
A Nimrud ivory showing a Nubian (?)
bearing offerings. *c.* 800 B.C.
The Metropolitan Museum of Art, Rogers
Fund, 1960.

dawn, before the sunrise, as 'the time when the birds twitter'. And when the Babylonian Noah wanted to find out if the waters had subsided he sent out successively a pigeon, a swallow and a crow to reconnoitre.

But the birds of prey are easier to recognize – the eagles and the vultures. Often the eagle is found grabbing its prey – goats, deer, even lions; or the eagle may be clawing on to the rump of its victim. It was on the back of this powerful bird that the mythical hero Etana tried to rise to heaven. The ruthlessness of vultures and their role as scavengers are clearly indicated on the stele known as 'The Vultures' from the beginning of the third millennium B.C., where they are carrying off in their beaks the heads of executed enemies, and again on an Assyrian bas-relief where a vulture holds in its claws the entrails of the van-quished.

There are numerous species of reptiles in Mesopotamia, and the vocabularies contain an impressive list of these. But here again we come up against difficulties of identification since serpents, just as birds and fishes, lend themselves readily to schematization. Snakes often serve as decorative motifs, such as that of the two intertwined serpents which adorn many objects. On an archaic impression from the Fara site there is a rearing snake from whose mouth a tortoise is hanging by its tail.

The tortoise, although quite common, was rarely represented. But, on the other hand, we often find scorpions, with their claws and their tail ending in the sting (fig. 30). Amulets – or figurines – in the shape of frogs are fairly numerous in all epochs. Some are tiny, in gold, silver, copper, lapis-lazuli or mother-of-pearl, and were used as pendants hanging from necklaces of coloured stones.

Fish formed part of the food-supply and there was no ritual prescrip-tion against the eating of fish. Both sea-fish and freshwater-fish are mentioned on numerous 'economic' tablets of the Archaic period. There are accounts from the town of Larsa, dating from the beginning of the second millennium B.C., mentioning deliveries of sea-fish made to a wholesale merchant. Thirty different species are named, with their prices, and they were sold either singly or by the basket. Salted or dried fish could be stored, and oil was also extracted. In this connection there is an interesting passage from Herodotus: 'Here are some of the Babylonian laws . . . there are in the country three tribes which consume no fish at all. After the catch people dry the fish in the sun and then cook them in the following manner: they throw them into a mortar, pound them with pestles, pass them through a piece of linen, and, according to taste, knead them to make a sort of porridge or bake them like bread.'[11] One must bear in mind the part that legends and erroneous tales play in the Greek historian's accounts which are nevertheless both valuable and enthralling.

Besides fish, shell-fish, both freshwater and salt-water varieties, were eaten, and shells left over from meals have been found on some sites.

Finally, there are the insects, so numerous and varied in the Near East but difficult to represent because of their small size. On many cylinders of the Kassite period one sees something that may represent a fly or a bee. The Mesopotamians, certainly, ate honey and used it for making pastries, but the honey came from wild bees and bee-keeping seems to have been unknown. Much less frequently shown, though certainly known, were locusts which at times might constitute a veritable

Fig. 30

Melishiru *Kudurru*. Beginning of twelfth century B.C.
Louvre Museum.

59

plague. In a letter found at Mari the writer addresses the King thus: 'Locusts often come to Terqa and the day they arrived the heat was torrid so they did not alight. But all the locusts that were taken I have sent to my Lord.' These insects were in fact much esteemed as a foodstuff, and on one Assyrian bas-relief servants are carrying a hare, birds and long pins of skewered locusts to a royal feast.

Here is an incantation. It is true that the interpretation is not very certain, but we cannot refrain from quoting it for it is very picturesque: it shows that mosquitoes were as irritating and disliked in ancient times as they are today. The first two lines of the text read thus: 'Zizzili, zizzili' – words which render well enough the irritating sound made by the insect and are translated 'Mosquito, mosquito' – 'fly away you intolerable little mosquito to [thy master?] Burlipi.'

MONSTERS AND FANTASTICAL ANIMALS   Monsters and fantastical animals are innumerable and many-shaped, both in the written documents and on the monuments. Indeed, the fertile imagination of the ancient Mesopotamians was for ever creating new creatures. This was done either by combining human and animal parts or by mingling together the characteristics of several different animals. For the ordinary people these monsters were awe-inspiring and very frightening. Even when the shapes are rather similar they may have radically different expressions and attitudes. Some grimace and gesticulate in a frightening fashion. These are the demons. Others, on the contrary, remain calm and serene, like the monumental bulls which, in pairs, guarded the palace gates of Assyrian Sargon at Dur-Sharrukin, the modern Khorsabad (fig. 31). The body is like a bull, or perhaps a bison (the thick hair, represented by curls on the breast, flanks and rump, seem to support the latter identification) but immense bird-wings spring from the joints of the fore legs, while the head is human, and that of a handsome, bearded man. The bull-ears are ornamented with ear-rings and on the head is a cylindrical tiara with two rows of horns, symbols of divinity. The whole conveys an impression of power and calm majesty. The motif of the man-headed bull (though without wings) occurs already at the beginning of the third millennium B.C. on bas-reliefs from Al 'Ubaid and on plaques from Tello and Ur. At the gates of other Assyrian palaces stood winged, man-headed lions. These genii were beneficent to the sovereign and the palace inhabitants, but threatening to intruders. Some Assyrian palace bas-reliefs are ornamented with winged genii who carry the vessel containing lustral water. These have a human body with the head of a bird of prey or of a lion. Sometimes instead of feet there are eagles' claws.

Here are a few more specimens of monsters: the lion-headed eagle, symbol of the god Ningirsu and blazon of the city of Lagash, the modern Tello. This emblem is often represented on the monuments and other objects from this town. Then there is the goat-fish, symbol of Ea, the god of the waters, where the fore-part is a goat and the hind-part a fish (fig. 30). And there is the man-scorpion (fig. 32), the man-fish, the man-bull (fig. 22), the many-headed serpent, and the serpent god with a human bust which merges into a long snake coiling round to form a base. The *mushrushu* dragon, the emblem of the god Marduk, has a long, slender, scaly body and the head of a horned serpent. There are other creations which later become famous in the Mediterranean area. The sphinx which appears in Kassite times, the centaur which is found on

Fig. 31
Monumental bull guarding palace gate of
Sargon II, King of Assyria (721–703 B.C.)
at Dar-Sharrukin (Khorsabad).
Louvre Museum.

the *kudurrus*, the winged horse which, though more uncommon, figures
on an Elamite cylinder of the Persian epoch.

Other monsters which inspired repulsion and terror represent demons.
There is the female demon Lamashtu which attacks infants and whose
naked but hairy body has the head of a lioness and the claws of a bird
of prey (fig. 33). In the texts she is sometimes described as having a
bitch's head. Her teeth, it was said, were those of a dog or an ass. Her
loins were spotted like those of a leopard, her poison was that of a snake
or scorpion. On the sculptured monuments she holds a snake in either
hand and these are sometimes two-headed. From her breasts hang two
small animals, a piglet and a puppy. She lived in the cane-brakes where
the wild beasts had their lairs, and in order to chase her away she must
be given provisions for the journey and an ass for transport. Her
companion, Pazuzu, the demon of the south-west wind, is as hideous as

61

Lamashtu herself. He is naked, furnished with two pairs of wings. His hands and feet end in claws. His head is that of a foetus.

In some cases the monstrous beings owe their origin simply to the artist's search for decorative motifs. Thus on cylinder-impressions from Fara (third millennium B.C.) there is a man whose legs form a lion's body with the head downwards. Or, again, there are elongated bodies of four lions forming a sort of swastika. A little later on and still in the engravings, a very artistic motif is formed by lions (or dragons?) whose very elongated necks are intertwined and whose tails intersect those of animals in a neighbouring group. The supple, sinuous serpents' bodies lend themselves very well to such decorative motifs.

The Mesopotamians' imagination is particularly well displayed in a collection of portents to be deduced from the births of monsters. This long text, which occupies several large clay tablets, describes all sorts of monsters to which women or female animals may give birth. Some of the monsters really did exist – like Siamese twins, or Mongoloid idiots for instance – but most of the examples raise problems – are they pure imagination or comparative examples? The method behind such a compilation was to examine all the possible cases of a certain set of circumstances. Thus, if a woman gives birth to a lion, a dog, a pig, an ass, a snake, a fish . . . if an infant has a dog's head or that of a lion, a pig, a snake, or a bird . . . if a ewe drops a ram-headed lion, or a lion with an ox's head or the eyes of a dog or a pig . . . with the mouth of . . . with six, eight, ten . . . legs . . . two, three . . . tails. Perhaps the following quotation will suffice: 'If the offspring of a mare has feet like those of a lion, a head like that of a dog, if it has one eye, six legs, bristles like a pig and no tail . . .', the portent announced by this monster is favourable for the monarch, but unfavourable for the owner of the creature, for that man will die.

Man and Animal. Fables and Divination

What significance did animals have for the Mesopotamians? In very ancient times wild animals were certainly a terrible menace, for men had to fight with very primitive weapons against ferocious beasts. Possibly in those days there existed an animal cult. However, the Apis Bull, for instance, does not appear to have had a counterpart in Mesopotamia. There may have been a totemic organization of society, but there is no clear evidence of this. Perhaps we may see a survival of totemism in animals used as divine attributes (see below) or in certain myths. As men became sedentary and as their agriculture developed the domain of the wild animals shrank, and some wild species became domesticated. Such domestic animals became the helpers and companions of man and contribute to the progress of civilization. The flocks and herds provided food and clothing. The beasts of burden made travelling, commerce and contacts with neighbouring people possible. Finally the horse arrived and revolutionized military tactics. Animals became an essential part of man's material life, and became too an important element in both his religious life and his literature.

In religion, animals were adopted as symbols. The Mesopotamian pantheon was a rich one. It contained, alongside the ancient Sumerian divinities, other gods introduced by the Semites after they settled in the Valley of the Two Rivers. Some gods possessed an animal attribute.

Fig. 32
Shell plaque from lyre, King's grave at Ur.
First half of third millennium B.C.
The University Museum, Philadelphia.

Fig. 33
Lamashtu plaque. Eighth to seventh century B.C.
Louvre Museum, Clercq collection.

62

The animal might be shown beside the god or with the god standing on its back, or – particularly on the Kassite *kudurrus* – the animal may be represented alone, replacing the god that it symbolizes (fig. 22). Thus the goddess Ishtar, the deity of war, has the lion as her animal attribute and she is sometimes shown standing upright and holding a leash which passes through the nostrils of the lion. As the goddess of love – especially in Phoenicia – she has the dove as her symbol. The dog is Gula's animal. She is the healing goddess, the patroness of physicians. Ea, the god of the waters, is represented by a fantastical animal, the goat-fish. The god of storms has, for his symbol, the bull of resounding voice and destructive strength. During Assyrian times, for instance, the deity is shown upright on a galloping bull. And there was also the scorpion, emblem of the goddess Ishhara, and the serpent which, on Gudea's goblet, represents the personal divinity of the prince Ningish-zidda.

In the literary works animals are often used as a form of comparison which gives us some idea of the character attributed to particular species and the esteem in which they were held. Thus the ass, mocked and despised in our civilization, was certainly held in high regard. Before the horse appeared it was the mount of kings and great personages. And even in the early days of the horse, it looks as though riding such a mettlesome and perhaps not very well broken-in animal was not considered compatible with the dignity of monarchs. A text dating from the middle of the third millennium B.C. informs us of how esteemed the humble and docile ass was. Gudea, the Governor of the city of Lagash recounts a dream in which his god appeared to him and gave him instructions about building a temple. In this dream, an ass was placed at the right hand of the god, and the goddess who interpreted the dream for Gudea said that the ass was Gudea himself, the loyal and faithful servant of the god.

As an example of literary comparison we may take the text of a treaty concluded between the Assyrian monarch Asarhaddon (680–669 B.C.) and several of his vassals. Curses are pronounced on those who violate the treaty, and in describing the punishments demanded for the offenders, references are made, among other things, to the animal kingdom. Thus we read: 'Just as the seed of a hinney [mule] is sterile, may your name, your seed and the seed of your sons and your daughters be destroyed from the land. . . . Just as a snake and a mongoose do not share one and the same lair [but] plot to kill each other so may you and your womenfolk not enter the same room without thinking of cutting off each other's lives. . . . Just as the caterpillar does not return to its cocoon so you will not return to your women, to your houses. . . . Like locusts devour . . . lice and caterpillars may they cause your towns, your land and your district to be devoured.'

In another treaty between Assurnirari V, King of Assyria (754–745 B.C.) and the Syrian king Mati'ilu, a passage occurs in which a sheep was brought to the spot where the treaty was concluded and the following was pronounced: 'If Mati'ilu sins against the provisions of this treaty, then, just as this sheep was taken from its pen and will not return there, so may Mati'ilu and his sons, his daughters and the people of his country, be removed from his land and not return there. This head is not the head of a ram, it is the head of Mati'ilu, it is the head of his children, of his notables, of the people of his land . . . if he does not keep his promises, just as the head of this ram is cut off . . . so may the

64

head of Mati'ilu be cut off.' The same ritual was performed for the ram's shoulders. As the words were pronounced the ram was slain, his head cut off and his shoulders torn away.

With the final allusions to animals in the texts, we move on to consider a different form of literature, the fables which touch very closely on our subject.

The stock of Mesopotamian fables was fairly extensive and we have a certain number of stories in which plants and animals are endowed with speech, which they use freely, usually in order to boast of their respective merits. There is not much action but plenty of dialogue. It is a sort of literary jousting which sometimes ends with a divinity pronouncing his verdict. The tablets are often in a poor condition, but as there exist several copies of the same text, a coherent story can be pieced together, although, in most cases, gaps remain. The 'Story of the Horse and the Bull' is an excellent example of the kind of dialogue that takes place. The two animals are looking at a flood that is at once destructive and productive of fertility. Then, as the fable goes on 'the Ox and the Horse became friends, their bellies were sated with the luscious pasture, in their pleasure they engaged in a dispute. The Ox opened his mouth and spoke, addressing the Horse, glorious in battle: "As I look around my omens are very favourable. From the beginning to the end of the year I find my pasture. The full flood has come early."' Then follows a description of the benefits of the flood and the Ox tells the Horse to come and join him. Most of the Horse's reply is missing because of a break in the tablet, but we gather that, as an excuse for refusing, the Horse points out his usefulness. The Ox states that he too contributes to a success in battle since the quivers and harness are made from his skin. The Horse retorts boasting of his pleasant life, how he is lodged near the King and great men, how choice and varied his food is and that his flesh is not eaten. These points indicate the esteem in which this animal was held and the value attached to it.

The Fox cycle, probably of Sumerian origin, is found on several tablets. On those which have come down to us we witness a dispute between the Wolf, the Fox and the Dog. The Dog accuses the others of attacking the flocks with which he is entrusted, and he takes advantage of the opportunity to vindicate himself and to boast with considerable complacency of his own merits. The Fox, cunning as always (he is represented in the same way at all times and in all places) manages to throw all the blame on the Wolf, and, in order to ingratiate himself with the god Enlil calls on him to decide the argument. The Lion occasionally appears but his role is not really clear. The Dog declaims: 'My strength is overpowering, I am the claw of the Anzu-bird, a very lion . . . in my pens the robber does not ravage.'

The fables must have been very popular since illustrations of them appear on the monuments. On small objects, cylinders or shell plaques, there are animals represented in the same attitudes as men, and in scenes on other monuments we find them with human protagonists. The best known is the long, thin shell plaque on the front of the harp from the King's Tomb among the Royal Tombs of Ur (first half of the third millennium B.C. (fig. 32). The plaque is divided into four registers. In the topmost one the hero Gilgamesh is subduing two human-headed bisons. Below this is a dog (or a jackal?) upright, with a knife in his belt and carrying a table with sacrificial dishes or a feast. He is followed by a lion, also upright, carrying a bowl and a jar with a handle. In the lower register there is a bear dancing to the sound of a harp played by a seated animal, the harp itself is in the form of a reclining bull, while a smaller animal is shaking a sistrum. At the bottom, alongside a man-scorpion, an upright gazelle holds two goblets which she has probably filled from a large jar behind her.

There are other 'humanized' animals on cylinder-impressions from Susa, small animals (mice?) are sitting in boats and paddling; or an upright bull is subduing two lions; or an upright lion lifts two bulls.

On a cylinder from Tell Asmar a lion and a horse are sitting on stools and drinking. On an impression from Ur a donkey plays the harp before a seated lion. This motif of the 'harp-playing ass' can be seen on the capitals of Roman columns. On a terracotta plaque a seated monkey plays the lyre.

We cannot, however, connect up these scenes with any of the fables that have come down to us. Perhaps they refer to stories or myths for which we have not, as yet, any texts, or perhaps such tales were transmitted by word of mouth.

Divination was one of the domains in which animals played a very important part. Haruspic is the art of divination by the examination of the entrails of animals sacrificed to the gods. In most cases the victim was a sheep. In a rigorously determined order the liver, lungs and other viscera (heart, kidneys, etc.) and the intestines were examined. The examination of the liver was the most important and there was a veritable 'science' (known as 'hepatoscopy') whose rules were the subject of a vast canonical treatise which is inscribed on many tablets to which commentaries, reports of consultations and also clay models of livers for the instruction and training of apprentice soothsayers were attached. The general appearance of the organ was carefully noted; attention was paid to any unusual marks it might present, depressions, furrows, spots and so forth. The aspect and position of the various parts and especially of the gall-bladder were studied. From this 'hepatoscopic chart' divinations relating to the person concerned or, in a general way, relating to the affairs of the king and country, were deduced.

Alongside this 'scientific' divination was another, popular sort which needed no preparation and did not require the direct intervention of a soothsayer. It was a divination deduced from the incidents of daily life and especially from the behaviour of animals. Here again we have a valuable collection of material which, according to Mesopotamian custom was entitled with the first line: 'If a town lies on a height . . .'. The reports are drawn up in the same way as those for the omens from monstrous births. In the parts dealing with animals a particular animal was considered (snake, scorpion, lizard, dog, pig) and its characteristics – size, colour, sex – were taken into account, as well as its behaviour, the place, and sometimes the date of its appearance.

The tablet devoted to snakes reads thus: 'If in the month of Nisan, the first day, a man sees a serpent, he will die in the course of the year . . . if in the month Nisan, the first day, a serpent falls on a man, that man will die during the course of the year . . . if in the month Nisan a serpent falls between a man and his wife, his sons will not live and his house will be destroyed . . . if in the month Nisan and in the street a serpent moves in a curve from the left to the right of a man, that man will die either from being gored by an ox or from the sting of a scorpion . . . if in the month Nisan serpents intertwine in a man's house, the master of that house will die.'

Glancing through the tablet devoted to the scorpion we find it stinging a man in various parts of his body – the enumeration proceeds from head to foot. The tablet about dogs tells us that if they assemble in the streets and howl it is a bad sign, so too if they lie down before a man, if they dig in the dust, if they defecate or urinate before or on a man. Such lists can be very tedious and it is difficult to draw from them any conclusions regarding the evil or the good influence of the animals whose behaviour is examined, for the influence would be good or bad according to the behaviour at any given time. Thus, while domestic dogs were valued as good and trusty guardians, stray dogs were suspect, and to meet one was not a good omen. It is evident that the presages were only taken into account when one wanted to know about the future and consult the omens. Clearly not all groups of howling dogs were dangerous – otherwise life would have become intolerable.

Evil presages might be averted thanks to magical acts which are indicated in the books of ritual. They give prescriptions for preparations to be drunk, or for objects to be carried about on the person. The composition of these is very similar to the medicaments ordered by the physicians. In these formulae, besides plants and minerals, there were some ingredients from the animal kingdom. We can give here only a few examples, for instance, so that 'the hand of the god' may not strike a child a tuft of wool enclosing a mixture of ass's slaver with the excrement of a pig and a black dog must be hung from his neck. In the treatment of sexual maladies and especially of impotence, drugs were employed containing certain parts of those animals noted for their virility – such as the bull, the stag and the bird known as the 'bird of the caverns'. These animals were also invoked in the incantations.

Black beasts, especially black dogs, were often used in magic. Thus two black dogs and two white dogs were put at the disposal of the she-demon Lamashtu and, in a ritual of exorcism against this terrible killer of children, it is prescribed that a clay dog should be prepared. A tuft of hair from a black dog must be placed on its head to form a mane, while its tail should be made of goat's hair. Animal hair, such as that from a virgin she-goat, is often mentioned in the ritual texts. The ingredients mentioned in one prescription, also against Lamashtu, include seven red threads, hair from an ass's beard (pulled from the right-hand side), hair from a she-ass's beard (pulled from the left-hand side), hair from the mane of an ass's colt, a white pig's bristle, a tuft of black hairs pulled from the right side of an ass's rump, the whole to be hung from the patient's neck.

Conclusion

This short account will show the important place occupied by animals in the life of the ancient inhabitants of the Valley of the Two Rivers. One sees how their tireless imagination, taking known species as a starting-point, created monsters and fantastical animals, some of which still survive and adorn the capitals of our cathedrals.

But the most striking feature is the number, the variety and the high artistic quality of the animal representations in Mesopotamian art. From the earliest drawings with figures on the pottery from the most ancient sites, when the human figure is either not represented or appears as a simple outline, animals appear, drawn skilfully, true to life, vivid, elegant or powerful, but always so beautiful as to win our admiration. These characteristics can be noted all through the centuries until they culminate in the masterpieces which adorned the palaces of the Assyrian monarchs. We can say without any exaggeration that the Mesopotamian artists were quite extraordinarily good at depicting animals.

4
ANIMALS IN EGYPT

RICHARD CARRINGTON

Egypt is one of the most rewarding countries in the world for the study of animals in archaeology. During the past 100 years it has perhaps been more extensively excavated than any other region and the pioneer work carried out by Flinders Petrie, Maspero and other eminent Egyptologists of the late nineteenth century was largely responsible for transforming archaeology from the hobby of antiquarianism into an exact science. Even to summarize what is known about animals in ancient Egypt in one short chapter would, therefore, be quite impossible and it is necessary to be strictly selective. I have chosen to concentrate on the relationship of animals and man in historical times, from the beginning of the First Dynasty to the advent of the Ptolemies. Within this time-span I shall be primarily concerned with the role animals played in the everyday life of the Egyptian people – in their agricultural economy, in their cults and religious beliefs, in their burial customs, as companions and quarry of the hunt and pets in their homes, and for labour both as beasts of burden and for traction.

The table below sets out the main historical periods, but as Egyptian chronology is notoriously difficult, the earlier dates must be regarded as only approximate.[1]

Divisions and Dates	Dynasties
Predynastic period (fourth millennium B.C.)	
Early Dynastic period (c. 3100–c. 2686 B.C.)	1–2
Old Kingdom (c. 2686–c. 2181 B.C.)	3–6
First Intermediate period (c. 2181–c. 2040 B.C.)	7–10
Middle Kingdom (2133–1633 B.C.)	11–13
Second Intermediate period (1786–1567 B.C.)	14–16
New Kingdom (c. 1650–1085 B.C.)	17–20
Late period (1085–525 B.C.)	21–26
Persian period (525–332 B.C.)	27–30
Ptolemaic period (332–30 B.C.)	

In Early Dynastic times the fauna of Egypt was much richer than towards the end of ancient Egyptian history, and vastly more so than it is today. Many animals which now only occur south of Khartoum in the Sudan were common in the Lower Nile Valley and their range

69

extended in some cases northwards to the Delta. Big game abounded, and included lions, hippopotamuses, giraffes, wild cattle and several species of large antelope. Among smaller mammals, hyenas, wolves, jackals, wild cats, porcupines, hedgehogs, mongooses, desert foxes, wild pigs and gazelles were all found. Reptiles included snakes, turtles, lizards and the much-feared crocodile, while among birds the ostrich, long since extinct in the region, was then a spectacular representative. Today, although many small mammals, reptiles, water-birds and birds of prey still make their home in Egypt, the only large and dangerous animal to occur there is the Nile crocodile, *Crocodilus niloticus*, which is itself becoming increasingly rare and is now found only along the river-banks just below and south of the new high dam at Aswan.

Stock-breeding

Cattle, sheep, goats, donkeys and pigs had all been domesticated before the First Dynasty but as the Old Kingdom ran its course animal husbandry reached new levels of sophistication and, with agriculture, formed the basis of the Egyptian economy (fig. 34). Some of the most common animals such as sheep and goats were not indigenous, being imported from western Asia, but many local species such as oryx, addax and gazelle were likewise built up into large herds. Strangely enough, the camel, which is now so typical of the region, was not imported from Asia until the Persian period (525–532 B.C.) in spite of its well-known tolerance of arid conditions; instead the donkey, which from the earliest times was much more than a farm animal, made a hardy and adaptable beast of burden, fulfilling most of the functions later performed by the camel. The horse also was virtually unknown until the Hyksos invasions (thirteenth century B.C.), and another late-

Fig. 34
Sow and piglets. *c.* 600 B.C.
British Museum.

comer was the strange hump-backed zebu, an Asiatic import which assumed considerable importance in the New Kingdom.

With a little imagination we can picture the scene on an Egyptian farm in the time of the earliest kings. The farms all lay within a few miles of the river or in such areas as the Fayum where water collected in depressions in the desert or emerged as springs to form oases. The annual inundation of the Nile, which lasted from late August to late November, was the life-blood of Egypt. Agriculture was impossible during the flood, but when the river subsided hoeing and ploughing began and the crops were sown for harvesting during the following spring. The natural moistening of the soil by the inundation was probably supplemented by artificial irrigation, and this was certainly done for the cultivation of gardens from the earliest times.

The rich harvest of wheat, barley and other crops that could be cultivated by irrigation was partly used to feed the livestock. Numerous pictures on the walls of ancient Egyptian tombs show the varied functions of the domesticated animals: donkeys and cattle treading out grain on the threshing-floor or carrying saddle-bags, peasants milking cows, cattle ploughing, sheep, goats, cattle and pigs being herded or driven across fields to tread in the seed, young stock being raised or carried and, in later times, after the Hyksos invasions, horses and mules drawing the landlord's chariot or carriage across his estate during the harvest (fig. 35, pl. 4). Selective breeding was already practised in very early times, as is well shown by the development from a single wild species of cattle (*Bos primigenius*) of at least two well-contrasted varieties – long-horned and short-horned – before the beginning of the Old Kingdom. In fact, Zeuner deduces from sculptures, paintings and hieroglyphs that there were as many as four distinct breeds descended from *Bos primigenius*: long-horned, short-horned, lyre-horned and hornless.[2]

Fig. 35
Scene showing the counting of cattle from the tomb of Nebamun, Thebes. *c.* 1400 B.C. British Museum.

Their colours varied from plain black and plain brown to brown and white, black and white and, according to Zeuner, 'possibly pure white, and white spotted with black like the Lascaux cattle'. To define the breeds of ancient Egyptian domestic cattle with any attempt at finality would be rash, but Zeuner's types, with a number of variations, are certainly well represented and show that stock-breeding had advanced to a very sophisticated level.

Hunting

The hunting of animals for sport was widely practised in ancient Egypt for excitement and recreation long after the grim realities of a life-or-death hunting economy had become obsolete with the development of agriculture and domestication. This is not to say that the quarry was not killed, captured or eaten, but the hunt was now mainly, as today, a social adjunct of a more settled way of life. Some of the domestic animals themselves, especially the dog, were enlisted to help their owners in the pursuit of the quarry.

There has been much learned argument about the descent of the domestic dog, *Canis familiaris*, but it is now fairly clear that it had a polyspecific origin in which both the European wolf, *Canis lupus lupus*, and the Indian wolf, *Canis lupus pallipes*, with possibly some admixture from the jackal, played a part.

Several different types, or breeds, are shown in the art-work of the time, at least three of which can be traced back to the Predynastic period. In the Old Kingdom, dogs ranging in type from mastiffs to pomeranians were all known and the kennels of hunting-hounds have been excavated among the outbuildings of rich estates, sometimes containing the bones of the dogs they housed. Dogs were among the many animals brought back from expeditions to the land of Punt (probably modern Somalia) and were also offered as tribute to pharaohs and nobles. Among the most striking dogs in appearance was the Egyptian greyhound, which is often depicted and whose descendants are still common in the Mediterranean region today. The inevitable mongrel, the product of accidental encounters or illicit forays by its more aristocratic relations, was as typical of ancient Egypt as it is of the modern world.

From the earliest Dynastic times we find that the pharaohs and their entourage often pursued the big game that then flourished in the Nile Valley. In the river itself the most dangerous quarry was the hippopotamus and the crocodile, and indeed King Menes, reputed to be the founder of the First Dynasty, is said to have been killed by a hippopotamus while hunting. Not much reliance should be placed on this story, however, for the Greek historian Diodorus Siculus gives a different and more fanciful version, namely that Menes was attacked by his own hunting-dogs but was saved by a crocodile which carried him across Lake Moeris to safety.

Although the hippopotamus was hunted for pleasure as well as the ivory of its tusks, its elimination from the Nile in the vicinity of inhabited areas was on balance desirable for purely economic reasons. Hippopotamuses are usually depicted wallowing amicably in the water, but at night they come ashore to feed, consuming vast quantities of vegetation. They were, therefore, very unpopular with the ancient Egyptian farmers, and Diodorus, whose visit to the country occurred in the

Plate 4
Wooden model of oxen ploughing. Middle Kingdom, *c*. 2000 B.C.
British Museum.

72

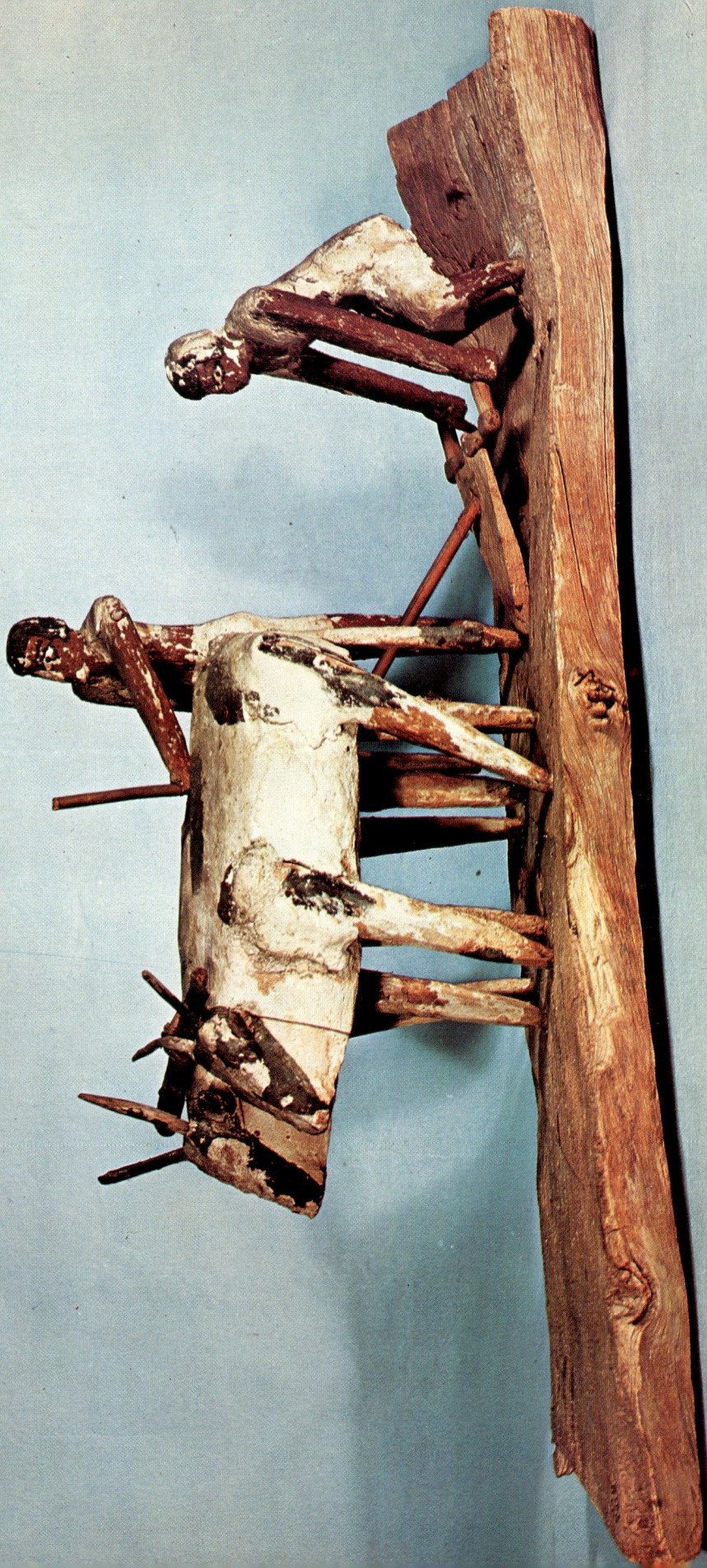

closing years of the pre-Christian era, surmised that if the hippopotamus was more common it would be a really serious threat to cultivation. 'It is hunted by many persons together, each armed with iron darts,' he writes.[3] This seems to suggest that hippopotamuses were still present on the lower reaches of the Nile in comparatively late times, but Diodorus leaves the locus of the hunt in doubt and it is possible that he is referring to regions further south. Most of the evidence seems to suggest that by the end of the Old Kingdom the numbers of hippopotamus in Lower Egypt were very much reduced, and although it continued to exist in the Delta into Ptolemaic times and even later it was by then a curiosity rather than a menace.

The crocodile, as is well known, was a sacred animal in many parts of Egypt, and the crocodile god Sobek is often depicted, sometimes carrying a mummified body. But in spite of the reverence in which it was held it was always regarded as symbolic of an inimical force hostile to both human and animal life. As such there seem to have been fewer inhibitions about hunting it than was the case with other sacred animals and it was a favourite quarry of those who wished to demonstrate their bravery. Hunting scenes show it being speared from small boats with obvious risk to life and limb, and even when it was killed or captured in less dramatic fashion it was always treated with respect. For instance, Herodotus writes: 'The modes of catching the crocodile are many and various. I shall only describe the one which to me seems worthy of mention. They bait a hook with a chine of pork and let the meat be carried out into the middle of the stream, while the hunter on the bank holds a living pig, which he belabours. The crocodile hears its cries, and, making for the sound, encounters the pork, which he instantly swallows down. The men on the shore haul, and when they have got him to the land, the first thing the hunter does is to plaster his eyes with mud. This once accomplished, the animal is dispatched with ease, otherwise he gives great trouble.'[4] It is not quite clear why plastering the eyes with mud should be considered less dangerous (especially for the plasterer) than dispatching the animal in the first place, but Herodotus would not be the writer he is if he did not titillate our curiosity with these mysteries.

Apart from the respect in which the crocodile was held for its ferocity and religious significance, it was also regarded as a symbol of virility and even, indeed, as a kind of reptilian Casanova. Wallis Budge quotes one of the famous Pyramid Texts of the Old Kingdom (the so-called 'Text of Unás') on the subject: 'He eats with his mouth, he voids water, he unites with women. He is the sower of seed who carries off wives from their husbands to the place which pleases him, according to the inclination of his heart.'[5] In the present century in the Sudan the genitals of crocodiles are often eaten as a supposed aphrodisiac, and very possibly these were one of the valued prizes of the crocodile-hunts of ancient Egypt. Certainly, on many counts the crocodile was one of the most important animals in the region and was even sent abroad when it was thought necessary to please a powerful foreign ruler. For example, in the Twenty-first Dynasty, when Tiglath Pileser I of Assyria began to make his power felt on Egypt's eastern frontiers, it was thought diplomatic to placate him with the gift of a crocodile, although whether this was alive or dead is not clear. Crocodiles were certainly captured alive on many occasions by the use of nets, and probably also by the pork and plaster technique described by Herodotus.

Among land animals the more spectacular quarry of the hunt included lions and the now-extinct wild ox, or aurochs. The pursuit of this big game required more elaborate organization than the hunting of river animals as well as a greater range of equipment. Spears, darts, lassoes, nets and boomerangs were all used, and the hunter was accompanied by a small army of attendants. Hunting on this scale was a rich man's sport, like big-game hunting today, and was largely the prerogative of the pharaoh and his courtiers. Apart from acting as beaters, armourers or dog-handlers, and carrying the equipment, the attendants also brought elaborate meals from the royal kitchens so that their masters could enjoy the luxuries of a banquet as a relaxation from the ardours of the chase. Nevertheless, many deeds of bravery were done (or at least reputed to have been done) and there are numerous pictures of pharaohs and other important members of the hunting-party slaying lions single-handed and otherwise proving their virility before the admiring gaze of the lesser fry who accompanied them (fig. 36).

Although many of the records of these hunts are suspiciously flattering in style, at least the prowess of the Eighteenth Dynasty pharaoh Thutmose III seems to be well established, and a graphic account of some of his exploits, which he apparently regarded as a change from killing human beings on his foreign campaigns, is prefaced by a reasonably convincing disclaimer of any sycophantic embroidery. The record occurs on a stele in the Temple of Erment, and the anonymous chronicler writes: 'I speak in accordance with what he actually did, there is neither deceit nor falsehood there, it was in the presence of the whole army, and there is no word of exaggeration in it. If he spends his time taking recreation in hunting in any desert, the number of his trophies is greater than the spoils of the whole army. He killed seven lions while out shooting in the twinkling of an eye. He secured a herd of twelve wild cattle in an hour, when breakfast-time came, their tails

Fig. 36
Lion hunting scene, casket from tomb of Tutankhamon.
Ashmolean Museum.

74

to be worn behind him. He dispatched 120 elephants in the mountain country of Nih, when coming from Naharin. . . . He bagged a rhinoceros when shooting in the southern desert region of Nubia. . . .'

An account of the pursuit of the aurochs by the Eighteenth Dynasty pharaoh Amenophis III is one of the most graphic to come down to us: 'A messenger came to tell His Majesty that there were wild cattle upon the desert in the district of Shetep. His Majesty thereupon floated downriver in the royal dahabiyeh *Shining-in-Truth*, at the time of evening, and after having had a good journey, arrived in safety at the district of Shetep at the time of morning. His Majesty mounted upon a horse and his whole army followed him. The nobles and the *ankhu* officers of the entire army were marshalled, and the children of the quarter were ordered to keep watch upon these wild cattle. His Majesty thereupon ordered that they should surround these wild cattle with a net and a dike and His Majesty then ordered that these wild cattle should be counted in their entirety, and the number of them amounted to wild cattle 190. The number . . . which His Majesty brought in by his own hunting in this day was 56. His Majesty rested four days in order to give spirit to his horses; then His Majesty mounted again upon a horse and the number of these wild cattle which were brought to him in hunting was wild cattle 20 plus 20; making the total number . . . captured 96.'[6]

Elephant-hunts were conducted by the ancient Egyptians on their Syrian campaigns, where the quarry was the Asiatic genus, *Elephas maximus*. Amen-en-heb, the biographer of the Pharaoh Thutmose III (1504–1450 B.C.), records one such exploit, which is confirmed by a similar account on the Barkal Stele. The Pharaoh, according to Amen-en-heb, 'hunted 120 elephants at their mud-hole. Then the biggest elephant began to fight before His Majesty. I was the one who cut off his hand [i.e. trunk – R.C.] while he was still alive, in the presence of His Majesty, while I was standing in the water between two rocks. Then my Lord rewarded me. . . .'[7]

Under the Ptolemies, elephants were domesticated for use in war and possibly also as ceremonial animals and hauliers. The Asiatic elephant was widely used in the armies of Alexander the Great and also by the Macedonian general Perdiccas who invaded Egypt in 322 B.C. after Alexander's death. The Ptolemies used captured Asiatic elephants in war, and also imported others from Syria, but it was obviously important for them to have a more secure source of supply on the African continent. Thus the African elephant, *Loxodonta africana*, which later featured so prominently in the Punic Wars and crossed the Alps with Hannibal, was also exploited by the ancient Egyptians. Originally regarded simply as a dramatic quarry on which the wealthy Egyptian courtiers could demonstrate their hunting prowess, it became sought after for more practical purposes. By the time its value in this respect was recognized, however, few if any elephants were left on the banks of the Nile below the Cataracts, and the Ptolemies had to send further afield. Two Egyptian trading-posts on the Red Sea, Ptolemias Theron (near the modern Agiq) and Adulis (near Massawa), were selected by Ptolemy II as headquarters for the capture of elephants in the region. The animals were trapped in pitfalls, transported to Egypt in specially constructed ships, and were first broken in by Indian trainers; these were later replaced by Egyptian trainers when they had acquired the necessary skill. Ptolemy III especially valued elephants in his armies and they contributed to the success of many of his campaigns. For instance, during the Third Syrian War his African elephants penetrated as far as Asia Minor, and an inscription at Adulis, set up by an officer in charge of the elephants, records that he also obtained examples of the Indian genus by capture from his Asiatic enemies.

The pursuit of big game such as elephants, either for sheer excitement or practical usage, was only one aspect of hunting in ancient Egypt. Less heroic but equally enjoyable pastimes were fishing and wildfowling, which were practised from the earliest times in Egypt much as they are today. The technical history of fishing is not well documented after the end of the Predynastic period when actual implements such as hooks and harpoons were quite commonly preserved, until the closing centuries of ancient Egyptian history when, in addition to the implements themselves, artists begin to show in considerable detail how the tackle was used. The fishing scenes depict, often in the most charming and human style, how the ancient Egyptians practised this time-honoured form of relaxation. From this evidence we can gather that the spear (or harpoon), the net, and the hook and line, with or without the aid of a rod, were all in use. Angling in Egypt also seems to have antedated angling in ancient China by many centuries, the first Chinese mention of the subject being *c.* 900 B.C.

At the present time there are rather more than 200 species of fish in the complex of lakes and rivers that make up the Nile system, of which at least 100 inhabit the river itself in Egypt. Probably about the same number existed there in ancient times, so there was a varied fish fauna for the Egyptian fisherman to enjoy. In addition the ancient Egyptians were certainly familiar with a large number of marine species, and fishing took place in the Red Sea, the Gulf of Aden and even probably to some extent in the open waters of the Indian Ocean. Many freshwater and marine fishes are depicted on the walls of the Temple of Queen Hatshepsut at Deir-el-Bahari near the present town of Luxor, and in other Egyptian works of art. Not all the reliefs at Deir-el-Bahari are identifiable, but there are unmistakable representations of such marine fishes as skates and rays and the swordfish, *Xiphias gladius*, as well as freshwater catfishes and such freshwater reptiles as the turtle *Trionyx*. An odd omission is the common Nilotic fish *Tilapia* which is, however, very clearly depicted at many other archaeological sites.

In ancient Egypt many birds were hunted for recreation and, one may be sure, for their gastronomic qualities as well. R. E. Moreau gives an admirable account of the species shown in Egyptian works of art, some of which were hunted, others of which were sacred, but all providing a strong aesthetic stimulus to the artist's imagination (pls. 5, 6).[8] The birds depicted include a great number of species ranging from ducks and geese of many kinds, all favourite quarry of the hunters, to pelicans and the odd-looking shoebill, *Balaeniceps rex*, which in ancient Egyptian times had a range extending to the lower reaches of the Nile but which is now restricted to the great papyrus swamp known as the Sudd region in the southern Sudan. One of the most remarkable pictures of water-fowl occurs on the famous coloured panel in the Tomb of Ne-fer-Maat at Medum, on which three species are represented with exquisite sensibility; all three are geese, and they are usually identified as the white-fronted goose, the bean goose, and the red-breasted goose, although opinions differ as to the exact identification of the first-named. This panel dates from the Old Kingdom and no later work of art

Plate 5
Fowling scene from the tomb of Nebamun, Thebes. *c.* 1400 B.C.
British Museum.

76

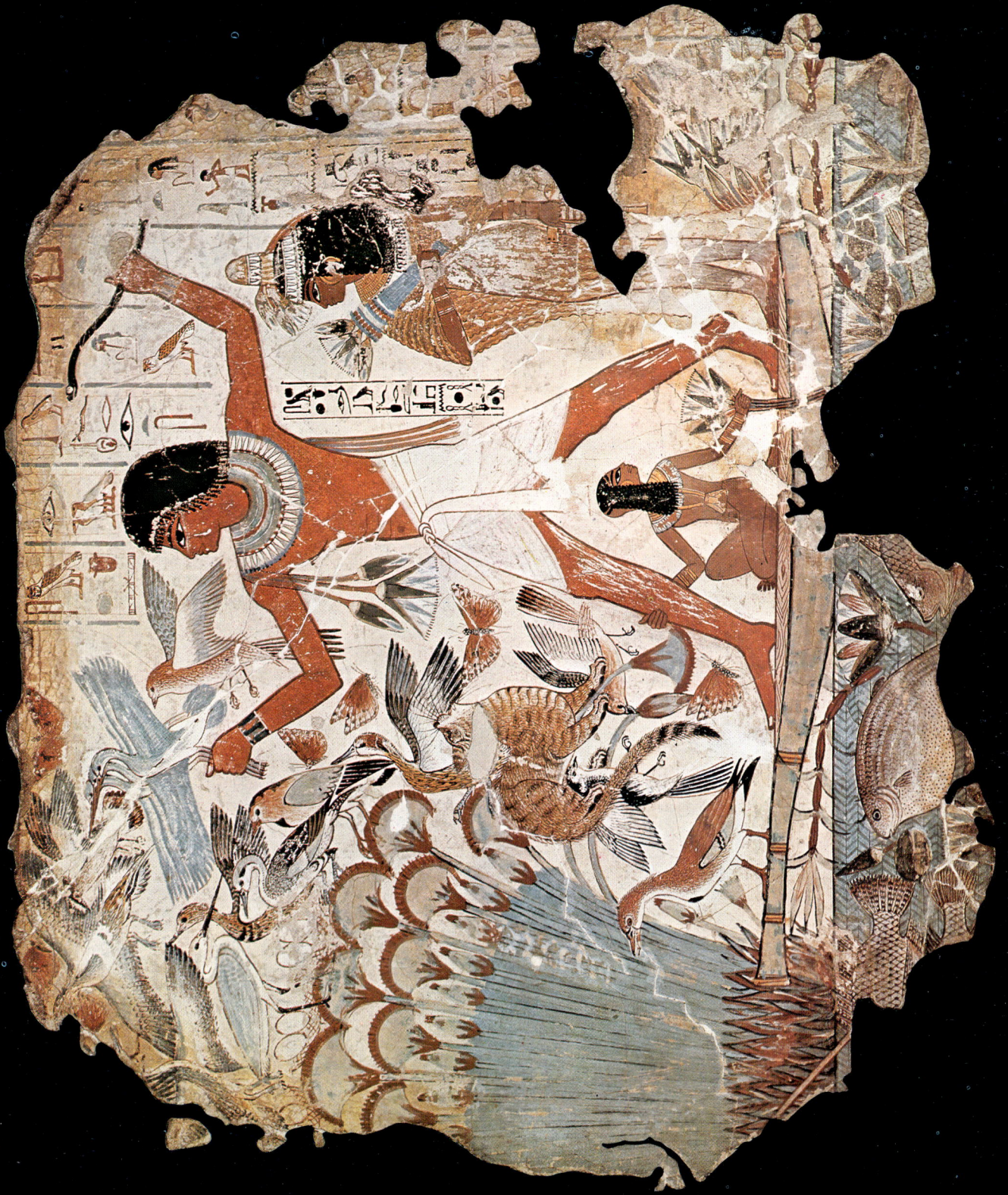

depicts these birds with a similar degree of exactitude.

Other birds which inspired the imaginations of ancient Egyptian artists include shrikes, swallows, nightjars, egrets, herons, spoonbills, ibises, cranes, quails and doves (fig. 37). There are also a number of representations of the ostrich, which only became extinct in Egypt during the nineteenth century, one of which shows a man grasping a young ostrich most confidently by the neck, suggesting that the ostrich was domesticated at that time. The purple heron, *Ardea purpurea*, which was probably the zoological inspiration of the phoenix legend, was a common species of which many beautiful paintings exist. The griffin-vulture, *Gyps fulvus*, is also the subject of a specially dramatic mural-painting at Thebes (the modern Luxor), surging with power and vitality. This graphic way of representing a bird of prey is exceptional in ancient Egypt, however; the pictures are in general highly conventionalized and, although they are frequently represented as hieroglyphs and on tomb-walls, it is normally very difficult even to hazard a guess as to what species is intended. An exception is the barn-owl, which is clearly shown on many hieroglyphic inscriptions. It also seems likely that pictures of the famous falcon god Horus were largely inspired by the peregrine falcon, *Falco peregrinus*, although buzzards, kites and eagles as well as other species of falcon may have played a part in its inspiration.

Fig. 37
Bronze statue of an ibis. Sainte-Ptolemaic period.
British Museum.

Animals as Pets

Before considering the sacred animals in Egypt something should be said about the role of animals as pets. Egyptology is often regarded as a somewhat arid and academic subject and it is too often forgotten that the ancient Egyptians were people of flesh and blood like ourselves. Nowhere were their human qualities better shown than in their regard for animals, not only for their practical use as a source of food or as beasts of burden, but as companions who shared their homes. The two most familiar pets of today, the dog and the cat, were regarded with equal affection.

Apart from their role in the hunt, dogs were valued as pets and household companions. Many pictures show them as part of the domestic scene. Figurines of bronze and ivory, among other materials, depict dogs in many lively attitudes, and children probably enjoyed the fun and pleasure of a puppy's companionship in those days just as much as they do now. The names of the dogs were often inscribed on their collars. Examples of the descriptive or whimsical names that have come down to us in this way are 'Grabber', 'Ebony' and 'Cooking-pot'. One ornate collar placed as funerary equipment in the tomb of a huntsman of the Eighteenth Dynasty was inscribed with the name 'Ta-en-nût', meaning 'She of the Town'. Many of the names include the word *abu*, which appears to be the Egyptian equivalent of our colloquial term 'bow-wow'. An example is a dog known as 'Abutin' of the Old Kingdom who so aroused the respect and affection of the Pharaoh who owned him that it was decreed at his death that 'he be buried ceremonially, that he be given a coffin from the Royal Treasury, fine linen in great quantity, and incense . . . and that a tomb be built for him by the gangs of masons'.[9]

Selective breeding created a vogue for miniature dogs. Representations of these dogs are quite distinct in character from those of ordinary puppies.

Dogs were also much valued as protective escorts, and were not only ready to guard their masters from human enemies, but also (if we are to believe an Eighteenth Dynasty army officer stationed on the Palestine frontier) from aggressive members of their own species. This officer writes a letter home in which he says: 'There are 200 large dogs here, and 300 wolfhounds, in all 500, which stand ready every day at the door of the house whenever I go out. . . . However, have I not the little wolfhound of Naheréh, a royal scribe, here in the house? And he delivereth me from them. At every hour, whensoever I sally forth, he is with me as a guide upon the road. . . .'[10]

Domestic cats were equally popular as pets, and statuettes and other representations are more common in ancient Egypt than those of any other domestic animal. The cat, with its feline grace and its erotic overtones, has come to be regarded by many people as peculiarly symbolic of the spirit of ancient Egypt. However, the domestication of the cat in Egypt seems to have occurred later than in other parts of the Middle East. Although representations of wild cats occur in the Middle Kingdom, the evidence for the animal's domestication before the Eleventh Dynasty is dubious and it is not until the New Kingdom that its frequent use as a subject of works of art prove its overwhelming popularity. Several New Kingdom tombs at Thebes and elsewhere contain the most lively pictures of cats showing them in typical feline

Plate 6
Marsh life, the Mastaba of Mereruka, chamber AI, North wall, scene 2. VIth dynasty, *c.* 2350–2190 B.C.
After *The Mastaba of Mereruka*, part I, Oriental Institute of Chicago, Chicago, 1938.

poses, or eating fish, or lying comfortably curled up under chairs. In the Metropolitan Museum in New York there is a particularly attractive exhibit showing polychrome faience kittens dating from the second half of the second millennium B.C., which are obviously elements of a necklace or collar. The popularity of the cat as a subject for works of art continued right through to Ptolemaic times, when statuettes of the typical Egyptian cat with rounded back and pointed ears, inscrutable and slightly sinister if not actually malevolent, occur in profusion (pl. 7). These cats are reminiscent in appearance of the modern Siamese, of which indeed it is a cousin, but its immediate wild ancestor was probably the so-called 'yellow cat' or 'sand cat', *Felis lybica*, of Africa.*

Apart from the dog and cat the ancient Egyptians also kept a number of more exotic pets. Gazelles with their delicate, graceful shape and soft soulful eyes were especially popular as pets for women. Often deep attachments seem to have been formed between the pet gazelles and their mistresses; for example, in the burial-pit of a Court singer of the Twenty-third Dynasty her pet gazelle was buried at her feet, its legs curled up under it in the attitude of peaceful sleep.

Monkeys were often kept as pets in ancient Egypt. Owing to the almost total lack of scrub or stands of wild trees no monkeys are now indigenous to the country, but in ancient times it seems that the Hamadryas baboon, *Papio hamadryas*, which is mainly a ground-dwelling species, had a range which extended several hundred miles north from the Cataracts. But this particular animal was of mainly religious significance, being sacred to the god Thot, and only the occasional female was kept as a pet. The monkeys which gladdened Egyptian homes by their vivacity and amusing antics all belonged to smaller species which were imported from the lands lying to the south. The exact identification of these little monkeys is difficult, as few of their representations in works of art can with certainty be referred to a particular species; in fact, many of the pictures seem to be compounded of several species, although the genus in most cases seems likely to be *Cercopithecus*. Both baboons and the smaller species of monkeys were often depicted in the same scene, one of the earliest examples being a baboon with red callosities shown with a yellow *Cercopithecus* at Medum, which dates from the Fourth Dynasty.

The Tomb of Achtoy, who was Chancellor under the Eleventh Dynasty pharaoh Mentuhotep II (2060–2010 B.C.), contains pictures of several monkeys disporting themselves in a most lively manner. As Achtoy used to travel widely in Nubia on the instructions of Mentuhotep we may surmise that he acquired a special interest in the monkeys of the region, and possibly the picture in his tomb is of a monkey-house he built to contain the animals brought back from his expeditions.

The affection with which some ancient Egyptians regarded animals, including monkeys, is most charmingly revealed by the story of Sen-mut, who was one of Queen Hatshepsut's most competent administrators. This distinguished official, who was also an architect in his own right, was apparently so deeply attached to his pet monkey, and also to a favourite mare, that he had them ceremonially buried; he even caused

* Incidentally, the Egyptian word for both the wild and domestic cat was *miu*, an unmistakable example of the derivation of an animal's name from the sound it makes.

a bowl of raisins to be placed in the monkey's coffin so that it might have food to enjoy in the afterworld.

It has been surmised that the cat was first allowed to enter the homes of the ancient Egyptians as a pest-destroyer and this is certainly true also of the mongoose, *Herpestes ichneumon*. Of the thirty-nine species of mongooses alive in the world today the Egyptian mongoose is exceptionally large, measuring about 3 feet from nose to tail; but it is quite as agile as all the members of the subfamily to which it belongs and, in Africa as in Asia, has always enjoyed a great reputation as a snake-killer. This well-known prowess has, incidentally, led to some picturesque stories about its methods of tackling its prey; for instance, according to Strabo, Plutarch and other Classical writers, it is alleged to roll itself in mud which it allows to dry into a defensive sheath before giving battle. Actually, of course, it is the animal's swift movements and thick fur which give it the advantage in its battles with snakes.

A further wild story concerning mongooses in ancient Egyptian times is that they were in the habit of running into the open mouths of basking crocodiles and eating out their insides before the astonished reptiles had realized what was happening to them. The mongoose would then emerge, smacking its lips, through a hole it bored in the crocodile's belly. Another superstition concerning the mongoose in ancient Egypt is based on a case of mistaken identity. The Egyptians, it seems, confused the animal with the much smaller and unrelated shrew *Crocidura* of the family Soricidae, which measures only a few inches in length. This seemingly unaccountable mistake has a quite simple explanation. The shrew is a nocturnal animal, whereas the mongoose is diurnal, and the Egyptians simply believed that when the sun set the mongoose shrank, remaining its new small size all night and only resuming its former proportions at dawn. A somewhat modified version of this odd belief survived until at least the ninth century A.D. when it is recorded in the work of Arab historians. For instance, Al-Gahiz, who died in A.D. 868, writes: 'In Egypt there is an animal called Nims. It is able to contract and to become smaller until it is like a mouse.' But this chronicler was fired to achieve even higher flights of fancy than the ancient Egyptians themselves, for he continued: 'If then a snake winds round it, it takes a deep breath, puffs itself up and so breaks the snake in pieces.'[11]

The most unexpected 'pet' (if we may use the word in this connection) to be encountered in ancient Egypt was the lion. Several pharaohs kept lions which, if not actually what we might call 'palace-trained', appear to have been at least semi-domestic. Thus pictures on the walls of temples show both Ramses II and Ramses III accompanied by lions which are obviously part of their establishments. The animals travelled with the pharaohs on their foreign campaigns 'doubtless hastening the enemy into retreat', as Dorothy Phillips aptly puts it.[12] The palace lions must have been quite as great an attraction to important foreign visitors and others whom the ruler wished to impress as were the wild beasts kept at the Tower of London during earlier periods of English history.

The ornamental fish-ponds established by the pharaohs and their wealthier courtiers are another example of pet-keeping in ancient Egypt. The Egyptians were very fond of gardens, and pictures of these are painted on the walls of several tombs so that the dead person might enjoy the pleasure of looking at them in the next world. The fish-ponds

Plate 7
Gayer-Anderson cat. ? Roman period.
British Museum.

80

were one of the most attractive features of the finer gardens and were stocked not only with fish but with many species of exotic water-fowl. According to Zeuner, Plato visited the royal fish-ponds in Egypt and mentions the 'taming' of fishes there.[13] Pools of other kinds were also constructed, although their inmates cannot always be strictly described as 'pets'. For example, one such pool in Thebes contained a number of hippopotamus. These animals were the subject of a stern message from the Hyksos ruler Apophis to his local vassal, complaining 'they permit me no sleep, day and night the noise of them is in my ear'.[14]

The Horse

The Hyksos were a group of Asiatic peoples who invaded Egypt during the Thirteenth Dynasty when the country was in a state of decadence and disruption. Although they were later expelled, their unifying influence brought their new subject peoples great benefits, not the least of which was the first introduction of the horse. As we have seen, in earlier times the main animal used for traction and as a beast of burden was the donkey. Although it was never superseded and, in fact, is one of the characteristic animals of Egypt in modern times, the arrival of the horse added a new dimension to the possible uses of domestic animals. Although the ancient Egyptians do not seem to have been great horse-riders, they harnessed them in pairs to chariots for use in war and in the hunt, and to draw rich men's carriages. In spite of some published statements to the contrary, there is no sound evidence for the domestication of the horse by Palaeolithic or Mesolithic man; it was first exploited in Neolithic times in Asia, the main centre of radiation apparently being Turkestan. From there its use spread westward, giving man a new degree of mobility, for it provided by its swiftness and stamina an invaluable aid to his warlike activities. If the elephant can be regarded as the tank of the wars of the ancient world, the horse was comparable to the jeep or the dispatch-rider's motor-cycle. Its introduction into the Nile Valley greatly improved the efficiency of the Egyptian armies as well as providing the pharaohs with a new and attractive animal to glamourize their processions and other ceremonial displays.

Other Animals

So far only the vertebrate animals of ancient Egypt have been mentioned – the mammals, the birds, the reptiles and the fishes; but the invertebrates, although generally smaller and less spectacular creatures, also played an important role in Egyptian life. The most obvious example is the beetle, which was a sacred animal in ancient Egypt and inspired the production of the magic charms, or scarabs (fig. 38). Many species of beetle occur along the banks of the Nile, but the ancient Egyptians were not sufficiently concerned with the subtleties of entomology to regard their differences as very important; their main criterion was size or attractive appearance. For this reason most of the scarabs are based on the larger beetles of the family Scarabaeidae, which contains such animals as the chafers and dung-beetles.

Wallis Budge, after remarking that the beetle is one of the commonest

Fig. 38
Large beetle, ? from temple at Heliopolis.
Ptolemaic period, *c.* 200 B.C.
British Museum.

amulets, says that their carved representations were often buried with the dead to assist with the restoration of their hearts. He recalls an instruction in a rubric to the sixty-fourth chapter of the *Book of the Dead* where it is stated that a green stone scarab set in a gold frame and anointed with myrrh should be placed in the mummified body of the deceased in the position normally occupied by the heart. During the anointing, which immediately preceded the insertion of the scarab into the body, an incantation was intoned over the dead person exhorting him to 'open his mouth' – that is to aid him to eat, drink and breathe and otherwise act as he did in the land of the living. This belief in the sacred qualities of the beetle still exists in Africa; Livingstone observed a large beetle hung up in the spirit-house of a burnt and deserted village, and the women in the modern Sudan eat beetles to make them more prolific. This Sudanese custom may be a direct survival from ancient Egyptian times when women in labour were given the shell of a beetle mixed up with oil and other substances to assist the birth of their child.

Another use of the beetle in ancient Egyptian burial customs differs somewhat from that given by Wallis Budge. It seems that in some cases the scarab was inscribed with a chant reading: 'Oh my heart, rise not up against me as a witness.' This was laid on the breast of the mummified body beneath the wrappings and it seems it was intended to prevent the dead person from giving away too many of his earthly sins when he came to the judgement hall before the great god Osiris. The beetle was, in fact, so important that it is often depicted as the head of the sun god Khepri, a particularly good example occurring in the tomb of Ramses I.

An invertebrate which had both practical use and religious signifi-

82

cance from the very earliest times in the Nile Valley was the bee. This was associated with the goddess Neith, whose temple at the town of Saïs in the Western Delta was known as 'the House of the Bee [*Hwt Bit*]'. Neith was especially revered by the kings of the First Dynasty and her cult probably goes back to Predynastic times. In fact, the pharaohs adopted her crown as a symbol of their sovereignty over Lower Egypt and employed the title 'He who belongs to the Bee'. Bee-keeping was widely practised, although owing to the shortage of wood in Egypt the hives were made of tubes of clay wider in the middle than at either end, arranged horizontally. When the bee-keeper wished to drive the bees temporarily from the hive in order to extract the honey he achieved this by blowing smoke into one end of the tubes, whereupon the bees hastily evacuated them at the other. Hives based on this ancient Egyptian model are still in use in many of the more arid regions of the Middle East.

Another less attractive insect which played a part in Egyptian life as it does today is the gnat, and we owe to Herodotus a most intriguing description of the methods adopted to mitigate the discomforts it apparently caused then as now. Although Rawlinson's translation describes the insect as the gnat it is probable that this rather loose term also included the mosquito. Herodotus describes the means of protection used in the fifth century B.C., means which are still employed nearly 2,500 years later. He refers first to an ointment made from the castor-oil plant, which was known to the Egyptians as *kiki*, which seems to have acted in much the same way as modern insect repellents, and seems to have been mainly effective by its disagreeable odour. But even more interesting is a device which seems to be the exact counterpart of the modern mosquito-net. Herodotus writes: 'In the marsh country . . . each man possesses a net. . . . By day it serves him to catch fish, while at night he spreads it over the bed in which he is to rest, and, creeping in, goes to sleep underneath. The gnats, which, if he rolls himself up in his dress or in a piece of muslin, are sure to bite through the covering, do not so much as attempt to pass the net.' Herodotus also states that outside the marsh regions 'the inhabitants pass the night upon lofty towers, which are of great service, as the gnats are unable to fly to any height on account of the wind.'*[15]

Animals in Art

The reader will have gathered that a very large part of our information concerning ancient Egyptian animals comes from their representation in works of art. This is especially true in the Dynastic period when paintings, sculptures and figurines reinforce and bring to life the facts we can learn from a study of the bones and other physical remains of the animals themselves.

Some of the nomes, or provinces, into which ancient Egypt was divided were often associated with particular animals whose representations appeared on the provincial standards. The number of nomes

* Of the effectiveness of this form of protection I am personally more sceptical unless the mosquitoes and other biting insects in ancient times were not such high-flyers as they are today; when, trusting Herodotus, I once slept on the twelfth floor on the open terrace of an apartment-house in Cairo when the Nile was in flood I was bitten to pieces.

cannot be strictly determined as they frequently merged or were sub-divided at different stages of Egyptian history, but the Sacred Lists suggest that there were normally forty-two, twenty in Lower Egypt and twenty-two in Upper Egypt. According to some authorities, the nomes carried on the traditions of Predynastic tribal settlements, and the animals associated with them may have had special significance in prehistoric totemism. But this is a subject on which it would be unwise to dogmatize as there are almost as many opinions as there are special-ists. Nevertheless, such animals as the jackal, the ibis and the hare were commonly associated with specific nomes and their use is suggestive of evolution from tribal badges. The use of these emblems in the nomes may, therefore, perhaps be compared to the use of animal symbols in more recent times by the North American Indians and other tribal societies.

As civilization became consolidated in the Nile Valley, and life grew, at least to some extent, more leisurely, the animal art of the Egyptians grew more sophisticated in style. Throughout Dynastic times the Egyptian artists seem to have derived great pleasure from the curious shapes and graceful movements of animals, and they often manage to communicate their own enjoyment with great sensitivity or gusto. Pictures of animals were almost always more free and naturalistic in execution than those of humans, whose representations were too often

rigidly stylized and made wooden and lifeless by adherence to traditional conventions.

One of the great periods of flowering of Egyptian animal art occurred in the Eighteenth Dynasty under the pharaoh Ikhnaton, often called 'the Religious Revolutionary'. Ikhnaton was possessed of exceptional artistic sensibility, and was even competent to give personal instruction to his painters and sculptors. Thus his Chief Sculptor, named Bek, was proud to include in his title the words 'Whom His Majesty himself taught.' As Breasted wrote of Ikhnaton, 'All that was natural was to him true, and he never failed practically to exemplify this belief, however radically he was obliged to disregard tradition.'[16] Encouraged by this attitude the artists of the time produced animal pictures of quite exceptional aesthetic quality. The leaping bull, the coursing hound, the game fleeing panic-stricken from the hunter, the water-fowl rising from the marsh with a flurry of wings, were all shown abounding with life, and even in representations of men and women the old formal conventions were very largely abandoned.

In the Nineteenth and Twentieth Dynasties the new ingredient of humour was added to some of the pictures. The serious affairs of daily life are shown in satirical vein with animals substituted for the human participants. Some of the best examples of this new form of animal art, which is the ancient Egyptian precursor of the modern Disney cartoon,

Fig. 39
Satirical drawings in which animals take the place of human beings in scenes inspired by tomb paintings. New Kingdom.
British Museum.

are preserved in a papyrus in the Turin Museum. Here we may see such scenes as an animal orchestra with a lion playing the lyre, a donkey the harp, a crocodile the lute, and a monkey the double pipes. A similar scene is shown on a papyrus in the British Museum (fig. 39). Cats are a favourite subject in some of the scenes; for example, one shows a cat herding a flock of ducks, another a number of cat bowmen desperately repelling the invasion of a fort by an army of determined mice. Some authorities have thought that these pictures illustrate episodes from some of the animal fables believed to have existed in ancient Egypt, but Professor Lepsius, the famous German Egyptologist, was sure that they are either parodies of contemporary life or of the stereotyped paintings found in many of the earlier tombs.

Apart from their aesthetic and emotional significance in works of art and funerary customs, pictures of animals were also widely used in ancient Egypt as purely practical symbols in hieroglyphic writing. Egyptian hieroglyphics are a system of picture-writing, or 'ideographs', which was originally restricted to concrete objects but was later applied to abstract ideas and verbs. As time went on, the hieroglyphic script was gradually simplified into a script more useful for everyday writing and the original pictures evolved into abstract signs. However, in pure hieroglyphic, which was used for formal inscriptions on tombs and monuments throughout Egyptian history, many of the ideographs were represented by animals of all kinds in more or less detailed form. The various animals did not necessarily represent themselves, although this was sometimes the case, but were used to signify some object or abstract idea. For example, the word 'son' was represented by a goose standing on the ground in profile, and a bird with outspread wings signified the concept of flight. Some of the hieroglyphic pictures simply represented a reference to the animal itself, others to the god with which it was associated.

A study of the royal cartouches of the pharaohs alone shows how commonly the animal symbols were used, and in many cases the species of the animal depicted is identifiable beyond any shadow of doubt. Figures of mammals, birds, reptiles and insects were all commonly employed, and among the unmistakable species are the lion, the wild bull, the jackal, the falcon, the ibis, the purple heron, the barn-owl, the vulture, the goose, the Egyptian cobra, and, of course, several species of the inevitable beetle, or scarab. Amphibians, which were a class of animals that seem to have been neglected as much in ancient Egypt as they are today, are not widely represented, but the cartouche of Ptolemy VI does contain a very clear picture of a frog in the act of jumping.

References to animals in Egyptian literature are more poetic and religious in inspiration than scientific; stories and philosophical dialogues which include animals as their principal characters also frequently occur. Nevertheless, as early as the Fifth Dynasty encyclopaedic lists of the names of animals and plants were already being recorded (for example, those describing the activities of the different seasons of the year in the Sun Temple of Nyuserre), which may be regarded as the forerunners of the natural histories of Classical and later times. In a less austere vein much of the literature of ancient Egypt shows that, for all their preoccupation with the cult of the dead, the writers of the time were capable of creating works of deep romantic and poetic significance. In many of these, animals played an important part in the imagery

86

employed, as is shown particularly in the following extracts from an Eighteenth Dynasty hymn composed by the young pharaoh Ikhnaton himself. This hymn was devised for use either for personal devotions or in the services in the temples, and was engraved by the nobles on the walls of their tomb chapels. It is generally entitled: 'Praise of Aton by King Ikhnaton and Queen Nefernefruaton'. Here, for instance, is a stanza entitled 'Day and the Animals and Plants':

> *All cattle rest upon their herbage,*
> *All tree and plants flourish,*
> *The birds flutter in their marshes,*
> *Their wings uplifted in adoration to thee.*
> *All the sheep dance upon their feet,*
> *All winged things fly,*
> *They live when thou hast shone upon them.*

The genesis of the name Aton who, although he evolved conceptually from the ancient sun god Ra, was more akin to the universal god of Christian religion, forms part of the extremely complex history of Egyptian religion and it would not be appropriate to discuss it here. But the whole of the hymn under discussion is filled with references to animals, and includes one other passage called 'Creation of Animals', with a simple charm that deserves quotation. It reads as follows:

> *When the chicklet crieth in the egg-shell,*
> *Thou givest him breath therein, to preserve him alive,*
> *When thou hast perfected him*
> *That he may pierce the egg,*
> *To chirp with all his might;*
> *He runneth about upon his two feet,*
> *When he hath come forth therefrom.*

In addition to such hymns the literature of ancient Egypt contains several animal fables, all of them graphic, some light-hearted, and others more in the nature of philosophical discourses embodying moral principles. While it must be admitted that the evidence for these fables is based on scripts written down in the Christian era when they may have been adulterated with Greek influences, it is reasonable to assume that no people as passionately addicted to the study, appreciation, and indeed the worship, of animals could have failed to originate many of the stories in which they are the principal characters.

Weidemann gives several examples of moral tales in which animals play the star roles.[17] One of these, which is quoted from a papyrus inscribed with the demotic script in the Leiden Museum, takes the form of a dialogue between a gigantic cat and a very small jackal. The cat takes the orthodox point of view, maintaining that the world is in the control of the gods, that good always triumphs, and that wrong-doing sooner or later meets with retribution. However dark the sky, however effectively the storm-clouds may temporarily block out the light, the sun will eventually break through to bring light and joy with his radiance. The jackal is more cynical. He maintains that might is right, that honour and loyalty are of no importance, that realism, not idealism, is the law of nature and that the wrong-doer will always be able to explain away his actions in a convincing manner that will be acceptable to himself and others. The author seems to favour the argument of the jackal, respecting the way his head rules his heart, although it is obvious that the jackal feels a wholesome respect for the tangible arguments of the cat's claws when its passionate response to the jackal's cold-hearted arguments is provoked. Perhaps fortunately, the papyrus is so damaged and incomplete that the outcome of the dialogue is inconclusive; we are left only with the instinctive feeling that the cat, for all his passionate exaggerations, has a nobler nature than the scavenging jackal.

So far, except by implication, little has been said about animals in Egyptian religion. This omission has been deliberate for, of all the aspects of animals in relation to the daily life of the ancient Egyptians, it is the most widely documented elsewhere. I do not therefore intend, in the present context, to do more than make a few brief generalizations on the subject.

Man being himself an animal, although of course with a higher level of awareness and sophistication, it is natural that he should have regarded the creatures that shared his environment with special interest. In its most primitive and practical aspect this interest was based quite simply on the use to which animals could be put, first as a source of food, and later, as the possibilities of domestication became more fully appreciated, as beasts of burden, means of transport, and collaborators in his hunting activities. But parallel with this evolution of thought about animals there occurred also a profounder kind of appreciation. At its simplest this was expressed in the recognition that animals were beautiful, decorative, essentially attractive, or simply fun to watch or rewarding, in their emotional response, to keep as pets.

But this was by no means the whole of the story. Some animals were seen to be so exceptionally powerful, dangerous, beautiful, or curious and mysterious in aspect and behaviour, that they inspired feelings of fear, admiration, wonder and awe. That is, they became symbolic of some of the profoundest emotions which to this day affect, and even sometimes inspire and exalt, the human heart. The identification of certain animals with these emotions has led quite logically in many societies at the early stages of their development to their endowment with metaphysical or supernatural powers and even to their deification. In no society is this natural and almost universal evolutionary trend more beautifully shown than in ancient Egypt.

The wonder that the Egyptians felt for animals began in the totemism of the Neolithic, and we can trace its evolution through the Predynastic period right down to the time of the Ptolemies. It was believed that the gods who decided the fate of men made their homes in the bodies of certain animals, and these animals thus became identified with the sacred beings who were believed to inhabit them. A full list of these sacred animals would be too long to enumerate, and in any case most of them are already well known, but they include such widely different species as the jackal, sacred to Anubis, the god of the dead; the cat, sacred to Bastet, the goddess of joy; the lion, sacred to Show, the god of the air, whom the Egyptians believed supported the sky; and the crocodile, sacred to Sobek, a god especially worshipped in the Fayum, where crocodiles then abounded.

Some gods, not content with a single species, had several animals sacred to them. Thus Thoth, a god of the moon and the sciences, was associated with both the ibis and the baboon, while Uto (the Greek Buto), a goddess of Lower Egypt, was believed at different times to

88

inhabit both the snake and its arch-enemy the mongoose. The most famous god of all was Horus, a sun god who received universal homage as the son of the still older sun god Ra, and whose sacred animal was the falcon. The Horus falcon appears constantly in hieroglyphic scripts on the walls of tombs and elsewhere, and to this day his majestically simple statue guards his temple at Edfu, where he was the patron of the pharaohs.

Animals associated with the gods were naturally the subject of special veneration and played an important part in numerous cults. The most famous example is that of the sacred bull, Apis, worshipped at Memphis. This was black with white spots and bore on its forehead a white triangle and on its flank a crescent. A succession of live bulls approximating to this ideal image of Apis in colour and the distribution of their markings was kept at the famous temple at Memphis; when the bull aged or sickened, emissaries were sent into all the surrounding regions to find its successor, whose owner was richly rewarded. When the previous bull died it was entombed with much pomp and circumstance in one of the gigantic sarcophagi that can still be seen in the Serapeum at Sakkara. This cult of the bull, which is obviously based as much on an appreciation of its physical strength and virility as on any mystical religious significance, is by no means limited to Egypt, and references will be found to it in several other contributions to this volume. Traces of its survival still exist in many primitive communities today, and even in such rituals as the Spanish bull-fight which has obvious emotional connections with the bull cults of earlier times.

In such a short account of animals in Egyptian archaeology I have scarcely been able to scratch the surface of this vast topic, even within the voluntary limitations I had to impose upon myself at the outset. There is not, for example, even space to refer to such a fascinating subject as the mummification of sacred animals, nor to the motivation and methods of animal sacrifice which was widely practised throughout Egyptian history. The literary sources for further information on the subject are virtually limitless, and some of these are listed in the Bibliography below. But my aim in writing this brief and essentially synoptic survey will be much better achieved if one reader is encouraged to visit the banks of the Egyptian Nile and savour the enchantment of its animal and human past.

5
ANIMALS IN THE AEGEAN

A. HOUGHTON BRODRICK

Behind the pantheon of the Classical Greek world lies a great heritage of more primitive beliefs, beliefs that go back to the Neolithic and sometimes even the Old Stone Age.

In Classical Greek mythology Artemis was the 'Mistress of Animals', of the hares and stags, the wolves and bears and lions and all the beasts of the wild, but most especially of deer. In the Greek temple at Ephesus on the coast of Asia Minor she was served not only by eunuch priests but also by priestesses and, during the ceremonies at the shrine, the priestesses were clad in the same way as the goddess herself is portrayed in Greek sculpture – buskins, a short robe drawn in with a girdle at the waist, the right breast bare, a quiver slung over a shoulder, a bow held in the hand. Here Artemis was 'Diana of the Ephesians', an Olympian goddess, but also a form of the Asiatic Earth Mother.

But Artemis, like all Greek deities, is a composite figure with varying attributes, differing aspects and embodying a number of local divinities whose origins were as diverse as ancient. Thus at another of her sanctuaries, Brauron, on the coast of Attica in Greece, the young girls were not dressed as huntresses but were disguised in the skins of bears and mimed the *arkteia* – the bear dance – with the shuffling, clumsy movements of *arktoi*, the bear. At Brauron the deity to whom the rites were addressed, the original divinity of the holy place, for sacred sites retain their sanctity throughout the ages despite changes in the hallowing spirit's name, was once a live she-bear who probably devoured the flesh of victims sacrificed to her. At another Artemis shrine a fawn dressed as a girl was immolated to her, a clear indication that at one time the deity was invoked with human sacrifices. Traces of such practices can be seen here and there amid the welter of Classical Greek myths and legends.

If the animals associated with Artemis were very numerous they were hardly 'sacred' to her in our sense of the term. She may have been the 'patroness' of beasts but the most acceptable sacrifice to a divinity is that of animals peculiarly associated with him, for worshippers by partaking of the flesh of beasts which in a measure share his divine nature, can enter into communion with him. Moreover, for the practical Greeks sacrifices might be the occasions for a good meat meal, were indeed more or less barbecues, except in the case of holocausts when the victims were entirely consumed by fire. Thus Artemis, in some places, was honoured, was placated and invoked with a holocaust in which animals of all sorts, together with the fruits of the earth, were cast alive on to a pyre there to be wholly charred and destroyed.

It is hardly surprising then that the goddess might sometimes assume strange forms. At Phigalia in Arcadia, a region where ancient beliefs and rites were especially rife, she appeared as a mermaid.

In the same town the goddess Demeter, not seldom represented as a dignified and matronly figure, a little sad maybe as though mourning for her lost daughter Persephone, had a temple that housed her venerated image. It was black. It had a mare's head. Its priests were known as 'foals'.

But in this case the horse-worship cannot have been derived from a very ancient stratum of the country's customs (although it is quite possible that the Mare-Demeter took the place of some earlier animal-divinity) since horses were unknown in Greece before the second millennium B.C.

'Unknown' is perhaps not the right word, since there were horses in Greece long before the year 2000 B.C., but it was a very long time before, during the middle of the last Ice Age. At that time horses roamed wild over the foothills of the Pindus Range and were hunted and eaten, together with woolly rhinoceros and deer, by Neanderthaloid man. There were horses on the Plain of Thessaly during the Ice Age, but the fine breed found in this area in later times were not their descendants. Between the two there was an hiatus, a time when there were no horses in Greece. The reason for this is mainly the changing climatic conditions. About 8000 B.C. European weather changed radically. The last Ice Age melted to an end. Glaciers sweated away, for the most part at least. The rainfall increased. Forests spread far and wide, interspersed with marsh and swamp – poor terrain for horses which do not like getting their feet wet and whose hooves are unsuited to a soggy soil. Horses are, by nature, creatures of the open spaces, steppes and prairies, and they can withstand a great deal of cold. So the horse moved off northwards and eastwards and flourished on the hard, grassy levels which stretch from the Ukraine to Turkestan. For thousands of years the horse was rare in most of Europe, and indeed, for the Classical Greeks, they remained rather exotic animals.

The great wild cattle, *Bos primigenius*, remained. These were the huge beasts portrayed by Palaeolithic artists in the caves of western Europe (see Chapter I). Already then they were symbols of supernatural power. In Europe the cave art ends with the end of the Ice Age, some 10,000 to 8,000 years ago. But the bull reappears again, this time in Anatolia, at Çatal Hüyük and Hacilar about 7000 B.C. (see Chapter 2). When we think of possible links between such art and that of the Palaeolithic cave-painters we may reflect that the fade-out of their pictorial activities which looks so sudden in the record may well have taken centuries to be consummated. The climatic switch did not occur overnight, and there must have been plenty of time for art traditions, and probably other traditions as well, to travel to more favourable climes.

The Neolithic Anatolians had shrines full of bulls' heads, horned pillars and paintings of animals. There is a great picture of a huge red bull being teased by a horde of small human beings. At Hacilar there

Fig. 40
Vaphio gold cup II showing bull captured by decoy cow, tholos tomb at Vaphio in Laconia. Upper diam. 10·8 cm. *c.* 1500 B.C. After S. Marinatos, *Crete and Mycenae*, Thames and Hudson, London, 1960.

is a bull's head frieze – things reminiscent of Crete where a bull cult and bull-sports were dominating cultural features – at least during the period for which we have statuettes, paintings, stucco reliefs, seals and decorated vases.

If we take the Aegean area to comprise mainland Greece, the islands of the Archipelago, the western coasts of Asia Minor and Crete, it is the last that is revealed as the laboratory where was developed the first Aegean – and European – civilization. Cyprus, though subjected to Aegean influences, lies rather outside the specifically Aegean region.

Crete also offers the only instance we know of where a high civilization was born and evolved not on a mainland but on an island – the example of Japan is not really valid since Japanese civilization was in its essentials imported from China. The first settlers in Crete must have arrived early in the sixth millennium B.C., if not before. They came probably from Asia Minor by way of Rhodes (from which on a clear day the summit of Cretan Mount Ida can be seen with the naked eye) and Carpathos. It is worth while stressing that Cretan culture had no deep roots in the island itself, that is to say there is no long record of human settlement going back to Palaeolithic times as there was in mainland Greece. The first Cretans found a deserted island as far as human inhabitants were concerned. We cannot say for certain what native fauna they found. Isolated islands do not, as a rule, have a very rich stock of animals and there seems no reason to think that the

92

indigenous beasts of Crete were more varied in species than those of
other Mediterranean islands situated at a comparable distance from
the mainland. At any rate, even before the ancient Cretans had begun
to make pottery they were keeping sheep, cattle, pigs and goats – the
last probably descendants of the native wild goat that still survives.
Much later on, in the heyday of Minoan civilization, the representations show a great variety of animals both real and imaginary, lions and
leopards, monkeys and cats, sphinxes and griffins, horses both winged
and wingless, wild boars and deer. The horses and the monkeys were
obviously imported and also the domesticated cats. Lions are so
frequently depicted in Cretan art that it has been supposed they roamed
the island even at the zenith of Minoan civilization, between 1700 and
1400 B.C. But this hardly seems likely. For even if wild lions had existed
in Crete, surely, over the centuries, a people with herds and flocks
(Cretan wool was famous and together with woven stuffs extensively
exported) would have exterminated the savage predators on such a
comparatively small island. The situation was, of course, quite other
on mainland Geeece. There is, moreover, no trace of lions on other
Mediterranean islands. Furthermore, many if not most of the Cretan
lion compositions closely resemble those of Mesopotamian or Egyptian
prototypes. It is just possible that during the heyday of Cretan prosperity lions and leopards were imported to grace parks or gardens.

The bull that played such a leading part in Cretan life was almost

93

certainly of domesticated stock, since cattle were, as we have seen, kept on the island from very early times. However, some, perhaps, were allowed to roam about in a semi-wild condition. There are Cretan scenes of capturing bulls but perhaps they were like the Spanish fighting bulls which have to be rounded up although they are not really 'wild'. The most famous of Cretan objects with bull scenes – the Vaphio gold goblets, showing the lassooing and the capture by means of a cow-decoy, were found in Greece, and though the objects were obviously made by Cretan artificers, they were not necessarily made on the island, and the scenes do not necessarily hold good for Crete itself (fig. 40). The Cretan bulls, as depicted in the frescoes, are piebald or dappled whereas wild cattle are of uniform colour.

The great preoccupation with bulls has left many traces in Crete (fig. 41). Skulls of huge bulls adorned the palace halls of Knossos as they did the walls of Neolithic sanctuaries in Asia Minor or the tomb of a First Dynasty pharaoh. The most consistent of Greek legends concerning Crete relates to the Minotaur, a monster, half-bull, half-man, reputed the offspring of Pasiphae and a white bull sent to King Minos by the god Poseidon. The numerous bull-headed human figures in Cretan art depict both the monster himself and probably also his priests wearing bull-masks.

Bulls were sacrificed, and there is a striking representation of a captive and dying bull from whose wound the sacred blood is pouring, to be used in libations and magico-religious ceremonies. The bull also figured in the chief of Cretan sports – no doubt also of some quasi-religious import – that of 'teasing' the animal (pl. 8). This sport was not bull-fighting as we understand it: the bulls do not appear to have been killed, at least there and then. The bull-sport was essentially an acrobatic display in which the bull was grabbed by the horns, men vaulted over his back and generally dared and played with him. The horns do not seem to have been blunted or capped (as in Portuguese bull-fights) and girls as well as young men took part in the dangerous game. There are representations of men leaping over deer or antelope, perhaps practising for the bull-arena on a more tractable sort of beast.

The Cretans also enjoyed chariot-racing – horses were kept but do not seem to have been very common – and their taste for wrestling-matches, boxing and for contests generally was passed on with so many other things to the Mycenaeans and from them to the later Greeks.

In the Cretan palaces spacious areas were set apart for magical, religious and sporting activities, all of which were probably closely connected. In the frescoes are representations of processions and dances as well as of the bull-sports. Crowds are shown watching, while elegant ladies lend a gay note to the scene.

The main divinity of the Cretans was a goddess, doubtless a form of the Earth Mother, and with her was associated a young god, maybe her lover, son or brother – or all three at once, since such apparent contradictions are common enough in ancient myths. We do not know what either of them had to do with the bull-sports or the Minotaur, but it is probable that these divinities were honoured with sacrifices.

The goddess is depicted with flounced skirt and crowned with a tall tiara and often with bare breasts, and there are scenes in which her priestesses or devotees are clad in the same way. That she was a deity of the earth and the nether regions is clearly indicated by her – and her

Plate 8
The bull-games, Palace of Knossos. Late Minoan I, shortly after 1500 B.C.
After S. Marinatos, *Crete and Mycenae*, Thames and Hudson, London, 1960.

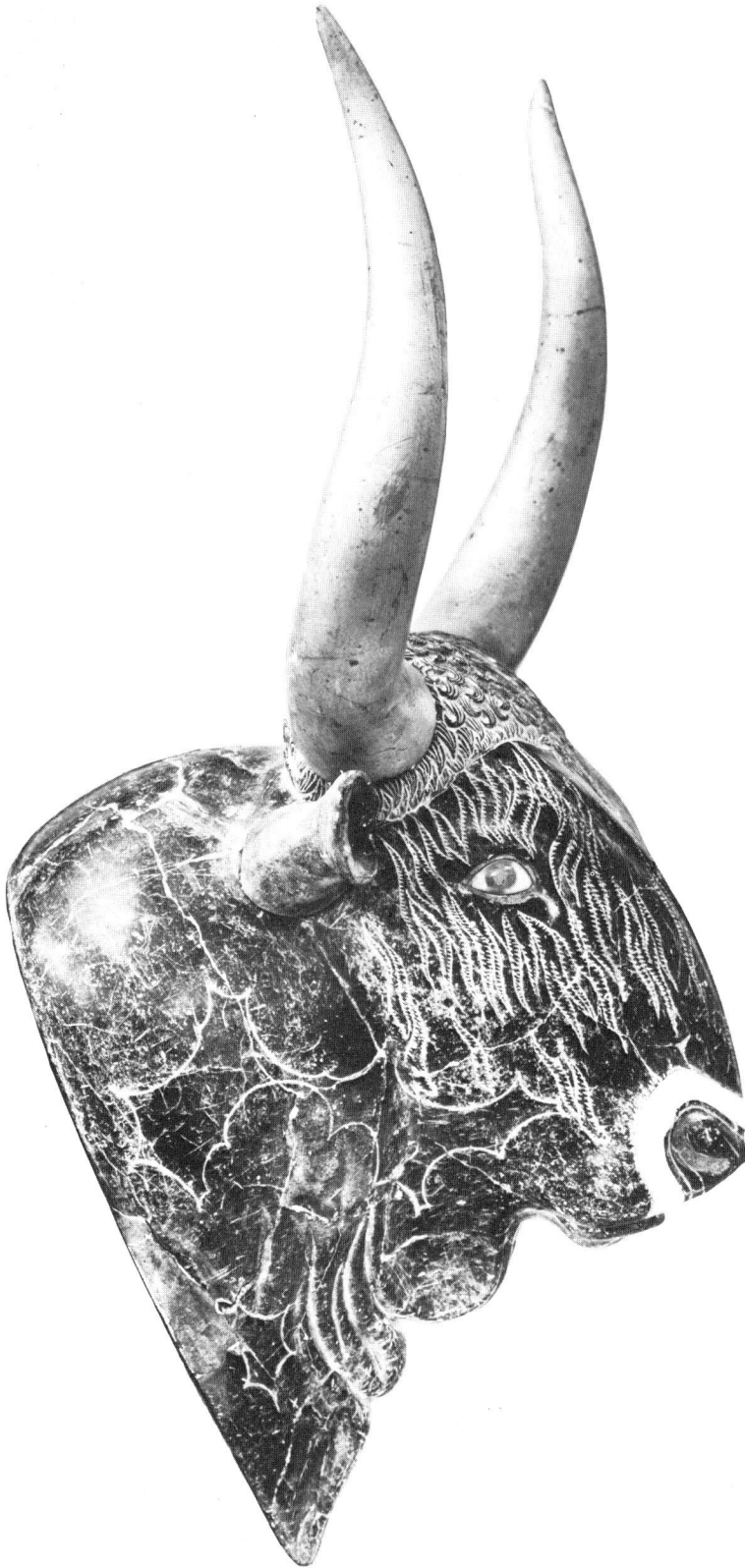

Fig. 41
Black steatite rhyton in form of bull's head, Little Palace at Knossos. Length without horns 20·6 cm. Late Minoan I, *c.* 1550–1500 B.C.
After S. Marinatos, *Crete and Mycenae*, Thames and Hudson, London, 1960.

Fig. 42
Earth goddess with snakes, underground
treasury of the central sanctuary in the
Palace of Knossos. Middle Minoan III,
c. 1600–1580 B.C.
After S. Marinatos, *Crete and Mycenae*,
Thames and Hudson, London, 1960.

devotees – holding serpents and having snakes entwined about them (fig. 42).

Snakes have healing and consecrating powers, they share a divine character since they are mysterious creatures which disappear and appear again, which die and are resurrected – that is they shed their skins. They are denizens of the nether world and thus peculiarly the creatures of chthonian, that is earth, deities.

The male divinity is depicted as a handsome youth, often with animals on either side of him, particularly lions, some of which are shown in a conventionalized and indeed stylized fashion which suggests that there were not always live models at hand for the artists to work from.

There is a good deal of evidence for a cult of the Dead, both from the tombs but also from the pictures in which we may see griffins, for instance, harnessed to a hearse. Maybe the fabulous creatures that figure so much in Cretan art – sphinxes, eagle-headed lions and the like, had some significance in connection with the cult of the Dead (pl. 9).

But our knowledge of ancient Crete is an archaeological one, for there is no ancient Cretan literature to lead or mislead us as the case may be. But there is an abundant art. It is true that the paintings, the most evocatory, belong only to a comparatively short period, from about 1700 to 1400 B.C., a time when the civilization was at its peak and had been enriched by borrowings from abroad. But Cretan art, if eclectic, was moulded by and stamped with the peculiar Cretan genius. A Cretan object – or one created under direct Cretan influence in mainland Greece or in the islands – is unmistakable. In the vase-decoration, the frescoes, the painted stucco reliefs (most of which have been extensively restored) there is a spring-like, a Renaissance quality that surprises and delights and seems to reflect the life of a people (or some of them) cheerful, peaceable and sensitive.

The earliest artistic representations are on vases. The early painted vases have floral motifs: plant forms and flowers, lilies, tulips, sweet peas and the like, admirably adapted to the curved surface but remaining naturalistic. Later there are vases with animal figures, marine creatures, fish, octopuses or insects, and then water-fowl (fig. 43). The floor of one of the Knossos palace apartments is also painted to represent the sea, with dolphins and other denizens of the deep. The Cretans were a seafaring people who lived on and from the sea.

Some time after the first development of painted pottery the frescoes adorning the palaces of Crete began to be painted. On these the Cretan artists left a panorama of animal life that is treated with an artistic feeling, a nice appreciation of form and colour that are hardly paralleled elsewhere in the ancient world. These compositions seem to have begun to be painted about 1550 B.C. There are rocky landscapes with flowers, lily gardens, birds and monkeys. There is an even earlier representation of monkeys on a seal which dates to 2000 B.C., if not earlier. Probably both the ivory for carved objects and the monkeys themselves were imported from Egypt. Monkeys can live out of doors for most of the year in Crete, at least at sea-level, and were obviously kept as pets, for in one of the paintings there is a representation of a monkey wearing harness. The creature's playful, mischievous attitude is well portrayed.

In another scene a feline, perhaps a leopard, stalks birds while a deer

bounds away in a flowery background. Hoopoes and partridges twitter in the foliage. Among brightly coloured lilies and crocuses a bull advances, a hare flees. In the Knossos 'House of Frescoes' a brilliant, evocatory blue bird wings off from amid rocks and lilies and wild roses in bloom.

With the exception of the bull-game scenes none of the paintings seems to tell a tale, they are just highly decorative things and aesthetically satisfying.

At their zenith the Cretans exercised an artistic, a cultural and possibly in places a political influence in the Aegean. A fresco of flying fish from the Cyclades might be Cretan work; Cretan-patterned sphinxes, deer, swans and griffins appear on the island vases. From Camiri in Rhodes comes a gold ornament showing a winged goddess flanked with two felines, lionesses or leopards, very like some representations of the Earth Mother whom the Greeks identified with Artemis, the Mistress of Animals.

The Cretans were skilful seal-cutters as well as ivory-workers. The seals of amethyst, agate, cornelian and other semi-precious stones show an immense variety of animals, both real and mythical (fig. 44). There is a sharp-looking cat; the original must have come from Egypt. There is an amusing scene of goats drawing a small cart, rather like those that used to be common at seaside resorts not so long ago. The goat-cart may just be a joke. The Cretans used asses and onagers to pull four-wheeled vehicles, and as pack-animals.

The seals show not only real animals such as lions and wild boars but also mythical creatures – griffins, winged and unwinged, sphinxes and harpies, tritons and sirens, human-headed bulls and, of course, bull-headed men, eagle-headed felines, birds with men's heads, most of them it would seem borrowed from abroad. It is hard to decide whether the animal and quasi-animal figures on the vases and in the paintings are significant or just decorative, but probably they had some quasi-magical import. In any case the figures on the seals certainly carried a meaning and not only a meaning but a menace. For seals were symbolical padlocks. And the image on the seal would have magical power. Whoever broke the seal would be breaking a taboo and would surely in some way or other suffer for his misdeed.

During the century from about 1400 to 1300 B.C. Crete declined and the cultural leadership of the Aegean passed to the Mycenaeans.

Mycenaean Greece

Recent discoveries have shown that up in the north, near Janina, men were living in huts as long ago as about 15,000 B.C., thus well within the last Ice Age. It is improbable that they had any domesticated animals except maybe dogs. These seem to be the earliest true men in Greece, inhabiting a country in which there had been no hominid population since the time of the Neanderthaloids who hunted deer, horses and woolly rhinoceroses on the slopes of the Pindus 30,000 years ago.

But there were Neolithic settlements at Nea Nikomedeia near the Macedonian frontier 8,000 years ago and possibly more. These people kept cattle, pigs and goats while in Thessaly, at about the same time, the inhabitants reared the same animals and also some sheep. These ancient Thessalians and near-Macedonians have left no art and, therefore, we know little about them. But there was a continuity of human settlements in Greece for many thousands of years, and each successive phase of culture must have influenced the following one. We may be pretty sure that beliefs, customs and even holy places were passed on from one generation to another.

The Mycenaean civilization, the earliest on the mainland, is so called from Mycenae, the fabled home of Agamemnon, where it was first recognized, but it spread far beyond the Mycenae region. It owed much, indeed, one is inclined to think, all, the essentials of civilization to Crete. In fact, the Mycenaean is really a provincial Cretan culture. There may even at one time have been a Cretan political domination over part of the mainland, and there must have been Cretan settlements or trading-stations. Possibly the Cretan penetration may have been comparable with that of China into Japan, that is to say bloodless, pacific and irresistible. Cretan civilization was obviously superior and so Cretan beliefs and customs must also be superior and fit to be imitated. None the less, the Cretan culture was grafted on to native traditions.

The cult of chthonian, that is earth, deities may be a Cretan legacy.

Fig. 44
Minoan gold signet ring with wild goats mating.
After S. Hood, *The Home of the Heroes*, Thames and Hudson, London, 1967.

The Earth Goddess in Cretan dress figures in Mycenaean art. Centaurs, harpies, tritons, sirens and griffins in Greek art and legend came, in part at least, from Crete, and it may be that ancient Aegean mysticism influenced later Greek ceremonies and cults.

If we are in doubt about the original fauna of Crete we know that that of Mycenaean Greece was abundant and varied. Lions and leopards, wild boars and bears, wild cats and wolves, lynxes and ibexes and probably wild cattle abounded. And in Mycenaean art many of these beasts are represented in an admirably naturalistic manner. Some, indeed, of the Mycenaean painting, sculpture, inlay-work and jewellery is excellent though some of it is coarse and even clumsy, and there was an artistic decline as time wore on. However, there is, for example, a scene of a lion-hunt (from Mycenae) that is particularly lively and lifelike (fig. 45). Spearmen on foot are attacking and one of the lions has fallen. On an inlaid dagger-blade from Pylos (Nestor's supposed capital) there is a representation of leopards chasing wild duck in what looks like a papyrus swamp (fig. 46). It is a very Cretan scene, though it is improbable that papyrus grew either in Greece or even in Crete. The motif may, however, have been a stock one with the swordsmiths, derived eventually from Egyptian prototypes and thus a status symbol. Imported objects have always a snob value on the home market.

The most famous Mycenaean animal figures are those decorating the 'Lion Gate' at Mycenae itself. The beasts represented are actually lionesses and are headless (the heads were apparently made separately) and are posed rampant in an heraldic attitude on either side of a

Fig. 45
a. Bronze dagger with inlay of lion hunt, grave IV, Citadel of Mycenae. Length 23·8 cm.
b. Detail of above.
After S. Marinatos, *Crete and Mycenae*, Thames and Hudson, London, 1960.

column. The execution seems rather clumsy, may be because the stone has weathered a good deal, but the beasts are impressive enough.

By about 1550 B.C. the Mycenaeans were using two-wheeled chariots, but there is no evidence that they rode on horseback. One of the Mycenaean sword-blades is decorated with figures of three galloping horses, probably the animals were kept out at grass and not stabled. At any rate, the inhabitants of ancient Hellas had chariots as early if not slightly earlier than the Cretans. Horses were first harnessed to war-chariots in Egypt, Mesopotamia and Hittite Asia Minor, so the Mycenaeans may have adopted horse-drawn vehicles from the Near East rather than from Crete.

We do not know much about Mycenaean religion or the part that animals may have played in it. On the so-called 'Nestor's Ring' from Pylos there is a great tree and round it some mysterious rites of initiation or purification are being performed. The newly discovered 'Sphinx Gate' at Pylos shows that the Mycenaeans took over, probably from the Cretans, the sphinx motif as well as those of other monsters. These survived into Classical Greece where, after the adoption of alphabetical writing and the development of language, such creatures were to be enveloped in legends (Fig. 47). The Mycenaeans adopted fresco-painting from the Cretans, although the pictures on the mainland are, on the whole, neither so evocatory or so finely executed as those on the island. But then the Mycenaean pictures are in an even worse state of preservation than the Cretan. The palaces of Tiryns, Thebes and Pylos were burned to the ground during the twelfth century B.C. when hordes of invading northerners, the ancestors of the historic Greeks, overran the country.

The Mycenaeans certainly adopted, among other customs, that of the Cretan bull-sport which probably retained the same significance, whatever that may have been. There is one picture of the bull-contest that is particularly lively. Lady *aficionadas* are sitting in a box and enjoying the entertainment just as they do in Spain today.

Fig. 46
a. Bronze dagger with inlay of hunting scene in papyrus swamp, grave V, Citadel of Mycenae. Length 16·3 cm.
b. Detail of above.
After S. Marinatos, *Crete and Mycenae*, Thames and Hudson, London, 1960.

Fig. 47a
a. Ivory plaque of winged sphinx.
b. Ivory plaque of bull attacked by a lion.
Both from Spata, east Attica. *c.* three times
life size.

Fig. 47b
After S. Marinatos, *Crete and Mycenae*,
Thames and Hudson, London, 1960.

Sometimes there is a pleasing note of interest in animals that is otherwise rare. A plaque from Tiryns shows a cow and her calf which can be compared not to its disadvantage with a faience plaque from Knossos showing a she-goat suckling her kids.

Mycenaean civilization, which had spread its influence even more widely than that of Crete, was blotted out at the source. Writing vanished from Greece (where the Cretan script had been used) and with it most of the arts and crafts. For several hundred years a cloud hangs over Greece. When it lifts a transformation has taken place. There had been an amalgamation of surviving customs and beliefs with new influences from the East. We are on the threshold of what the French call *le miracle grec* – 'The Greek Miracle'.

Classical Greece

The part played by animals in Greek life, art, religion and literature was a very considerable one. Our knowledge of their role in the Classical world derives not only from archaeological sources but from literary evidence, though it is somewhat dangerous to formulate the Greek ways of life and the manners and customs of the mass of the people from the evidence of books written in fifth-century Athens.

The archaeological evidence is, indeed, from some points of view rather disappointing for a civilization so important and imposing as that of Classical Greece. First of all, with the exception of the painted vases, we have few examples of ancient Greek pictorial art. The vase-paintings are precious, of course, and throw a certain amount of light on everyday life. But they are monochrome, either black figures on a red background or red figures on a black background; there is no perspective, and there is a continuous repetition of the same themes, almost *ad nauseam* – the Labours of Herakles, the Exploits of Theseus, the Rape of Europa and the many episodes of a complicated mythology, but not many pictures showing us how the people really lived (figs. 48, 49). The Greeks did have a flourishing pictorial art and many famed artists, but of their work we know only what ancient writers have described, and their comments are about as useful as those of a modern art critic in enabling us to visualize a painting we cannot see.

Again, Greek sculpture is not perhaps so informative about animals as might be hoped or expected, but we have to bear in mind that most of the 'Greek' sculpture that fills the museums is, in fact, Roman copies, often remarkable but all the same executed by, and addressed to, a people fundamentally differing from the Greeks in outlook, ways of life, philosophy of living, religious ideas and artistic genius.

The Greeks of Classical times were scattered about among a considerable number of different sovereign States whose inhabitants were in the main both poor and superstitious. Moreover, there were great contrasts between the customs and beliefs in the varous regions of Hellas. Ionia, especially, on the western coast of Asia Minor, was penetrated with Oriental influences.

But foreign divinities were always assimilated and merged into the figures of gods and goddesses already existing in any given locality. And this was a constant process throughout Greek history. Much was absorbed. Little was discarded.

The Greek deities whatever their origin had one thing in common:

Fig. 48
Caeretan *hydria* showing Herakles delivering the hound of Hades, Cerberus, to his master Eurystheus. *c.* 530 B.C. Height *c.* 43 cm.
After J. Boardman, *Greek Art*, Thames and Hudson, London, 1964.

they were all associated with, or accompanied by, animals. Animal stories form part and parcel of Greek mythology as a whole. The legends of the great Olympian deities themselves, as reworked, embellished and enriched by generations of poets, were informed with beliefs having their roots in a remote past. Side by side with decorous ceremonies in the great temples, there were popular religious rites and orgiastic cults.

The gods, indeed, often assumed animal forms themselves as well as changing mere mortals into beasts. Some of the epithets of the gods (for an 'epithet' indicated generally that the god had absorbed another

104

Fig. 49
Detail from Athenian black-figured
amphora showing Herakles wrestling with
the Nemean lion. *c.* 520 B.C.
After J. Boardman, *Greek Art*, Thames and
Hudson, London, 1964.

divinity) show their original animal origins. Thus the cow was 'sacred'
to Hera who was also styled 'cow-faced'. Athena's favourite bird was
the owl, but she might also be 'owl-faced'. Dionysus favoured, among
a host of other beasts, the goat, and on occasion he was a he-goat.

The Greeks mocked the Egyptians for their adoration of animals, but
Greece itself was filled with divinities of animal origin.

The bull was the chief among the Grecian magic beasts and the most
spectacular victim that might be offered in sacrifice to the gods; its
outstandingly sacred character was of immense antiquity. So persistent
was the holy nature of the bull that at some bull-sacrifices the officiating
priest was regarded as a potential criminal who must be purged of his
guilt. In Athens consecrated cakes would be presented to the victim,
ostensibly so that by eating them he might seem to merit death for
sacrilege, but in reality to increase his sanctity. After the beasts had
been immolated the priest had to undergo a mock trial at which he was,
of course, acquitted. It was the axe that was adjudged guilty and it must
be flung into the all-corrupting sea. At Tenedos, the officiant, after he
had sacrificed a young bull, had to flee under a hail of stones.

A bull immolated at Delphi became known as the 'Sanctifier', for
bulls' blood makes holy and is powerful magic. Indeed, to drink of the
blood of a sanctified and sacrificed bull was to court death, so virulent
were its properties, for the immanent 'virtue' of the sacrificed beast
resides in its blood, and also in its hide. To be asperged with bulls' blood
was to be purged of guilt and assured of good fortune.

Great Zeus himself would often assume the form of a bull, and one of the most famous of his amorous exploits was the rape of Europa whom he carried off to Crete, the Land of the Bull. No doubt some of the bull-complex of Greece was an inheritance from Crete through Mycenaean Greece, but stretching back beyond that the symbolic significance of the bull can be seen in the Neolithic art of Asia Minor and beyond that in the Palaeolithic art of western Europe 20,000 years ago.

Perhaps the most spectacular and dramatic of bulls in Greek sculpture is that known as the 'Farnese' (in Naples) showing Dirce about to be tied to the beast's horns while an attentive dog stretches upwards and watches with curiosity the development of the tragedy. Although the group was extensively restored (by Michelangelo no less) it was carved out of one huge block of stone and is very possibly a Greek original and no Roman copy. It forms a splendid frontispiece to the bull in the archaeology of Greece.

The Classical Greeks do not seem to have indulged in the bull-sports and acrobatic displays that featured so prominently in Cretan and Mycenaean civilizations. But bull-fights were held both in Thessaly, the Land of Horses, and in Ionia in honour of Poseidon, a national god of the Ionians. At his festivals at Ephesus his cupbearers were known as 'bulls' and the god himself invoked as the 'Bull Poseidon', no doubt in his character as a chthonian or underworld deity. On occasion not only were black bulls, as well as boars, rams and horses offered to him but also, sometimes, in early days, human victims.

But Poseidon, known mainly in later Greek times as the 'God of the Sea', never lost his peculiar association with horses. He seems to have been one of the divinities brought south from the northern home of horses by the invading 'proto-Greeks', who would not have had much use for a sea god, but who no doubt found one in Hellas who then became identified with Poseidon.

We noted that horses travelled eastwards to the great plains thousands of years before the beginning of Greek history, and there is a fourth-century B.C. Greek silver vase found in south Russia which is decorated with vivid scenes of the steppes' horsemen. They are dressed in their barbarian costume suited for a cold country, trousers and thick jackets. These men are shown lassoing horses, taming them, talking to them, bridling them, breaking them in. It was probably in these areas that horse-riding first began. It might well be that the invading 'proto-Greeks' may have owed some of their success to their cavalry especially if the enemy only had chariots and no mounted men.

Not only did the horsemen of the steppes invent bridles but they had bone bits, and some of these have been recovered from southern Russian sites dating from about 2000 B.C.

Possibly the invaders brought with them some sort of horse cult as well as the god Poseidon, the 'Earth-Shaker'. A thundering herd of half-wild stallions, mares and foals galloping over the steppes can give a pretty good imitation of an earthquake. Nothing would be more natural than to associate the horse god with earth tremors especially when he got to Greece, a land of frequent earthquakes.

Poseidon was doubtless originally a horse, The Horse, the embodiment of all horses, their god and their lord. Later on in Greek legend he created horses when he was already the god of the sea. He struck his trident on the ground and the first horse sprung out of the earth. In this story there is no trace of the thundering herds of the steppes.

Frequently in Greece Poseidon would assume the form of a stallion. At Haliarnus in the heart of Boeotia there was an ancient pre-Hellenic sacred site where a 'nymph' or earth-spirit changed herself into a mare when pursued by Poseidon, but he, as a stallion, overtook her and possessed her. At Thelpusa in Arcadia Demeter took on the form of a mare and by Poseidon-Stallion became the mother of the divine horse Areion. From Medusa's blood sprang the winged horse Pegasus. The winged-horse fables may owe their origin in part to 'explanations' about winged horses that figure on Cretan pictures though no doubt the Cretans did not have such rich legends about these creatures as did the Greeks.

Horses were far too valuable to be much used in sacrifice, but on occasion they were offered up to Poseidon. On such occasions they were drowned and not slaughtered. So, too, in ancient India at the great horse-sacrifice the victim was strangled and no blood shed. The flesh of the horses offered to Poseidon would not, in any case, be eaten, for though the Scythians on the Russian steppes ate horse-meat and drank mares' milk, farther south and west there was a long-standing taboo against the eating of horse-flesh.

At Rhodes each year there was a ceremony in which a white horse harnessed to a chariot on fire was cast into the sea in order to aid the sun in recovering his strength after his winter weakness. Here again the horse was drowned not slain, and it was white because offered to a deity of the upper world.

For the Classical Greeks not only was the horse always something of an exotic animal but it was also an expensive and a rather rare one. Greece is not a good country for horse-breeding. It is a land of rocky soil, it is mountainous and poor in pasture, and the little that existed was needed for sheep. So it was that the horse-breeding regions were few in number. The most important of them was Thessaly, about the only part of the country with extensive plains. Alexander's favourite steed, Buchephalus (the 'ox-headed'), was Thessalian bred. And it was in Thessaly that Poseidon was especially honoured. In these regions the horses were probably selectively bred and reasonably well fed. As a result, whereas other animals tended to decline in size on being domesticated because of the limited and rather poor fodder, the horse increased in size.

Horses were costly to keep. Moreover, they were not really suitable either as pack-animals or for drawing carts. They were unshod, and horse-collars were not invented until medieval times. Horses could be harnessed to light chariots and they could be ridden. All in all we may say that horses in Greece were relatively no more numerous than are the race-horses, hunters, or the mounts of the Household Cavalry with us. It is quite possible that one might have travelled for days in rural Greece without ever seeing a horse. In the countryside asses were the all-purpose beasts of burden. Even in the narrow, rather sordid streets of fifth-century Athens horses must have been rare. They were for rich men and were indeed a symbol of social status. The Greek chariot-races were an ostentatious display. Thus Alcibiades, in Thucydides' history, says that the chariot-race victory in 416 B.C. raised the city's prestige among the Hellenic peoples, and Herodotus mentions that certain Athenian families found that a chariot-race victory at Olympia was a political asset in the city.

Greek chariots figure in profusion on the Greek vases. They were light vehicles with standing room for two persons at most. They generally had very large wheels and were hitched so close to the horses that they looked rather like trotting-cars. In war, chariots were mostly used to carry the warriors to and from the battlefield but not in action.

Xenophon's treatise on horses and horsemanship fills in the gaps which appear if we confine ourselves solely to the monuments. Xenophon was a country gentleman and a cavalry officer who wrote primarily for his own class; his descriptions of the cavalry corps supplements what we can learn from the pictures that have come down to us.

The Greeks, as all the ancients, rode bareback, or rather with just a saddle-cloth. Saddles and stirrups were unknown (they seem first to have been used in China) but a rider might slip his feet between the girth and the horse's body. The Greeks used bridles and bits – some of the latter pretty harsh instruments. But still it must have been almost an acrobatic feat to keep one's seat, especially in a cavalry mêlée, as we may see in the lively mosaic of Alexander at the Battle of Issus (a Roman copy but probably of a Greek original) or in a relief from a sarcophagus representing the Battle of Granicus (fig. 50). In both pictures there are plenty of horsemen toppling off their steeds. The horses were, of course, stallions, for gelding is a late invention, and mares cannot be used in company with stallions.

No animal figured more than the horse in Greek art. Possibly the mettlesome, prancing stallions on the Parthenon frieze show Greek horses in a rather idealized fashion, since in reality most of them seem

Fig. 50
Detail from 'Alexander sarcophagus' from royal cemetary at Sidon in Phoenicia. Late fourth century B.C. Height of frieze 58·5 cm. After J. Boardman, *Greek Art*, Thames and Hudson, London, 1964.

to have been rather on the small side. But in legend and mythology the horse was a commanding creature. It drew the chariots of the gods and is represented in magnificent sculpture. The head of Selene's horse from the pediment of the Parthenon is one of the finest animal portraits in existence, though possibly rivalled by the very best of the T'ang carvings in China.

Horses were, with dogs, about the only animals the Greeks regarded with any degree of what we might call sentimentality. For the Greeks were not given to keeping pets, though they did keep cicadas in cages for the cheerful sound of the insects' chirping. Indeed, the Greeks left pets to their gods.

There are plenty of representations of deities not only accompanied by animals but carrying them or a small image of them. Poseidon may hold as a sort of badge a miniature horse's head in his hand. Athena will have a small owl. Hermes may have a small lamb tucked under his arm, indicating his role as the protector of flocks and herds. Artemis may be fondling a little fawn when she is not holding up a deer by its antlers.

But dogs are rarely associated with the gods. Dogs were man's particular companions. Remains from ancient sites show that the dog was almost certainly one of the first animals to be tamed and domesticated. However, the first more or less domesticated dogs may have resembled wolves rather closely. Persistent wolf-legends, including the werewolf theme, show how common the wolf was for ages in Greece. In Arcadia there was a legend that a man transformed into a wolf might regain his human shape if he abstained for ten years from eating human flesh.

But whatever the appearance of the first domesticated dogs it is likely that they chose men rather than vice versa, for dogs seem instinctively to like human beings whose odour may be agreeable to them. And not only were dogs useful right back in Early Neolithic times and possibly before, as scavengers and for helping in the chase, but they were also comfortable bed-fellows. A couple of dogs snuggled down beside a sleeping man were as good as a thick blanket.

Maybe dogs have been man's companions for so long that they were not ranged as mysterious or divine. In any case in Greece dogs do not seem to be detectable in the persons of any divinity. There are no canine deities and although dogs did accompany some gods they were not often sacrificed nor were human beings often transformed into dogs, though Hecuba did get turned into a bitch.

In Greece there is little evidence of the contempt and even loathing for dogs so common in the Near East. There may have been some Persian influence affecting the Greek attitude, for in ancient Persia some dogs at least were accounted as sacred.

Even the philosophical name 'Cynic' did not imply scorn for dogs. Diogenes himself regarded them as brave, faithful, with no false shame and with few needs, thus admirable. And Pythagoras put a dog to the mouth of a dying disciple so that the animal might catch the man's last breath and perpetuate the virtues of the dead pupil. The *Greek Anthology* contains a number of epitaphs written in memory of dogs. There is one little poem that recounts the prowess of a favourite hound. But the regret for the loss of a loyal companion is tempered by the recollection of how much the 'wild beasts feared him'.

The Greeks had several breeds of dog. There were the half-starved curs that infested the city streets; there were watch-dogs, and there were the ferociously savage beasts that guarded flocks and herds and were perhaps the ancestors of the present-day sheep-dogs to which the prudent traveller gives a wide berth. Not for nothing was one of Hermes' epithets the 'Dog-Strangler'. There were war-dogs too and there is a scene showing some of them with Greeks in a battle against the Cimmerians. But the most prized dogs were what we should call 'hounds' and were similar to the *salūqi* of North Africa and the Near East today. They were short-haired beasts with good muzzles and of sturdy but graceful form, fleet of foot and used in hare-coursing as well as other field-sports.

The Greek story is filled with tales about dogs. There was Argos that recognized the returning wanderer Odysseus but was too feeble to do more than wag its tail and gaze fondly up at its master. Alexander the Great was so attached to his dog Perditas that when it died he not only gave it a sumptuous funeral but raised a monument to its memory. The Greeks, however, regarded Alexander, the Macedonian, as at least half-barbarian and such a display of sentimentality must have shocked Greek practical sense.

There were also 'sacred' dogs in Greece but they served a useful purpose. Dogs might be healers and as such were particularly associated with Asclepius, the god of medicine at whose 'shrine-hospitals' (for the treatment was psychosomatic) there were dogs to minister to the patients. At Epidaurus, for instance, the animals were trained to lick the sick back to health. Maybe the dogs' saliva served to keep wounds clean, and then the animals' evident commiseration might have had a tonic effect.

Occasionally, dogs were offered up in sacrifice. Ares, the god of war, a rather shadowy figure in Greek mythology and originally a foreigner from Thrace, received offerings of dogs (probably rounded up from the stray kind) while Hecate received sacrifices of both black lambs and black puppies. She was a deity of magic and spells, of darkness, of the nether world, and she was at home in Thessaly, though she too may have originally come from Thrace, even more a land of the black arts then Thessaly. She is often also identified with Artemis and is, indeed, one of the 'aspects' of the 'Mistress of Animals'.

There is an attractive fourth-century relief found at Crannon in Thessaly where Hecate-Artemis is shown as a graceful yet sturdy figure with a torch in her left hand while with her right hand she gently caresses the forehead of a delightful little mare, obviously pleased by these marks of affection. Behind the goddess is a shapely bitch of the *salūqi* type, patient, attentive, expectant even, though she may be destined as a sacrifice in the Grecian land of horses and magic. In any case the carving is an attractive picture of the two animals most prized by the Greeks.

In another scene two men are shown sitting and holding two animals by leashes and matching them, presumably to encourage them to fight (the Greeks also liked cock-fights). One of the beasts is obviously intended for a dog. The other has been identified as a cat, presumably a wild cat; if it was the dog would have had a bad time of it when it came to the showdown.

There were certainly wild cats in Greek forests and on the mountains, but such beasts are accounted quite untameable and it is unlikely that the Greeks had domestic cats.

There are pleasing statuettes of children playing with cocks, dogs and goats but no cats. The Greek word *ailouros*, generally translated as 'cat', would apply to any animal with a long tail. It is probable that the ancient Greeks used the 'marten-cat' to keep down vermin, or else the genet, which is easily tamed if caught young and makes an excellent ratter.

Egypt was the classical home of cats where they were revered and often mummified. The Egyptians did not like people carrying off or maltreating their cats and there is an exemplary tale of a Greek tourist in Egypt who killed, accidentally he averred, a cat and got himself thereby into all sorts of trouble.

Alongside the 'healing' dogs at the shrine-hospitals there were medicinal snakes. Snakes were also often used to consecrate offerings in some of the mysteries. At the same hospital-sanctuary in Epidaurus where the healing dogs operated, healing snakes were allowed to slither over patients and coil round them and so help to cure them of their ills.

The snake, symbol of the earth deities and of the nether world, of the land of the dead and the lords of death, was ever-present in the Aegean area, and a semi-divine creature, elusive and mysterious.

Holy places retain their sanctity throughout the ages and before Apollo could take Delphi as his high sanctuary he had to slay Python, the great she-serpent that was the goddess of the place, a deity of the nether world, a chthonian divinity.

In some reliefs Zeus, in his character as Meilichios 'The Placator', appears not as a glorious figure in human form but as a huge snake, and a bearded snake at that, towering above a crowd of worshippers, a fearsome god indeed. Erechtheus the legendary King of Athens had snakes instead of feet; indeed, in the earlier version of his story he was a snake.

The snake cult in Greece was one expression of a most widespread and ancient religion. In Arcadia, Artemis sometimes held snakes in her hands, as did the Earth Mother in Crete. The mare-headed statue of Demeter at Phigalia was draped in a long black robe to which snakes were attached, while in one hand she held a dove. Snakes belong to the nether world and its deities, while doves belong to the upper world and its divinities. In some places, at the Festival of Demeter and her daughter Persephone, women worshippers carried with them in procession not only phalli modelled out of dough but also live snakes – symbols of generation and regeneration.

Almost any animal might be an acceptable sacrifice to the gods. A cock (symbol of virility) to Asclepius or a white bull to Zeus. But some beasts were rarely offered because they were too expensive, while other animals lingered on in the wilds and never appear as sacrificial victims. Of the domestic animals, the commonest offerings were goats and swine, both, of course, good to eat.

In the Aegean lands domesticated goats are found in the earliest Neolithic sites. Goats need little attention; they can scratch a living almost anywhere and ravage woods by eating foliage and even tree-bark (and so are a pest today in lands such as North Africa). These anti-social habits of the goat made him precious to men 8,000 years ago and more. Goats helped to clear the ground at a time when chopping-tools were not very effective. Goats were domesticated or semi-domesticated before sheep, for sheep need more attention.

Sheep in Greece were not particularly associated with any god, except that Hermes 'protected' them in his role as guardian of flocks and herds. But rams' heads did adorn the shrines in Neolithic Asia Minor and may well have been of wild animals. In Greece sheep were kept for their wool and their milk was used for making cheese, although, at least in later Greek times, goats' milk cheese seems to have been more common.

Goats, however, unlike sheep, play a considerable part in Greek legend. The rural divinities, the spirits of the wild, partake of a goat-like nature. Dionysus would frequently appear as a goat. Pan was half-goat as were satyrs and other imps of the forest.

With the wild goats ran the wild swine. Wild boar survived for a long time and probably still exist in more out-of-the-way places, and they afforded excellent sport. The Greeks did their pig-sticking on foot.

The wild swine completed the goats' work of ground-clearing by rooting up young trees and not merely stripping them.

Pigs might be sacrificed to almost any deity and especially to Aphrodite. Pigs' blood was very effective in purification ceremonies – though not as magical as bulls' – and it was pigs' blood that cleansed Orestes from the guilt of matricide. Moreover, it looks as though one of the divinities merged into the figure of Demeter was a divine sow.

The most mysterious of the creatures of the wild was the bear. It is not obtrusive in Greek legend and history and was possibly never common in Classical Greek times. There may still be bears at large in the Balkan mountains as there are in the Alps and Pyrenees. Undoubtedly there existed a bear cult among early inhabitants of Greece and the bears' skins for the dances to Artemis must have come from somewhere, but the fact that the skins were fairly early on replaced by saffron garments suggests that the supply of skins was drying up. In this connection it can be noted that the Artemis bear-dances in Cyrenaica, where they were introduced by Greek colonists, kept to real skins long after they had been discarded at Brauron. Bears, as far as they exist in Africa are confined to a relatively small area in the north-west of the continent.

A great deal has been written about the antiquity and supposed ubiquity of bear cults, and they may well have existed in the Old Stone Age.

Some authors have held that even the Neanderthaloids practised some sort of bear cult since in a few central European caves there are supposedly 'ritual' arrangements of bears' bones but the evidence is not conclusive (see Chapter I). If it were we might reflect that the little devotees honouring Artemis at a sanctuary near the Athens of the glorious fifth century were engaged in a ceremony whose origins are to be found some 30,000 years ago, a splendid pedigree for any ceremony or ritual.

Among the animals he thought might be attacked by mounted men, Xenophon lists leopards, lynxes and panthers, and also bears and lions, but this does not mean that these animals were to be met with in Greece. Xenophon was a great traveller and we have no reason to suppose all these animals could be found on a day's sporting expedition from Athens.

Lions certainly existed in Greece in Mycenaean times, but Aristotle mentions them as still being found in Macedonia, so presumably no longer in Greece. We are perhaps somewhat inclined to think that animals in the past must have flourished only in climates like those of their present-day counterparts, but there were cave-lions in Europe during the last Ice Age. We picture to ourselves leopards as beasts snaking their way through tropical jungles, but there are snow-leopards in the high mountains of eastern Asia.

The lion survived in Greece, not as a god or as a sacrifice to a god (though in Lydia, in Asia Minor, where Greek myths often suffered a sea-change, Herakles was a lion) but as the symbol of valour and victory. It is true that on occasion some gods would assume a lion's form, and there is the most ancient theme of a god or goddess flanked by lions, and there are a variety of mythical lions in Greece as well as in Crete, but the lion in Classical Greece is, above all, a symbol of victory. It is notable that the lion statues erected to commemorate victories were mostly of lionesses which are generally regarded as more daring, enter- prising and generally intelligent than their mates, as indeed is the case with nearly all the cats great and small. It may also be that a lioness was thought more suited as a symbol of and a monument to honour the goddess Nike – Victory – who usually had wings so that she could swiftly change sides. Nike Apteros, the 'Wingless Victory', had her shrine on the Acropolis, but she was a rare deity indeed.

Winged creatures, the birds, mysterious and perhaps endowed with supernatural powers, disappearing and reappearing, undertaking long journeys to far-off lands and perhaps bringing back strange knowledge, figured largely in Greek mythology and popular superstition. In his famous comedy Aristophanes tells of what might happen if the birds united and built a city in the air from which they could rule both gods and men. For if they devoured all the seed on the earth they would paralyse and starve all mankind and abolish the beasts which, when sacrificed, nourished the immortal gods. Then there would be a silent spring.

Some birds were acceptable sacrifices to the deities. A white fowl might be offered to Zeus and a cock to Asclepius, for domestic fowl were kept by the Greeks before 500 B.C. while pheasants were brought back, it was said, by the Argonauts from the Caucasus.

Other birds were accounted sacred, sacrosanct. In Aristotle's time it was accounted a heinous crime to kill storks, which are still regarded in many parts of Europe as bringing good luck. In the courting season the storks indulge in a grotesque kind of dance which was regarded, evi- dently, as of magic import. In any case at Delos a sacred stork-dance was performed in which the participants imitated the movemets of the birds and maybe at one time were disguised as birds. There is a curious parallel to such bird-ceremonies represented on the walls of Neolithic Çatal Hüyük in Asia Minor: two human vultures or vulturine human beings, possibly priestesses in some cult, seem to be executing a dance.

Magic and religion were so closely intertwined in Greece that it is often impossible to distinguish the one from the other. Magic might be defined as having been, for the mass of the people, the practical applica- tion of religion to the everyday affairs that concern men most. There was a strange use of the wryneck (a sacred bird it would seem in Egypt and Assyria) which, if fastened to a wheel that was revolved, was thought capable of turning the hearts of men, thus acting as a love charm.

Some great birds seemed freed from all servitude that bound men and most animals to the earth; the eagle could fly right up to Zeus and carry Ganymede to the chief of the gods. And some human beings were metamorphosed into birds, as the women who mourned for Meleager were changed into guinea-fowl. The numerous winged creatures, the monsters that figure on Cretan vases and appear all through Greek art, the flying horses, and lions and griffins, are symbolical of beings that transcended the limits to movement to which are condemned all creatures but birds. Birds, or some of them, were then undoubtedly in a measure supernatural, but not menacing or frightful. They were creatures of the air and the light and the upper regions and some of them could triumph over serpents, the horrid, yet revered, age-old servants of the Earth Mother in her most redoubtable aspect.

Conclusion

There is no region of the ancient world which is more significant for us than the Aegean, where the first European civilization arose and its descendant Classical Greece formed the basis of so much of our own civilization. In the Aegean animals played a role of the first importance and the legends and beliefs relating to them had their roots in a most remote past. We can know but little of the traditions, the rites and the ceremonies of peoples who left no pictorial art, much less writing, so that it is hardly an exaggeration to say that we are better acquainted with some aspects of the life of the Old Stone Age men who left the pictures, designs and engravings on cavern-walls than we are with the ways of Neolithic peoples of ancient Greece thousands of years later. But to a certain extent, the evidence from Asia Minor fills the gap between the Old Stone Age and the New. It is evident from the Anatolian sites that the Neolithic people who inhabited them 8,000 or 9,000 years ago already possessed a highly complex culture, with sculpture, painting and weaving, domestic animals and the beginnings of agriculture. And this culture obviously included animal cults; bulls and rams and vultures had some religious significance. It is probable that an Earth Goddess was revered and certainly sacrifices were offered up. Horned pillars were part of the sanctuaries' furnishings as they were in Crete. In fact, we may take it that the essentials of a religion in which animals were closely associated existed in Asia Minor by 7000–6000 B.C. and that this religion in many of its characteristics reappears in Crete and to a certain extent in Bronze Age Greece.

The myths and legends and religious ideas of the historical Greeks were, no doubt, derived from a number of sources, but among them the legacy from Neolithic and Bronze Ages times was always present. Perhaps this little sketch, necessarily condensed and selective, may serve to indicate that in the Aegean, from the earliest times we can visualize, right up to the zenith of Greek civilization in the Golden Age of Athens, beliefs regarding animals and ceremonies involving animals formed an essential part of the culture.

6 ANIMALS IN INDIA

JEANNINE AUBOYER

The importance attributed to animals in Indian civilization is so great that it has sometimes rivalled or even surpassed the attention given to mere mortals. The same attitudes have, moreover, survived to some extent to this day – at least in the rural areas of many of the regions that make up the immense Indian Sub-continent.

This long-lasting survival of beliefs superstitions and even conceptualizations about the world, is due to many factors which are well worth some examination. First of all, as in many other cultures, animals, or some of them, played a mythical and symbolical role in prehistoric times, though it is not clear whether this prehistoric population and civilization were the direct forerunners of historical Indian society. The Indus Valley sites, and those of other regions have seals with writing on them, but it has not been deciphered, and we cannot tell whether the animals represented on these steatite seals were associated with religion and, therefore, indirectly, with man. It is clear, however, that the vast majority of the representations are of animals rather than human beings. One well-known type of seal shows a personage seated cross-legged with two horns on his head, flanked by animals. Such figures have been compared with those of the god Siva, but the identification is not certain.

When, in the historic period, objects made of non-perishable materials appear, a representation of animals form an important element in the plastic arts. But, again, we can only guess at the allegorical allusions and are not justified in elaborating any hypotheses. This art style takes the form of isolated columns erected for commemorative purposes. Their bell-shaped lotus-capitals support a tambour decorated with perambulating beasts in turn surmounted by one or more animals, which, in some cases, hold a wheel (*chakra*), symbol of the Law (*dharma*), of the Cosmic Order and of Imperial Power. From this time, about the middle of the third century B.C. onwards, animals are depicted with a remarkable accuracy.

From this period onwards we can begin to appreciate the part played by animals in both the public and private lives of the people, their role in religion and traditions. Indeed, there are literary texts which explain and supplement the sculptured and painted representations. These two sources, literature and representational art, illuminate each other and reveal the multiplicity and the survival of the ancient, ancestral traditions regarding animals. They allow precious insights into the relationship between man and animal.

This relationship is astonishingly close, both in everyday life and in the spiritual domain. No doubt the rural way of life, still that of 80 per cent of the Indian people, was at the basis of this relationship, as well as the custom of going into retreat in hermitages in the wilds far from inhabited areas. Familiarity with animals, and the observations which naturally result from this, no doubt determined man's attitude towards the animals surrounding him and with which he lived every day of his life. This familiarity most certainly profoundly influenced his concept of the universe in that it presented an appearance of unity and one could make analogies between the different animal species. The undeniable poetic gifts of the Indian peoples helped to refine these notions and to render them accessible to all classes of society, so that even today such an attitude is highly characteristic of Indians.

The close communion which in traditionalist India exists between animals and men is at once the cause and the result of a belief in the transmigration of souls. It is a belief which goes right back into the old Vedic substratum and was widely accepted at the time of the Upanishads' composition in about the sixth century B.C. The essentials of this doctrine are that the soul, or rather the individual 'self' (*âtman*), survives bodily death and transmigrates into another body until the termination of the sum of acts (*karman*) that causes this survival. The chain of rebirths runs on, like the tireless turning of a wheel (*chakra*), until the soul, liberated from the burden of its evil deeds, rejoins the Universal Self. In essence, although there are variations among the different sects, one dies only to be born again, indefinitely. In the course of successive rebirths the same soul is reincarnated, according to its merits, in an animal or a man.

The doctrine, then, implies the integration of animals into the same 'cycle' as man, in an inferior rank, no doubt, but by no means an unworthy one. Indeed, this participation of animals within the cycle, the wheel of transmigration (*sâmsara*), gives them a relatively privileged position, the degree of privilege depending on the place assigned them, on the basis of their specific characteristics, in the animal hierarchy. Thus some are despised, even rejected, while others are exalted to a noble, even sacred, rank. This scale of values is seen in the lists of fines inflicted on those found guilty of causing an animal's death. The fines are often comparable to those for homicide, where the amount varies according to the caste or social class of the victim.

As might be expected in a rural society the cow is at the top of the scale. To kill a cow was considered a very grave crime, as serious, indeed, as the murder of a high-caste man. The expiation was harsh, not only must the guilty man spend three months as a member of the herd, have his head shaven, wear nothing but the skin of the animal he has killed, drink nothing but a concoction of barley, but he had also to supply ten cows and a bull, or pay the price of them, failing which all his belongings were confiscated. At the other end of the scale came the dog, the killing of which was comparable to the murder of a *chândâla* (pariah or 'Untouchable') – regarded as the lowest of mankind. In this case the punishment was very slight. Two animals, the horse and the elephant, have a particular place, because of various qualities they were held to possess. These two will be considered separately after we have dealt with the domestic animals.

Thus, just as human society was divided into classes, so also was the animal world. This accords with the Indian belief that the divine, human and animal worlds are organized according to a similar social system, a regal system, and that both obey similar laws, it being understood that man was the basic criterion. As the possible host of a migrating soul the animal is held to possess the same feelings as a man and the same ability to express them. Its acts, like those of a man, are good or bad, in terms of the reduction of the sum of *karman*, either holding the soul prisoner in an inferior body or permitting it to be reborn in a higher state.

When, from the sixth century B.C. Buddhism began to spread throughout India, it perpetuated these same ideas and incorporated them into the Buddhist system founded on charitable relations between all beings. Popular literature drew abundantly from this traditional source and the stories of the former lives (*jâtaka*) of the Buddha offer explicit proof of this. The *jâtaka* were compiled in about the second century B.C. and from that time onwards were illustrated in a delightfully spirited fashion. At Bhârhut and other sites we find innumerable animals which act, speak and behave like men, with whom they participate in the scene. From these one has a feeling of a great fraternity united in an almost Franciscan tenderness, with just the occasional malicious comment and picturesque asides. The Buddha himself is incarnated in many animals and the list of them is significant – fish, crab, cock, woodpecker, partridge francolin (the black partridge of Persia and northern India), quail, pigeon, goose, crow, zebu, buffalo, monkey, elephant, antelope, deer and horse.

This intimacy between man and animal, this profound belief in the fellowship that links all living creatures, the concept of the transmigration of souls – all these led to a respect for even the humblest animals, since it formed part of one great community. To these conceptions Buddhism added the notion of friendship, even of love.

Professions which entailed the killing of animals were forbidden to Brahmins, priests by right of birth. Thus they could not become a farm-labourer, since in ploughing the soil he kills insects and other small living creatures, or a hunter, a fisherman or fowler, butcher, or even a tanner or currier. Such people were held in as great contempt as hangmen, grave-diggers and those conducting funerals. Slaughter-houses were banished to sites beyond a city's limits, though perhaps, in part, for hygienic reasons. Indeed, everything relating to the death of animals was condemned.

It was in such a spirit of reverence for animal life that the Emperor Aśoka (about 264–227 B.C.), who was converted to Buddhism in approximately 252 B.C., had a number of edicts engraved and set them up in various places throughout his Empire.[1] In these proclamations he declared that he himself had renounced the pleasures of the hunt and he encouraged his subjects to follow his example. He ordered that the slaughter of animals should be much curtailed, and to set a precedent he prohibited the daily killing of 'several hundreds of thousands of beasts' for the Imperial Palace. Only three might be killed for his table, 'two peacocks and a gazelle' and even these not 'constantly'. In a later edict he went so far as to state that he had renounced flesh-eating for himself and had become a vegetarian.

Even if all the sovereigns of ancient India did not imitate Aśoka they did at least found hospices for old and sick animals. These rulers had their zoological gardens stocked by hunters and professional fowlers; and reserves where animals lived without constraint and where visitors were admitted to wander about freely.

The extraordinarily close relationship between man and animals led naturally to the inclusion of animals in the pantheon. Indeed, this occurred so early that it probably falls within the prehistoric period. Some authors, indeed, have held that animals preceded anthropomorphic beings among the dieties, but that, later on, the animals became subordinate and became sacred mounts or vehicles, acolytes, messengers and servants. Whatever the evolution of the mythological animals may have been, they were certainly subordinate by the time they were described in the sacred writings, even though in the hymns addressed to one or other of them their position is often almost as exalted as that of the great divinities. This is a similar phenomenon to that by which, in the eyes of his votaries, a minor deity is credited with characteristics which are also attributed to the most powerful gods.

The rose-pink Cows of the Dawn, the Horses of the Sun, the bull Nandin of Śiva, the goose (*hamsa*) of Brahmâ, the Garuda bird of Vishnu, the peacock of Skanda and many others figure in the pantheon. Then there is the monkey Hanumâna, celebrated in the epic poem of the *Râmâyana* for his prowess, and the object of a special cult. Other celestial animals are purely mythical such as the *makara*, an aquatic monster, part crocodile and part fish; the *nâga* serpent of many hoods; the *vyâlaka*, a species of horned lion; the *sarabha*, a cervine animal, both he-goat or ram at the same time. All with innumerable representations in temple decoration.

The Hindu pantheon also contains deities that are partly anthropomorphic and partly zoomorphic like Ganeśa, the son of Śiva, with an elephant's head, or, above all, the various 'aspects' of Vishnu assumed during his redeeming 'descents' (*avatâra*) when the great god is shown successively with the head of a lion, a wild boar, a horse and with the body of a fish or a tortoise.

Even this brief review shows that the role of animals, whether mythical or not, was very important in Indian tradition.

We may now elaborate on some of these themes.

Domestic Animals

The most important of these are the flocks and herds, the main preoccupation of the rural population and the main source of wealth. The flocks and herds were very varied, bullocks, cows, buffaloes (both male and female), rams, sheep, ewes, pigs, dogs and sometimes even horses. These were under the guardianship of the village headman who protected them against bandits, ferocious beasts and even armies in the field. The beasts were carefully branded each springtime and led and watched over by herdsmen.

Indian artists, unlike those of other countries, never depicted flocks and herds as such, that is as a rather disorderly and jostling mass of heads, legs, bodies and tails. However, the presence of herds is sometimes suggested, particularly on some of the bas-reliefs, of which the finest are undoubtedly those on the gateways (*torana*) of stûpa I at Sânchî, dating from about the beginning of our era. Here there are buffaloes enjoying a bathe in a lotus-covered pool. Only their heads and imposing horns show above the surface of the water.[2] There are also cows and goats wandering peacefully about among the thatched dwellings. It was not until the eighteenth and nineteenth centuries that the Râjput artists depicted herds, often most successfully, in order to illustrate the pastoral life of the god Krishna among the female cowherds (*gopî*).

On the other hand, the animals we have just mentioned were frequently shown either in isolation or as part of a scene. They are represented with all the skill the Indian sculptors possessed, sometimes, perhaps, somewhat ingenuously but always in a very naturalistic style. The well-marked characteristics, the carefully observed forms, and the simple planes all combine to give these animals a very lively appearance.

Among them, humped cattle and cows occupy a place of honour. The ox figures as early as the third century B.C. on one of the pillar-capitals of the Maurya epoch. This piece was discovered at Râmpurva and is now in the Rahrapati Bhavan, New Delhi. This magnificent statue is one of the masterpieces of Indian sculpture. The animal, firmly planted on well-modelled legs, stands calm and motionless. The sculptor has very successfully rendered the vigour of a splendid male animal and, while simplifying the relief, has retained all the essentials. Later on, after the Maurya epoch, oxen often appear in Indian art. These animals served then, as they do today, for tilling the fields. They were yoked together in pairs to a plough, the ploughman standing upright on the share to weigh it down. The animals were urged on with whips. They cut furrows not only in the fields but also during the symbolical spring ceremonies in which the king took part. A ploughman and his team are shown on a half-medallion decorating one of the balustrade-posts surrounding the Bodhgayâ sanctuary, a site more sacred than any other since it was there that the Buddha experienced his Awakening and began his holy career (fig. 51). With great economy the sculptor has presented the essentials of a ploughing scene, which may perhaps be identified as one of the episodes which occurred before the Illumination (*bodhi*) of the Buddha.[3]

Oxen were also used to draw chariots, wagons and light carts. The various vehicles, both heavy and light, were furnished with a pole ending in a yoke resting on the beasts' necks, between the nape and the dorsal hump. Four long pegs of turned wood were driven upright through the yokes and framed the neck of each ox, which was also restrained by a halter. In order to calm these temperamental beasts a cord was passed through their nostrils. Their tails were carefully attached to their flanks so as not to inconvenience the driver or allow them to relieve themselves during the journey. This type of harness may still be seen today. It is often represented in ancient art especially at Bhârhut (about 150–100 B.C.), at Mathurâ (second century A.D.) and at Goli (approximately third century A.D.) in the south-east (fig. 52).[4, 5, 6]

Sometimes the ox is shown in his wild state, unbridled and running at full speed, for example in some friezes of the Amarâvatî school, about the first and second centuries A.D., where the modelling is remarkably fine. In contrast, in other scenes the ox is adorned as though for some

Fig. 51
Bodhgayā. Labourer with plough drawn by
a pair of humped cattle. *c.* beginning of
first century A.D.
Indian Museum, Calcutta. Author's
photograph.

ceremony (fig. 53). For example, at Mathurâ (first century A.D.) his
horns are sheathed in a gilded and chased metal casing, and a heavy
collar hangs down over his chest.* The ox appeared in such finery at the
royal coronations, where it symbolized the riches of the husbandman
whose wealth was computed in head of cattle and who calculated, by
ox or cow, sums due and owing. It is quite probable that a monetary
unit was eventually named after these animals.

The cow, valuable for both its milk and other products, which,
moreover, were used in the Brahmanic rituals, also frequently figures
in ancient art. The finest of all the representations is perhaps that
sculptured in the seventh century A.D. in the 'Cavern of Krishna' at
Mahâbalipuram to the south of Madras (fig. 54). The artist composed
a huge picture to illustrate the pastoral life of this god and placed in the
foreground a magnificent cow with lyre-shaped horns (still found in
India today). A cowherd squats in front of her and milks her while she
lovingly licks her calf. This theme of the cow licking her calf is often to
be found in medieval Indian art. In such creations one sees all the
tenderness the Indian felt for the cow nurturing its young, the animal
he has venerated for more than 2,000 years.

The lusty and ardent ram, a solar symbol as well as a symbol of the
flock's well-being, was valued for his wool and his leather. He is often
represented either as a draught-animal (in the Gandhâra art of the
third century A.D.) or as a trained fighting ram. Ram-fights were much

* The sculpture was found at Kauśambî and is conserved in the Museum
at Allahâbâd (no. 9/5).

enjoyed by the humble, the noble and the king himself. The ancient sculptors at Bhârhut (about 150–100 B.C.) represented some charmingly naïve portraits of rams, though this animal does not seem to have inspired any masterpieces.[7]

Dogs were considered as part of the flocks and herds. By order of the master of the household they were fed after each midday meal. They wandered about freely within palace or villa enclosures but had to be chased away from the kitchens when they were daring enough to try to slip by.[8] In packs, they accompanied hunters. But although they were on such familiar terms with men, they were accounted unclean and their barking might be interpreted as an evil omen. The somewhat rare pictures of dogs show them as rather starved creatures with short, yellowish coats and turned-up tails. In fact, they resemble in every way the dogs that swarm round the Indian villages today. Some dogs already figure in scenes at Bhârhut and we find them again at Begrâm (first to second century A.D.) with a hunter.[9, 10] At Mathurâ they are following a caravan of carts and we come across them again at Ajantâ in a fresco in cavern XVII, dating from about the fifth century A.D.[11, 12]

Other domestic animals also lived in close contact with their masters. Cats were depicted on the roof-tops lying in wait for birds.[13] Peacocks, geese and parrots, whose cries gave the alarm that snakes were about, figure prominently in art. Whereas the mongoose, tamed by men of low caste, which also attacked snakes, fought courageously with them, and killed them, were never, as far as we know, represented by the old Indian artists.

Fig. 52
Mathurā. A convoy of chariots drawn by humped cattle. *c.* second century A.D. National Museum of India, New Delhi. Author's photograph.

121

Fig. 53
Kauśambī. Adorned bull, beside Lakṣmī.
Second century B.C.
Archaeological Museum, Allahābād.
Author's photograph.

Fig. 54
Mahābalipuram. Krishna cave. Milking
scene. Seventh century A.D.
In situ. Author's photograph.

Peacocks, whose flesh, in the times of the Maurya, was served up on royal tables and whose sumptuous plumage was used in making garlands for festive occasions, were taken alive by the fowlers and then released to adorn and ornament gardens and parks. Platforms were built for them, each one held up a post and on these the peacocks would execute their pavan to the strains of the palace orchestra accompanied by the rhythmical clapping of the women and the jingling of their anklets. Such scenes are often described in the classical Indian literature and are depicted in plastic art; among the earliest examples are a number of ivories dug up at the Begrâm of Kapiçî (first to second century A.D.).[14] (Fig. 55.) They were also trained for peacock-fights.

But the favourite pets of the princesses were geese and tame parrots. They were regarded as souls on their way to the moon. They followed their mistresses everywhere. They played with her, nibbled mischievously at the tips of her flowing locks. Such delicate compositions are often represented – especially at Begrâm and Mathurâ.

The parrot, like the myna,* was much admired for its ability to imitate the sounds of human speech, and was exported to other countries. Parrots and mynas were snared in nets by the fowlers and then put into ivory cages which were hung up at windows or on the walls of the courtyards of house and of schools. Or the birds might accompany their mistresses on walks. On a second-century sculpture

* A member of the starling family.

Fig. 55
Bhārhut. A peacock in full display.
Second century B.C.
Indian Museum, Calcutta (no. 125).
Author's photograph.

from Mathurâ a smiling and graceful girl, healthy and plump, holds a cage in her hand while the parrot at liberty pecks at the fruits his mistress has stuck in her hair.[16] One of the favourite pastimes of lovers was to teach the birds affectionate words which they could repeat to the lover or his mistress when they were separated. This poetic and literary theme is abundantly represented in the sculptures. It is very beautifully treated on one of the finest ivory plaques found at Begrâm where the bird, released from his cage, perches on the hand of his mistress who rewards him with a titbit (fig. 56).[17] This subject, in fact, continues to be used in Indian art right until the present time.

Although they were neither trained nor even tamed, doves and pigeons lived among men. In the towns the canopied dormer-windows went by the attractive name of 'pigeons' shelters' (*kapotapâlikâ*). The birds are often shown on house-roofs where they symbolize the love uniting people living below. The story is told of a cook who was so fond of a particular pigeon that he kept it in a basket hung up on the door of his kitchen. The scene is represented at Bhârhut.[18] A pigeon is also the hero of a very well-known story often illustrated by the ancient artists. It is the *Śibi-jâtaka* in which the Bodhisattva cuts into the flesh of his own thigh so that a starving bird of prey shall spare a wretched pigeon it was about to kill and eat. This moral tale in which the pigeon plays the 'star' role includes a number of participants including, of course, a servant with a pair of scales. The pigeon is placed on one side of the scales and on the other a piece of the Bodhisattva's august flesh. But, to test his sanctity, the gods cause the pigeon to go on increasing in weight so that eventually the Bodhisattva has to sacrifice nearly all his

Fig. 56
Mathurā. Lady with her pet.
c. second century A.D. Sandstone. Height 17 cm.
Archaeological Museum, Mathurā (no. 1307). Author's photograph.

body. It goes without saying that on account of his virtue, and before he was wholly sacrificed, his body was once more restored to him intact.

Ravens lived, as they do today, near to habitation sites. Greedy, talkative and always hungry, they would flock down after each meal to see what they could scavenge. Ravens were thought to be able to transmit love-messages confided to them, and also to pronounce oracles.

Other less familiar birds are often referred to in Indian literature – the cuckoo (*kokila*) which with its languorous cries awakes desire; the partridge (*chakora*) reputed to feed on moonbeams, and many others thought to possess supernatural powers and to be associated with the solar and celestial realms. Some birds, though the precise species is not known, were taken on board ship for ocean voyages. They were kept on deck so that the pilot who had trained them could make use of them at the right moment, for in order to discover the whereabouts of the nearest land he would release them on the high seas. If no coast was in sight the birds returned.

On the fringe of the human world but still frequently encountered were deer and monkeys. The stag was royal game and hunted by the king in person. This noble animal is often mentioned in literature and depicted in works of art. There is a famous story, the *Ruru-jâtaka*, remarkably illustrated at Bhârhut in which a stag is an incarnation of the future Buddha, remarkable both in his self-abnegation and in the grandeur of his attitude towards ungrateful men (fig. 57).[19] The gazelle, also destined to grace royal tables, was again one of the incarnations of the Bodhisattva. The Indian artists excelled in reproducing her aristocratic and graceful bearing. One of the most beautiful representations is a sixth-century fresco in cavern XVII at Ajantâ and another, still more famous, and remarkably executed, is at Mahâbalipuram. It forms part of the astounding seventh-century monumental composition illustrating 'The Descent of the Ganges'. The gazelle, drawn from life, is shown in a characteristic attitude, rubbing its muzzle with its hoof (fig. 58). The picture is one of the highlights of the Indian animal paintings.

There are also many early representations of the antelope. These were much in demand for their hair which was used for weaving thick garments and for their venison, but they were also captured alive and used to stock gardens and zoological parks. In order to capture them the professional hunters would discover their favourite haunts, spread honey on the plants the creatures most enjoyed, keep watch on them for a long time, then, little by little, show themselves so that the animals became accustomed to the sight and smell of man, and so finally capture them. Antelope skins were used as clothing for young Brahmanic initiates sent to complete their education in the forest hermitages; their horns were used in the royal coronation ceremonies as rhytons (libation-vases).

From early times onwards monkeys figured in popular stories. They lived in groups, led by courageous leaders. They were famous for their boisterousness and their small intellect, their impudent curiosity, their fickleness and their insolence. They are endlessly referred to in the Buddhistic tales – with both indulgence and disapproval. Indeed, the future Buddha did not disdain to incarnate himself as one of the monkey leaders.

Many monkeys were taken alive, even up in the Himalayas. They were trained and sold, some in fact exported by the caravans supplying

Fig. 57
Bhārhut. Ruru jātaka.
Second century B.C.
Indian Museum, Calcutta (No. 128).
Author's photograph.

Fig. 58
Mahābalipuram. Detail from 'The descent
of the Ganges' showing two antelopes and
a tortoise.
Seventh century A.D.
Photograph V. Goloubew (photographic
archives, Guimet Museum).

126

ports that traded with the West. Numerous monkeys were kept for their clever performances. Among the Jaina, monkey bones were considered efficacious and they were made up into necklaces for children.[20] There are numerous representations of monkeys in the arts of India. Already at Bhârhut there are several *jataka* scenes with humorous depictions of monkeys and they are equally popular in the later Brahmanic art (fig. 59). They are found among the animals in the lower levels of the god Śiva's abode, Mount Kailâsa, and, above all, they play a leading role in the celebrated *Râmâyana* epic where the monkey chieftain Hanumâna and his brother Sugrîva play a very important part.

Alongside all these animals which were generally regarded with good-will, there were others either feared or but little respected, or even detested. We have seen that a dog's bark might sometimes be regarded as an ill-omen. The ass (of which no representations are known) was adjudged both evil and lewd. Its braying might foretell bad harvests. A Brahmin's wife, found guilty of adultery, was placed upon an ass's back, with her head facing towards the animal's tail. With her head shaven she had to make public expiation by riding thus through the streets.

The jackal, represented only, it would seem, at Bhârhut and very unskilfully at that, was also a beast of ill-omen since it haunted the graveyards, the corpse-strewn battlefields and the cross-roads at which condemned criminals were executed. Hyenas were the companions of jackals. Vultures and all the birds of prey that feed on the putrifying flesh of dead animals were placed in a similar category.

Fig. 59
Bhârhut. Buddhist fable showing the training of an elephant by a group of monkeys.
Second century B.C.
Indian Museum, Calcutta. Author's photograph.

The Horse

From Vedic times, which link up with prehistory, the horse was associated with the idea of universal sovereignty. The sacrifice of a horse (*avamedha*), a ritual possibly of remote Indo-Iranian origin, was performed by a king when, through conquest, his realm attained the dimensions of an empire. This power was thus consecrated in the eyes of all men. The ceremony extended over an entire year. First of all a horse was very carefully selected according to very precise specifications: it had to be a fine stallion, a splendid racer and with no physical defects. In February/March the horse was let loose among a herd of geldings. Guarded by a party of young nobles headed by the heir to the throne, the horse set off (traditionally in a clockwise direction) and wandered about freely wherever he liked. The ground that he covered within the year was considered to have become the king's property and anyone who attempted to question this royal right was immediately attacked, and, of course, overcome, by the young warriors accompanying the stallion. His passage through the kingdom and beyond its frontiers was compared with that of the sun. It was a solemn confirmation of the king in his role as Regent of the Year, and was also an exaltation of the valour of the warrior caste (*kshatriya*).

Then, when a year had gone by and the horse had returned to his starting-point, the preparation for the sacrifice came to an end. Twenty-one sacrificial posts (*yûpa*) had been erected on a wide, open space, as well as ritual huts for the officiating priest and his wives. Numerous animals were tethered to the posts while the central post was reserved for the stallion now returned from his imperial tour. After the performance of various rites,[21] the animals were sacrificed and their blood was allowed to flow on to the ground. On the second day the victorious stallion was in his turn immolated, but by suffocation, and was offered up to *Prajâpati*, the personification of the Universal 'Self' of which it was the analogue. According to the *Brihadâranyaka-upanishad*, a series of comparisons prove this analogy, for each part of the sacrificed stallion corresponds to a part of the universe and of Cosmic Time. The animal's 'soul' (*âtman*) is the Year, his limbs the seasons, his joints the months and fortnights his hooves the days and nights, his belly the atmosphere, his back the sky, his eye the sun, his bones the constellations his lower parts the earth, his flanks the regions of space, his ribs the intermediary regions. He was born of the Primordial Ocean when it had been churned up by the gods and demons, his flesh symbolizes the clouds, the contents of his intestines the sand, his guts the rivers, his liver and lungs the mountains, his hair the plants and trees, his neighing the lightning, his shuddering the thunder, his urine the rain his breath the wind. Thus the consecrated horse contained in himself the Year and its divisions, the cosmos and all its spatial and terrestrial components. By sacrificing the stallion the king identified himself with it, he recomposed the great, dispersed Whole so as to render himself master of it, and from thenceforth he was the Universal Sovereign.

The great horse-sacrifice was very costly. It was performed by the Maurya emperors in the third century B.C. and then by one of their successors, the Śunga Pushyamitra in about 176 B.C. It then fell into disuse, but was restored to honour by the Gupta dynasty, whose members, moreover, claimed descent from the Maurya – Samudra (A.D. 333–75), Kumâra (about A.D. 415–54) and Âdityasena (second half of the seventh century A.D.). The last horse-sacrifice was held, it seems, in Orissâ during the ninth century.[22]

The solemn ceremony seems never to have been depicted. Our knowledge of it is derived solely from texts and inscriptions which confirm that it was performed right up into medieval times.

On the other hand, horses are represented in the earliest stone sculptures, from the time of the Maurya, and very naturalistically. There are horses galloping on the tambour of the lion-capital found at Sârnâth and preserved in the Museum there. Thereafter horses figure often in the art of all the Buddhist schools, as the mounts for kings, nobles and warriors, or harnessed to war-chariots or pulling covered carts (fig. 60).

Although forming part of the herd, the horse appears to have always been a luxury and very expensive, its price being double that of a zebu or humped ox. No doubt this was because the best horses were imported at great cost, formed part of the entourage of kings and noble warriors (*kshatriya*) and required experienced grooms. Moreover, they were particularly vulnerable during the rainy season. One of the main sources of supply was central Asia, especially the region of Khotan, and each year, at the beginning of the dry season, great convoys of some 500 animals, led by horse-dealers, would set out to make the long and perilous journey in order to furnish the princely courts of India. There

Fig. 60
Bhārhut. Horse with armoured rider.
Second century B.C.
Indian Museum, Calcutta. Author's photograph.

the dealers were sure to earn high profits, especially if, on their return trip, they stole the best horses they had sold on their way out – as they were sometimes accused of doing.[23]

The horse played an important role in the aristocratic life of India. By tradition the kings were inclined to pay very high prices for the finest animals.[24] The nobles imitated them and gamblers hoped to win horses at play. The horse was, moreover, evoked during the blessing pronounced at the erection of the central pillar, the king pillar, each time a new dwelling was constructed. It was considered proof of social advancement.

Kings and nobles trained, at a very early age, to become 'horse experts' (aśvâdhyaksha). Those found worthy of this envied title were entrusted with the task of training the wild horses. The technical treatises show the methods adopted to make the animal manageable. The horse was tied to a post by a cord which was progressively shortened and it was forced to trot and gallop by whipping, beating with a stick, prodding with a goad and flicking with thongs. The animal was thus forced to go round and round in a circle that was continuously reduced in circumference. This method should tame the most restive of horses. But it demanded on the part of the experts a profound knowledge of the effects of bridle and bit on the mouth, nostrils, forehead and ears of the animal.[25]

The king visited his stables each day. They were situated in the first courtyard of the palace and sheltered both saddle- and draught-animals. They were under the general supervision of qualified overseers and required a numerous staff – grooms and stable-boys, veterinary surgeons and various assistants. They were required to prove that they had the technical knowledge, and also the moral qualities, which justified complete confidence being placed in them – so highly were the horses valued. Everything was carefully verified, the state of the harness no less than the kind of fodder provided. This was made up of barley, peas and oats, with, on exceptional occasions, root vegetables steeped in honey[26] or, during military campaigns, the addition of some wine to 'dope' the animals. Each horse had its own name, yet further proof of how highly they were esteemed.

When he left his palace, the king was on horseback. He was preceded by an equerry wearing a livery patterned on the costume of the central Asian grooms, who were often retained to care for the horses they had accompanied from their distant home. It consisted of a tunic with long sleeves, tailored and caught in at the waist with a belt and cut low at the bottom of the neck, breeches and leather sandals. The equerry ran in front of the Royal Horse and held a ring in which could be seen the chakra, a formidable missile and symbol of royalty.[27] Numerous carvings of the Amarâvatî school of the third to second century B.C. show this scene with the Bodhisattva leaving his father's palace in order to make a secret retreat to the forest to begin his life of meditation. His faithful horse, Kanthaka, is the very image of one of those royal and princely steeds of which their owners took such good care. Kanthaka, endowed with intelligence and even speech, participates with 'human' emotions in the famous scene of the 'Great Departure'. He leads his master to the forest, then, with the equerry, returns to the royal palace to share in the general consternation. For the Departure, as for all royal outings, Kanthaka is richly apparelled – a saddle-cloth, a saddle-girth, a head-stall sometimes ornamented with a plume. His tail is plaited or covered with a metal sheath, probably gilded. There were no stirrups but sometimes, for example at Mathurâ (first century A.D.), the rider slips his toes under the girth. In the fifth and sixth centuries, for example at Ajantâ, cavern XVII, and perhaps even before then, a saddle was placed on the saddle-cloth. This was a comfortable 'English'-type saddle, but there were still no stirrups.

Although the king owned many horses, one particular horse was selected as the royal steed, and this 'Royal Horse' was counted among the 'Seven Jewels' (*saptaratna*) which denote a Universal King (*chakravartin*). As the palladium of the empire, the Royal Horse occupied a special stable decorated with gold and crimson hangings. He had his own staff to watch over his health and security. The theft of a Royal Horse was punished with death. Like a spoilt child the State Horse indulged in plenty of caprices, detailed in the *Giridanta-jâtaka*[28] and illustrated at Begrâm.[29]

From the earliest historical times the horse was associated with the idea of universal sovereignty. Thus, indeed, was the significance of the *digvijaya* rite – the triumphal procession of a newly crowned king, first round his capital, then round his kingdom – a distant memento of the conquering course the stallion traced in the preparation for the horse-sacrifice.

Associated with sovereignty, the horse was also the symbol of the warrior aristocracy. It took part in all the military campaigns which were, indeed, the *raison d'être* of the nobles (*kshatriya*). Until about the third century the Indian armies consisted, traditionally, of four corps – the chariots, the elephants, the cavalry and the infantry. The chariots, resembling the *bigae* and *quadrigae* of Etruria, made up an élite corps whose defeat would inevitably be followed by that of the whole army. The chariots were drawn by the best-trained horses (fig. 61). Each driver was recruited from among the aristocrats of the Royal Court. His task was perilous since he was exposed, without any defence, to the missiles of the enemy; his responsibility was very great since the safety of the king or of the leader he was charged to protect depended upon his skill in changing course according to the fortunes of battle. Furthermore, the chariots were easily bogged down in mud and were not very effective in the face of fast, unexpected tactics. It was probably for these reasons that the use of chariots was eventually abandoned.

On the other hand, the cavalry was the most adaptable arm of the forces. Success depended, of course, largely on the quality of the horses and on their training. Cavalry was used for reconnaissance purposes for sudden attacks, for pursuing the enemy in flight and for capturing the enemy's reserves. The horsemen were armed with lances or swords, sometimes a bow and they wore breast-plates. The game of chess represents an army in battle array and was invented by the Indians in order to work out different strategies. Among the pieces were a horse and a chariot, the latter was afterwards replaced by a ship.

The horse was thus a cosmic and a solar symbol, the emblem of sovereignty, of the aristocracy and of the warrior's valour, the mark of wealth and prosperity. Throughout the history of India, it continued to be associated with human activity, in terms of victory and prestige. Even today the Indian bridegroom rides on a sumptuously caparisoned horse through the streets of towns and villages and plays, for a day, the part of a conqueror and an aristocrat. We shall see that the horse also had a place in the world of spirits and gods.

Fig. 61
Sāñchī. Royal elephant leaving a town.
c. beginning of first century A.D.
In situ. Author's photograph.

The Elephant

The elephant was as highly prized as the horse. In the most ancient schools of Indian art the elephant is reproduced with both skill and naturalism. Its gigantic size, massive body and familiar poses inspired the artists (fig. 62), and there are innumerable representations of elephants throughout the whole course of Indian art.

Already in the earliest representations, among others those of Bhârhut (about 150–100 B.C.), the elephant is among the most carefully studied and the most finely depicted. Especially at Bhârhut, but also in the works of the Śunga school, one finds wild elephants paying homage to the Buddha in the forest.[30] Carved in profile, they display an easy mastery based on close observation. There are also tame elephants, harnessed and adorned, taking part in many scenes, most of which illustrate *jâtaka*. In the next phase of Indian artistic development, about the beginning of the Christian era, the elephants of Sâñchî are found in comparable scenes, but seem to be more skilfully integrated into the compositions which themselves have become more cleverly constructed. The reliefs in the Udayagiri Caves, Orissâ (about the first century A.D.), show an easy and free treatment. The school of Mathurâ (first to second centuries A.D.) did not initiate any great changes although there is a certain clumsiness in the treatment of scenes and animals. This is not true, however, for the works of the Amarâvatî school, of the second and third

132

Fig. 62
Sārnāth. Adoration of the stupa of Rāma-grama.
Second century B.C.
Archaeological Museum, Sārnāth (CB-9).
Author's photograph.

centuries A.D., where elephants are depicted with much skill. One of the best scenes is on the famous medallion preserved in the Government Museum at Madras, which illustrates the episode of the 'furious elephant'. The naturalness and the dynamic movement make this a miniature masterpiece.[31]

A little later on, in the Gupta and post-Gupta periods of the fifth and sixth centuries A.D., elephants are depicted with much artistic ability in the frescoes of Ajantâ and Bâgh. Every device is employed to accentuate the imposing impression conveyed by the animal but at the same time there is grace in its mighty form.

In the seventh century the sculptors of Mahâbalipuram again show great interest in the elephant theme, whether in the high-reliefs of the monolithic temples or in the great composition already mentioned, 'The Descent of the Ganges'. Here an elephant family – male, female and two young, advances towards the crevice from which the sacred waters gush forth to quicken the earth. Soberly modelled, majestic, natural, these elephant portraits are among the most beautiful in all the art of India. In the eighth century, at the Kailâsa of Ellorâ the elephant appears once again in full relief, as at Mahâbalipuram, and also on a very fine plinth forming the lower storey of the building. Though still skilful, these sculptures are neither as beautiful nor as natural as those of an earlier period.

In the medieval epoch, the tenth to eighteenth centuries, the elephants portrayed in relief are much less fine. They continue to be painted and appear in the scenes decorating the lower courses of temple-walls, but are much more mannered, as are all the works of this period, a feature which becomes more and more pronounced as Indian art declines.

The elephant, like the horse, though perhaps even to a greater extent, occupied a place of the first importance in the kingdom. Like the horse, the elephant counted as one of the Seven Jewels of the Universal Monarch, and anyone who was convicted of stealing a State Elephant was condemned to death.

The king when hunting avoided killing elephants, but the animals were sought out by professional hunters who wanted to obtain the tusks. For the ivory market in ancient India was one of the most flourishing, rivalling that of Africa. Moreover, in addition to demands from abroad there were those of the different Indian communities who required ivory for a wide variety of uses. Despite the high taxes, some 50 per cent levied by the State on the raw material, the ivory-workers plyed a flourishing trade. Their skill was highly reputed and is often mentioned in the texts and tales. A large hoard of carved ivory plaques of Indian origin, from the first and second centuries was discovered in the years 1936-7 and 1939 by Joseph and Ria Hackin at the Begrâm of Kapishî, in Afghanistan. They show that the reputation of the Indian ivory-carvers was well deserved.

The ivory was collected by specialists, highly skilled in the dangerous sport of elephant-hunting. The hunt is described in detail in a celebrated Buddhistic story, the *Shaddanta-jâtaka*.[32] This tale is, moreover, very often illustrated in ancient sculpture and painting, to honour the abnegation of the Bodhisattva who was incarnated in a six-tusked elephant (*shad*, 'six', and *danta*, 'tooth'). The Buddhist artists' affection for this story resulted in some very fine representations of the noble animal kneeling before the hunter who is sawing off the precious tusks.

But many elephants did not fall victims to hunters. They were taken alive, either to be trained or to be exported to some foreign country where they would be kept in zoological parks. The animals were captured in the same way as today, using a tame elephant as a decoy to lure the wild beasts into an enclosure where the training took place.[33] This training was undertaken by 'elephant experts' (*gâjâdhyaksha*) who taught the elephants the various tasks they had to perform, helping woodmen during the felling of trees by rolling and transporting timber and loading it on carts,[34] military tactics, how to kneel down and rise with a howdah on their backs, how to fight in single combat and so forth.

Once it had been well trained an elephant could be sold at a very high price, the same price as a slave, and four times that of a horse. The king owned many elephants and their stalls were placed, like the stables, in the first courtyards of the palace with the storerooms for the howdahs and harness. Each day the elephants were led out to an exercise area and then to the river or a pool to bathe. They rested for the remainder of the day and the king visited them daily during the cooler hours.

Elephants trained for war composed one of the four army corps, represented in the game of chess by pawns, and were covered with trappings made of metal plates. Each animal carried three archers as well as the mahout (*mahaut*). Sometimes the elephants were protected by three horsemen. The elephant corps formed the vanguard and its task was to force a passage by trampling down obstacles, to jump over embankments and holes so as to avoid traps, and to protect the army's flanks by forming a continuous front to enemy attack. All this is described in technical treatises attributed to the fourth century B.C. and has been confirmed by history; thus in 327 B.C. Alexander the Great had to face an imposing formation of elephants drawn up against him by one of the Indian sovereigns, Pôros (in Sanskrit Pûru). About twenty years later, Seleucus Nikator while negotiating with the Maurya emperor, Chandragupta, was offered 500 elephants in exchange for several provinces situated in what today is part of Afghanistan.

Needless to say, the State Elephant, the palladium of the Empire like the Royal Horse, was chosen with the greatest care and with close attention to certain characteristics which were thought to confirm the animal's royal and sacred origin. Thus he had to have a very light grey colour skin which qualified as 'white'. The king paraded the elephant through the streets of the capital and was followed by a solemn procession. After that the king consecrated the animal by a ritual baptism and declared it to be specially reserved as a royal mount.[35] From that day onwards the State Elephant occupied a stall of its own where the king came to visit it each day. A staff was allocated to the white elephant which took part in every festival and in the royal pilgrimages. During the coronation ceremonies the new monarch, seated on the State Elephant's back in a fine covered howdah, made him walk clockwise round the capital. The gates of the city were made tall enough for the elephant and its howdah to pass through.

For these ceremonies the elephant was sumptuously adorned. The literature and the illustrations agree in the description of this finery. The elephant's back was covered with a splendid striped or chequered carpet held in place by a girth; clusters of jewels hung from its ears; its head was ornamented with a gilded bridle and crowned with a golden diadem. Its neck was encircled with a wide collar and on its legs were hung rings of precious metal. Attached to the breast-plate were two cords hanging down to the animal's knees and bearing bells, large and small, which, by tinkling and jangling at each step, announced the State Elephant's approach.

The Elephant of State indeed was believed to be born of a cloud and was compared with Airâvata, the mount of the king of the gods, Indra. His strength and wisdom were vaunted, his steadiness and prudence praised.

Indeed, elephants, because of their obvious qualities, have always been considered exceptional animals in India. As far back as the Satapatha-brâhmana epoch (about 1000–800 B.C.) they were said to have been born of Purusha or the 'Cosmic Soul' whose nature they share. Again in Buddhism they played a very important part, incarnating the future Buddha during the Conception. This scene, often illustrated in ancient paintings and sculpture, shows a young elephant, white in colour, descending from the heavens to Queen Mâyâ as she sleeps. He was to enter into her womb and be born again as a man, in the person of a young prince, Siddhârtha, who, when he reached man's estate, was to be the Buddha Sâkyamuni himself. This theme, repeated again and again, has given rise to many beautiful illustrations through all the long course of Buddhist art, not only in India itself, but also in the countries converted to Theravada Buddhism.

Another Buddhist theme frequently treated throughout ancient

Indian art, most notably at Sânchî, in the first and second centuries B.C., represents two elephants each holding a jar with its trunk and sprinkling a woman, either seated or standing. Comparisons are easy to find. Not only does the woman seem to symbolize the Goddess-Mother, either Lakshmî in Brahminism or Mâyâ in Buddhism, but the attitude of the elephants recalls the rite of royal baptism (*abhisheka*).[36]

Since the elephant was the royal animal *par excellence* it was only logical that it should be assimilated with the sovereign. The symbolic character of the elephant was maintained for a long time and it was associated with other animals, no less symbolical, in the decoration of Buddhist thrones.

Snakes

Snakes, regarded as both fearsome and beneficent, were often represented in Indian art. They appear in two forms: zoomorphic (the less usual) and anthropomorphic. In the latter their reptile nature was only indicated by the presence of one or several hoods above the head of a personage, or else, as at Mathurâ, by a human being standing with his back against a coiled serpent whose many hoods rise like a nimbus behind his head. No creature was, perhaps, so closely connected with human nature and none, moreover, gave occasion for such beautiful examples of plastic art. To understand how this came about one must, perhaps, first consider the traditional data we have regarding serpents.[37]

Some of them, generally cobras (*nâga*), lived near men and were regarded as the protectors of the domestic hearth. Each dwelling had a snake which was regularly fed and was regarded as the tutelary genius of the home. When it disappeared it was thought that the home was doomed. Moreover, in many villages, there were little temples, shaped like pavilions, that sheltered a cobra. Daily devotion was rendered to the snake, and the villagers brought it offerings of milk, rice, fish, meat and even strong drink. This cult was particularly observed during the rainy season, the four months when, attracted by the humidity, the snakes come forth from their lairs and might be aggressive.

This aggressiveness was proverbial. The soldiers of Alexander the Great who had advanced into India were terrified by the sinister hissing of serpents at the entrance to caves and by the flashing eyes 'as large as Macedonian shields'.

Snakes were thought to have many powers. As the guardians of subterranean treasure they could either offer it to men or keep it for themselves. They were ferocious when attacked and would take immediate vengeance when offended; they might even exterminate a whole people by distilling the mortal poison of their fangs or by strangling their victims in their coil. They could also blind men with their foul breath, kill by a single glance, or reduce a city to ashes.

There were numerous charms thought to conciliate snakes and to preserve men from them. Anyone who picked up the discarded skin of a serpent could make himself invisible or attain longevity or even immortality, for the casting of the skin symbolizes the soul freeing itself from evil and from the cycle of rebirths. Some men specialized in capturing snakes and in charming them, and serpents figured among the exports from India to countries of the West. The snake-charmers, as they do today, carried their snakes about in cylindrical wickerwork

baskets, depicted in a seventh-century fresco at Ajantâ, cavern I, and earned a little money with their act.

Serpents, it was said, were people of the subterranean world, at the bottom of the waters. There they possessed a resplendent capital called Bhogavatî, 'The Rich in Enjoyment'. Their sovereigns were reputed very powerful and noble. And their kingdom communicated with the world of man by means of caverns or ant-hills which play an important part in the popular traditions of India.

Snakes often assume human forms. This was so widely admitted that in the ordination ceremony of a Buddhist monk he was always asked the strange question 'Art thou a man or a *nâga*?', since some highly favoured individuals maintained they were descended from the serpent race while others claimed they had received certain magical formulae from snakes endowing them with extraordinary powers. There are numerous legends about women-serpents or *nâgî* appearing among men and arousing passionate desire by their great beauty. But each night the *nâgî* has to regain their reptilian form and because of this were forced to resort to a multitude of ruses and subterfuges.

The feared and respected *nâga* were above all, venerated as the 'givers of rain'. Since they were especially numerous at the time of the monsoon and because they had a preference for damp places they were regarded as having some direct connection with water. Thus statues to the *Nâga* king (*nâgarâja*) were erected near springs and pools to act as

Fig. 63
Sāñchī. Episode from Buddha' life: the nāga with five heads protecting the seated master (invisible) on the altar-throne in the sanctuary of flames.
c. beginning of first century A.D.
In situ. Author's photograph.

137

the protectors of such places. They were represented upright and backed by a coiled serpent raising its fabulous hood with five or seven heads, in their left hand they held a covered cup (for they were reputed to be great wine-drinkers) and with their right hand they pointed up to the sky – a gesture to attract the fertilizing rains. This subject was treated in masterly fashion by the artists of the Mathurâ school of the second, century A.D. in sculptures of the local pink sandstone, displaying a marvellous feeling for proportions and harmony of forms.[38]

These mysterious beings, thought to be able to render sterile women fertile and to enrich men with subterranean treasures, were incorporated into Buddhism and there are numerous legends in which serpents play a part. No doubt the most celebrated of these stories is that introducing the *nâga* Muchilinda. It concerns an episode in the life of the Buddha Sâkyamuni, who, while plunged in profound meditation, was attacked by the Demon who raised a great storm to destroy him. Now the *nâgarâja* lived near by and when he saw the danger to which the Master was exposed, he hastened to his aid. He coiled his body under that of the seated Buddha so as to raise him above the waters, which, as is usual in tropical storms, rose at a fantastic rate. He spread his hoods over the Buddha's head to preserve him from the furious winds and the waterspouts. This theme, often treated in the works of the Amarâvatî school of the second to fourth centuries A.D., reached its maximum perfection in the Khmer art of the eleventh to thirteenth centuries (fig. 63).

Mythical and Divine Animals

So far the animals dealt with, whether domestic or not, formed part of the world of man. The natural world and the supernatural were intertwined. The gods walked among men, the genii lived in their forest homes, in the waters, in the most common objects, at the cross-roads and even in the fire of the domestic hearth. The invisible seemed as real as the visible and revealed itself on many occasions, in so many different aspects, and often in forms so similar to those of the visible world, that it was easy to be mistaken.

This supernatural world was composed of many gods, genii, spirits and phantoms, not to mention wizards and witches, ogresses *e tutti quanti*.

In the world of the gods, which was conceived in the image of the world of men, particular animals were associated with certain deities. Each great god was provided with a 'mount' or 'vehicle' (*vâhana*) sacred to him – the elephant Airavâta for Indra the sovereign of the gods, the bull Nandin for Śiva 'the destroyer' (fig. 64), the Garuda bird for Vishnu 'the preserver', the sacred goose (*hamsa*) for Brahmâ 'the creator', the peacock for Skanda, the god of war (known as Subrahmaniar in southeastern India), the rat for the god Ganeśa or Ganapati, the lion for the goddess Durgâ, and so forth.

It has been held that these *vâhana* were the most ancient gods of India and that, little by little, they were ousted by the anthropomorphic deities conceived of at a later date. The older animal-divinities then survived as sacred 'vehicles'. Whether or not this theory is well founded, it brings out the importance that animals had in Vedic times for the Hindus, and also throws light on the animal cults of later times. Among these 'vehicles' the bull Nandin assumed an increasingly great impor-

Fig. 64
Kodambalur. Muvarkovil temple. Detail of roof showing the bull Nandin, the sacred mount of the god Śiva.
c. Eighth century A.D.
Author's photograph.

tance.[39] Special sanctuaries were erected to him and his gigantic statue is often sheltered under a columned pavilion adjoining the shrine of Śiva. Frequently this arrangement was still adhered to in medieval times.

Another *vâhana* worthy of special mention is the Garuda bird, the 'vehicle' of Vishnu.[40] He is a solar bird of a hawk-like nature and is the traditional enemy of the *nâga* which he carried off in his powerful beak. Curiously enough when the *nâga* is in human form, the representations of this theme strikingly resemble those of Ganymede being carried off by the eagle. This is very noticeable in the early sculpture from Pakistan (Gandhâra) and even as far away as Sinkiang.[41, 42] Treatment of this subject is found over an immense area, from the Russian steppes to Cambodia and Indonesia.[43] In Cambodia, especially, it was remarkably popular in the Bayon-style art of the second half of the twelfth century A.D. In India itself it appears early, and here the Garuda bird and the *nâga* surmount two commemorative columns. One such monument was erected to Vishnu at Besnagar during the reign of the Sunga by Heliodôros, the envoy of King Antialcidas who reigned at Taxila towards the end of the second century B.C. The same theme is found at Sânchî on the middle architrave of the eastern *torana* of stûpa I, dating from about the beginning of the Christian era. The Garuda bird in these monuments is a fabulous bird, rather like a parrot, holding a serpent in its beak. Later on, under the Gupta – and after – the Garuda bird becomes a hybrid, as much man as bird. But it must be admitted that the Indian artists, unlike their counterparts in south-eastern Asia, did not produce any masterpieces on this particular theme.

The god Vishnu who, with Brahmâ and Śiva, makes up the great Hindu Trinity, has one remarkable peculiarity, that of having, on several occasions, assumed the form of an animal. According to Brahmanic conceptions Brahmâ created the world; after some time had passed Śiva shook the world and threatened to destroy it. Meanwhile, Vishnu, reclining on the great Serpent of Eternity, Śesha, in the midst of the Primordial Ocean, awaited the moment to intervene and restore the world to order and peace.

By this myth of threefold action the Hindus explain the alternation of cosmic periods. In order to play his part Vishnu 'descends' onto the earth and each time assumes a different aspect, these are the *avatâra* of which there are ten principal ones. Sometimes Vishnu appears in the form of an animal (successively wild boar, lion, tortoise, fish and horse) and at other times in the shape of a man (giant, dwarf, child-god and so forth). It is by no means impossible that the animals whose form Vishnu is said to have assumed may, earlier on in the course of Indian religious evolution, have been the objects of individual cults. The Brahmins, anxious to divert popular religious devotion towards their great god Vishnu, may have found their task made easier by closely associating him with some of the deified animals.

The representations of Vishnu's animal *avatâra* show him sometimes in the form of the whole beast, sometimes as a man with an animal's head, or again with a man's trunk tapering off into the lower part of an animal.

When he was transformed into a boar (*vahâra*) Vishnu saved the goddess Prithivî who had fallen to the bottom of the Ocean. This subject was often treated by the Indian sculptors (fig. 65). One of the finest compositions illustrating this episode is to be seen at Udayagiri (Bhopâl, fifth century A.D.) where the god with the boar's head is holding up the little goddess with his left tusk while, with powerful strokes he rises to the surface of the waters. The exaggeratedly great stature of the god, compared with the size of the onlookers watching the miracles, invests Vishnu with an impressive majesty.[44] Another very well-known relief at Mahâbalipuram (seventh century A.D.) illustrates the same scene in the rather formal style characteristic of this site. It shows great mastery and the unusual couple are depicted with a real tenderness.[45] Later on, in the tenth and eleventh centuries, at Khajurâho, the god takes the form of the whole animal in a monumental and powerful statue whose cosmic character is indicated by a multitude of small figures carved in serried ranks and representing 'all' the Brahmanic gods.[46] This *avatâra* has been endlessly reproduced up until the present day, with greater or lesser success.

Fig. 65
Varahāvatara. The god Visnu with a boar's head bringing up the Earth from the bottom of the ocean.
Fifteenth century A.D.
Pondicherry.

Another theme that occurs almost as frequently as that of the boar is that of Vishnu the Man-Lion (Narasimha). According to the legend Vishnu assumed this terrifying appearance, unlike his usually peaceful character, in order to overcome an impious king, his fierce adversary. But the Man-Lion was not satisfied with having overcome the king in single combat; he slit up the wicked man's belly with his claws and ferociously disembowelled him. Here again was a subject that inspired the sculptors and some of them produced masterpieces. The most remarkable of these is no doubt the eighth-century A.D. example from the Ellorâ caves where the god and the miscreant are shown face to face in a finely, well-balanced composition.[47] But Narasimha is also represented in repose, in the attitude of meditation. A tympanum from Deogarh (fifth to sixth centuries A.D.) shows him thus, as do numerous south Indian bronzes of a later epoch. The medieval sculptors concerned themselves more with the depiction of the savage scene of the god devouring the guts of his enemy.

The other animal *avatâra* of Vishnu have not been dealt with in so masterly a fashion. In his fish-incarnation (Matsya) the god rescues the Veda and the centre of the universe from the destruction caused by the Flood. In the incarnation of the tortoise (*kûrma*) he carries on his shell the Mount Mandara, pivot of the world, with the aid of which gods and demons (*asura*) churn up the Primordial Ocean. These two *avatâra* did not provide much inspiration for the Indian artists. On the other hand, there are very fine examples of the 'Churning of the Sea of Milk' in Khmer art, notably at Angkor Vat (first half of the twelfth century A.D.). Vishnu was also incarnated as a horse (Kalkin) but this *avatâra* is never represented on its own.

The celebrated monkey of the *Râmâyana*, Hanumâna, the son of the Wind Vâyu, also belongs to the Vishnuite cycle; but in early Indian art he occupies a much lesser place than in the later arts of Cambodia and Java. All the same, from the medieval period onwards Hanumâna was represented in statues, especially of bronze. He is shown as almost human in aspect, but with a simian face and a long tail. Sometimes he is shown making the gesture of respect, placing his hand in front of his mouth.

The cult of Ganeśa, the elephant-headed deity, seems to have existed by the beginning of Gupta times (fourth century A.D.) and perhaps even earlier, though there is no mention of him in the inscriptions. He is usually called the 'Chief of the Gana' (Ganapati), thus of a class of genii. He was thus related to popular divinities, and became the main object of devotion for the Ganapatya, members of one of the five recognized Hindu sects. His origin is probably very ancient and one can detect several attempts to introduce him into the cult of more powerful deities. Finally, he ended up as the son of Śiva and Pârvatî. From the medieval period onwards Ganeśa became the object of especial veneration by the merchants and businessmen in Hinduist India, and so remains today. And althought his cult never attained a pre-eminent rank, none the less worship is rendered to him at the beginning of each religious ceremony and also on special occasions.[48] In this way, then, the elephant, royal, sacred and useful, was also incorporated into the Hindu pantheon.

Side by side with these divine animals, whose morphological characters are those of natural beings, there were others which were as much monsters as mythical animals. Thus, in the ancient representations we find centaurs (notably at Mathurâ, first to second centuries A.D.), griffins, and two-headed eagles (both found at Mathurâ and Begrâm), and even grylles (Begrâm) showing that there were contacts with Hellenized Iran.

Indeed, a whole collection of mythical animals appeared in the first and second centuries A.D. and later, but they were mainly decorative, though, at the same time, they were invested with symbolism. There are the men-birds (*kinnara*) and their spouses (*kinnarî*), charming musicians with hardly any connection with the Classical harpies; they played a sort of zither (*vînâ*) made out of bamboo. They were the rivals of the Wind Vâyu whose symbol is the bamboo. These celestial musicians are represented during the first centuries of figurative art and, during the Gupta period (fifth century A.D.) they become extraordinarily graceful, their human bust terminates in a feathered tail of flowing curls.[49] There are the *makara*, marine monsters combining the forms of crocodiles, elephants and fish.[50] The *makara* are mentioned as among the animals peopling the Ocean which, in Sanskrit literature is called 'the abode of the *makara*' (*makarâlaya*). These creatures have formidable jaws like those of crocodiles. Sometimes their snout ends in an elephant's trunk. Their ears are like fins, and they have paws, while their bodies are covered with scales and their tails are those of a fish. According to the Buddhist stories, one *makara* of gigantic size, called Timingala, living in the midst of the Ocean had an insatiable appetite. He terrorized the vessels that ventured on the high seas, for each time he opened his mouth he raised a whirlpool and sucked in both the ship and the men on board.[51]

The *makara* was frequently used as a subject by the early artists, especially at Bhârhut, and little by little the beast was incorporated into the repertoire of architectural decoration. *Makara* appear on the ends of the lintels of the gateways (*torana*) at Begrâm, Mathurâ, Amarâvatî in the first to third centuries A.D. and on the back of Buddhistic thrones.[52] Although their use as part of the *toran* decoration was fairly short-lived, they survived for a very long time as part of the seats. They ornament the extremities of the bar that demarcates the upper part of the back, and seem to symbolize the base of the celestial regions and to have some connection with cosmic stratigraphy as envisioned by the Indians. The *makara* are also used in another theme where they were shown facing one another while a semicircular arch unites their open mouths. This theme has been interpreted as symbolizing the rainbow which, according to some conceptions, joins heaven to earth. The *makara* always retains an aquatic character and it is also associated with the goddess Gangâ, the River Ganges, represented as a beautiful young woman standing upright upon the back of the monster (Begrâm, Mathurâ and in the Gupta and post-Gupta styles).

Finally, the lion appears frequently in the early representations. Already in the Maurya epoch, third century B.C., it appears in a naturalistic form. Lions adorn, four times repeated, the famous capital at Sârnâth. Four seated lions touching each others' hind quarters support a great wheel (*chakra*). There is little doubt about the symbolism of this capital which surmounts a commemorative column. The *chakra*, symbol of the Law (*dharma*), is the image of the sun as it traverses the world like a monarch's triumphal chariot. Lions, themselves sovereign beasts, and by tradition likened to the sun, are the most evident emblems of the universal domination of the Law whose depositary is the monarch. This is the *chakra* which today serves as the symbol of an independent India and figures on the national flag.

From the Maurya epoch onwards the Buddhist artists adopted the lion to symbolize the Buddha Sâkyamuni, known also as 'The Lion of the Sâkya'. In the first representations of the Buddha, which do not appear until about the second century A.D., the lion is shown between his feet as though it were his *vâhana* (Mathurâ, second century A.D.).[53] Or, again, the beast stands at the corner of his throne, recalling similar Egyptian, Assyrian, Iranian, Greek and Roman thrones.

The Lion Throne (*simhâsana*) is explicitly a royal and imperial seat so that the fact that it was attributed to the Buddha seems to indicate that his votaries wished to invest him with the character of a sovereign.

Later on, from the time of the Amarâvatî school (second century A.D.), the seat becomes more ornamental and while still supported by two seated lions also includes two other lions along the arms. Then during the Gupta period (fourth and fifth centuries A.D.) the composition becomes more detailed and amplified. At the height of the seated personage's thighs, can be seen the foreparts of two elephants. Above this two lions rampant form the verticals of the back of the throne, while two *makara* terminate the horizontal bar at the top of the back. The lion rampant did not remain naturalistic for very long. In Gupta art his head sports horns either twisted like those of a ram or ribbed like those of a goat. The body became more arched and the muzzle lengthened, the paws sometimes end in claws but also sometimes in hooves, and progressively between the eighth and twelfth centuries A.D. the lion becomes a hybrid creature closer to a goat or a ram than to a wild beast. This slow evolution was not only due to the fantasy of the sculptors and painters, but also represents an evolution in symbolism towards uniting a number of disparate elements thought to be comparable and all relating to solar symbolism.

These mutations resulted in the birth of a mythical animal, the *vyâlaka*, linked, through time and space, with all the composite animals in other ancient civilizations (fig. 66). The *vyâlaka* appears not only on the backs of thrones but also in architectural decoration, supporting columns, ornamenting the space between pilasters, running along friezes, mounted by young women, etc. The *vyâlaka* is one of the distinguishing marks of the medieval style that lasted until the eighteenth century.

Conclusion

At the conclusion of this short review of an immense subject, we must try to weigh up the evidence. The persistence of beliefs in Indian civilization is an almost unique phenomenon, a continuity from prehistoric times to the present day. Archaeology and art give ample evidence of the important place which animals occupied at the very core of Indian life throughout some 5,000 years. Whether useful or domestic, sacred or symbolic, animals are always and everywhere associated with everyday life, with religion, with ritual, and even with royal and imperial ceremony. We must stress once more that it is impossible, in so short a study, to detail the whole of this subject.

However, what one finds is close union between man and animal, and that the animals may be highly respected or even venerated. If one objects that this is an exaggeration because in India, as elsewhere, human cruelty towards animals existed, and still exists, one must recall that in no other part of the world is there so marked a fraternity between man and animal, a fraternity expressed in many actions beginning with the adherence to a strictly vegetarian diet as early as the third century B.C. (and still an important tenet for the orthodox), and continuing with the foundation, in the second century B.C., of hospices for sick and aged animals.

India, always a land of paradox, is true to itself in its attitude towards

Fig. 66
Bhuvaneśvara Mukteśvara temple. A queen
serpent. Tenth century A.D.
Author's photograph.

animals. But animals have been honoured and even exalted. Indian
artists have been among the most skilled depicters of animals, they
created masterpieces which could never have existed without the strong
bond of affection towards the whole animal world.

7
ANIMALS IN CHINA

M.TREGEAR

Animals figure in archaeology in many roles – as remains giving clues to the climate and conditions in a palaeontological sense; as adjuncts to human settlement giving clues to the character of society and its agriculture; represented in art when they bridge the spheres of the archaeologist and the art historian. This brief survey touches on all these roles which of course overlap, and in the latter two roles the Chinese have distinctive attitudes to animals both real and mythical as much part of their culture as rice-eating and the wearing of silk.

That 'Mankind is the proper study of Man' has been very much the Chinese historian's view of his subject and, in a culture so voluminously documented from a very early period, this study has involved almost exclusively the use of written records. These, however questionable in authenticity, extend back into the Shang dynasty (1766–1111 B.C.), and scholars throughout the long span of historical studies in China have shown little interest in prehistory – in the sense of pre-written history.

There have, of course, been notable exceptions, among them the indomitable historian and recorder Ssu-Ma Ch'ien (145–c. 86 B.C.).* Commissioned by the ruler to make an official inspection of the newly conquered territories of Ssechwan and Yunnan, he travelled widely, and, on the death of his father the Grand Astrologer, he also took over and completed the writing of the *Shih Chi* or Historical Record. In the *Shih Chi* he recorded all the history of the country that he regarded as verifiable and included ancient sites which he had checked. His first hand descriptions lend a freshness which is still evident today and many of his identifications of ancient sites have proved correct, notably that of the 'Wastes of Yin' in the present-day Anyang region which mark the capital of the later Shang dynasty. Although not an excavator, Ssu-Ma Ch'ien was unusual as an historian who took note of archaeological evidence.

However, perhaps the earliest archaeologist who has left records was Yuan K'ang who, in his *Yüeh Chüeh Shu* ('Record of Yüeh'), quotes an explicit periodization of the development from the Stone Age

---

* Ssu-Ma Ch'ien was a native of Lung-men, Shensi. His father was Ssu-Ma T'an, the Grand Astrologer.

146

to the Iron Age which must have been based on archaeological observations.*

In general, however, interest in the very early settlement of the country was not awakened until the excavations in the early twentieth century at the large Middle to Late Shang sites at Anyang which, even today, remain incomplete.[2] This was followed in the 1920s by the discovery and publication of widespread Neolithic sites and of the *Homo erectus pekinensis* finds at Chou K'o Tien near Peking.[3] The latter aroused great interest in 'early man' and in the origins of Chinese culture. This question of origins, as yet unsolved, and the introduction of modern palaeontological techniques has opened up a wide area of study. Although perhaps more rightly termed 'human' palaeontology, this work has inevitably led to the recording of fauna found on ancient sites. This study of animal distributions is naturally of great importance for the analysis of climate and general environment. Information on the distribution of fauna is now available for the Late Pliocene and post-Pliocene periods (chart, page 148).†

The fauna of northern China during the Pliocene period is regarded zoologically as the eastern extension of an assemblage that covered the northern region from the Atlantic to the Pacific. This seems to indicate a similarity of climate and environment over this vast area. The Pliocene seems in general to have had a mild temperate climate characterized, according to Teilhard de Chardin, by *Hipparion* fauna. The *Hipparion* is an extinct horse-like animal and the animals found associated with it include hyenas, wolves, rhinoceroses, deer and birds.[4] This fauna also suggests that in the earlier part of the Pliocene period there was considerably more water, in the form of lakes and marshes, than is present in northern China today. Finds of gravel and sand layers give evidence of extensive lakes and running water, particularly in the Yellow River area. However, excavations have also shown that a progressive desiccation took place later in the Pliocene leading to an increase in browsing animals and the appearance of such trees as the poplar.

In the Pliocene period the Ts'in Ling mountain range already marked the division between northern and southern China, a divide which, with the Nan Shan, is still of great geographic and climatic significance today (map, page 151).[5] To the south of this range was a warmer and more forested area which, in this period, shared many animals in common with the Indo-Malay forest fauna. Here apes, stegodon and rhinoceros (both *pre-orientalis* and *monocerine*) are characteristic of a fauna better known in the forest regions of the northern Malay peninsula. The K'ai Yuan forest ape found in 1957 with fossil remains of mastodon, a large mammal somewhat resembling an elephant, in the Pontian coal-beds in Yunnan might be an early ancestor of both ape

* In the *Yüeh Chüeh Shu* an eastern Chou philosopher, Feng Hu Tzu is quoted as reporting to the King of Yüeh: 'In the Age of Hsüan Yüan, Shen-nung and Hê-hsü weapons were made of stone for cutting trees and building houses, and were buried with the dead. . . . In the Age of Huang-ti weapons were made of jade for cutting trees, building houses and digging the ground . . . and were buried with the dead. . . . In the Age of Yü, weapons were made of bronze, for building canals . . . and houses. . . . In the present time weapons are made of iron. . . .'[1]
† The Pliocene and post-Pliocene or Pleistocene are geological epochs. The Pliocene began some 12 million years ago, the Pleistocene probably 1 or 2 million years ago.

CHART SHOWING THE MAJOR ARCHAEOLOGICAL SITES OF THE PLIOCENE TO HOLOCENE PERIODS AND THE VERTEBRATES FOUND IN NORTH AND SOUTH CHINA

Geological period	NORTH Fauna	Sites	SOUTH Fauna	Sites
PLIOCENE				
Pontian	*Hipparion* fauna including:		India/Malay forest fauna including:	
Pao-te beds, north China	*Hipparion*, horse-like Perissodactyl		Rhinoceros – *monocerine*	
deposition of	Rhinoceros – *Dicerorhinus*		Mastodon – primitive elephant,	
Lower Red clays	Sabre-toothed tiger – *Machairodus*		small with large tusks	
Lower Red earths	Wolf – *Felis*		Apes	K'ai Yuan, Yunnan
	Hyena licenti			
	Boar – *sus lydderski*			
widespread lakes	Deer – *moschus* and *cernulus*			
gradual desiccation	Birds, including ostrich			
	Gazelle			
Fen-ho erosion	Bovid – *Sprioceru*s } Steppe	Chou K'o Tien,		
	Rodents }	location 14		
PLEISTOCENE				
Lower	*Hipparion* (dying out during this period)			
Corresponding to	*Proboscihiparrion*, this period only			
Villafranchian formation	Horse – *Equus sanmeniensis*	K'e He, south Shansi		
	Elephas – *meridionalis*	(Palaeolithic)		
	namadicus			
	planifrons			
	Stegodon zdanski (primitive elephant with very small tusks)			
	Deer – *Euryceros flabellatus* and *pachyostus*			
	Rat – *siphneus*			
Huang Shui	*Lamprotula antiqua* (warm-water clam)		*Rhinoceros indicus*	Liu Ch'eng Kwangsi caves
Middle	*Sinanthropus pekiniensis*	Lan T'ien	Deer	
(*c.* 600,000 years ago)	*Equus sanmeniensis* (disappearing)	500,000–600,000	Tapir – *Tapirus*	
widespread deposition	*hemionus* (appearing mid	years ago	*Stegodon pre-orientalis*	
of Red earths.	period)	Chou K'o Tien	*Elephas namadicus*	
At least two semi-arid	*Hyena sinensis*	location 1	Orang-utan	
phases related to	'Red dog' – *Kuon alpinus*	500,000 years ago	Gibbon	
Himalayan	Leopard		Water-buffalo – *Bubalus teilhardi*	
Second Glacial	Tiger			
Second Inter-glacial	*Elephas namadicus*			
Third Glacial periods	Wolf			
	Corsac fox			
	Badger – *Meles taxus*			
Ch'ing shui erosion	Lynx – *viveridae*			
(*c.* 150,000 years ago)	Sika deer – *Pseudaxis grayi*			
Upper	*Homo sapiens* – Neanderthal		Tapir	
Loessic (*c.* 100,000 years ago)	*Sinanthropus pekinensis*	Shui T'ung kou	Deer	Ma Pa Kwangtung
Cool semi-arid	Onager – *Equus hemonius*	Sjara Osso Gol		Tzu Yang
	Elephas primigenius and *namadicus*	Sungari		
Corresponding to	*Rhinoceros tichorium* (woolly)	(50,000 years ago)	*Bubalus wonsjocki* – water-buffalo	
Himalayan Fourth	Cow – *Bos primigenius*		Giant Panda – Ailuropoda to Tibet	Chang Yang, Hupei
Glacial period	Sika deer – *Pseudaxis grayi*	Microlithic	*Stegodon* disappear	Lungtan, near Nanking
	Camel – *Camelus knoblochi*	Ting Ts'un	Orang-utan disappear	Tientsin
	Wolf			
	Hyena spelaea		*Lamprotula*	
	Badger – *Meles taxus*	Chou K'o Tien		
	Ovis ammon (central Asia big horned sheep)	(upper cave)		
RECENT HOLOCENE				
	Extinction of 'cool' fauna, e.g. *Rhinoceros tichorium*			
General rise in mean	Onager – *Equus hemionus*			Kwangsi caves
average temperature	*Elephas primigenius indicus*			Mesolithic type
	Bison – *Bos namadicus*			artefacts
	Moose			
	Sika deer			
	Euryceros			
	Père David's deer			
	Menzies deer	Neolithic sites		
	Porcupine	*c.* 5,000 years ago		
	Bamboo rat			

Zoological information and terms follow A. S. Romer, *Vertebrate Paleontology*, 1966. Acknowledgements and thanks for advice on this to Miss Caroline Pond.

and man.[6] There is, however, insufficient evidence on which to build any safe theories of the development of early man in China.

The list of the *Hipparion* fauna of the Pliocene period shows that many ancestors of modern animals were already present in northern China, though some, notably the ostrich and rhinoceros, have since moved away. The horse-like *Hipparion* and the related *Proboschipparion* both died out before or during the Lower Pleistocene. The development of the horse in northern China is of peculiar interest because of its great social and military importance and its fascination for artists in later periods. The *Equus sanmeniensis* appeared right at the end of the Lower Pleistocene and continued into the Middle Pleistocene. This horse-like animal then became extinct and was replaced by the *Equus hemionus*, a half-ass or onager, which survived into the Holocene and may even have overlapped with the first true horse in China, *Equus caballus ferus* (known as 'Przewalski's horse) which is found in the Shang burials. This type of horse had a very wide distribution in the more northerly areas of Asia. However, at least by the Han period, the Chinese were importing the so-called 'Heavenly Horses' from Fergana;* these seem to have been the tarpan from southern Asia which were regarded as spirited beasts by the Chinese. The large horse of the T'ang tomb figures came to China from Parthia.†[7] Thus all the admired horses in China have been imported horses valued for their qualities as cavalry, mounts as distinct from the small chariot-horse in common use and found over north China.

The early presence of the boar, *Sus lydderski*, is also of significance, for Chinese agriculture has from the earliest times been based upon the pig and the chronology of development of settled communities must depend to a certain extent upon the history of the domestication of this animal. The picture is by no means clear but bones of a type of domesticated pig are found in the middens of the Early Neolithic settlements and these are related to the earlier boar found among the bones in the caves of Palaeolithic man at Chou K'o Tien.

The development of man is of interest to the present study in so far as he represents an animal that developed fast and eventually dominated most of the other species, domesticating many to his own agricultural needs. Recently, sites have been reported that show evidence of Palaeolithic 'settlement' even earlier than that of *Homo erectus pekinensis* at Chou K'o Tien. Notable among these are the sites at K'e He in southern Shensi found in 1960. No hominid fossils were found but discoidal scrapers and chipped quartzite tools give evidence of hominid visitation to the marshy river-crossing, perhaps to collect mollusc and edible plants and to find pebbles for tools.[8] These sites lie within a grey level below 20 to 40 metres of red earth cross-bedded with sand typical of the *Homo erectus*/Middle Pleistocene period and above a red marly Lower Pleistocene clay. On these sites the animal fossils include stegodon, Zdanski elephant (a Pliocene pre-*Homo erectus* animal) and the two deer, *Euryceros flabellatus* and *Euryceros pachyostus*, which are also found in the early Chou K'o Tien cave, location 14, and are thus also pre-*Homo erectus*. The presence of a warm-water clam, *Lamprotula antiqua*, now extinct, points to a warm, damp surrounding different from the present-day conditions in this area.

The other site recently reported is at Lan T'ien, 50 miles south-east

* Fergana is a city-state north of Samarkand on the River Taxartes.
† Parthia, the State south of the Caspian Sea, to the west of Bactria.

of Sian.[9] Here the fossil remains of the earliest 'ape-man' yet found in China seem to indicate a hominid related to both *Homo erectus pekinensis* and to the Java man of the Djetis beds, perhaps closer to the latter. The Lan T'ien find has been dated to between 500,000 and 600,000 years ago. This places the site slightly earlier than Chou K'o Tien, location 1, the *Homo erectus* cave. The animal finds at Lan T'ien are of typical Middle Pleistocene fauna and include tiger, elephant, Sika deer, boar and the red dog, *Kuon alpinus*, said to be still living in remote parts of north-east Russia.

Finds of *Homo erectus pekinensis* (Peking man) in the north and in the south show a hominid occupation developing over a wide area. The northern finds, notably at Chou K'o Tien, reveal a hunter using simple tools. His animal prey was mainly the smaller mammals as one might expect, and there is no evidence of domestication. It is interesting that this 'man' might be the ancestor of the present-day inhabitants of this area with whom he shares certain characteristics of skull formation and the 'shovel-shaped' teeth present in many mongoloid peoples.

The environment and fauna of the northern region of China changed radically in the Upper Pleistocene period due to the onset of a process still active today, though to a much-reduced extent. The movement of the loess, a wind-blown soil, in the Yellow River Basin area is still not fully explained but it started during a period corresponding to the Himalayan Fourth Glacial period and may be connected with the climatic changes which probably took place at that time. The talc-fine soil was laid down to a great depth, in some places exceeding 250 feet. The area is large, extending both sides of the southward loop of the Yellow River, with the north-west boundary following the general line of the 15-inch isohyet (map, opposite). The origin of the soil is still under discussion but the wind which brought it seems to have come from the north-west and the initial effect was to produce a widespread inhospitable desert of dry sand, smothering remains of marsh settlements and apparently scattering animal populations in their search for food and water. Archaeology today produces an incomplete picture of some peripheral human settlements and animal remains on the edges of the loess, but very little to indicate animal occupation of the loess area itself during the period of deposition. Excavation and surface investigation have primarily been concerned with sites to the north of the loess and here a great variety of animals has been reported by Teilhard de Chardin, Licent and others. These are perhaps more readily associated with central Asian fauna than with that of China proper.

Animal habitation in the loess region itself during the period of maximum loess deposit seems unlikely, as the area must have been subject to bitter winds and suffocating sandstorms. However, with the stabilization of conditions the animal population soon moved back, for, being porous and well drained, this loess soil is extremely fertile. River-valleys tend to be deep and to become deeper, but where there is a water-supply vegetation flourishes and food is plentiful for animals and man alike. The post-Glacial sites, exemplified by the upper cave at Chou K'o Tien, show a mixed hominid occupancy with signs of fire and many animal species clearly the prey of man. These include mainly smaller mammals such as badger, wolf and deer. It is perhaps safe to assume that by this time a human population had expanded over a wide region and that a mixture of races from widely separated origins had already begun. The finding of primitive tools and signs of fire,

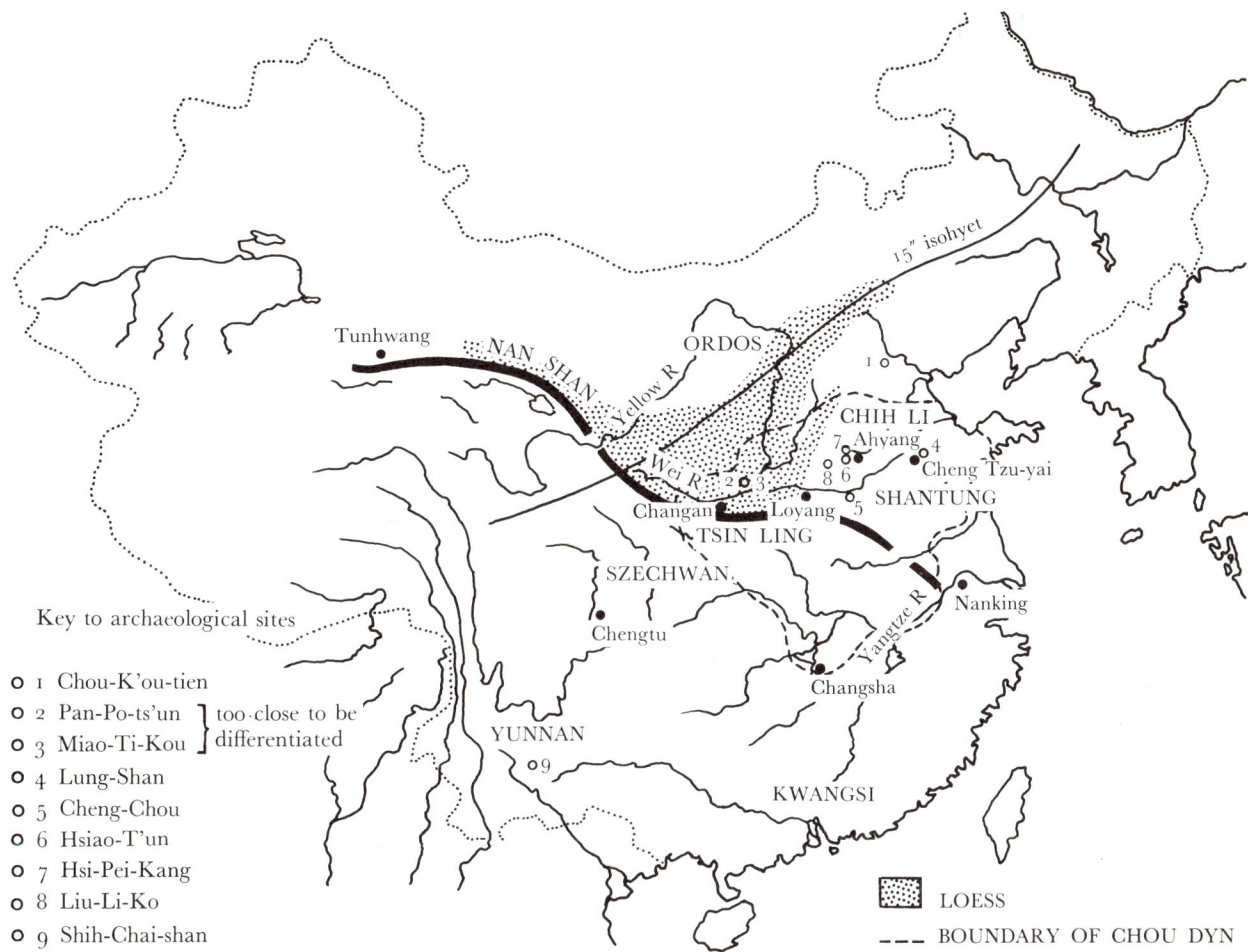

Key to archaeological sites

o 1 Chou-K'ou-tien
o 2 Pan-Po-ts'un ⎤ too close to be
o 3 Miao-Ti-Kou ⎦ differentiated
o 4 Lung-Shan
o 5 Cheng-Chou
o 6 Hsiao-T'un
o 7 Hsi-Pei-Kang
o 8 Liu-Li-Ko
o 9 Shih-Chai-shan

▦ LOESS
--- BOUNDARY OF CHOU DYN

Fig. 67
Map of China showing the principal geographical features and archaeological sites mentioned in the text.

together with both adult and child remains, suggest a Palaeolithic settlement of some duration at this site.

With the end of the Pleistocene and a general warming up of the climate one finds the extinction of the 'cool' fauna of the north, notably the woolly rhinoceros, while in the south the giant panda had already retreated to Tibet and the foothills of south-west China, where it is found today. The stegodon and orang-utan had disappeared, but the water-buffalo, *wonsjocki*, had appeared and many of the modern fauna in both north and south China were already established.

Thus from this time forward the archaeologist's interest in animal finds shifts to their place in society and the light which this may shed on that society. As arts and crafts develop this evidence becomes more subtle for representations of animals both real and mythical are in many ways more direct clues to the complex web of beliefs and attitudes which accrue to any civilized society.

There is still an archaeological gap between the Palaeolithic finds of the Upper Pleistocene and Early Neolithic man. The Neolithic settlements reported in the loess area have been dated to about 3000 B.C. This area of fertile soil and ample rainfall clearly encouraged settlement. The extensive Yellow River valley, often called 'The Cradle of Chinese Culture', sees an early development of agriculture apparently short-circuiting the more usual progression from hunting via herding to husbandry. The 'nuclear area' of this Neolithic culture appears from recent excavation and reports to have been in the Wei Shui Valley, for example the Miao Ti kou site, Shen hsien, Honan.[10] Neolithic man in this region lived either in subterranean dwellings cut into the loess, as is done to this day, or in round pit-dwellings which were roofed over with thatch.[11] Pan-p'o ts'un on a tributary of the Wei Shui represents a Neolithic settlement showing some planning, with a pottery area and cemetery separate from the dwelling-houses (fig. 68). Settlement remains show middens near to the houses and enclosures probably for chickens and pigs, the bones of which abound in the middens. Dogs were domesticated but appear to have had no ritual significance, for they were not included in burial. Hunting continued to be part of man's life and the Sika deer, *Pseudaxis grayi*, wild boar and moose were among the prizes of the hunt. Deer appear as part of the burial ritual and antlers furnish material for needles, fish-hooks and simple tools. The presence of the remains of grain in some of the burnished painted pots of the period, together with the evidence of hoes, adzes, axes and other implements, indicate some attempt at cultivation. One can picture a primitive agricultural society dependent, to a degree almost comparable with that of present-day China, on cereal production and domesticated animals, notably the pig. The horse does not appear to have been domesticated. Despite the value placed on the horse for military purposes by the Chinese, it has never become the universal work- or pack-animal of many other parts of the world. This is probably at least partly due to

Fig. 68
Excavation of a dwelling site at Pan P'o Ts'un, Shensi.
After W. Watson, *China before the Han dynasty*, Thames and Hudson, London, 1961.

climate, and indeed in the north the camel filled much of the role of pack-animal, while in the south the water-buffalo has proved far better adapted for both draught and transport. The date of the domestication of the camel is not known, perhaps it originates much later, associated with the northern tribes of the Liao-ning area where camels are represented on eastern Chou bronzes (771–221 B.C.).

The earliest Neolithic culture of northern China, the Painted Pottery culture is now thought to give way to the Black Pottery culture which is found in much the same region and overlies or even, occasionally, is mixed with Painted Pottery culture remains. The Black Pottery culture has an agricultural base much the same as its predecessor but has more sophisticated settlements, sometimes encircled by tamped mud walls. With more sophisticated pottery-kilns, this culture is distinguished by the very elegant black burnished pottery, wheel-made and entirely without figurative decoration. Geometric motifs replace the swirls and zoomorphic fish and frog motifs used by the Painted Pottery people. Remains of the same sorts of domesticated and wild animals killed by hunters are found in middens at village sites, of which Lung-shan, Shantung, seems to be a representative example (map, page 151). Interestingly, these people practised scapulamancy* – even though they had no writing the ox scapulae were clearly prepared and used in the same way as those of the later Shang dynasty.

There is a further archaeological gap between the Neolithic settlements found over a wide area of northern China, dating probably to between 3000 and 2000 B.C., and the sites of the Mid to Late Shang dynasty, dating to 1500 to 1111 B.C., found in the same area. The Mid Shang capital at Cheng Chou (1500 to 1300 B.C.), and the near-by sites of Lo Ta Miao and Erh Li Kang, bear a strong resemblance to the later capital of the State, the great sites at Hsiao T'un, Ayang (1300 to c. 1111 B.C.).[12, 13] These two capitals, though naturally more elaborate than the settlements of the ordinary people of the same period, show an urban people dwelling in quite extensive groups with some division into craft groups. Even so, each household still retains its pigs and chickens and possibly dogs.

The elaborate royal tombs at Anyang contain many horses thought, in the absence of detailed reports on the bones, to be the Przewalski horse (fig. 69). The horses are now harnessed to war-chariots but there is no sign of bit, saddle or stirrups, so that they were not ridden. The development of the chariot itself is a question as yet unsolved. Pre-Shang burials give no evidence of the presence of a chariot in China, or even of any use made of the horse. However, the chariot is present in the Mid Shang and there is no clear indication of its origin. Questions of foreign introduction still await settlement, perhaps in the excavation and study of Early Shang sites in northern China.

During the Shang dynasty the royal household was buried along with the ruler and among his retinue was a charioteer with his two or four horses. Other more exotic animals were also represented in the 'Imperial entourage', an elephant with its mahout was found at the royal cemetery

---

* Scapulamancy is the custom of telling oracles or foretelling the future by the use of bone, usually the scapula, which is cracked by the application of a hot point and the resulting crack is read by the oracle-taker. In its simpler form this is unreadable, of course, by any other person. Later when writing was developed the question and sometimes even the answer was incised on the bone.

Fig. 69
Shang burial of a charioteer, chariot and two horses at Ta Ssa Kung near Anyang, Honan.
After W. Watson, *China before the Han dynasty*, Thames and Hudson, London, 1961.

at Hsi Pei Kang near Anyang. Monkeys, dogs and chickens are among the most common animals slaughtered for burial. Such animals were part of the daily scene of the capital city, but not only were they killed and buried as part of the royal household but the presence of animal and human skeletons under the central chamber of the large tombs indicate that they were also used for ritual sacrifices. The custom of both animal and human sacrifice is also found in lesser tombs and is associated with some of the larger buildings. Here pits containing slaughtered animals, dogs, pigs, horses and human beings, are found below the floor-level or placed at the corners of the building denoting a consecration ceremony. The animal most commonly found is the dog, buried singly or in groups of five. This use of sacrifice is typical of the Shang period and appears to die out quite soon after the fall of the dynasty. Interestingly, the exception to this is the use of the dog as a sacrificial animal, a custom which continued throughout the Chou dynasty (1111–255 B.C.) over a large area of China.

Further archaeological evidence of a different kind is found in the Shang period with the discovery of inscribed oracle bones at the Shang sites at Anyang (fig. 70).[14] These, found in large storage-pits, are of ox scapula or of tortoise plastron, one material being used in preference to the other at different periods. The bone was prepared with regularly placed oval depressions cut out of the reverse surface, and the question to be asked was inscribed on the obverse face. A hot point applied to the appropriate depression formed an angled crack, and the oracle was read. The questions, written in extremely succinct form, are usually inquiries about military strategy or about prospects of crops, hunting or rain. The ideographs used are the earliest known forms of many characters used today, and can therefore be interpreted. The name of the oracle-taker is often recorded, and by correlation with the ruler's name, also often recorded, a chronology has been reconstructed which makes the oracle bones a rudimentary historical record of the Shang

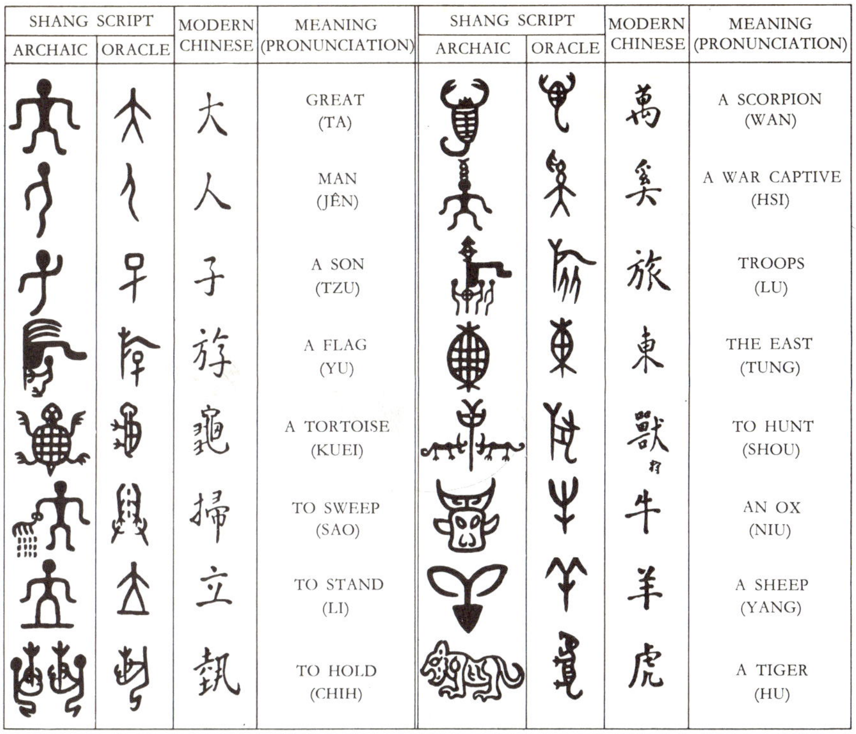

SHANG SCRIPT		MODERN CHINESE	MEANING (PRONUNCIATION)	SHANG SCRIPT		MODERN CHINESE	MEANING (PRONUNCIATION)
ARCHAIC	ORACLE			ARCHAIC	ORACLE		
		大	GREAT (TA)			萬	A SCORPION (WAN)
		人	MAN (JÊN)			奚	A WAR CAPTIVE (HSI)
		子	A SON (TZU)			旅	TROOPS (LU)
		斿	A FLAG (YU)			東	THE EAST (TUNG)
		龜	A TORTOISE (KUEI)			獸	TO HUNT (SHOU)
		掃	TO SWEEP (SAO)			牛	AN OX (NIU)
		立	TO STAND (LI)			羊	A SHEEP (YANG)
		訊	TO HOLD (CHIH)			虎	A TIGER (HU)

Fig. 70
Oracle bones excavated at Anyang.
After Cheng Te K'un, *Shang China*, Heffer, 1960.

period. Inscriptions mention animals in connection with hunting, and we can identify the names of deer, elephant, etc, while inquiries about ritual mention animals for sacrifice, including pig, goat, dog and ox. Although this adds nothing to our knowledge of animals present, indeed those recorded are fewer than those that archaeological researches have found, they do throw light on the place of animals in the society of the time; they were kept for food, hunted for sport and killed for sacrifice or for the reading of portents. Thus begins a long-lived tradition of the place of animals in China. In that country there has been no St Francis and little even casual interest in, or admiration for, animals except as food, as curiosities, or because of a superstititious belief that some had special powers.

In the brutal Shang kingdom, obsessed as it seems with blood sacrifices and ritual, animals clearly had a significance beyond that of objects of ritual slaughter. The ritual bronzes, objects of great artistry and technical finesse, are elaborately decorated with animalistic designs. Some are strikingly realistic while the majority show a handsome ferocious formalism (fig. 71). The motifs, usually of bird or quadruped, are arranged in typical Chinese fashion in bands round the vessel. The impelling *t'ao-t'ieh* masks appearing at the angles or above the legs already in the Mid Shang pieces are a feature of this early animal style which has not yet been fully explained. Especially in the later pieces these masks are composite and formed of stylized animals, whole or dismembered, arranged in a confronted design (fig. 72). The result is a monster-mask, the earliest of many monsters invented by Chinese artists. A large part of the bronze décor is formed from the small creature called a *ku'ei*; it may be two-legged in which case it is defined as a dragon *Ku'ei lung* or one-legged with a plumed tail when it is defined as a phoenix *ku'ei feng*. This is, however, a later terminology and reflects later dynasties' concern with the dragon and phoenix as

155

Fig. 71
Bronze vessel, *tsun*, in the form of a
monster with victim. Shang dynasty style.
Eleventh century B.C. Height 24·6 cm.
Sumitomo collection Kyoto. After W.
Watson, *Ancient Chinese Bronzes*, London
1962.

Fig. 72
Chih bronze vessel. Chou dynasty. Height
17·9 cm.
British Museum.

supernatural creatures of multiple significance. It is interesting that
neither form in this early period bears any similarity to the later
creatures known as *lung* and *feng*. Indeed, the Shang animals, though
formalized, refer to real creatures and range from the tiger (which was,
of course, still well known in north China) to the ox, elephant, long-
tailed bird, owl, cicada and many others. Vessels made in the shape of
these animals appear to have been intended for a similar use to those
in more conventional shapes. But the fact that all decorative motifs of
this period derive directly from animals, often clearly recognizable and
always expressed with an awesome ferocity, seems to indicate a superstitious society obsessed with a ritual closely related to the animals, each
of which perhaps had some significance to that ritual. We have few
indications of the precise form of ritual practised, but it does not
continue in the following dynasty, when slaughtered animals are no
longer encountered in the tombs. The progressive disappearance of the
animalistic ferocity of bronze decoration again underlines a change in
customs and in outlook.

More light-hearted works of the Shang dynasty, if such a term can be
applied to this rugged period, are small carvings made of slices of jade.
These are all of animal shapes showing great variety, birds, fish and
animals. They are usually pierced as though for threading, and, though
now termed 'amulets', the method of their application to the garments
or to the person is not clear. It is perhaps permissible to regard them as

decorations probably treasured for more than their representational significance.

After the fall of the Shang dynasty, the emergent Chou State covered a still greater area, reaching south of the Yangtse, west of the Wei River and north to Chihli, and forming a loosely knit kingdom embracing more diversified cultures than had as yet been evident in China. While the central kingdom clearly took over many of the attributes of the previous culture, some characteristics changed, notably the already mentioned apparent discontinuation of many of the sacrifice rituals. During the long Chou dynasty changes in art styles mark the cultural variations within the enlarged State. Animals remain the chief motifs of decoration but differing styles of treatment begin to appear. Contact with the steppe nomads of the north gives rise to an 'animal style' bronze tradition sometimes difficult to distinguish from the Asiatic variants but always lively and, even in its stylization, retaining a sense of realism and vivid observation of the animal and its characteristics. These bronzes show a hunting basis still alive in this part of China (figs. 73, 74).

A further variant of bronze decoration more closely within the old tradition is presented by the interlaced dragons of the north. Dragons have become snake-like and writhe in complex knot patterns which eventually, in some cases, degenerate into geometric motifs (fig. 75). This is a form of stylization which tends to evolve into the meaningless and often stiff spiral and whorl, which is a strand in the fabric of Chinese decorative tradition perhaps also related to a mid-Asiatic tradition. The writhing snakes of Honan seem to have no cult significance and, indeed, the bronzes of this area, though handsome and finely cast, have none of the zoomorphic strength of their predecessors.

However, in the Ch'u State to the south and east, in the much lusher region south of the Ts'in Ling range and in the wide Yangtse Valley, the animal representations have a clear and impelling importance. Cult-objects dating from the later Chou period found at and near Changsha are of carved wood painted in bright lacquer colours.[15] Antlers appear to have a special significance and are often real horns mounted in a wooden stand. The long-tongued human face with horns is a very striking example (fig. 76). Equally fine are the feline animals and long-legged birds standing on writhing snakes. All are stylized, but with an inherent vitality and grace typical of the work of the artists of Ch'u. These people had not only a strong artistic sense but a poetic sensibility evident in the beautiful poem *Li Shao** by Ch'u Yuan, and a religious animal cult as yet unexplained. This cult has, until recently, been thought to be quite different from anything in the north, but objects from excavations at Hsi Yang in Honan show a similar grotesquery in carving and imagery which perhaps points to a link in beliefs if not in artistic traditions.[16]

The very splendid productions and many artistic techniques of the Ch'u peoples had a great influence on the work of later generations, and their vivid representations of animals are among the most beautiful in the whole span of Chinese art. Throughout the later Chou dynasty one is conscious of the influence of lacquer-painting on bronze design: the introduction of the sinuous line and metal inlay make for a quite

* Ch'u Yuan (fourth century B.C.), a poet whose collection of lamentations is known as the *Li Shao*, 'Falling into Trouble'; written in very free metre the poems contain many vivid descriptions of the wilder regions of the country.

Fig. 73
Yen Hou Yu excavated at Hai Tao Ying
Tzu, Ling Yuan Hsien, Jehol. Chou
dynasty. Height 22·1 cm.
National Museum, Peking. After W.
Watson, *Ancient Chinese Bronzes*, London,
1962.

new style of decoration admirably shown in the exquisite pieces found
in the Hui Hsien area of Honan.

Excavations of Chou burials, particuary the fine site at Liu Li Ko,
Hui Hsien, Honan (fourth century B.C.), show chariots and horses
(fig. 77).[17] The small Przewalski horse was still used, but the harness
changed from the old choker style of the Shang dynasty to the breast-
strap harness which allows the horse to take the strain more effectively
on the shoulders and chest. This antedates the appearance of such a
harness in Europe by some seven centuries and would account for the
effective chariot-fighting of the period, for the chariot with the cross-bow
and Chinese short sword was the chief military equipment of the time.
The introduction of iron, thought to be effective towards the end of the

Fig. 74
Ordos Bronze plaque, a tiger and a deer.
Seventh to sixth century B.C. Height
10·1 cm.
British Museum.

Chou dynasty, accounts for the many changes which are apparent in the Han dynasty archaeological finds (206 B.C.–A.D. 220).

Following the unification of the country by Ts'in Shih Huang-ti, the First Yellow Emperor Ts'in (255–206 B.C.), and the rationalization of communications carried out during his brief but active rule the Han Chinese further expanded their sphere of influence. A distinctively Chinese culture was carried to districts as far separated as Kwangtung, Manchuria, Yunnan and Ssechwan. Many of these areas were occupied by Neolithic-type cultures, but with techniques and customs introduced from the metropolitan area they moved into a metal age with local variants which excavation is now beginning to underline.

The wall-paintings in Liao-yang, Manchuria, show little horse-carriages much as in the Chou dynasty, with the small horse in a breast-strap harness. This is also clear in the Wu Liang shrine reliefs in Shensi dated at A.D. 147. The same type can be seen at Tun Huang used for bovine harness with modification to take advantage of the hump of the water-buffalo, much as it is still used today for ploughing. It seems possible that the foot-stirrup was introduced during this dynasty, although the evidence is controversial. Dr Needham considers that this derived, through Buddhist links, from the toe-stirrup used in India.[18] The dating of the use of the foot-stirrup is at present dependent on artistic representations and rests on the reading of the now weathered

Wu Liang shrine reliefs, the nineteenth-century rubbings of which seem to indicate a foot-stirrup. The stirrup certainly seems to be present in the clay models of mounted figures excavated from a tomb dated to the fourth century A.D. in Changsha. At all events horses were ridden in the Han dynasty when, presumably, combat had been transformed by the introduction of the long iron sword. At this time an interest in strong, spirited horses was aroused in China and the so-called 'Heavenly Horses' make their appearance in art. Possibly the sturdy slightly larger tarpan of south Asia, these horses are portrayed with flames breaking from their shoulders and mark perhaps the beginning of a long tradition of imported cavalry horses. They certainly represent a tradition of the idealization of the horse in many media. Probably the most famous example is the horse standing over a captive in the Ho Ch'u-pin tombstone figures found in Shensi and dated at *c.* 117 B.C.

The Ordos area in the north was at this time, as always, the frontier between the agriculturists and the nomads (map, page 151). At this period the art of the nomads, mainly horse-trappings and personal ornaments cast in bronze, dominate the artistic production. Very lively animal art, closely related in style and technique to the many other nomadic tribal arts of Asia, was produced in some quantity in the Ordos area and is well known from the rich collections made in the early years of this century in Europe. These pieces were not excavated and have no carefully recorded provenance and are, therefore, of little archaeological significance, but they are evidence of a strong cultural affinity surviving complete absorption into Chinese culture throughout the Han dynasty. They show feline and deer-like animals fighting, and hunting scenes.

Tombs of the Han period excavated in Ssechwan, mainly in the vicinity of Chengtu, show a different pattern of life.[19] A more settled agricultural system seems to be indicated, a more varied existence where men till the soil and harvest grain, mine for salt, enjoy feasts and the entertainment of jugglers and dancers. When man goes hunting he goes on foot and takes along a dog, he fishes in ponds which appear to be very well stocked. In this district, despite the very sketchy artistic impressions on brick, the animals are vividly portrayed and one can see that duck and geese were the birds they hunted and that deer were the object of the chase. Pigs and chickens remain the chief domesticated animals and the basis of animal husbandry.

Contrasting with this far western province are the finds from excavations at Sse Chai Shan in Yunnan.[20] Here the richly ornamented bronze drums depict a society with a very different structure. The busy scene of the village with its pigs and dogs is dominated by one or more matriarchal figures on a larger scale; on one drum a ceremonial execution appears to be taking place, while on others a bull is chased and the bull-killer is clearly an important personage. These lively scenes, showing, in some details, a relationship to the Miao tribes of the present day in this region, surely illustrate an existence not entirely Sinicized and perhaps more nearly related to the culture to the south in North Vietnam or Burma. The animal bronzes of this area show feline animals in combat, but no deer, and the animal 'loops' on the larger pieces seem to be tigers rather than the dragons of the north.

Burials of the Han dynasty in the metropolitan China area of Loyang contain many ceramic replicas showing large homesteads with outbuildings housing pigs, sheep, goats, hens and dogs.[21] The herding of sheep and goats differentiates this northern area from the south.

Fig. 75
Gold dagger handle of interlocking dragons. Fourth century B.C. Length 10·9 cm.
British Museum.

Fig. 76
Wood carving of an antlered head with
long protruding tongue, excavated at
Changsa, Hunan. Third to second century
B.C. Height 80·0 cm.
British Museum.

Animals were now regarded as curiosities and were collected in parks and zoos. The rhinoceros, which had existed in northern China but had probably become extinct by the beginning of the historic period, about 1700 B.C., was sent, as a tribute during the Han dynasty, to the Court in Loyang. It is just possible that the two-horned rhinoceros related to the two-horned Sumatran rhinoceros survived a little longer in the south.[22] Rhinoceros horn had considerable significance in China for a variety of superstitious powers attached to it. Chief among these is the quality attributed to it of dissolving in poison which made it a favoured material for special cups. Moreover, it was one of the substances believed to have properties as an aphrodisiac and although this significance is not of such overwhelming importance as in some other cultures it does account for the importation of horn in some quantity from Africa. The elephant was also a curiosity in China; the live animal became associated with Imperial ceremonial and animals sent as tribute from the south were kept at various times. Ivory was much favoured as material for carving and, at least to begin with, the main source was mammoth ivory imported from Siberia. The elephant became extinct in northern China by the historic period (1700 B.C.), but finds of mammoth tusk, *Elephas primigenius*, in Siberia kept the Chinese craftsmen supplied for many centuries. They did not associate this ivory with the tusks they saw on the elephants or those which they eventually imported from Africa but regarded the Siberian material as coming from some form of giant rodent. It is now impossible to distinguish the worked material. The elephant stables at the Palace in Peking were in use until the end of the nineteenth century when it is reported

Fig. 77
Earth 'ghosts' of chariots excavated at Liu li Ko, Hui Hsien. Fourth century B.C. After W. Watson, *China before the Han dynasty*, Thames and Hudson, London, 1961.

that an elephant ran amok and killed a man. The animals were used in Buddhist ceremonial and notably in the ceremonies at the Altar of Heaven on the sixth day of the sixth month.[23]

The introduction and establishment of Buddhism in northern China during the Han dynasty and the concern to establish a comparable 'church' of Taoism led to the crystallization of many beliefs of long standing, and it is in the Han period that a cosmogony with full icons makes its appearance. This makes an equation of colours, seasons, elements and the four directions. These are also bound in with the theory, of *yin-yang*. This propounds the balance of opposites: negative and positive, cold and hot, passive and active, female and male. Thus the winter, when all is dormant and cold, is the time of maximum *yin* and the summer of maximum *yang*. Naturally enough animals are chosen to symbolize these four divisions governed by the *yin-yang* theory. The black tortoise of the north, sometimes more poetically translated as 'the Dark Warrior', is the representative of winter. This dark-blooded, slow-moving creature had from early times, when the plastron was used in oracle divination, been of special significance in China and it makes an admirable symbol of winter. There was also a belief that all tortoises are female and that they are mated with snakes; this accounts for these two creatures often being depicted together, the one entwined round the other. The green dragon of the east is the symbol of spring, the beginning of the year, the season of rain and growth. The dragon can move equally in the elements of air and water and on land and was regarded as the controller of rain and consequent floods. It is easy to understand how this beast was of supreme importance to an agricultural society in a land subject to devastating floods. The dragon symbolizes the rising *yang* quality which then reaches its maximum in the summer heat and harvest, symbolized by the red bird of the south. This showy creature may derive from one of the magnificent pheasants of China. The name is a direct translation of the term *chu-niao* which seems sometimes to be used in Chinese interchangeably with *feng-huang*, a term usually translated in English as phoenix and referring also to the elegant long-tailed bird. The name *feng-huang* has the further meaning of referring to a bisexual bird, which, however, is sometimes divided to make a pair, as in the Han tile carvings of Ssechwan. The white tiger of the west opposes the dragon and is the symbol of autumn, the decrease of *yang* and the bringer of desolation to the countryside.

These animals appear to this day in contexts which have some reference to ancient beliefs, with the many accretions added over the years. The most striking are perhaps the dragon and the phoenix which became eventually the emblem of the emperor and empress respectively. The ability of the dragon to move through air, water and on land make it a ready symbol of the Imperial role as intermediary with the gods. The emperor's main function was, by carrying out the correct ritual, to maintain the right relations between man and the gods, his own ancestors. It may be assumed that the phoenix, a later adoption, was chosen primarily for its showy and decorative appearance, and also because the two creatures together represent the most auspicious combination of the 'Four Guardians'.

A further example of the Chinese genius for creating monsters or mythical animals is seen in the magnificent stone chimera found in the area around Nanking and dating from the fourth to the sixth century A.D.[24] These represent a large part of the comparatively undeveloped

164

art of sculpture in China. They are large figures which strut proudly with puffed-out chest, handsome ruff, and tongue hanging to the chest. They were originally guardians for tombs and are now preserved standing solitary in the countryside. There seems some case for a theory of derivation from the winged figures of the Near East but this has not been archaeologically proven. Stone sculpture, rare though it is in China outside the Buddhist setting, accentuates the Chinese artist's preoccupation with a very few animals, notably the horse, primarily as a cavalry animal, and with mythical monsters and dragons and chimera usually set up as guardians at tombs. The camels and elephants at the Ming tombs are the shining exceptions to this.

With the increasing wealth of a cosmopolitan society in the T'ang dynasty the vogue for burial figurines of glazed pottery reached a climax in the mid and late ninth century. Tombs excavated at Loyang include enormous quantities of these colourful models.[25] The sociological interest of these pieces is perhaps equal to their artistic value for they show many aspects of the life of the wealthy classes of the time. The dancers, musicians, servants and foreign slaves illustrate some aspects of this most outward-looking period of Chinese history. The horse again figures largely and is the huge beast coming from Parthia, a true horse for the first time in China, often with its own foreign groom and by its opulent and handsome trappings clearly a highly prized possession. The camel appears as a beast of burden, and sheep, dogs, now sometimes as pets, chickens and pigs are still present.

Since the establishment of an agricultural society based on the cultivation of cereal, and pig- and chicken-rearing, both that pattern and the position of animals in that society have remained constant. With the exception of the working animals, the cavalry horse, the camel and the water-buffalo, all animals, including the pet cats, song-birds and the ubiquitous watch-dog, have been regarded as potential food. In a land of recurrent famine this must be so. In a culture with very little curiosity about the living things surrounding man extraordinarily little notice was taken by artists of the native animals. Once the pattern of settlement is established, archaeology gives little clue to any but the most essential animals to man except through the arts. Thus in China a few of the more decorative animals, tree-shrews, cats, butterflies and insects find their way into the decorative paintings and poetry. But the main preoccupation of the artist is with the wider panorama of the whole landscape and man and animals alike take their place as incidentals in a larger scene. The near vegetarianism of a large proportion of the population is due to poverty, for it is allied to a callousness not associated with the devout Buddhist. This is not to say that there are no pets in China, there is ample evidence in paintings and in tomb models of pet cats and dogs in the wealthy homes, but the names of none of these is known and there is no evidence that they were more than accessories to their owners.

REFERENCES &
BIBLIOGRAPHIES

2

General

Bordes, F. (1968). *The Old Stone Age*. London.
Boule, M. and Vallois, H. (1957). *Fossil men. A text book of human palaeontology* (transl. by M. Bullock). London.
Clark, G. (1967). *The Stone Age Hunters*. London.
Howell, F. Clark (1966). *Early Man*. Time-Life International, Netherlands.
Leakey, L. S. B. (1965). *Olduvai Gorge 1951–61*. Cambridge.
Leroi-Gourhan, A. (1961). Les fouilles d'Arcy-sur-Cure (Yonne). *Gallia Préhistoire*, *4*, pp. 3–16.
Leroi-Gourhan, A. and A. (1964). Chronologie des grottes d'Arcy-sur-Cure (Yonne). *Gallia Préhistoire*, *7*, pp. 1–64.
Leroi-Gourhan, A., Bailloud, G., Chavaillon, J. and Laming-Emperaire, A. (1966). *La Préhistoire*. Paris.
Piveteau, J. (1957). *Primates. Paléontologie humaine.* (*Traité de Paléontologie*: Tome VII. *Vers la forme humaine. Le problème biologique de l'homme. Les époques de l'intelligence.*) Paris.
Sonneville-Bordes, D. (1961). *L'Age de la pierre*. Paris.

Palaeolithic Art

Laming-Emperaire, A. (1962). *La signification de l'art rupestre paléolithique. Méthodes et applications*. Paris.
Leroi-Gourhan, A. (1964). *Les religions de la préhistoire (paléolithique)*. Paris.
Leroi-Gourhan, A. (1965). *Préhistoire de l'art occidental*. Paris.
Ucko, P. J., and Rosenfeld, A. (1967). *Palaeolithic cave art*. London.

Source References

1. Bate, D. M. A. (1940). The Fossil Antelopes of Palestine in Natufian (Mesolithic) Times, with Descriptions of New Species. *Geological Magazine, 77,* 418–42.
2. Solecki, R. S. (1963). Prehistory in Shanidar valley, northern Iraq. *Science, 139,* pp. 179–92.
3. Perrot, J. (1960) Excavations at 'Eynan' ('Ein Mallaha). *Israel Exploration Journal, 10,* pp. 14–22.
4. Hole, F. (1962). Archaeological Survey and Excavation in Iran, 1961. *Science, 137,* pp. 524–6.
5. Solecki, R. S. (1961). New anthropological discoveries at Shanidar, northern Iraq. *Transactions New York Academy Science,* Ser. II, *23,* pp. 690–9.
6. Hole, F. (1962). *op. cit.*
7. Braidwood, R. J. (1960). Seeking the world's first farmers in Persian Kurdistan. *Illustrated London News,* p. 695.
8. Hole, F. (1962). *op. cit.*
9. Kirkbride, D. (1961). Ten thousand years of man's activity around Petra. *Illustrated London News,* pp. 448–51.
10. Reed, C. A. (1960). A review of the archaeological evidence on animal domestication in the prehistoric Near East. *In* Braidwood, R. J. *et al., Prehistoric Investigations in Iraqi Kurdistan.* Oriental Institute of the University of Chicago: Studies in Ancient Oriental Civilization No. 31. Chicago. pp. 119–45.
11. Troels-Smith, J. (1960). Ivy, Mistletoe and Elm – Climate Indicators – Fodder Plants. *Geological Survey Denmark,* IV Ser., *4,* no. 4.
12. Clark, G. and Piggott, S. (1965). *Prehistoric Societies.* London.
13. Reed, C. (1960). *op. cit.*
14. *Ibid.,* p. 143.
15. Perkins, D. (1964). The fauna from the prehistoric levels of Shanidar Cave and Zawi Chemi Shanidar. *INQUA report of the VIth International Congress on Quaternary,* Warsaw, 1961. Lodz. Vol. II, pp. 565–71.
16. Reed, C. (1961). Osteological evidences for prehistoric domestication in southwestern Asia. *Zeitschrift für Tierzüchtung und Züchtungsbiologie, 76,* pp. 31–8.
17. Hole, F. and Flannery, K. V. (1965). Early agriculture and animal husbandry in Deh Luran, Iran. *Current Anthropology, 6,* pp. 105–6.
18. Hole, F. (1962). *op. cit.*
19. Rodden, R. J. (1962). Excavations at the Early Neolithic site at Nea Nikomedeia, Greek Macedonia (1961 season). *Proceedings of the Prehistoric Society, 28,* pp. 267–88.
20. Zeuner, F. E. (1955). The Goats of Early Jericho. *Palestine Exploration Quarterly,* pp. 70–84.
21. Hole, F. and Flannery, K. V. (1965). *op. cit.*
22. Mortensen, P. (1964). Additional remarks on the chronology of early village-farming communities. *Sumer, 20,* pp. 28–36.
23. Hole, F. and Flannery, K. V. (1965). *op. cit.*
24. Clark, G. and Piggott, S. (1965). *op. cit.,* p. 161.
25. Reed, C. (1960). *op. cit.,* p. 135.
26. Zeuner, F. E. (1963). *A History of Domesticated Animals.* London.
27. Jewell, P. (1961). The wild sheep of St. Kilda. *New Scientist, 11,* pp. 268–71.

28. Herre, W. (1963). The Science and History of Domestic Animals. *In* Brothwell, D. and Higgs, E. (eds.), *Science in Archaeology*, London, pp. 235–48 (p. 245).
29. Reed, C. (1961). *op. cit.*
30. Clutton-Brock, J. (1962). Near Eastern canids and the affinities of the Natufian dogs. *Zeitschrift für Tierzüchtung und Züchtungsbiologie*, *79*, pp. 326–33.
31. Degerbøl, M. (1961). On a find of a Preboreal domestic dog (*Canis familiaris* L.) from Star Carr, Yorkshire, with remarks on other Mesolithic dogs. *Proceedings of the Prehistoric Society*, *27*, pp. 35–53.
32. Clutton-Brock, J. (1963). The Origins of the Dog. *In* Brothwell, D. and Higgs, E. (eds.), *Science in Archaeology*, London, pp. 269–73.
33. *Ibid.*
34. Behrens, H. (1964). *Die Neolithisch-Frühmetallzeitlichen Tierschelettfunde der alten Welt*. Berlin.
35. Zeuner, F. E. (1963). *op. cit.*, p. 260.
36. Behrens, H. (1964). *op. cit.*
37. Graziosi, P. (1961). A new masterpiece of Palaeolithic art discovered in Italy: a superb bull of 10,000 B.C. carved in a Calabrian rock-shelter. *Illustrated London News*, pp. 578–9.
38. Mellaart, J. (1965). *Earliest Civilizations of the Near East*. London (p. 79).
39. Mellaart, J. (1963). Excavations at Çatal Hüyük 1962, Second Preliminary Report. *Anatolian Studies*, *13*, pp. 43–103 (p. 67).
40. Leroi-Gourhan, A. (1964). *Les religions de la préhistorire*. Paris.
41. Mellaart, J. (1963). *op. cit.*, p. 52.
42. Garstang, J. (1953). *Prehistoric Mersin*. Oxford (p. 33).
43. Mellaart, J. (1966). Çatal Hüyük Excavations 1965. Lecture at Institute of Archaeology, London University, 15 March. Unpublished.
44. Mellaart, J. (1961). Excavations: Hacilar. *12th Annual Report of the British Institute of Archaeology at Ankara*, pp. 5–8.
45. Garrod, D. A. E. and Bate, D. M. A. (1937). *The Stone Age of Mount Carmel*. Vol. I. Oxford (p. 100).
46. Rodden, R. J. (1964). Early Neolithic frog figurines from Nea Nicomedeia. *Antiquity*, *38*, p. 295.

Other Selected References

Braidwood, R. J. (1958). Near Eastern Prehistory. *Science*, *127*, pp. 1419–29.
Braidwood, R. J. (1958). The Old World: Post-Palaeolithic. *In: The Identification of Non-artifactual Archeological Materials*. National Academy of Sciences Publication 565, Washington, D.C., pp. 26–7.
Braidwood, R. J. (1961). The Iranian Prehistoric Project. *Science*, *133*, pp. 2008–10.
Butzer, K. W. (1964). *Environment and Archeology*. Chicago.
Cole, S. (1963). *The Neolithic Revolution*. London.
Hole, F. and Flannery, K. V. (1962). Excavations at Ali Kosh, Iran, 1961. *Iranica Antiqua*, *2*, pp. 97–147.
Mellaart, J. (1962). Excavations at Çatal Hüyük. *Anatolian Studies*, *12*, pp. 41–65.

Mellaart, J. (1964). Excavations at Çatal Hüyük 1963, Third Preliminary Report. *Anatolian Studies, 14,* pp. 39–119.

Mellaart, J. (1964). A Neolithic City in Turkey. *Scientific American, 210,* pp. 94–104.

Reed, C. (1958). Zoology. *In: The Identification of Non-artifactual Archeological Materials.* National Academy of Sciences Publication 565, Washington, D.C., pp. 43–4.

Reed, C. (1959). Animal Domestication in the Prehistoric Near East. *Science, 130,* pp. 1629–39.

Rodden, R. J. (1964). A European link with Chatal Hüyük: uncovering a 7th millennium settlement in Macedonia. *Illustrated London News,* pp. 564–7, 604–7.

Solecki, R. S. and Leroi-Gourhan, A. (1961). Palaeoclimatology and Archaeology in the Near East. *Annals of the New York Academy of Science, 95,* pp. 729–39.

3

1. Landsberger, B. (1934). *Die Fauna des alten Mesopotamiens nach der 14 Tafel der serie Har-ra-Hubullu.* Des XLIII bandes der Abhandlung der Philologisch-historischen Klasse der Sächischen akademie der Wissenschaften. *VI.* Leipzig.
   Oppenheim, A. L. and Hartman, L. F. (1945). The domestic animals of Ancient Mesopotamia according to the XIIIth tablet of the series ḪAR. *ra/ḫubuḷḷû. Journal of Near Eastern Studies, IV,* pp. 151–77.
   Van Buren, E. G. (1939). The fauna of ancient Mesopotamia as represented in art. *Analecta Orientalis, 18,* Rome.
   Bodenheimer, F. S. (1960). *Animal and man in bible lands.* Leiden. (Ch. 2:2, The animal in the life of ancient Mesopotamia, pp. 87–117).

2. Van Buren, E. D. (1939). *op. cit.*

3. Parrot, A. (1953). *Archéologie mésopotamienne.* Paris. II: *Technique et problèmes,* p. 132, Fig. 25.

4. Labat, R. (transl.) (1961). Epopée de Gilgamesh, tablette VI. *Les écrivains célèbres.* Paris.

5. Luckenbill, D. D. (1926). *Ancient records of Assyria and Babylonia.* Chicago.

6. Parrot, A. and Dossin, G. (gener. eds.) (1950–4). *Archives royales de Mari.* Vols. I–VI, Paris.

7. Birot, P. and Dresch J. (1956). *La Méditerranée et le Moyen Orient.* Paris (Ch. II).

8. Contenau, G. (1931). *Manuel d'archéologie orientale.* Vol. II, Paris (p. 626).

9. Contenau, G. (1931). *Manuel d'archéologie orientele.* Vol. III, Paris (p. 1201).

10. Dyson, R. H. (1960). A note on Queen Shu-Bad's 'onagers'. *Iraq, 22,* pp. 102–4.

11. Herodotus. Godley, A. transl. (1946). *Histories,* Vol. I, Book I, para. 201, London and Cambridge, Mass.

4

1. Baumgartel, E. J. (1965). Predynastic Egypt. *Cambridge Ancient History*. fasc. 38. Cambridge.
   Edwards, I. E. S. (1964). The early dynastic period in Egypt. *Cambridge Ancient History*, fasc. 25. Cambridge.
   Stevenson Smith, W. (1965). The Old Kingdom in Egypt and the beginning of the First Intermediate period. *Cambridge Ancient History*, fasc. 5. Cambridge.
   Breasted. J. H. (1909). *A history of Egypt from the earliest times to the Persian Conquest*. London.
   Murray, M. A. (1964). *The splendour that was Egypt*. London.
2. Zeuner, F. E. (1963). *A history of domesticated animals*. London (pp. 221–9).
4. Herodotus. Godley, A. transl. (1946). *Histories*, Vol. I, Book II, para. 70, London and Cambridge, Mass.
5. Budge, E. A. Wallis (1911). *Osiris and the Egyptian resurrection*. 2 vols. London.
6. Phillips, D. W. (1955). *Ancient Egyptian animals*. New York.
7. *Ibid.*
8. Moreau, R. E. (1930). The birds of ancient Egypt. *In* Meinertzhagen (ed.), Vol. I, pp. 58–77.
9. Phillips, D. W. (1955). *op. cit.*
10. *Ibid.*
11. *Ibid.*
12. *Ibid.*
13. Zeuner, F. E. (1963). *op. cit.* (p. 479).
14. *Ibid.*
15. Herodotus. Godley, A. transl. (1946). *Histories*, Vol. I, Book II, para. 95.
16. Breasted, J. H. (1909). *op. cit.* (p. 378).
17. Wiedenmann, A. (1902). *Popular literature in ancient Egypt* (transl. J. Hutchison). London.

Other Selected References

Conrad, J. R. (1959). *The horn and the sword: the history of the bull as a symbol of power and fertility*. London.

Davies, N. M. (1936). *Ancient Egyptian paintings*. Vols. I and 2 colour plates; Vol. 3 descriptive text. Chicago.

Davies, N. M. (1954). *Egyptian paintings*. London.

Desroches-Noblecourt, C. (1962). *Egyptian wall paintings from tombs and temples*. New York.

Drioton, E. and Vandier, J. (1946). *L'Egypte*. Part 4 of *Les peuples de L'Orient Mediteraneén*. Paris.

Hinton, H. E. and Dunn, A. M. S. (1967). *Mongooses: their natural history and behaviour*. Edinburgh and London.

Kees, H. (1961). *Ancient Egypt: a cultural topography*. London.

Lucas, A. (1962). *Ancient Egyptian materials and industries*. London.

Meinertzhagen, R. (1930). *Nicoll's birds of Egypt*. 2 vols. London.

Murray, M. A. (1931). *Egyptian temples*. London.

Posener, G. (1962). *A dictionary of Egyptian civilisation* (transl. A. Mac-Farlane). London.

Radcliffe, W. (1921). *Fishing from the earliest times*. London.

Ranke, H. (1936). *The art of ancient Egypt*. Vienna.

Reed, C. A. (1959). Animal domestication in the prehistoric Near East. *Science, 130*, pp. 1629–39.

Stevenson Smith, W. (1958). *The art and architecture of ancient Egypt*. Harmondsworth.

Wilkinson, J. G. (1878). *Manners and customs of the ancient Egyptians*. 3 vols. London.

Zoology of Egypt (1898–1907). Vol. I: *Reptilia and Batrachia* by J. Anderson (1898). Vol. 2: *Mammalia* by J. Anderson, revised and completed by W. E. de Winton (1902). Vols. 3 and 4: *The fishes of the Nile* by G. A. Boulenger (1907). London.

5

Boardman, J. (1964). *Greek Art*. London.

Caskey, J. L. (1965). Greece, Crete and the Aegean islands in the Early Bronze Age. *Cambridge Ancient History*, fasc. 24. Cambridge.

Guthrie, K. C. (1961). The religion and mythology of the Greeks. *Cambridge Ancient History*, fasc. 2. Cambridge.

Hood, S. (1967). *The home of the heroes*. London.

Hutchinson, R. W. (1962). *Prehistoric Crete*. London, Reading.

Marinatos, S. (1960). *Crete and Mycenae*. London.

Matz, F. (1964). Minoan civilization: maturity and zenith. *Cambridge Ancient History*, fasc. 12. Cambridge.

Stubbings, F. H. (1965). The rise of Mycenaen civilization. *Cambridge Ancient History*, fasc. 18. Cambridge.

Vermeule, E. (1964). *Greece in the Bronze Age*. Chicago and London.

Weinberg, S. (1965). The Stone Age in the Aegean. *Cambridge Ancient History*, fasc. 36. Cambridge.

6

1. Bloch, J. (1950). *Les inscriptions d'Aśoka*. Paris (edict on stone no. 1, edict on pillar no. 4, 7).

2. Marshall, J. and Foucher, A. (1940). *The monuments of Sâñchî*. Calcutta (Vol. II, Pl. LXV *a*, I).

3. Foucher, A. (1949). *La vie du Bouddha*. Paris (pp. 92–4). Coomaraswamy, A. K. (1935). La sculpture de *Bodhgayā*. *Ars Asiatica*, Vol. XVII, Pl. XLIX, 5.

4. Cunningham, A. (1879). *The stûpa of Bhârhut*. London (Pl. XXVIII, 3; XXXIV, I; LVII).

5. Vogel, J. P. (1930). La sculpture de Mathurâ. *Ars Asiatica, XV* (Pls. VIII *b*; LVII *a*).

Sivaramamurti, C. (1942). *Amâravatì sculptures in the Madras Government Museum.* Madras (p. 140).

6. Ramachandran, T. N. (1929). Buddhist sculptures from a stûpa near Goli village, Guntur District. *Bulletin of the Madras Government Museum,* New Series, *I.*

7. Cowell, E. B. (1895–1913). *The jâtaka.* Cambridge (Vol. III, p. 41: Kanavera-jâtakano, 318).
   Coomaraswamy, A. (1956). *La sculpture de Bhârhut.* Paris (Pl. XLVII, Figs. 192 and 194).

8. Foucher A. (1955). *Les vies antérieures du Bouddha.* Paris (p. 287: jâtaka no. 537).

9. Coomaraswamy, A. K. (1956). *op. cit.* (Pl. XXXVI, Fig. 104; half-medallion no. 218, Museum of Calcutta).

10. Hackin, J. (1954). *Nouvelles recherches archéologiques à Begram,* Paris (II, Fig. 123: ivory no. 192).

11. Vogel, J. P. (1930). *op. cit.* (Pl. LVII *b*).

12. Yazdani, G. (1930–55). *Ajanta.* Hyderabad (Vol. IV, Pl. XXXIII *a*).

13. Hackin, J. (1954). *op. cit.* (Figs. 22, 25, 659, 660).

14. *Ibid.* (Fig. 30).
    Upadhayaya, B. S. (1947). *India in Kâlidâsa.* Allahâbâd (p. 254).

15. Hackin, J. (1939). *Recherches archéologiques à Begrâm.* Paris (Pl. VIII, no. 53).

16. Vogel, J. P. (1930). *op. cit.* (Pl. XIX *a*).

17. Hackin, J. (1954). *op. cit.* (Fig. 233).

18. Cunningham, A. (1879). *op. cit.* (Pl. XLV, 7).

19. *Ibid.* (Pl. XXV, 1).

20. Jain, J. C. (1947). *Life in ancient India as depicted in the Jain Canon.* Bombay (p. 100).

21. Dumont, P. E. (1927). *L'Asvamedha.* Paris-Louvain.

22. Basham, L. *Journal of the Andhra Historical Research Society,* X (p. 14).

23. Foucher, A. (1955). *op. cit.* (p. 125).

24. Cowell, E. B. (1895–1913). *op. cit.* (Vol. II, pp. 199–203, *jâtaka* no. 254).

25. Dikshitar, V. R. R. (1944). *War in ancient India.* Madras (p. 176).

26. Foucher, A. (1955). *op. cit.* (p. 130).

27. Auboyer, J. (1964). Quelques réflexions à propos du cakra, arme offensive. *Arts asiatiques,* IX, I, pp. 119–30.

28. Cowell, E. B. (1895–1913). *op. cit.* (Vol. II, pp. 67–8, *jâtaka* no. 184).

29. Foucher, A. (1947). Deux *jâtaka* sur ivoire. *India Antiqua.* pp. 124–30.

30. Coomaraswamy, A. K. (1956). *op. cit.* (Pl. III, Fig. 6).

31. Stern, P. and Benisti, M. (1961). *Evolution du style indien d'Amarâvatî.* Paris (Pl. LXIV).

32. Cowell, E. B. (1895–1913). *op. cit.* (Vol. V, pp. 23 ss., *jâtaka* no. 514).

33. Dikshitar, V. R. R. (1944). *op. cit.* (pp. 168 ss.).

34. Cowell, E. B. (1895–1913). *op. cit.* (Vol. II, p. 14, *Alînachitta-jâtaka*).

35. *Ibid.* (p. 16, *Alînachitta-jâtaka*).

36. Coomaraswamy, A. K. (1956). *op. cit.* (Pl. XL, Fig. 124).

37. Fergusson, J. (1873). *Tree and Serpent worship.* London.
    Vogel, J. P. (1926). *Indian serpent-lore on the Nâgas in Hindu legend and art.* London.

38. Vogel, J. P. (1930). *op. cit.* (Pl. XLI).

39. Banerjea, J. N. (1956). *The development of Hindu iconography.* Calcutta.

40. *Ibid.* (pp. 529–34).
41. Foucher, A. (1905–51). *L'art gréco-bouddhique du Gandhâra.* Paris (Vol. II, pp. 36 ss.).
    Combaz, G. (1937). *L'Inde et l'Orient classique.* Paris (Vol. I, p. 159).
42. Le Coq, A. von. (1925). *Bilderatlas zur Kunst und Kulturgeschichte Mittelasiens.* Berlin (Fig. 147).
43. Leroi-Gourhan, A. (1943). *Documents pour l'art comparé de l'Eurasie septentrionale.* Paris.
44. Banerjea, J. N. (1956). *op. cit.* (Pl. XXV).
45. Jouveau-Dubreuil, G. (1937). *Iconography of southern India.* Paris.
46. Auboyer, J. and Zannas, E. (1960). *Khajurâho.* La Haye. (Pls. CXXV–CXXIX).
47. Smith, V. A. (1962). *A history of fine art in India and Ceylon,* Bombay (Pl. 81 *a*).
48. Banerjea, J. N. (1956). *op. cit.* (pp. 354–64).
    Getty, A. (1936). *Ganeśa, a monograph on the elephant faced god.* Oxford.
49. Marcel-Dubois, C. (1941). *Les instruments de musique dans l'Inde ancienne.* Paris (pp. 144 ss.).
50. Vogel, J. P. (1929–30). Le Makara dans la sculpture de l'Inde. *Revue des Arts asiatiques, VI,* 3, pp. 133 ss.
    Combaz, G. (1937). *L'Inde et l'Orient classique.* Paris (pp. 152 ss.).
    Viennot, O. (1954). Typologue du makara et essai de chronologie, *Arts asiatiques, I,* 3, pp. 189 ss.
51. Foucher, A. (1905–51). *op. cit.* (pp. 50 ss.).
52. Auboyer, J. (1949). *Le trône et son symbolisme dans l'Inde ancienne.* Paris.
53. Vogel, J. P. (1930). *op. cit.* (Pl. XXVIII *a*).

7

1. Kwang-Chih Chang. (1963). *Archaeology of ancient China.* Yale (p. 2).
2. Institute of History and Philology, Academia Sinica (1929–33). *Excavations at Anyang.* Peking (Chinese: Anyang Fa Chueh Pao Kao).
   Hu Hou-hsuan (1955). *Excavations at Yin Hsu.* Shanghai.
   Shih Chang-ju (1947). Important recent finds at Yin Hsu, and the stratigraphy at Hsiao T'un. *K'ao Ku Hsüch Pao, 2.*
3. Black, D., Teilhard de Chardin, P., Young, C. and Pei, W. C. (1933). Fossil man in China. *Geological Survey of China,* Memoirs, series A, *II.* Peking.
4. Teilhard de Chardin, P. (1941). *Early man in China.* Peking.
5. Tregear, T. R. (1965). *Geography of China.* London.
6. Institute of Archaeology (1962). *Archaeology of New China.* Peking (p. 3).
7. Zeuner, F. E. (1963). *The domestication of animals.* London.
8. Chia Lan-po *et al.* (1962). *Ke He.* Peking.
9. Cheng Te-k'un (1966). *New light on prehistoric China.* Archaeology in China series. Cambridge (pp. 5–6).

10. An Chih-min, Cheng Nai-wu and Hsieh Tuan-chi (1959). *Miao-ti-kou yu San-li-ch'iao*. Peking.
11. Cheng Te-k'un (1966). *op. cit.* (pp. 17–22).
    Institute of Archaeology (1962). *ibid.*
12. Honan Wen Hua Chu (1959). *Cheng Chou Erh-li-kang*. Peking.
13. Cheng Te-k'un (1960). *Shang China*. Archaeology of China series, Vol. II. Cambridge.
    Creel, H. G. (1963). *Birth of China*. London.
14. Cheng Te-k'un (1960). *op. cit.* (pp. 177–94).
15. Chiang Yuen-yi (1949–50). *Ch'ang-sha*. Shanghai.
    K'ao-ku Yen-chiu So (1957). *Changsha excavation report*. Peking.
    Institute of Archaeology (1962). *ibid.* (p. 60).
    Cheng Te-k'un (1963). *Chou China*. Archaeology of China series. Vol. III (pp. 1962–9).
16. Kwang-Chih Chang (1963). *op. cit.*
17. Sun Wang-lieh (1956). Hui Hsien finds. *K'ao Ku Hsüch Pao*, *2*
18. Needham, J. (1964). Science and China's influence on the world. *In The Legacy of China*. Ed. R. Dawson. Oxford (pp. 268–70).
19. Rudolph, E. C. (1951). *Han tomb art of west China*. California.
20. Yunnan Provincial Museum (1959). *The group of ancient tombs at Shih Chai Shan near Chin Ning, Yunnan province*. Peking.
21. Loyang District Excavation Team (1959). *Han tombs at Shao Kou, Loyang*. Peking.
22. Jenyns, S. (1954–5). The Chinese rhinoceros and Chinese carving in rhinoceros work. *Transactions of the Oriental Ceramic Society*. London (pp. 31–59).
23. Tun Li-chen (1936). *Annual customs and festivals of Peking* (Yen Ching Sui-shih-chi), (transl. D. Bodde). Peking.
24. Matsubara, S. (1969). Ornamental stone sculpture – stone animals. *In Chinese art*, ed. M. Tregear. Tokyo.
25. Ando, K. (1969). Tomb figures. *In Chinese art*, ed. M. Tregear, Tokyo.

Additional Bibliography

Li Chi (1957). *The beginnings of Chinese civilization*. Seattle.
Pei Wen-chung (1948). *Studies in Chinese prehistory*. Shanghai (Chinese).
Watson, W. (1960). *Archaeology in China*. London.
Watson, W. (1961). *China before the Han dynasty*. London.
Watson, W. (1966). *Early Chinese civilization*. London.
Watson, W. (1969). Early animal domestication in China. Early cereal cultivation in China. *In the domestication and exploitation of plants and animals*, ed. P. J. Ucko and G. W. Dimbleby. London, pp. 393–402.
Willets, W. (1965). *Foundations of Chinese art*. London.

INDEX

Index of Sites

Index of Animals